K YLEY

As Full as the World

When I want
Shooting stars,
Foreign cars,
Ancient wars,
Or matadors;
When I want
Prairie schooners,
Eclipses lunar,
Olympic races,
Or loaded bases;
When I want
Treasure chests,
Eagles' nests,
A runaway horse,
Or epics Norse—
I open a book
And take a look
At pages unfurled,
As full as the world.

—Dawn L. Watkins

Reading6 for Christian Schools®
Second Edition

BJU PRESS

GREENVILLE, SOUTH CAROLINA

This textbook was written by members of the faculty and staff of Bob Jones University. Standing for the "old-time-religion" and the absolute authority of the Bible since 1927, Bob Jones University is the world's leading Fundamentalist Christian university. The staff of the University is devoted to educating Christian men and women to be servants of Jesus Christ in all walks of life.

Providing unparalleled academic excellence, Bob Jones University prepares its students through its offering of over one hundred majors, while its fervent spiritual emphasis prepares their minds and hearts for service and devotion to the Lord Jesus Christ.

If you would like more information about the spiritual and academic opportunities available at Bob Jones University, please call
1-800-BJ-AND-ME (1-800-252-6363).
www.bju.edu

NOTE:

The fact that materials produced by other publishers may be referred to in this volume does not constitute an endorsement by Bob Jones University Press of the content or theological position of materials produced by such publishers. The position of the Bob Jones University Press, and the University itself, is well known. Any references and ancillary materials are listed as an aid to the student or the teacher and in an attempt to maintain the accepted academic standards of the publishing industry.

READING 6 for Christian Schools® Second Edition
As Full as the World

Produced in cooperation with the Bob Jones University School of Education and Bob Jones Elementary School.

for Christian Schools is a registered trademark of Bob Jones University Press.

© 2003 Bob Jones University Press
Greenville, South Carolina 29614

First edition © 1986 Bob Jones University Press

Printed in the United States of America
All rights reserved

ISBN 1-57924-542-0

15   14   13   12   11   10   9   8   7   6   5   4   3   2   1

Contents
Perspectives

Victories

Ventures

Distant Realms

Overcomers

Acknowledgments

A careful effort has been made to trace the ownership of selections included in this textbook in order to secure permission to reprint copyrighted materials and to make full acknowledgment of their use. If any error or omission has occurred, it is purely inadvertent and will be corrected in subsequent editions, provided written notification is made to the publisher.

Of the following publishers, authors, and other holders of copyright material:

A portion from *Call It Courage* by Armstrong Perry. Reprinted with the permission of Simon & Schuster Books for Young Readers, an imprint of Simon & Schuster Children's Publishing Division. Copyright 1940 by Macmillan Publishing Company; copyright renewed 1968 by Armstrong Perry.

"First Chronicles 21:24-29" taken from *Expositor's Bible Commentary: Old Testament,* Vol. 4, by Herman J. Austel; Frank E. Gaebelein; J. Barton Payne. Copyright © 1988 by the Zondervan Corporation. Used by permission of Zondervan Publishing House.

"Jerusalem" taken from *Zondervan Pictorial Encyclopedia of the Bible* by Merrill C. Tenney. Copyright © 1975, 1976 by the Zondervan Publishing House. Used by permission of Zondervan Publishing House.

"Ornan" taken from *The New Strong's Exhaustive Concordance of the Bible* by James Strong. Copyright © 1995, 1996. Used by permission of Thomas Nelson, Inc.

"The Secret Pitch," by Earl Chapin. Reprinted by permission.

"The Sparrow Hawk," by Russell Hoban. Reprinted by permission of Harold Ober Associates Incorporated. Copyright © 1968 by Russell Hoban.

"Stickball," by Virginia Schonberg. Reprinted by permission of HarperCollins Publishers.

"Sunrise," by Emily Dickinson. Reprinted by permission of the publishers and the Trustees of Amherst College from *The Poems of Emily Dickinson,* Thomas H. Johnson, ed., Cambridge, Mass.: The Belknap Press of Harvard University Press, Copyright © 1951, 1955, 1979 by the President and Fellows of Harvard College.

"Threshing Floor" taken from *The New Unger's Bible Dictionary* by Merrill F. Unger, Moody Press, 1988.

"Wind-Wolves," by William D. Sargent. Reprinted by permission of Scholastic Inc.

Project Coordinators
Vicky L. Burr
Janice A. Joss
Susan J. Lehman
Jeri Massi
Amy Miller
Karen T. Wooster

Project Editor
Debbie L. Parker

Designers
Holly Gilbert
John Bjerk

Cover
Noelle Snyder

Composition
Carol Larson

Photo Acquisition
Tara Swaney

Photo Credits

The following agencies and individuals have furnished materials to meet the photographic needs of this text-book. We wish to express our gratitude to them for their important contribution.

1999-2001 © www.arttoday.com
AP/WIDE WORLD PHOTOS
Corel Corporation
Digital Stock
Eastman Chemical Division
Library of Congress
National Archives and Records Administration (NARA)
National Baseball Hall of Fame Library, Cooperstown
PhotoDisc, Inc.
Sanela Tutaris
Tara Swaney
Unusual Films
Visual Image Presentations

Introduction
Corel Corporation i-xiv

Unit 1
PhotoDisc, Inc. 1 (opener), 14, 15, 16; Corel Corporation 1 (opener background); Unusual Films 14 (top right)

Unit 2
PhotoDisc, Inc. 137, 163 (all), 168-81 (backgrounds); NARA 148-53; Library of Congress 190 (both), 191; National Baseball Hall of Fame Library, Cooperstown 192, 193; Eastman Chemical Division 194 (Babe Ruth); AP 194 (McGuire/Sosa); Corel Corporation 195; Unusual Films 198, 199

Unit 3
Corel Corporation 227 (background), 243-44, 246-47 (background), 249-55; PhotoDisc, Inc. 227 (opener), 241, 247, 283 (background); Unusual Films 283

Unit 4
PhotoDisc, Inc. 305, 325-33, 338-59 (bottom border); Corel Corporation 305 (background); Unusual Films 334-35, 337

Unit 5
Corel Corporation 415 (both); 1999-2001 © www.arttoday.com 476, 477 (inset), 481 (top); PhotoDisc, Inc. 477, 479 (inset, top), 479 (inset, bottom left and right), 480, 481 (bottom left) 483 (all); Sanela Tutaris 482, 484, 488, 491 (all); Digital Stock 487

Unit 6
Digital Stock 495, 553, 555, 556; Corel Corporation 495 (background), 588-89; Library of Congress 504; PhotoDisc, Inc. 540-42, 554, 557, 562; 1999-2001 © www.arttoday.com 565

Glossary Art
Corel Corporation 609-651 (all background and borders); 1999-2001 © www.arttoday.com 610, 615, 622, 632, 640, 646, 648 (top), 650-51; Digital Stock 629; PhotoDisc, Inc. 644, 648

PERSPECTIVES

Jake Sparks and THE CASE OF The Missing Monkey

Sharon Hambrick
illustrated by Paula Cheadle

No Time to Lose!

Jake Sparks leaned back in the soft brown recliner. He locked his hands behind his head and stared at the old photograph of his great-grandfather, Edmund Wilton Sparks, that hung on the living room wall. The photograph was fading behind its glass, but Great-Grandfather Sparks's stern face gazed intently at Jake.

"Okay, Great-Grandpa," Jake said aloud. "I've got a new mystery for you. How would you find a missing monkey?"

"Great-Gramps can't hear you, Jake," his little sister Bridget said. "He's been dead sixty years."

"Sixty-five."

"Anyway," Bridget said, "you know he didn't help you with the last

mystery you solved. I did that!" Bridget beamed triumphantly at Jake.

It was true, and Jake knew it. It had been Bridget who'd nudged him in the right direction last time when he had been searching for the lost goldfish.

"I admit it. But I'm going to solve this one. I'm bending all my mental powers on this one problem. You'll see; I'll figure it out."

Bridget mumbled something about Jake thinking he had all the answers. Then she grabbed a doll from underneath the couch and wandered out of the living room. Jake leaned back in the chair and thought about how the case of the missing monkey had begun.

2

It was the first day of school. Jake thought it seemed like every other first day of school he'd ever seen. There were the brand-new clothes and the squeaky-clean back-packs. There were schoolbooks that still looked shiny and new shoes that were not yet scuffed up.

Jake and his friend Nathan walked from the sixth-grade room at Philpot Christian School to the Philpot Public Library as they had done the first day of school for the last two years. They counted their steps as they walked. Last year, it took nine hundred and seventy-five steps, but this year, since their legs were longer, it didn't take as many.

"Nine hundred fifty-two!" Jake and Nathan said together as they stomped up to the front door of the library. "Hi, Miss Hancock," Jake said, and, "We're here!" Nathan said, probably a little too loud for a library.

"It's good to see you," Miss Hancock replied. She tucked a wisp of her gray hair behind her ear and smoothed her skirt down. "Are you going to be joining the Library Club again this year, Nathan?"

"Yes, ma'am," Nathan said smiling. "That's why I'm here. Mom says it's my civic duty to help you and to read to little kids."

"And what about you, Mr. Sparks?" Miss Hancock asked. "Are you joining the library club too?"

"Yes, ma'am," Jake said. "Mom says I can join if I'm home in time to do my chores in the evening."

"That will be perfectly fine," Miss Hancock said. "What chores do you have to do?"

"I feed the chickens. I tend a big plot of tomatoes. I'm supposed to, anyway. Dig out the weeds, watch for bugs, that sort of thing. Plus keeping the garage cleaned up, prac-ticing, doing homework. You know, all the regular stuff."

"Sounds like a lot of regular stuff," Miss Hancock said, smiling. Jake loved the library, and he loved Miss Hancock. Miss Hancock would help you find any book you needed, and if you wanted to keep it longer than it was checked out for, she didn't care. She could also help you with your homework and could work out long division problems in her head.

Miss Hancock had been the Philpot Library's librarian since be-fore Jake was born. But she wasn't the only wonderful thing about the library. There was also Barney, Miss Hancock's pet monkey. Usually Barney would sit on the floor doing nothing, but sometimes he would shriek suddenly and scare everyone, though they usually ended up laugh-ing when they calmed down from the fright. Jake knew there probably wasn't another public library like Philpot's in the whole country.

"Well, don't stand outside in the heat," Miss Hancock said. "Come on in." She held the door open for them, and they walked into the cool of the library.

A few minutes later the first meeting of the Junior Library Club at the Philpot Public Library was called to order. Miss Hancock tapped a wooden gavel[1] on her desk.

"This meeting will come to order," she said. "I'd like to officially welcome you to this year's Library Club. I'm counting on all of you to help me reshelve the returned books in the right places, read to little children in the children's room, and generally make the Philpot library a happy place. Are we all agreed?"

Fifteen heads nodded yes.

"Good. Now, let me call Barney. As you know, Barney's my dear friend and confidant.[2] If I hear you've been naughty, I'll whisper it in Barney's ear, and he'll eat your homework!"

All the kids laughed, and Jake wondered if Barney wasn't the only thing unique about Philpot's library. Maybe Miss Hancock was a bit out of the ordinary too.

"Barney," Miss Hancock called. There was no answer, so she tried again. "Barney!"

Jake and the other kids got up and looked around, but Barney was nowhere to be found.

"Well, don't worry," Miss Hancock said, "he never misses dinner, and tonight I'm serving his favorite salad and a big bowl of mashed potatoes. He'll be home in time for that, I know!"

Barney did not return by dinner time, and the next day found Miss Hancock fluttering with anxiety. She was unable to speak to the library clubbers, though she smiled at them as they went about their tasks of putting books back on shelves and straightening magazines.

"He's lost," some kids said.

"He's stolen," others whispered.

By the second day, there was no doubt. Barney was missing for good. A reporter from the *Philpot Stew* showed up at the library for an interview with Miss Hancock. Jake Sparks watched from the children's room where he pretended to be interested in reading a book to several toddlers when what he really wanted to be doing was rushing out to tell the reporter to sound an urgent alarm for the return of Barney. There was no time to lose! The fact was, he'd seen Miss Hancock crying, and he didn't like that one bit.

That was the night Jake sat in the recliner and asked his long-deceased[3] great-grandfather's picture for help. Of course, no help came.

---

[1]gavel—a mallet that a judge strikes on his desk for order or attention
[2]confidant—one to whom secrets are told
[3]deceased—no longer living; dead

The next morning, Jake was transfixed[4] by the front page of the *Philpot Stew.* Above the news of a hurricane in Alabama and a fire in Montana was a picture of a distressed Miss Hancock and this headline: "Beloved Librarian Offers Two Hundred Dollars for Barney's Safe Return!"

That evening Jake absentmindedly poured Italian dressing on his French fries and ketchup on his salad. He said "yes" when his father asked how his day had been, and handed his mother the pitcher of lemonade when she asked him to please pass the tomato slices. Bridget giggled into her hand, but didn't say anything.

"Is something wrong, Jake?" Mr. Sparks asked.

"Tuesday," Jake said.

"Jake, look at me," his father said. Jake looked up. "Are you all right?"

"Yes, sir; sorry sir," Jake said. "I'm thinking about Barney and how I can find him. If I rush out right after dinner tonight, I think I can find him. Dad, there's a two hundred dollar reward!"

"What about your chores?" Mr. Sparks asked. "If you're monkey-hunting, when will you finish them? And what about your homework and your trumpet practice?"

---

[4]transfixed—motionless in amazement

"But, Dad, what's a couple of days of homework or practice when you consider two hundred dollars? I could start my college fund. I could buy a new skateboard. I could—"

"He's in the tomatoes," Bridget said.

"Who?"

"Barney."

Jake poked at the sliced tomatoes on the plate and said, "No, Sis; he's not. Look, Dad, I've figured it all out. Monkeys are jungle animals, right? That means they want to be in the jungle. Philpot isn't exactly a jungle, so Barney's run away from the library to find a jungle. All we have to do is look in the jungliest-looking place around here, and there will be Barney."

He wiped his mouth with his napkin and beamed around the table at his family.

"See, it's simple, Sis," he said to Bridget. He tapped his head. "You've just got to use your noggin."

Jake stood up. "So, I'm off to the park, Dad," he said. "I've got a monkey to capture."

"Not so fast, Son," Mrs. Sparks said. "There's the small detail of your evening chores."

"Chores, s'mores," Jake said. "When I've got that two hundred dollars, I'll hire a maid for you, Mom. I'm doing this for all of us."

Dad turned a stern gaze on Jake. Jake swallowed hard. "Sorry, Mom," he said. "What I meant to say was, 'May I please look for Barney after I do my chores?'"

"After your chores and after your homework if it isn't too late."

It was too late. By the time the chickens were fed and the weeds were pulled, it was eight o'clock. By the time Jake had practiced and finished up his math homework, it was bedtime.

Maybe tomorrow, he thought.

What's the Reward?

The next day was the same. While other kids poured out into the afternoon in bunches of threes and fours to look for Barney, Jake trudged home with Bridget so they could do their chores and their homework, their music practice, and their family devotions.

"Never mind, Son," Mr. Sparks said. "Your job is not to get rewards. I'm sure Barney will be found soon. Your job is to do your work well and trust God to take care of all your needs."

"But Dad, I'd get two hundred dollars if I found him."

"And if you didn't find him, you'd be behind on your homework, behind on your trumpet practice, and behind on your chores. The vegetable garden would completely fall apart, and your chickens would starve to death."

"But, Dad—"

"No buts. There are plenty of kids looking for Barney. We need your help here at home. No wild monkey chases for you."

"What about me, Daddy?" Bridget said. She was sitting in the rocking chair, braiding her doll's hair. "Can I find Barney? He's in the tomatoes."

"The tomatoes?"

"She said that last night," Jake said. He snickered, but he didn't admit that he'd looked all through the tomato plants before school that morning. There was no monkey there, just a few broken plants where a dog must have run through and some half-eaten tomatoes the birds had been after.

The Library Club hadn't met since Barney got lost. Miss Hancock was distracted and frantic. She roamed around the library looking in corners and peering out the windows. She cried often. Jake felt uncomfortable around her and stayed away.

On Friday, Nathan caught up with him as he walked home from school. Nathan carried a large cage made of chicken wire and led an enormous dog on a leash.

"Come on, Jake," Nathan said. "See, I've got a monkey-catching cage and my rottweiler Hamlet. We're going to plop the cage on top of Barney and then make Hamlet sit on it until the police arrive."

"Sorry," Jake said. "I can't. Chores."

Another boy ran by with a rope. "I've been practicing with the lasso. I'm going to catch that monkey by his tail and drag him into town."

Saturday's *Stew* revealed that although hope was growing dimmer for Barney's safe return, many people were still looking diligently.

Jake felt foolish that he couldn't help out, but he knew he had to obey his father. He felt worse when he read that the reward money had been increased by Miss Hancock's assistant librarian and now stood at three hundred dollars.

"Coming with us today?" Nathan asked on Monday.

"You know I can't," Jake said. "My dad says I have to do my regular homework and chores."

"That's too bad," Nathan said, "because I can feel it in my bones—today's the day I'm going to sneak up on that critter and bag him!"

"What happened to your cage and the big dog?"

"It was too flimsy," Nathan said. "Hamlet sat on it and crushed it. Besides, I never did see Barney."

While his friends went monkey-hunting that day, Jake Sparks studied alone in the Philpot Library. He wrote his spelling words into sentences, made a list of thirty-five adjectives, and filled in blanks on a worksheet about the ancient Sumerians.

He didn't say much at dinner. There didn't seem to be anything to say. Everyone else had been out looking for the monkey, and he had been tossing corn to chickens! Bridget said, "He's in the tomatoes," again, but Jake glared at her.

Tuesday's edition of the *Stew* featured a color picture of Mayor Stubbs and the town council smiling over the diminutive[5] form of Miss Hancock. The caption read, *Council Aids Leading Citizen.* Jake read the article and sighed deeply. The leadership of Philpot had pitched in to help.

"She has been a pillar[6] in the community of Philpot as long as any of us can remember," Mayor Stubbs was quoted as saying. "Barney was a gift of the Junior Library Club several years ago. He has been a wonderful companion for Miss Hancock, and we are deeply grieved that he is missing. We have all contributed to the Find Barney Fund, which has now reached a total reward of five hundred dollars for the safe return of Barney, Philpot's most prized monkey."

Jake swallowed hard. Five hundred dollars! Even his father would have to admit that was worth having!

"Mom, did you see this?" Jake held out the picture. "How can I get Dad to let me join the search teams?"

"Yes, I saw it Jake, but I don't think Dad's going to change his mind. Rushing out to make a quick dollar isn't the way to prosperity[7] for most people. Dad wants you to be steady and responsible. Maybe if you finish everything up early tonight, we can all go out and look around for that monkey, but not for the money."

5diminutive—of very small size; tiny
6pillar—(figurative) one who has an important position
7prosperity—success, especially in money matters

"Why not for the money?"

"That's not why you should look for Miss Hancock's monkey, Son."

The next day, Jake went to see Miss Hancock.

"I'm sorry about your monkey, Miss Hancock," Jake said.

The two of them sat in the library on plush couches. Miss Hancock always said it was better to read in comfort than in pain.

"I don't think he'll come back, you know," she said. "He's been gone a long time now, and, after all, maybe a monkey should be free. Maybe he didn't like living in a house alone with an old lady like me. You know I'm almost seventy years old, Jake, and maybe a lady of seventy shouldn't tie her affections up in a monkey. Maybe Barney knew it was time to make his own way in the world."

Jake laughed a little, but sadly.

"I'd look for him, but my Dad won't let me," he said. "He said I should work hard at my regular chores and homework and not rush off for get-rich schemes."

"Get-rich schemes?" Miss Hancock sat up straight. "Do you mean the kids are all looking for Barney just for the reward, not because I miss him? Not because he's lost?"

Jake cringed under her gaze. "I guess so," he said. "I don't really know."

"Can you believe she canceled the reward and called the search off?" Nathan said. The Library Club was full again, and the kids put books back on shelves and read stories to small children instead of spending their afternoons on the monkey search. "That money was practically in my pocket," he said. "I know I was just about to find old Barney."

"Never mind that monkey," a girl said. "It's over, so it's over. Let's read."

Jake looked over at Miss Hancock who sat behind the book check-out counter. She seemed older and sadder than she had been the day before.

"Dad, I've got to find that monkey," Jake said at dinner.

"What's the reward up to?" Mr. Sparks asked.

"No reward," Jake said. "But Miss Hancock really misses Barney. She needs him."

Mr. Sparks looked up from his dinner plate and gazed deeply into Jake's eyes. Jake was a little bit afraid of what his father would say— after all, this was the third time he'd asked permission to look for Barney—but he didn't look away.

Mr. Sparks smiled. "Let's clean up dinner and think about where a monkey would hide. We'll do this to-gether. For Miss Hancock."

"He's in the tomatoes," said Bridget.

"Stop with the tomatoes, okay?" Jake said, his voice rising. "Why do you keep saying that?"

"Because he's in the tomatoes. I saw him."

"You saw him?"

"I've been trying to tell you all along!"

Half an hour later, Mr. and Mrs. Sparks, Bridget, and Jake sat quietly in the back yard, each of them at a corner of the large tomato plot. They sat perfectly still. Time ticked slowly by. No one spoke.

At last a dark something moved quickly through the plants. Jake's heart pounded. He heard a sharp gasp from Bridget, but knew not to say anything. They must all be as quiet as possible.

Snap. Splat.

There! Ten feet away from him sat Barney the monkey chewing tomatoes!

Snap. The tomato branch broke. *Splat.* Barney bit right through the juicy tomato.

Jake saw his mother's shadowed figure slip quietly back toward the house. It was her job to call Miss Hancock if they spotted Barney.

It seemed like forever, but proba-bly only a very few minutes passed before Jake sensed the small pres-ence of Miss Hancock standing next to him. She was trembling with ex-citement.

"Barney boy," she whispered, "come to Mama. Come on, sweetheart. It's time to come home."

The snapping and splatting stopped.

"Barney, sweetie," Miss Hancock said, "Don't you want to come home now?" Her voice was quivering. Jake thought she might burst into tears.

And then, all in a rush, Barney flung himself onto Miss Hancock, and Miss Hancock wrapped him up in a great hug. He twined his arms around her neck and shrieked, his mouth wide open in a great monkey grin.

"It's not fair," Nathan said. He tossed his school books down on the library's reading table and elbowed Jake in the ribs. "If she'd kept the reward on, we would've kept looking for him too."

Jake smiled. He knew that Miss Hancock's joy in having Barney back was gift enough, though if he was strictly honest, he would have to admit that five hundred dollars would have been nice.

"Don't worry about it, Jake," Bridget said that evening as the two of them sat in the living room playing checkers. "You can't help it if you've got a brilliant little sister living down the hall."

Jake leaned back in the soft brown recliner and looked at Great-Grandpa Edmund hanging as stern as always on the wall.

"Hey, Grandpa," he said, "do you have any advice for dealing with smart little sisters?"

"He can't hear you," Bridget said. "He's been dead for sixty years."

"Sixty-five," said Jake.

A Visit with a Humorist: Sharon Hambrick

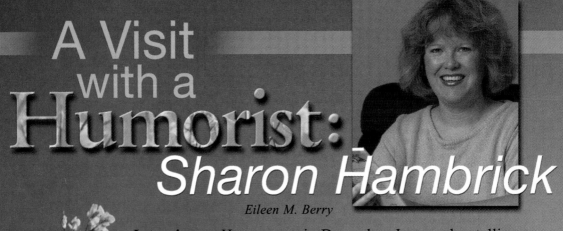

Eileen M. Berry

Interviewer: How long have you been interested in writing?

Hambrick: It's been a lifelong interest. I sent my first story to a magazine at age eight. It was a Christmas story written from the donkey's viewpoint, and I sent it to the magazine in November, hoping they would publish[1] it in December. I remember telling my mom not to read it as she typed it for me. I wrote my first novel in the late 1980s, but it was never published. I also wrote plays, stories, and songs for my students while I was a teacher.

[1]publish—to print material to be sold to the public

Interviewer: When did you publish your first novel?

Hambrick: I published *Arby Jenkins* in 1996.

Interviewer: Your novels are famous for their humor. What ingredients do you believe a good humorous story is made up of?

Hambrick: Humor has to include the unexpected. The outcome of a situation or of a dialogue[2] should take us by surprise, like the punch line of a joke. We also tend to laugh at other people's misfortunes—especially if those misfortunes are exaggerated and not really tragic. Humor almost always involves a universal[3] situation that everyone can understand and identify with. I think the reason some stories are not as funny as the author intended is that he is trying too hard to be funny. Humor becomes the whole focus at the expense of a good plot. That's what slapstick is.

Interviewer: How much do you rely on your personal experience as you're thinking about ideas for plots and characters?

Hambrick: Completely. You really have to *know* what you're writing about. In a way, I think all my characters are *me*—either how I would be in a certain situation or how I would like to be. But at the same time, I try to make my characters, especially my adult characters, good role models. I want to give kids a picture of what grown-ups *ought* to be.

Interviewer: How much planning do you do before you begin writing a novel?

Hambrick: Not very much. Usually, when I decide to write another book, my husband and I go out to dinner and talk about ideas. I always make sure I know what my character's main problem is. Characters need to have both internal and external problems. After I have my idea, I outline the book chapter by chapter. But I always find that sometimes things just happen as I write.

Interviewer: What is the average length of time it takes you to write a novel?

Hambrick: Three to four months, usually. However, I wrote *Arby Jenkins* in thirty days.

---

[2]dialogue—speaking parts of a play or story
[3]universal—applying to all members of a group

Interviewer: Do you have a favorite place to be when writing?

Hambrick: Alone at my computer. No music.

Interviewer: What do you find most challenging about writing a humorous story?

Hambrick: Getting the cadence[4] right. There's a certain pace to humor: you have to start out funny, then go to the more serious or philosophical,[5] then bring the humor in again. You also have to have a balance between action and humor. If a story's just funny all the time, it has no depth. It needs to have something underneath to keep it going.

Interviewer: Do you have a favorite humorous novel or author of humor?

Hambrick: James Thurber is the greatest American humorist.[6] He wrote mostly short stories and essays. "The Night the Bed Fell" and "The Day the Dam Broke" are two of my favorites.

Interviewer: What other books have influenced you most greatly as a writer?

Hambrick: All good writing inspires me. I like to read Tolstoy and Twain. And some of my favorite children's authors are Patricia MacLachlan, E. B. White, Donald Sobel (who wrote the *Encyclopedia Brown* series), and Robert McCloskey (who wrote the *Homer Price* books).

Interviewer: What advice would you give to young writers who would like to write humorous stories?

Hambrick: I would tell them to first learn to *write.* Don't try to write jokes and read joke books. Learn the serious techniques of writing—plot, characterization, theme. Also, learn to see the world with an eye to what is funny without being cruel. Above all, learn not to take yourself too seriously.

[4]cadence—rhythmic flow
[5]philosophical—of philosophy (a person's own beliefs about life and the world)
[6]humorist—writer of humorous or funny material

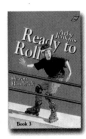

The Squire's Bride

Peter Christian Asbjörnsen

and Jorgen Möe

translated by George Walle Dasent

illustrated by Timothy Banks

Once upon a time there was a rich squire who owned a large farm and had plenty of silver at the bottom of his chest and money in the bank besides; but he felt there was something wanting, for he was a widower.[1]

One day the daughter of a neighboring farmer was working for him in the hayfield. The squire saw her and liked her very much, and as she was the child of poor parents, he thought if he only hinted that he wanted her she would be ready to marry him at once.

So he told her he had been thinking of getting married again.

"Ay! One may think of many things," said the girl, laughing slyly. In her opinion the old fellow ought to be thinking of something more proper for him than getting married.

"Well, you see, I thought that you should be my wife!"

"No thank you all the same," said she, "that's not at all likely."

The squire was not accustomed to being contradicted,[2] and the more she refused him, the more determined he was to get her.

But as he made no progress in her favor, he sent for her father and

---

[1]widower—a man whose wife has died
[2]contradicted—stated the opposite of

told him that if he could arrange the matter with his daughter, he would forgive him the money he had lent him, and he would also give him the piece of land which lay close to his meadow into the bargain.

"Yes, you may be sure I'll bring my daughter to her senses," said the father. "She is only a child, and she doesn't know what's best for her." But all his coaxing[3] and talking did not help matters. She would not have the squire, she said, if he sat buried in gold up to his ears.

The squire waited day after day, but at last he became quite angry and impatient. He told the father of the girl that if he expected him to stand by his promise, he would have to put his foot down now, for he would not wait any longer.

The man knew no other way out of it but to let the squire get everything ready for the wedding; and when the parson[4] and the wedding guests had arrived, the squire should send for the girl as if she were wanted for some work on the farm. When she arrived, she would have to be married right away, so that she would have no time to think it over.

The squire thought this was well and good, and so he began cooking and baking and getting ready for the wedding in grand style. When the

[3]coaxing—getting something by being nice or gentle
[4]parson—a clergyman or minister

guests had arrived, the squire called one of his farm lads and told him to run down to his neighbor and ask him to send him what he had promised.

"But if you are not back in a twinkling," he said, shaking his fist, "I'll—"

He did not say more, for the lad ran off as if he had been shot at.

"My master has sent me to ask for what you promised him," said the lad, when he got to the neighbor, "but there is no time to be lost, for he is terribly busy today."

"Yes, yes! Run down into the meadow and take her with you. There she goes!" answered the neighbor.

The lad ran off, and when he came to the meadow, he found the daughter there raking the hay.

"I am to fetch what your father has promised my master," said the lad.

"Ah, ha!" thought she. "Is that what they are up to?"

"Ah, indeed!" she said. "I suppose it's that little bay mare of ours.

You had better go and take her. She stands there tethered[5] on the other side of the pea field," said the girl.

The boy jumped on the bay mare and rode home at full gallop.

"Have you got her with you?" asked the squire.

"She is down at the door," said the lad.

"Take her up to the room my mother had," said the squire.

"But master, how can that be managed?" said the lad.

"You must do as I tell you," said the squire. "If you cannot manage her alone, you must get the men to help you," for he thought the girl might turn rebellious.

When the lad saw his master's face, he knew it would be of no use to contradict him. So he went and got all the farm-tenants who were there to help him. Some pulled at the head, and the forelegs of the mare and others pushed from behind; at last they got her up the stairs and

---

[5]tethered—tied up

into the room. There lay all the wedding finery ready.

"Now, that's done, master!" said the lad; "but it was a terrible job. It was the worst I have ever had here on the farm."

"Never mind, you shall not have done it for nothing," said his master. "Now send the women up to dress her."

"But I say, master—!" said the lad.

"None of your talk!" said the squire. "Tell them they must dress her and mind and not forget either wreath or crown."

The lad ran into the kitchen.

"Look here, lasses," he said; "you must go upstairs and dress up the bay mare as a bride. I expect the master wants to give the guests a laugh."

The women dressed the bay mare in everything that was there, and then the lad went and told his master that now she was ready dressed, with wreath and crown and all.

"Very well then, bring her down!" said the squire. "I will receive her myself at the door," said he.

There was a terrible clatter on the stairs; for that bride, you know, had no silken shoes on.

When the door opened and the squire's bride entered the parlor, you can imagine there was a good deal of tittering and grinning.

And as for the squire, you may be sure he had had enough of that bride, and they say he never went courting[6] again.

___

[6]courting—trying to win love or affection

The Scullery Boy

from The Foundling *by Linda Hayner*
illustrated by Steve Mitchell

In seventeenth century London, it was not uncommon to find abandoned children on church doorsteps. During this period of war, soldiers drove respectable peasants from their homes in the country. Forced to flee to the city of London, many of these peasants ended up begging and eventually found themselves unable to feed their own children. To avoid further misery, these peasants often decided to let the parish church care for their children and place them in homes where they would be fed and clothed. These abandoned children were known as foundlings.

One such foundling, named Will, was discovered at the age of four and was taken into the temporary care of a kind gentleman named James Perry. During Will's brief stay, Master Perry and his closest friend and employee, Rodgers, gain an attachment to the young foundling. After finding a nurse, Mistress Bessie, to care for Will, Rodgers continues to visit him and to keep up with his progress. Following the death of Mistress Bessie, Rodgers and Master Perry place Will under the care of the local Vicar.[1] Rodgers and Perry agree to pay the Vicar a monthly sum to provide Will with food, clothing, and education. However, the Vicar gives him only loose straw for a bed, takes away his nice clothes and toys, and gives him the dirtiest jobs of the household. Also, the Vicar instructs Will to stay out of sight when visitors come. As a result, Will begins to think Rodgers has forgotten him.

Will resigns himself to living in this cruel situation and does what he is told. But one day he finds a way to escape from the harsh world in which he lives, though the escape is only in his imagination.

---

[1]Vicar—a clergyman of the Church of England who is paid by the government

Delightful Discovery

Will fetched the last scuttle[2] of coal and went to the library. He had never been in the room before. It was small and dominated[3] by a large fireplace. After laying the fire and sweeping up the coal dust that always flew about no matter how careful he was, Will looked around. Two chairs flanked[4] the fireplace. Their cushions were a deep purple and looked soft and comfortable. In front of each chair was a footstool, and by the right arm of each was a small table with a candlestick for reading. Along one wall stood a small desk covered with papers and books. Most of them were in Latin. The Vicar's scrawling handwriting covered some of the papers. At the top of one was written "Sermon for the Lord's Day, September 23." Will didn't like the Vicar's sermons much.

He straightened up; he'd already spent too much time here. Then he spied a piece of furniture almost hidden in a corner. It was a beautifully carved bookcase with glass doors. And it was full of books whose leather bindings gleamed in the fading afternoon light. If only I could open the doors, he thought, I could read the titles better. He pressed the door with his finger.

When he took his finger away, the door opened with a snap that made him jump and glance toward the library door. No footsteps. The family was still at supper.

The bookcase door squeaked a bit when he pulled it open. Will ran his fingers along the spines. He breathed in the warm smells of leather and parchment,[5] paper and ink. Most of the titles were in Latin, but he pulled out a small volume anyway to look at it and enjoy its feel. He opened the book and ran his fingers over the heavy vellum,[6] leaving a smudge of coal dust that would not come off no matter how he rubbed it. When he bent to replace the book, he saw another book behind it. In fact, there was a whole row of books behind on every shelf. The Vicar had lots more than a hundred books.

Will reached in and pulled out one of the back books. It was in English, and it was about King Richard and the Crusades. He pulled out several more books of stories, legends, tales of foreign lands, and exploration.

Footsteps sounded in the dining room. Dinner would soon be over. Quickly, Will replaced the books, making as little noise as he could. He picked up the last one and read

---

[2]scuttle—a container for carrying coal
[3]dominated—positioned in an obvious or prominent place
[4]flanked—placed on each side
[5]parchment—writing material of sheepskin or goatskin
[6]vellum—fine parchment made of lambskin or kidskin

the title again. He looked over his shoulder, then slipped the volume about King Richard into his shirt. He closed the squeaky bookcase door slowly, hoping it wouldn't be heard. At the library door he checked both ways and sped quietly down the hall and into the kitchen.

"Where have you been, you bone-idle scamp?" Cook slammed down a large pot. "Begin cleaning the kitchen. You'll get no supper tonight for your laziness."

Will ran to his cubby, wrapped the book in his extra shirt, and shoved it under his straw bed. He didn't care about supper. He would clean so fast and so well, Cook wouldn't be able to complain. Then he could read.

But it was two hours before he crept into his cubby. He carried a long splinter of wood from the kitchen fire to light a candle. He'd never used any of his candles before, so he grabbed one from the small pile near his bed, lit it, and stuck it to the floor with some melted wax. Will kicked the straw into a pile, spread his blanket over it, and lay down. He reached out and pushed the cubby door shut. Almost reverently,[7] he unwrapped and opened the book. The leather felt warm and smooth, but the pages were cool under his fingertips. Will rubbed his hands on his blanket to clean them. He turned page after page, enjoying the contrast of black ink on the creamy vellum. When the anticipation was unbearable, he started to read.

Soon he was lost in the world of King Richard I and the Third Crusade. It didn't matter that he already knew the story from the beginning to end from the times when he and Mistress

[7]reverently—having feelings of deep respect

24

Bessie had read it together. The walls of the tiny cubby disappeared, and he walked through castles and rode through the forests of England and Europe all the way to the Holy Land. With King Richard he charged the Moslems[8] and made a treaty with Saladin the Turk so Christian pilgrims could travel safely in the Holy Land.

He read on and on, shifting from elbow to elbow, rolling on his side, then on his back. Sitting up to read wasn't easy because he had to put the book on the floor between his feet and bend over it to have enough light. Only when the candle guttered did he look away from the page before him and realize where he was and how stiff his muscles were. With a sigh, he

closed the volume, wrapped it up again, and hid it behind the door of his cubby. The candle flared up one last time and went out.

The next morning Cook had to pound on his door to waken him. Why wasn't he up and working? Was he sick? No? Well, then, best have breakfast and get to work.

Will rubbed his eyes. He thought they'd never open. His muscles made him wince when he rolled over. He limped into the kitchen, rubbed his sore shoulders, and stretched his stiff back.

Over the following weeks, Cook wondered at the difference in the scullery[9] boy. He often had a faraway expression and was tired in the morning. But he never had to be told to take the heavy scuttles upstairs. She did not notice the occasional bulge beneath his shirt.

---

[8]Moslem—a person who believes in the religion of Islam
[9]scullery—a room for cleaning kitchen dishes and utensils

By the end of December, Will's supply of candles was nearly gone. Fortunately, the holiday parties and celebrations provided a new supply of partially burned candles, too many for the housekeeper or Cook to count. But holidays that brought him the extra candles also made it more difficult to get into the library because of the Vicar's many guests. Will was happy when everyone finally left and the household settled back into its routine.

During the next three months, he read of Marco Polo's visits to the court of Kublai Khan and a book on the Hundred Years' War between England and France. Will felt rather sorry for Joan of Arc. She was so brave leading the French army that he thought it too bad the English army captured her and burned her as a witch. He found a book by a man named Langland who had walked all over England and written down what he saw. It wasn't as exciting as reading William Shakespeare's plays, however. Then he found a volume of Chaucer's *Canterbury Tales*. The "Knight's Tale" was the best of all, and Will set himself the task of memorizing the passages of the great battles. He memorized up to the last battle of the knight Arcite, who had fallen from his horse, hit his head, broken his ribs, and lay dying. Will would have finished, but by the end of March, he was nearly out of candles again. This time it was Cook

herself who helped him out. She sent him to clean all the candlesticks in the house and put new candles in them. At any other time Will would have hated cleaning the wax left behind by dripping candles. Now he picked up the large basket and went through all the rooms collecting candlesticks without complaining.

He entered the room of Elspeth, the Vicar's daughter. Will did not like her at all. She was always calling him a maid because he cleaned the pots and pans in the scullery. She bullied him every chance she had and made him do all sorts of irksome[10] tasks for her. Today, however, he decided to be nice, because it was her turn to contribute to his candle collection.

"I say, there. What are you doing?"

Will spun around with a candlestick in his hand. She really is sneaky, he thought. Aloud he said, "Taking this candlestick to be cleaned. It's awfully messy."

"It also has nearly half a candle in it." Her eyes closed ever so little when she smiled. "Are you selling the ends back to the candle maker and keeping the money? I shall tell Father at once."

"No, I haven't been selling the ends back to the candle maker," Will said mimicking her. "You can ask Cook. She sent me to collect and

---

[10]irksome—annoying

clean these. Now if you don't want this one cleaned . . ." He left the sentence unfinished, shrugged, and moved to replace the candlestick on the mantle.

"Oh, no. Please do clean it," Elspeth fairly purred. "I'm going to follow you, though, until I find out whether or not you're selling those candle bits. This will be more fun than my embroidery and music lessons."

Will watched her.

"You may go." She motioned him away.

From then on Elspeth appeared at the most unexpected times and places. Will started looking around corners and peeking through doorways before he took another step. Still she surprised him, once with a full coal scuttle. He spun around so fast, lumps of coal went rolling onto the floor, scattering black dust. Elspeth stood over him while he picked up the coal and wiped the floor. She also visited the kitchen more often, much to Cook's annoyance.

Spying Elspeth

Lady Day came and Will went with the other parishioners[11] to hear another of the Vicar's sermons. Lady Day was not only the day the angel told the virgin Mary she would be the mother of Jesus but March 25 was also New Year's, the first day of 1653. After the service everyone ate in the churchyard and played games. The Green Man visited, decorated with leaves and vines from the woods, to wish good crops for the farmers. When the sun set, a huge bonfire lit the churchyard, and the young people sang and celebrated the end of winter. A late shower did not dampen their spirits. It only sent the older folks home to tuck the children into bed.

Shortly after Lady Day, Will finished memorizing his favorite parts of the "Knight's Tale." When the days grew longer and he spent more time tending the herb garden, he recited the battles over and over again. When he escaped down the lane, he used stick knights and horses and set up whole battlefields.

When summer came, Will frequently went and sat on the hill overlooking the London Road. He took his book with him because he was now memorizing the exploits[12] of King Richard the Lion-Hearted in the Third Crusade. The rumble of the traffic, the shouts and calls of the

[11]parishioners—members of a parish (a church district)
[12]exploits—heroic or daring deeds

people became the clamor of great campaigns. And as long as he didn't look up from the story, he lived at the end of the twelfth century and rode at King Richard's side.

Later on he went back to the library and took the volume about King Arthur. So much of King Arthur's trouble was caused by the wicked witch, Morgan le Fay. She reminded Will of Elspeth because they were both sneaky.

Elspeth's spying had kept him from returning to the library as often as he liked. Only by going very early one morning was he able to return the volume about Arthur and remove the history of Charlemagne. Even then, he was certain he heard the rustle of cloth. The squeak from the hinge on the bookcase door sounded like a scream when he pushed the door shut. Will tucked the new book into his shirt and tiptoed down the stairs toward the kitchen.

His hand was out to open the door. Then he froze where he was.

"Elspeth, you leave that boy alone!"

"You can't tell me what to do. This is my house. You merely work here!"

Will stepped back into the corner behind the door. Maybe Elspeth had seen him go into the library. Maybe he hadn't just imagined the noises. He had no time to put his newest book back now. Besides, he wanted

to hear everything that was going on in the kitchen. Elspeth was no match for Cook.

"Your scullery boy is stealing everyone's candles."

"Really?" Cook smoothed her voice to the consistency of honey. She frequently found the Vicar's children a nuisance, but Elspeth wanted bunging[13] out the kitchen door for all her high and mighty ways. "I allow him all the candle ends he digs out of the candlesticks."

"Look what I found in his cubby! Several candle ends and half a good candle as well! I think he's selling the ends to the candle maker."

Will clutched the book in his shirt. What if he had not taken his book back this morning? She would have found it. His heart began to beat so hard that he was sure the whole house could hear. He held his breath and crunched himself farther into the corner.

"That's his half candle he gets each week. If you must know, I give him the odd broken ones as well. Now stop being a silly goose."

"Why does he need these candles? Have you thought of that?"

"You've been into his cubby. How many windows did you count?" Cook snapped back.

"He's up to something. He sneaks around the house, you know."

[13]bunging—(British) flinging or tossing

"And who's creeping about?" Cook's eyebrows flew up. "Put those bits and pieces of candle back where you found them." Cook's knife expertly quartered an onion for the evening's meat pie.

"I'm not going in there. It stinks."

"You went in there to pry."

Elspeth stood at the door and tossed the candles into the cubby.

"Now you'll go in there and sort those candles out and leave them as you found them. Then you'll leave my kitchen, or I'll put you to work in the scullery." Cook's words were slow and calm. Even if Elspeth didn't realize that Cook had reached the end of her patience, Will knew. From his corner he wondered if Cook would really thrash Elspeth. He hoped so, and he moved closer to the door so he wouldn't miss anything.

"Ugh!" Elspeth came out of the cubby shaking her skirts. "Doesn't he ever change his straw?"

"Once a month or as often as your father allows him new."

Elspeth stood silent for a moment. She knew, as well as Cook, that it was her mother who ran the house. She pinched every penny and would never allow new straw every month. Elspeth had enough trouble wheedling a new bodice[14] for the midsummer celebrations next week.

"Well, doesn't he ever bathe?"

"Once a week except in winter. And if you recall," Cook's tone was not friendly, "it was a long, cold winter." Her knife chopped a carrot in two. "Now, off with you; out of my kitchen."

Elspeth flounced[15] through the door, hitting it so hard that it cracked against the stone wall behind. Will didn't dare move until she reached the top of the stairs. He reached out for the door handle, but thought better of it. He didn't want to have to explain to Cook why he had been upstairs so early in the day. So he tiptoed back up the stairs, slipped out a side door, walked around through the garden, and entered the kitchen through the back door.

"Get about your business, boy."

Will stepped into his cubby to hide his new book. It definitely did not stink in there.

"Get to work, I say." Cook watched Will go into the scullery. When she heard pots and pans clanging and the steady scrubbing of sand against metal, she turned back to the vegetables.

---

[14]bodice—a woman's vest worn over a blouse
[15]flounced—used bouncy, exaggerated movement

The long summer days passed slowly for Will. Cook decided that every inch of the kitchen needed cleaning. Will emptied all the cupboards and moved them so the walls and floors could be washed down. Then he dusted the cupboards and polished them with beeswax. He was surprised that Cook didn't make him wipe off the ceiling beams. Even the fireplace and chimney received a cleaning. Will breathed a sigh of relief when a chimney sweep came to do that.

When he wasn't in the kitchen, Will worked long hours in the gardens. There were berries, apples, and pears to be picked. The herb garden needed constant attention to keep the weeds from taking over. The gardener was as hard a taskmaster as Cook, and he soon had Will lopping branches off trees and trimming the bushes and hedges[16] as well.

Will decided he liked the outside work the best. It was easier to stay away from the Vicar's family, particularly Elspeth. It was easier to recite the passages from his books too. He had only to look into the tangle of a hedge to imagine himself in a forest. Sometimes he finished his work hardly remembering what he'd been doing.

He tried hard not to think too much of Rodgers anymore. In the

[16]hedges—rows of closely planted shrubs or small trees

year since Mistress Bessie had died and he'd lived at the vicarage, Rodgers had never come visiting once. And when visitors did call, Will was always sent to the scullery or on a long errand. It soon became clear that he was never to be around when guests arrived. So when the wagon wheels crunched in the driveway, or horses' hooves clattered up to the front gate, Will left his work and disappeared for an hour or two.

One late August afternoon when he heard a rider stop, Will picked up his book and set off down the lane. The day was warm under a blue sky dotted with only a few small clouds. In the lane, wildflowers bloomed in the tall grasses and the smell of freshly cut hay blew over the low stone walls.

He sat on the hill overlooking the highway, reading and memorizing until his eyes began to close. Then he leaned back on his elbows to watch the world passing below him. A few minutes later a man carrying a small boy on his shoulders caught his eye. They were very poor. Their clothes had holes and didn't fit very well. The boy drooped over the man's head, not even bothering to hang on. The man shuffled at the edge of the highway, never slowing down or hurrying along no matter who shouted at him.

Rodgers carried me like that on our way to Mistress Bessie's, Will thought. He could still remember sitting on Rodgers's shoulders and being able to look down on all the people around him. He recalled turning into the lane that led to Mistress Bessie's cottage. Will's mind filled with pictures of the cottage, of Button, the cat, curled up on the warm hearth, and of Mistress working in her rose garden. He thought of their trips to market for groceries and clothes. He glanced down at his shirt and breeches. His wrists and an-

kles stuck out because he had grown so much, and he'd had only one new shirt and pair of shoes all winter.

I had proper clothes at Mistress Bessie's, he thought, and all I wanted to eat of bread and preserves and thick stews and meat pies. The memories faded into the churchyard where he had stood with Rodgers at her grave.

When he finally sat up, the traffic moved as it had before under the yellow sun. Nobody looked in his direction. Oxen still bellowed, and dust drifted up from the wheels of the carts and wagons they pulled. Whips cracked. Horses whinnied. Draymen[17] shouted. Will took a deep breath.

"So this is where you come!"

Will jerked up and looked over his shoulder. Elspeth! The book tucked inside his shirt pressed against his ribs. He turned back to the road and slid the book more securely into his waistband.

"Go away."

"I knew I'd find where you ran off to if I followed you long enough." She stood over him. "You should be working."

"Cook doesn't need me until afternoon. Besides, someone called at the vicarage, and I always get sent away."

"The gardener was looking for you."

---

[17]draymen—drivers of a dray (a heavy cart used for hauling things)

"He can do his old garden himself."

"I shall tell Father you've been running off. You'll be locked in your cubby—with no candle ends at all."

A carriage of some important man caught Will's eye. Four horsemen protected it. Once it reached the wild countryside, robber gangs might attack. He studied the horses prancing and tossing their heads. They wanted to gallop straight away. Elspeth was still talking, and her tone became angrier. Will's eye was drawn to the livery[18] worn by the outriders. The purple and silver cloth, shining buttons, and jaunty

hats with huge feathers were grander than any he had ever seen.

"Ow!"

Elspeth had his ear and was dragging him up. She pinched harder when he slapped her hand.

"Let go!" Will tried to get up to relieve the pressure on his ear. He couldn't get his feet to catch up. When her skirt caught on a piece of rusted metal, she yanked it free without missing a step.

Will reversed tactics. Instead of pulling away from Elspeth, he ran straight at her, his fists waving. He swung twice, but she straightened her arm and held him away. He thought his ear would be torn off. A picture of Mistress Bessie holding

---

[18]livery—uniform worn by male servants of a household

tightly to Peter's ear flashed through his mind. He laughed out loud.

Elspeth stopped. "Laugh at me, will you?" She brought her other hand around to slap Will, but the sudden movement allowed him to slip free. He ran back toward the vicarage, half-laughing, half-crying, holding his ear with one hand and the book in his waistband with the other. He ran through the garden gate, around the vicarage, and stumbled into the hedge at the side of the house.

"You, boy! Get out of there and back to the scullery!"

The Vicar turned to his guest, who had just arrived. "I hardly know what to think of the world today. . . ."

The guest wasn't listening. He was staring at the scullery boy. The Vicar cleared his throat for a more authoritative tone.

"Be gone, boy. You know you're not to be seen when we have visitors."

The guest's eyebrows flew up, and he looked quickly from the Vicar to the boy who was fighting to free himself from the hedge. "I say, isn't that—"

"My apologies, my friend. Such carryings on are simply not permitted in my household. Mrs. Richards takes all the help in hand to teach each one his place, but some are more difficult than others." The Vicar coughed apologetically. "Elspeth?"

The Vicar's daughter came round the side of the house, brandishing a switch. Her cap was askew[19] and wisps of straight, brown hair hung to her shoulders. Part of her hem trailed in the grass.

"Where is he? Slap at me, run away from me, laugh at me, will he? Where is the little toad?" She paused for breath. "I'll give him a lesson he'll soon not forget." She tripped over a tree root and fell against the house.

Will collapsed in the hedge and laughed until his sides hurt.

Elspeth righted herself and raised the switch. "I'll sort you out!" She was nearly shouting.

Will tore himself free of the hedge, ducked Elspeth's switch, and ran to the back of the house and into the kitchen. He stumbled into his cubby and collapsed on the straw, still laughing.

Meanwhile, the Vicar was trying to bring some order to what he could only describe as a social disaster.

---

[19]askew—not lined up or straight

"Elspeth . . . my dear! Elspeth, my pet. We have a visitor."

Elspeth stopped in midstride and whirled around. She looked up. Her face registered her thought: handsome! Elspeth dropped the switch and ran her fingers around her cap, trying to tuck her hair in, and kicked the trailing hem behind her. She approached the two men with what she believed was her most becoming expression, a slight smile that just showed her teeth and made her dimples appear. She'd practiced it in front of her glass for hours.

Rodgers looked past her. "I'd like to see the . . . toad . . . if I may."

The Vicar harrumphed. "Yes, indeed. . . . Are you quite sure? Yes, of course you are. Ah, Elspeth, who was that . . . that?"

"He's the scullery boy, Father." Elspeth never took her eyes from Rodgers.

"Oh, yes . . . quite." The Vicar led Rodgers up the garden walk. "If you please, sir. Elspeth, please bring us refreshments in the library."

Will didn't care if the Vicar beat him for running from Elspeth or appearing when a guest was present. It was worth it to see that girl all mussed and tattered. He rubbed his sore ear. He still owed her for that.

Not Forgotten!

Cook called him. "The house-keeper wants you to clean the fire-places this afternoon. See that you don't scatter ash all over. Put any live coals in the kitchen fire."

Will took the canvas, bucket, and shovel and started up the stairs. Ahead of him he could hear the Vicar holding forth on the evils of an unlettered[20] younger generation, and that was why he consented, at great inconvenience to himself, mind you, to take in local youngsters and set them on their way with lessons in reading and writing, both English and Latin. He played no favorites as some did, but taught boys and girls alike. Of course, the girls didn't need as much education. . . . The Vicar warmed to his topic.

Will spread the canvas on the dining room hearth. He was supposed to have had those lessons.

"And how is Will coming along? I have been disappointed that he has not been here whenever I have visited." Will turned to stone at the sound of that voice.

Vicar Richards said in his most reassuring voice, "Oh, famously, quite. In a few more years, he'll be ready for the university if that's

---

[20]unlettered—illiterate; unable to read well

36

your intention, or ready to be put to apprentice[21] much sooner."

Will knelt in front of the fireplace, shovel in hand. Rodgers! He's been here before! I've been sent off every time, he thought. Will held his breath.

"And has the allowance been sufficient for all his needs?" Rodgers asked.

"Of course, of course. I immediately turn all monies over to Mrs. Richards, you know. My wife and the housekeeper discuss each child's needs and strive to meet them within the limits of the fees. I must say they do extremely well."

Will wanted to jump up and shout to Rodgers that he was in the dining room. And he might have done it, if he hadn't looked down at his dirty and ill-fitting clothes. Suddenly, he was embarrassed and didn't want Rodgers to see him at all. Not looking like this!

Rodgers spoke again. "You have other children staying with you? Do they get on with Will?"

"None at the moment, but when they're here, they do tend to get on well together. I like to think it's the loving atmosphere of the house. Aha!" Will could hear the smile in the Vicar's voice. "A case in point. My daughter and the light of my life."

"Oh, Father."

Will could imagine her curtseying to Rodgers and wearing that silly expression. He sat waiting for the conversation across the hall to resume.[22]

"No, it's true, my dear." In the stillness of the old house, Will heard the Vicar pat his daughter's hand. "A good match you'll be for any young man. Raised with love, yet well educated. A good match." The Vicar paused. "Don't you agree, sir?"

"Quite." Rodgers said. "I'm sure she'll be more than a match for any young man."

"Wouldn't have to be a young man, would it my dear? It is frequently advantageous for a young lady to . . . ah . . . marry a man somewhat beyond her years, a man settled in his work with more than two coins to rub together. Someone more like yourself, sir."

"Surely, there's a man perfect for her," Rodgers said briskly. "Now about Will—"

"Will you pour, Elspeth, before you return to your duties?"

The clatter of cups and saucers was followed by Elspeth's retreating footsteps.

"Some people have hard hearts, and no mistake, but not that girl. Worrying herself over a stray kitten just yesterday, she was."

"Now about Will." After a moment of silence, Rodgers raised his voice a bit. "The boy!"

"What? Yes, what about him? I believe I've told you all I can."

---

[21]apprentice—person who learns a skill or trade by working for a skilled craftsman
[22]resume—to begin again; continue

"I demand to hear him recite his lessons before I leave. I do have a bit of personal interest in him, as does Mr. Perry, and so far we've no satisfaction that he's doing as well as you say he is."

Not forgotten! Will's heart pounded. Not alone! And Rodgers wants to hear me recite! I could read to him from King Richard, but it's in my cubby. I could recite from the "Knight's Tale." That's what I'll do— the part where Arcite dies. Or maybe—

In the library, Rodgers leaned forward and put his cup and saucer on the tray.

"What has he been studying, if you please?" Rodgers said. "He always loved knights, dragons, and all sorts of exploration and adventure."

"Just so." The Vicar wheezed as he rose from his chair. "I'll show you the library available to the boy as soon as he's ready for it. Quite the

follower of such reading myself, I am. Mind I keep those volumes in the back. Don't want to appear frivolous[23] or put them before my other, more learned theological studies." He opened the bookcase. "How odd. It appears these volumes have been moved. And just a fortnight[24] ago I found a truly bad smudge on one of the pages of my Tacitus. Most distressed I was and took it right to the printer, for it looked like the result of poor quality ink. Horrible smudge. I'm very particular about who handles my books." He pulled some from the front row. "Notice the quality. Each year I personally set them all in front of the fire to dry the vellum. It absorbs the damp so. What's this? One is missing! Someone has taken a book!"

---

[23]frivolous—not serious or important
[24]fortnight—two weeks

The Vicar pulled out book after book. Rodgers held the growing stack until it threatened to topple.

"Might I just put these on your desk?"

The Vicar's voice rose. "Look! Look at the condition of these bindings—finger marks, water spotted, pages soiled. Now who—" He ran to the library door and shouted, "Elspeth, Mrs. Richards, come here at once, and bring the housekeeper. Bring everyone! I will know who's responsible for this. Whoever it is will pay dearly."

Footsteps hurried from several rooms. Elspeth arrived first. "Father, Father," she nearly shrieked, "look what I found in Will's cubby! Your volume of King Richard. And look at the stains on it, Father; he should be whipped! How dare a scullery boy steal, or even presume[25] to read your books!"

Will cringed. Did he dare run? Could he hide?

Mrs. Richards joined her daughter. "Why, Rodgers, good day to you. And how are the Perrys? I understand they've just added a son to their family."

Rodgers bowed slightly. "Thank you for your interest. The Perrys have indeed a new son, a welcome addition, I assure you."

"And the twins?"

[25]presume—to act without permission or authority

"Very well, thank you. They've just turned five."

"Madame!" exclaimed the Vicar. "Kindly bring the amenities[26] to an end. I've called to discover who might have been in my bookcase without permission. Just look at the damage!" He waved the volume of King Richard in front of her face. When she tried to take it, he handed it to Rodgers. "Just look at that!"

"Mother, he'll have an apoplexy!"[27] Elspeth said.

The Vicar's voice nearly rattled the windows. "Where did you say you found this book?"

"The scullery boy. I told you I found that book in his cubby. I knew he was up to something with all those candles."

"Eh? What candles? Look at my books! Get him. Now! Bring him here. I'm of a mind to have him arrested right after I give him the beating he deserves. He'll work off every penny of their value. He'll be in the scullery until he's fifty!"

"Yes, Vicar, let's see this scullery boy named Will." Rodgers snapped the words across the room. "I believe we'll find more problems than a few well-read books." He went to the door and called so the whole house shook. "Will! Will. It's Rodgers. I must speak with you now!"

Will slowly stepped from behind the dining room door and into the hallway.

Rodgers motioned with the book he held. "Will, come into the library . . . Yes, come along." He motioned them all to chairs. "You too, Will."

"No, he mustn't sit on the cush—" Mrs. Richards began.

"Get him out of my sight. He's worse than a thief." The Vicar sat on the edge of his chair.

"He'll stay while I speak," Rodgers began. "It was with the distinct understanding when you took Will on after Margaret Bessie's death that you would treat him as a family member and continue his lessons."

Rodgers held up his hand at the beginning of a protest from the Vicar's wife. "Master Perry provided you with ample funds for his room, board, and clothing. Indeed I have three pounds, fourteen shillings, six-pence in my pocket to pay last quarter's charges."

"It'll not begin to cover the cost of my books!"

Rodgers ignored the interruption. "Instead what I find is a dirty, poorly fed, abominably clothed boy forced to do the heaviest household labor and to forgo his lessons as well." He turned to Will. "How many lessons have you had this past year?"

"None," Will said and rushed on, "that's why I took the books—"

---

[26]amenities—pleasant or polite conversation; "small talk"

[27]apoplexy—(ăp´ə plĕk´sē) a stroke or sudden attack on the brain

"Shh." Rodgers addressed the Vicar and his wife. "If you two were in a proper business, you'd be imprisoned for embezzlement[28] and breach[29] of contract. Don't get red in the face. I believe you've misspent the money meant to support Will. Heaven only knows what you've done with the clothing provided for him.

"Because you have not honored your commitment to Will for this past year and more, you will receive no more of Master Perry's money. Nor will he, I should add, recommend you as a teacher in the future. Will, go collect your belongings."

Will looked down at his clothes and shrugged.

"That's it? You have nothing more? . . . One should not leave such a hospitable home with such a thin valise."[30] Rodgers held up a book. "I believe he's earned this and one other of his choice many times over, don't you, Vicar?"

"No, I do not. He's earned nothing and been nothing but trouble. I'll have the constable on you!"

Rodgers stood. "Master Perry could take you in suit before the law for what you've done here."

"My dear, no!" whispered Mrs. Richards from her seat. "I was depending on the last quarter's fees to cover the expenses of a new gown and party for Elspeth for her sixteenth birthday. If we lose our position here at the vicarage, how can we afford—"

"Hush, Barbara!" Vicar Richards looked at Will, then Rodgers. "All right, take the boy and the book and good riddance."

Rodgers smiled and held up two fingers. "Two books."

"He's not touching my books again."

"Very well." Rodgers stepped over to the stack of books on the desk. "Which one, Will? And I will take it for you."

[28]embezzlement—the act of stealing money in the course of a job
[29]breach—breaking, as of a rule or contract
[30]valise—small suitcase or luggage

Will stepped over to the desk and bent his head sideways so he could read the titles. "The third from the bottom."

"Of course, you want the thick one at the bottom." Rodgers set the other books aside. "Chaucer, eh? Beautiful binding. Great stories, aren't they? 'Wife of Bath' interest you?"

The Vicar fairly exploded. "Not the Chaucer!"

"The 'Knight's Tale,'" Will answered.

"Not my Chaucer!"

"Correct, it is no longer *your* Chaucer. Let's be off, Will. It is clear we are in no proper Vicar's house."

Will returns to the temporary care of Master Perry and Rodgers until a suitable arrangement can be made. Perry and Rodgers decide to go ahead and apprentice Will to an ironmonger, or blacksmith, even though he is still a bit young and small. Once more, Will loses contact with Rodgers, this time under the agreement of his apprenticeship.

Will does well with his new trade and even befriends three other apprentices. However, he unintentionally leads them into trouble, which results in a great adventure. This adventure proves the true friendship of Rodgers as he once again rescues Will in his time of need.

The Dewey Decimal System

The author of *The Foundling* probably spent some time in the library looking up information before she started writing. She would have looked for books about England's history and orphaned children in the 1600s. Perhaps she used the card catalog or a computer to search by title, author, or subject. If her library used the Dewey decimal system, she would also have had the choice of investigating a whole section of books on English history.

Learning About the Dewey Decimal System

The Dewey decimal system of cataloging books could easily be called "the browsing system." Melvil Dewey, a Christian librarian, developed the system in 1876. He continued to revise and update it until his death in 1931.

Melvil Dewey lived from 1851 to 1931.

In the Dewey decimal system, books are classified in one of ten general subject areas. Each subject has a three-digit number to represent it. Notice that each general subject on the following chart begins with a multiple of one hundred, such as 100, 200, 300, and so on.

000–099	Generalities (encyclopedias, general reference works, computing)
100–199	Philosophy, psychology, logic, ethics
200–299	Religion and mythology
300–399	Social sciences (government, education, etiquette)
400–499	Language
500–599	Natural sciences, mathematics, physics, chemistry, biology
600–699	Technology (Applied sciences—medicine, engineering, manufacturing)
700–799	The arts (painting, music, sports)
800–899	Literature, rhetoric (novels, short stories, plays)
900–999	Geography, history, travel, biography

Each three-digit number can be used to narrow a search for information. Within each number, the digits in the hundreds, tens, and ones places identify a more specific topic.

These numbers allow each of the general subjects to be divided further. Each general subject is broken down into ten topics that deal with that specific subject. Consider the 900s as an example. The general subjects for the 900s are history, geography, biography, and travel. Like the other nine general subjects, the 900s are broken down into ten smaller and more specific topics. Look at the example of the way the 900s are divided further.

Topics within the General Subject

900 General history
910 General geography
920 General biography
930 History of the ancient world to A.D. 500
940 History of Europe
950 History of Asia
960 History of Africa
970 History of North America

Subtopics

970 General information on North America
971 Canada
972 Middle America; Mexico
973 United States, Historical Periods

973.1 Discovery Period

973.11 Primitive America
973.12 Chinese Discovery
973.13 Norse Discovery
973.14 Welsh Discovery
973.15 European Discovery

973.2 Colonial Period
973.3 War for Independence

974 Northeastern United States
975 Southeastern United States
976 South Central United States; Gulf Coast
977 North Central United States
978 Western United States
979 Great Basin and Pacific Slope

980 History of South America, Latin America, Spanish America
990 History of Oceania, polar regions

A person who wants to browse through books on United States history could find the 900s section in the library and then locate the 970s. But again, even the 970s would be broken down into ten more categories having to do with North America.

Understanding Decimals

As you see, the Dewey decimal system has ten main subjects with multiples of one hundred to represent each. The ten subjects are each divided into ten topics, and every topic is divided into ten subtopics.

Beyond these divisions, decimals are used for more specific information. A person wanting to glance through books on United States history would immediately go to the 900s. He would find his subject by looking at the 970s for North America and then by checking 973 for the history of the United States itself. He would then discover that the 973 topic is subdivided. Books in the 973.1 section are about the dis-covery period of America. The 973.2 books deal with the colonial period, and books in the category of 973.3 are about the War for American Independence. Notice how decimals are used on the chart.

The divisions using decimals continue with each specific subject about the United States. The discovery period of America (973.1) is broken down into books about primitive America as well as into books about Chinese, Norse, Welsh, and European claims of discovering America. Look at the chart to see where these belong within the topic of "United States, Historical Periods."

The Dewey decimal system may seem a bit complicated at first, but for people who enjoy reading, it is the perfect system. It lets a person browse through the library shelves, scanning through books on his favorite subjects—anything from orphans in England to Christopher Columbus!

Listening to Katey

Louise D. Nicholas

illustrated by Johanna Ehnis

Easy Money

As I see it, all my troubles started in history class. Ike, my best friend, says history class had nothing to do with the whole mess. But Ike never has been strong on cause-and-effect reasoning.

Ike thinks maybe we should have listened to Katey. Now, I ask you—why should two sixth graders listen to a ten-year-old girl? Don't get me wrong. My little sister is just about the best a guy could ask for, but Katey simply has no imagination.

Take for instance the time our family went to a family reunion down in Tennessee. Katey was five then, and I was seven. Uncle Luke's place is way out in the country, a real log cabin with a split-rail fence around the yard and a barn, two sheds, a chicken coop,

and an outhouse. Beyond that is pastureland and woods for miles.

Soon as I got there I said to Katey, "Let's take off and see what we can find that's adventuresome." She said, "No, let's go in the cabin." Go in the cabin! What could possibly be adventuresome in a cabin? So I went on to the barn to scout around, and Katey went into the kitchen with Grandma, Mom, Aunt Louise, Aunt Betsy, Aunt Mildred, and however many cousins. You can see that a man of adventure would have been out of place in the kitchen.

I say *would have* because normally a kitchen offers little in the way of true excitement—discounting, of course, Aunt Louise's chocolate pie. But this time, as it is many times

46

with Katey, when she does not seek out life, it seeks her out.

Katey was sitting in the rocking chair by the window watching that particular kind of hubbub that can be created only by a dozen women getting a supper ready at a reunion. And then she saw a snake, a wily, shiny green one, put his head around the edge of the open back door. He flickered his tongue once and then oozed the rest of him over the threshold[1] and in along the wall. Katey studied him a while, until he disappeared behind the stove.

Then she went to Mom who was sitting at the table shelling peas. She tugged at the sleeve of Mom's cotton dress. "Mama—"

"Now, Katey, I said you had to stay back out of the way," Mom said. "Go on, honey, and sit in the rocker."

"But, Mama—"

"Go on, Katey."

Katey went back. In a little while, the snake slid out of his hiding place and traveled in that liquid way of snakes over toward Katey. Then he turned suddenly and went down behind the water heater just as smooth as a Slinky.

Katey got up and this time went to Grandma. "Grandma, there's a snake in here."

"What!" Grandma always took things calmly.

"A snake went behind that tank," said Katey.

"Oh my land!" said Grandma. "Louise, get Luke in here!"

"Wait," said Mom. She pulled Katey over to her gently. "I think Katey is just saying that to get attention. I suppose I shouldn't have made her sit in the chair so long. I'll get Pete to take her for a walk."

"But, Mama—"

"Hush, Katey."

And so that's when I heard my name, loud and distinct, all the way up to the edge of the woods. It came to me on the wind, and it came *Peter*, not *Pete*, which means in my mom's code that any dawdling in the response will be regarded as a felony[2]. I still give my mother the credit for my holding the record for the fifty-yard dash at school. Without her calling me in all the time, I would never have gotten so much practice.

Anyway, I arrived at the back door to see what the summons was for. Grandma was saying to Katey, "You can tell Grandma, sweetheart. Did you make up a story?"

I said to Mom, "What's going on?"

"I want you to take Katey out with you. She's bored in here."

I thought to myself that I could see how that would happen.

"What did she do?" I asked, not so much out of curiosity as out of a

---

[1]threshold—the floor or ground at an entrance or doorway
[2]felony—a serious crime

sense of research. If I knew what Katey had done, I might be able to avoid doing the same thing myself.

"Oh," said Mom, "she told Grandma there was a snake behind the water heater." Mom almost smiled telling me this. I started to smile too, but I stopped. Even as my mother spoke, I caught a glimpse of something moving, slow and smooth, around the rocker.

"You mean that one?" I said, pointing toward a large green creature coming our way.

Rarely in my life has a sentence from my mouth sparked such an instantaneous and gratifying[3] response. My grandmother yelled "Luke" at such an amazingly high pitch that for a second I thought perhaps the water heater had blown up. My mother swept up Katey and stood her on the table, all the while saying, "Peter, Peter, get back." Aunt Betsy went into some kind of high-stepping dance over by the sink, and Aunt Mildred whipped open the bedroom door and waved at us wildly. "Everyone into the bedroom," she kept saying, as if it were a bomb shelter.

The snake meanwhile had tried to make a straight shot for the back door. Aunt Louise sidetracked the snake with an empty frying pan and

---

[3]gratifying—pleasing

a spatula, which she threw with surprising accuracy in its direction. I tried to make a grab for the snake as it turned back toward my mother who had suddenly joined Katey on the kitchen table. I might have got it too, except Aunt Louise's next missile—a kettle lid—bounced off me instead of the snake.

Uncle Luke stood transfixed[4] in the doorway, seeing every available surface above floor level occupied with screaming women and his wife throwing kettle lids at his favorite nephew. "What's going on here?" he roared, as the snake slipped right past him out the door.

There was suddenly silence and calm. Katey, who had been watching quietly all the while, smiled at Uncle Luke. "There was a snake in here," she said.

But to get back to the story I had set out to tell you. All of us kids wanted to go to the new amusement park that had opened about an hour's drive away from our town. It was called the Kingdom by the Sea, and the ads for it in the paper just fairly made your head swim. There was everything in the world to do there. You could go on a safari, with a real safari helmet but with a camera instead of a gun, of course. If you got the most pictures on your safari, you would win a dinner for your whole family at the restaurant there called The Ten-Gallon Hat that served barbecued beef and Texas chili.

You could also ride elephants, rent costumes to wear, and see fireworks and watch a parade every evening. And of course there were all the usual rides and games of an amusement park there too. The only trouble was, it cost a lot of money to get in. Forty dollars a ticket.

"I'm sorry, son," Dad had said. "I'd like to give you and Katey the money, but it'd be eighty dollars plus another twenty for the bus ride. I'm afraid I just can't do it."

Katey and I tried to look as if it didn't matter to us one way or the

[4]transfixed—motionless in amazement

other. I looked over at Katey; I hoped I was doing a better job of not looking disappointed than she was.

"But," he said, "the grand opening's still a month and a half away. Maybe you can earn the money yourselves."

Katey beamed out one of those smiles of hers, and I felt inspiration carry my heart up like a helium balloon.

The next day I said to Ike, "So all we have to do is come up with a quick way to earn the ticket money."

"How are we going to do that?" Ike wanted to know. "We don't have any talent."

"Ike, Ike, Ike," I said. "You don't need talent for this, just brains. "

He nodded solemnly.

"Just keep your eyes open for a good plan," I said. "We'll think of something."

Katey, lacking our sense of enterprise[5] and adventure, went around asking our neighbors for housecleaning jobs. Mrs. Bittner hired her to pick strawberries instead.

"Why don't you come along," Katey said to me. "We could pick twice as many berries and make twice as much money."

"No," I said, appalled.[6] "Men do not pick strawberries. And besides,

---
[5]enterprise—willingness to undertake risky projects
[6]appalled—surprised and dismayed

that's too slow a method. Ike and I are going to make money fast."

"How?" said Katey, her big green eyes looking up at me with admiration.

"Well, we're not sure of our plan yet, but I'll let you know."

Method Madness

For the next week, Katey got up early every morning to go pick strawberries. I would hear her alarm go off and then in a little while her door would open quietly, and down she'd go to the kitchen. I could hear her get some cereal, the bowl and spoon clicking, the cupboard doors opening and closing. Then the back door opened and closed quietly, and in my mind I could see her stepping out into the dew and shadows. And then I felt sorry for her because there was no way she could earn enough money picking berries.

Ike and I tossed around several plans. None seemed entirely satisfactory. We thought we might try to invent a new soft drink, but we didn't have enough money to buy the ingredients to experiment with. We tried mixing soda, orange juice, and apple cider, but when Mom found out about that scientific endeavor,[7] she revoked[8] our inventors' licenses. We also had to pay for the wasted groceries. I say *wasted* because we hadn't come up with a combination we thought would sell. Ike said it might possibly go as an insect repellent, but he didn't know of anything else.

The grocery penalty nearly wiped out my allowance. With the two dollars I had left I bought a used book entitled *How to Make Money at Home*. What I learned from reading that book was that the best way to make money at home is to stay there and write a book on how to make money at home and sell it to people who are looking to make money. Ike asked if he could read the book, and I let him, but he didn't get any ideas out of it either.

Ike and I sat down on the porch steps and watched the traffic go by in front of the house.

"Well," said Ike, "we better come up with a plan pretty soon."

This thought had also occurred to me. "Let's try to think of all the ways we ever heard of someone getting very rich very quick. Maybe we can do what they did then."

"Striking oil," said Ike.

"Getting an inheritance," I said.

"Finding a treasure," said Ike.

That last had a ring to it. "I wonder if there's any treasure to be found around here?"

Ike looked at me hopefully a moment, then drooped. "If there was, Mr. Jackson would have already dug it up."

I nodded. Mr. Jackson was our history teacher. He knew everything there was to know about local history—or any history for that matter. Once he told us how he had worked all one summer with some people who were looking for some

---

[7]endeavor—major effort or attempt
[8]revoked—took back or took away

Pharaoh's brother's tomb. They never found it; but if they had, they would have all been famous.

"Hey!" I said, and Ike jumped. "We could look for artifacts[9] in that empty lot at the end of the cul-de-sac.[10] Mr. Jackson said there used to be Indian villages here. If we found a couple of arrows or tomahawks, we could sell them to a museum."

Ike looked doubtful.

"Come on," I said. "Those kinds of things go for a lot of money. One good tomahawk and we're into Kingdom by the Sea for sure. Are you with me?"

For several days we worked the lot with shovels and spades. We managed to create a rather large hole on the north side. In fact, when we stood in the hole, we could rest our elbows on the top edge of the rim. We uncovered a few interesting things, among which were a handle off a fancy china cup and the sole of a boot. We also uncovered three or four dozen worms and some slugs.

"Maybe we could open a bait shop," Ike said, as he held up one tremendously long worm for me to admire. "I think I'll save a few of these." He dropped the worm into a rusty can and put a stone on it for a lid.

[9]artifacts—ancient manmade objects
[10]cul-de-sac—dead-end street

The digging got harder as the hole got deeper, and Ike and I found we had to stop more and more often to check on the welfare of the captive worms.

During one of our worm breaks, Katey came by.

"Petey," she called down to me. "Petey, can you help me carry a box home from the post office? I don't want to wait until Daddy comes home. Mama said to ask you if you weren't too busy."

"Ah, Katey, I got things to do here. Can't you wait for Dad?"

"I guess so," she said. Like I said, Katey is a really good sister. "I was just worried he'd be late like sometimes and the window would be closed."

Ike said, "Oh, let's go help her. We aren't finding anything here anyway." I had noticed Ike's interest in the project was dwindling.[11]

"Sure we are," I said, mostly for Katey's benefit. "What about this?" I held up the remains of an umbrella. It was a true relic,[12] its bare steel ribs sticking out at odd angles.

Katey studied it briefly. "I didn't know Indians had umbrellas."

"They didn't," Ike said, putting up the plank we now had to use to

---

[11]dwindling—growing less; becoming smaller
[12]relic—something that survives from the distant past

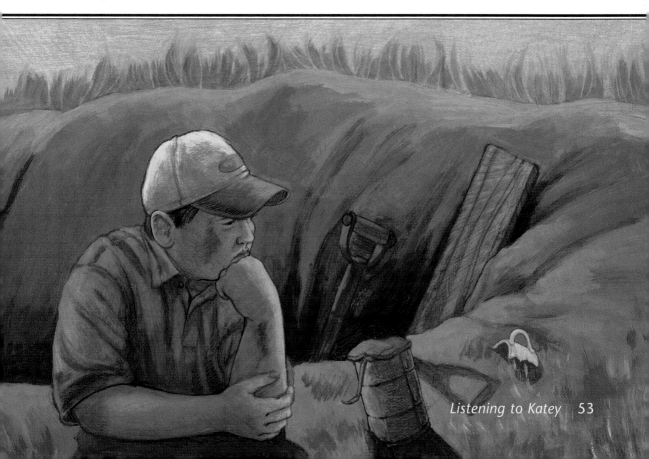

get out of the hole and looking at me as if to say "Ha!"

Katey's box at the post office was heavy. "What's in here?" I asked her.

"Stationery. Writing paper. And recipe cards."

I looked at Ike to see if he was thinking what I was thinking. "Why did you buy so much writing paper?" I said to Katey.

"I'm going to sell it," she said, as if the question surprised her.

I shook my head. "Katey, did you spend your strawberry money on this?"

"Only a little of it. I put the rest in the bank."

Ike and I carried the box home. The whole way I felt sorry for Katey. These little methods of hers were never going to get her into Kingdom by the Sea. Maybe, I thought, if Ike and I struck it rich enough, I could lend Katey some money.

After supper that night, Ike came over to our house to talk to me. He brought the can of worms. We took them up to my room.

"We aren't going to find any artifacts in that hole, you know," he said, kind of disgusted-like. "We need another plan. Maybe we should do like your sister and work."

"Work! What do you call all that digging we've been doing for days now?"

"Craziness," he said.

"Come on, Ike," I said. "We'll find something."

"Maybe. But I don't think there's much of a market for dead umbrellas and squashed coffee cans."

That was the trouble with Ike. He never could just envision a thing. He always wanted proof. I could see there would be no talking to him. Besides, I was getting tired of digging there myself.

"All right," I said. "I have been turning over a new idea, now that you mention it. And one that will make some use of all that work we did at the vacant lot."

"Yeah?" His eye had that spark I liked to see.

I was about to explain how the plan would work when Katey came to the door of my room. "Do you guys want to share my stationery selling? I'll split the money with you if you go with me so I can walk farther up town."

"Katey, men do not sell writing paper. Can't you sell around here?"

"Yes," she said, a little sadly. Then she brightened. "I'll pay you then, to walk with me. You don't have to go in or sell anything."

I was afraid her big green eyes would sway Ike's already wavering[13] loyalty. Anyway, I needed a little capital[14] to back my next venture, and so although I hated to take money from my sister, I took her up on her offer.

"All right," I said. "Two evenings a week."

She clapped her hands in delight. "You're so wonderful, Petey. Thank you." With that she left the room.

"Now then, back to the new plan," I said to my fellow adventurer. "This is the best idea yet."

Ike smiled a crooked little smile, which I ignored.

"Remember Mr. Jackson telling us about the fur traders? And how much money they made?"

Ike nodded, somewhat like a fellow nods when he thinks you might be trying to trick him.

"Well, I figure there are lots of animals in the woods back of the cul-de-sac, you know. All we have to do is catch them. Then we can sell the fur."

Ike sat there as if he expected me to say more.

"That's it," I said. "That's the plan. We'll use that big hole to keep the animals in until some company comes for them."

Ike just stood there, smiling. "What company?"

Proof, proof, always proof. "A fur company." What company did he suppose would buy fur?

"Name one," he said. There was no malice[15] in this statement, just the sad tone of a fellow who had seen too much hardship in his life.

I said brightly, "You worry too much, my friend. Just leave it to me. We'll be so rich you'll have to hire people to carry your money to the bank."

Ike must have tried to stifle a sneeze just then because he made the oddest snorting sound I'd ever heard him make.

---

[13]wavering—uncertain; faltering
[14]capital—money or property that is invested to produce more money
[15]malice—ill will; spite

The Best Plan Yet

The next evening Ike and I walked with Katey when she went uptown to sell her stationery. We took turns pulling the wagon—my wagon once, but Katey's now—along the curb until we passed the shopping square. Then the sidewalks widened and evened out; so we brought the wagon up on the sidewalk and crossed over into the land of the rich.

The walk was pleasant enough, and there was plenty to see. Some of the houses at the other side of town were as big as our whole school, handsome white two-stories with pillars from the ground clear to the roof. The lawns looked as if somebody cut every blade of grass with fingernail clippers. And the flowers gushed out from every-where, over fine wood fences, down white latticed[16] arbors,[17] through trellises,[18] beside garages, around high front steps, and between statues of Roman soldiers and of ladies pouring water out of stone jars.

The first house we stopped at had eleven marble steps up to the front door. Katey walked right up and rang the bell. Ike and I hung back a little. We could have gone up if we had wanted, but we didn't want to.

---

[16]latticed—decorated with a framework of strips of wood or metal woven with spaces between
[17]arbors—shaded places or garden areas
[18]trellises—frameworks used for training climbing plants

A woman in a black dress with a thin white apron over it that would not have kept it clean for a minute in our kitchen answered the bell.

"May I help you?" she said, looking down at Katey kind of stiff, like her neck hurt her.

"Hello," said Katey. "I'm selling stationery to earn money for a ticket to King—"

"No, thank you," said the woman. She closed the door.

Katey did not turn around to us. She just kept staring at the door.

"Come on," said Ike. "Lots more houses on this street, right, Pete?"

"Sure," I said.

Katey put on a brave smile for us. I decided right there that I had to sell enough furs to get Katey a ticket too.

We went on to the next house, and the next, and the next. The fourth time the door closed coldly against Katey, Ike said, "I've never seen so many white aprons in my life."

Katey was beginning to lose some of her polish and perk. "Let's go back home," she said, running her finger slowly along the side of the big box of stationery in the wagon.

I looked up the street a way. There was one house nearly at the end of the street that had a pretty white fence with a gate swung open and an unruly rose garden taking over the walk. The house was smaller than the others but twice as grand, its red shutters standing out proudly against the white clapboard.

"Let's try one more house," I said. "I think there's one that looks nice on down."

Katey looked at me only a little hopefully. "Okay," she said.

The red front door came fully open, and an old lady, older than Grandma, smiled out on us. She had shiny white hair, like the angel hair Mom puts under the china carolers at Christmas, all swept up and away from her face into a loose knot on the top of her head. She must have had a hundred wrinkles going out from the corners of her eyes to the edge of her hair, and her large glasses had gold frames only along the top. She wasn't much taller than Katey.

"Hello, children," she said in a way that made me think of music boxes, but I couldn't tell why. "What do you have in that wagon? Candy?"

"No, ma'am," said Katey. "I have writing paper and recipe cards. Would you like to see some?"

"Why, I believe I would, my dear. Now if you had said it was candy, I would have had to say I didn't need any. But a person always seems to be almost out of writing paper, doesn't he? Come on in and show me what you have." She held the screen door open for Katey.

Ike and I handed Katey a few boxes from the wagon and then sat down on the porch.

"Don't you boys want to come in too?" said the lady, coming back to the door.

"No, thank you," said Ike. "We aren't selling anything."

She laughed lightly. "All right." I heard her say to Katey, "Now then, what's your name, child? Oh, this is pretty paper. How much is this?"

In a few minutes the door opened again, and Katey came out with a ten-dollar bill in her hand and a smile on her face that we could have used for a flashlight if we were late getting home.

"I need two more boxes of the blue paper," she said, businesslike.

"And one box of recipe cards with the lines on them."

Ike bent to his work and produced the merchandise. Katey handed the boxes over to the lady. "Thank you, Mrs. Norwood," she said.

"Let me know how you like Kingdom by the Sea. Maybe I'd like to go myself," said the woman. "And have your mother call me if you want the job, my dear."

We said good-bye, Ike and I looking sideways at Katey but asking no questions until we were out the gate and past the house.

"What job?" I said, only one half second ahead of Ike.

"Mrs. Norwood needs someone to help her clean for a few weeks. Her regular cleaning lady is going to be gone for a couple of weeks. She says I'd get good pay." Katey was nearly skipping, and Ike and I had to hurry a little to keep up with her.

"Katey," I said, "you don't even know this woman. How come she asked you?"

"She said she liked a person who believed in working for what he wants. She needs a cleaning lady, and I need money. Why not?"

We couldn't find out right away what Mom thought about the job because she was too busy hunting the worms that had somehow escaped from under the rock on the can in my room.

"Peter Jonathan Bates!" My mother's voice rolled down from upstairs with a good deal of chill in it as I entered the kitchen. "You get up here this minute. There are worms everywhere in here!"

That was a slight exaggeration. They weren't *everywhere*. They were mostly on the floor, and there were a few on the dresser. I felt sorry for them because they were getting dried out. I started putting them back in the can as quickly as I could.

"All they need is a little mud, and they'll be good as new," I said to make Mom feel better. "I'll get a can with a better lid too."

"That won't be necessary," said Mom. There was an awful calmness in her tone that made me turn around. She stood in the hallway holding a trash can into my room.

I was horrified. "But Mom, I can't throw these worms away! They're our sideline business!"

The trash can did not waver. Neither did my mother's resolve.[19] Slowly, sadly, I dumped the worms into the trash can, thinking how much money I had just thrown away. My only consolation[20] was that few people fished in our town anyway.

It was much later that evening that Katey finally got a chance to ask about the cleaning job. Dad thought it would be fine. Mom was not so sure.

"That's all the way uptown," she said. "Someone will have to take her and pick her up. And besides, Katey is only ten years old."

"Let's let her try," said Dad. "Pete, you'll walk her up there, won't you?"

I wanted to tell Dad about my trapping plans, but the worm incident was still so fresh in everybody's mind that I just nodded meekly.

[19]resolve—determination; firm decision
[20]consolation—comfort

The next afternoon, Ike and I rigged up a covering for our animal trap. It was a wonderfully inventive arrangement of old boards and binder twine, which we carefully covered with lots of grass and some of the dirt. We had plenty of dirt.

"Now," I said, "no animal will notice that hole until he's in it! Shall we go see what we can scare up?"

Ike was agreeable; so we sallied[21] forth, the Lewis and Clark of Alton Heights, out across the prairie and into the heavily wooded mountains beyond.

The dense forest turned out to be only a thin strip of birch trees and overgrown witch hazel.[22]

"I don't see too many foxes in here," said Ike. "Maybe it's the wrong time of day."

"Maybe."

"Have you ever seen any foxes around here?" There went Ike again, needing to see something before he believed.

"Well, no," I said. "But that doesn't mean there aren't any."

We walked through to the other side and looked out on another street of houses just about like ours.

"Hey," said Ike, "I didn't know that this woods came out over here. That's amazing, isn't it?"

I didn't think it was amazing. I thought it was flatly discouraging. What animal worth his pelt would live in such scrawny woods as these? We stood there a moment, Ike reveling[23] in his geographical discovery and I wondering if I could come up with another plan to replace this one that was rapidly going the way of our archeological excavation.[24]

Suddenly, perhaps having stood the suspense as long as he could, a rabbit burst forth from the underbrush right beside us, springing high into the air and stretching out long and lean. He hit the ground about a yard in front of us. Finding himself suddenly in a clearing, he veered back in our direction.

"After him," I yelled triumphantly, as he sped back between us into the small wood.

Ike and I thrashed after the fleeing rabbit in wild excitement, battling the low branches and the tangles around our ankles. The rabbit broke into the open lot on the cul-de-sac with Ike right behind him. Zigzagging better than a sewing machine, the rabbit outmaneuvered both of us and shot away

---

[21]sallied—set out
[22]witch hazel—type of shrub or small tree with yellow flowers
[23]reveling—delighting in
[24]excavation—the act of digging or digging out

toward—I could hardly believe it—the trap.

"Head him in," I yelled with the little breath I had left, trying to get free of some kind of prickly vine that had snared me just below the knee. I jerked my leg up. The vine let go, but not without taking part of my pant leg with it. I briefly considered that this accident might cause some unpleasantness at home. But as I looked out toward Ike and the rabbit again, I realized a torn pant leg was going to be insignificant compared to what was about to happen.

Ike in his wild chase had followed the rabbit straight for the trap. He had whipped off his cap and was waving it in great circles and whooping something that sounded vaguely like "little doggie." The rabbit charged across the trap cover and bounded up the pile of dirt on the other side. Ike neither slowed down nor swerved.

"Ike!" I hollered. "Ike! Look out for—"

But it was too late. One instant I saw him running headlong onto the trap cover, and the next I saw only a blue and gold baseball cap dropping out of the sky and disappearing into the earth.

I raced to the hole, tearing away the boards, the

twine, the grass, the dirt. "Ike! Ike! Are you alive? Ike!"

My friend, my fellow adventurer, rose up slowly in the pit, bits of grass making him look like a ruffled porcupine. He picked up his cap with much dignity, slapped it against his knee, and put it back on his head. Then he looked up at me and said, "You're right. We covered this trap real good."

When we entered the kitchen, my mother gasped. "Oh, what happened? Are you hurt? Whatever happened?"

She hurried around getting washcloths and medicine and bandages and other remedies dear to mothers. Actually we looked worse off than we really were. I mean, once Ike got the grass and dirt off him, you could hardly tell he had fallen into a six-foot hole at a dead run. He did limp a little, but only for a day or two.

Well, as you can imagine, our enterprising days were brought rather quickly to an end. After Ike quit limping, we had to go put all the dirt back into the hole where we had found it. Then we had to call the man who owned the lot and apologize for digging up his property. All in all, I decided that being a trapper was not in my future. Ike said he wished it hadn't even been in his present.

In the meantime, Katey had sold all of her stationery to Mrs. Norwood's rich friends and put the money in the bank. With her cleaning-job money, she says she thinks she'll have enough saved to buy tickets to Kingdom by the Sea—for all three of us. I hate to borrow money from my poor little sister, but she says Ike and I were so kind to walk her uptown that she thinks it's only fair.

Besides, Mrs. Norwood is going to hire Ike and me—on Katey's recommendation—to do yard work for her. So by the end of the summer we should be able to pay Katey back. The pay is good, but the work has no adventure to it. But we're taking the job anyway. This time, Ike says, we're going to listen to Katey.

The Apple of CONTENTMENT

Howard Pyle

illustrated by Lynda Slattery

Traditional stories from English and European folklore often contain elements that come in threes, such as the three pigs, the three billy goats, or more often, three brothers or three sisters. These stories usually have the two older children enjoying themselves at the youngest one's expense. Howard Pyle, a popular author who lived in the nineteenth century, has written a tale about three sisters. It may seem familiar to you as you read it. What story does it remind you of?

There was a woman once, and she had three daughters. The woman loved the first daughter and the second daughter as she loved salt, but the youngest daughter she loved not at all.

The first sister and the second sister dressed in their Sunday clothes every day, and sat in the sun doing nothing, just as though they had been born ladies, both of them.

As for Christine—that was the name of the youngest girl—as for Christine, she dressed in nothing but rags and had to drive the geese to the hills in the morning and home again in the evening, so that they might feed on the young grass all day and grow fat.

The first sister and the second sister had white bread (and butter besides) and as much fresh milk as they could drink; but Christine had to eat cheese parings[1] and bread crusts, and had hardly enough of them to keep Goodman Hunger from whispering in her ear.

This was how the churn clacked in that house!

One morning Christine started off to the hills with her flock of geese, and in her hands she carried her knitting, at which she worked to save time. So she went along the dusty road until, by-and-by, she came to a place where a bridge crossed the brook, and what should she see there but a little red cap, with a silver bell at the point of it, hanging from the alder branch. It

---

[1] parings—outer portions that are removed from fruit, vegetables, or cheese

was such a nice, pretty little red cap that Christine thought she would take it home with her, for she had never seen the like of it before.

So she put it in her pocket, and then off she went with her geese again. But she had hardly gone a step when she heard a voice calling her, "Christine! Christine!"

She looked, and what should she see but an odd little gray man, with a great head as big as a cabbage and little legs as thin as young radishes.

"What do you want?" said Christine, when the little man had come to where she was.

Oh, the little man only wanted his cap again, for without it he could not go back home into the hill—that was where he belonged.

But how did the cap come to be hanging from the bush? Yes, Christine would like to know that before she gave it back again.

Well, the little hill man was fishing by the brook over yonder when a puff of wind blew his cap into the water, and he just hung it up to dry. That was all that there was about it; and now would Christine please give it to him?

Christine did not know about that; perhaps she would and perhaps she would not. It was a nice, pretty little cap. What would the little underground man give her for it?

Oh, the little man would give her five dollars for it, and gladly.

No; five dollars was not enough for such a pretty little cap—see, there was a silver bell hanging to it too.

Well, the little man would give her five hundred dollars for it, and gladly.

No; Christine did not care for money. What else could he give for this nice, dear little cap?

"See, Christine," said the little man, "I will give you this for the cap." And he showed her something in his hand that looked just like a bean, only it was as black as a lump of coal.

"Yes, but what is that?" said Christine.

"That," said the little man, "is a seed from the apple of contentment. Plant it, and from it will grow a tree, and from the tree an apple. Everybody in the world that sees the apple will long for it, but nobody in the world can pluck it but you. It will always be meat and drink to you when you are hungry, and warm clothes to your back when you are cold. Moreover, as soon as you pluck it from the tree, another as good will grow in its place. Now, will you give me my hat?"

Oh yes; Christine would give the little man his cap again. He put the cap on his head, and—puff!—away he was gone, as suddenly as the light of a candle when you blow it out.

So Christine took the seed home with her, and planted it before the window of her room. The next morning when she looked out of the window she beheld a beautiful tree, and on the tree hung an apple that shone in the sun as though it were pure gold. She went to the tree and plucked the apple as easily as though it were a gooseberry, and as soon as she had plucked it another as good grew in its place. Being hungry she ate it, and thought that she had never eaten anything as good, for it tasted like pancake with honey and milk.

By and by the oldest sister came out of the house and looked around, but when she saw the beautiful tree with the golden apple hanging from it you can guess how she stared.

Presently she began to long and long for the apple as she had never longed for anything in her life. "I will just pluck it," said she, "and no one will be the wiser for it." But that was easier said than done. She reached and reached, but she might as well have reached for the moon. She climbed and climbed, but she might as well have climbed for the sun—for either one would have been as easy to get as that which she wanted. At last she had to give up trying for it, and her temper was none the sweeter for that, you may be sure.

After a while came the second sister, and when she saw the golden apple she wanted it just as much as the first had done. But to want and to get are very different things, as she soon found, for she was no more able to get it than the other had been.

Last of all came the mother, and she also tried to pluck the apple. But it was no use. She had no more luck of her trying than her daughters. All that the three could do was to stand under the tree and look at the apple, and wish for it and wish for it.

They are not the only ones who have done the like, with the apple of contentment hanging just above them.

As for Christine, she had nothing to do but to pluck an apple whenever she wanted it. Was she hungry? There was the apple hanging from the tree for her. Was she thirsty? There was the apple. Cold? There was the apple. So you see, she was the happiest girl betwixt all the seven hills that stand at the ends of the earth; for nobody in the world can have more than contentment, and that was what the apple brought her.

One day a King came riding along the road, and all of his people with him. He looked up and saw the apple hanging in the tree, and a great desire came upon him to have a taste of it. So he called one of the servants to him, and told him to go and ask whether it could be bought for a potful of gold.

So the servant went to the house and knocked on the door—rap! tap! tap!

"What do you want?" asked the mother of the three sisters, coming to the door.

Oh, nothing much; only a King was out there in the road, and wanted to know if she would sell the apple yonder for a potful of gold.

Yes, the woman would do that. Just pay her the pot of gold and he might go and pluck it and welcome.

So the servant gave her the pot of gold, and then he tried to pluck the apple. First, he reached for it, and then he climbed for it, and then he shook the limb.

But it was of no use for him to try: he could no more get it—well—than I could if I had been in his place.

At last the servant had to go back to the King. The apple was there, he said, and the woman had sold it, but try and try as he would he could no more get it than he could get the stars in the sky.

Then the King told the steward[2] to go and get it for him; but the steward, though he was all man and a strong man, could no more pluck the apple than the servant.

So he had to go back to the King with an empty fist. No; he could not gather it, either.

Then the King himself went. He knew that he could pluck it—of course he could! Well, he tried and tried; but nothing came of his trying, and he had to ride away at last without having had so much as a smell of the apple.

---

[2]steward—person who manages another's household

After the King came home, he talked and dreamed and thought of nothing but the apple; for the more he could not get it the more he wanted it—that is the way we are made in this world. At last he grew melancholy[3] and sick for want of that which he could not get. Then he sent for one who was so wise that he had more in his head than ten men together. This wise man told him that the only one who could pluck the fruit of contentment for him was the one to whom the tree belonged. This was one of the daughters of the woman who had sold the apple to him for the pot of gold.

When the King heard this he was very glad. He had his horse saddled, and he and his court rode away and so came at last to the cottage where Christine lived. There they found the mother and the elder sisters, for Christine was away on the hills with her geese.

The King took off his hat and made a fine bow.

The wise man at home had told him this and that. Now to which one of her daughters did the apple tree belong? asked the King.

"Oh, it is my oldest daughter who owns the tree," said the woman.

So, good! Then if the oldest daughter would pluck the apple for him he would take her home and marry her and make a queen of her. Only let her get it for him without delay.

Prut! that would never do. What! was the girl to climb the apple tree before the King and all of the court? No! No! Let the King go home, and she would bring the apple to him all in good time; that was what the woman told him.

Well, the King would do that, only let her make haste, for he wanted it very much indeed.

As soon as the King had gone, the woman and her daughters sent to the hills for the goose-girl. They told her that the King wanted the apple yonder, and that she must pluck it for her sister to take to him. If she did not do as they said they would throw her into the well. So Christine had to pluck the fruit; and as soon as she had done so the oldest sister wrapped it up in a napkin and set off with it to the King's house, as pleased as pleased could be. Rap! Tap! Tap! She knocked at the door. Had she brought the apple for the King?

Oh yes, she had brought it. Here it was, all wrapped up in a fine napkin.

After that they did not let her stand outside the door till her toes were cold, I can tell you. As soon as she had come to the King she opened her napkin. Believe me or not as you please, there was nothing in the napkin but a hard round stone!

[3]melancholy—sad; gloomy

The Apple of Contentment 69

When the King saw only a stone he was so angry that he stamped like a rabbit and told them to put the girl out of the house. So they did, and she went home with a flea in her ear, I can tell you.

Then the King sent his steward to the house where Christine and her sisters lived.

He told the woman that he had come to find whether she had any other daughters.

Yes; the woman had another daughter, and, to tell the truth, it was she who owned the tree. Just let the steward go home again and the girl would fetch the apple in a little while.

As soon as the steward had gone, they sent to the hills for Christine again. Look! She must pluck the apple for the second sister to take to the King. If she did not do that they would throw her into the well.

So Christine had to pluck the apple and give it to the second sister, who wrapped it up in a napkin and set off for the King's house. But she fared no better than the other, for when she opened the napkin, there was nothing in it but a lump of mud. So they packed her home again with her apron to her eyes.

After a while the King's steward came to the house again. Had the woman no other daughter than these two?

Well, yes, there was one, but she was a poor ragged thing, of no account, and fit for nothing in the world but to tend the geese.

Where was she?

Oh, she was up on the hills now tending her flock.

But could the steward see her?

Yes, he might see her, but she was nothing but a poor simpleton.[4]

That was all very good, but the steward would like to see her, for that was what the King had sent him there for.

So there was nothing to do but to send to the hills for Christine.

After a while she came, and the steward asked her if she could pluck the apple yonder for the King.

Yes; Christine could do that easily enough. So she reached and picked it as though it had been nothing but a gooseberry on the bush. Then the steward took off his hat and made her a low bow in spite of her ragged dress, for he saw that she was the one for whom they had been looking all this time.

So Christine slipped the golden apple into her pocket, and then she

---

[4]simpleton—person without good sense; a fool

and the steward set off to the King's house together.

When they had come there everybody began to titter and laugh behind the palms of their hands to see what a poor ragged goose-girl the steward had brought home with him.

"Have you brought the apple?" said the King, as soon as Christine had come before him.

Yes; here it was. And Christine thrust her hand into her pocket and brought it forth. Then the King took a great bite of it, and as soon as he had done so he looked at Christine and thought that he had never seen such a pretty girl. As for her rags, he minded them no more than one minds the spots on a cherry; that was because he had eaten of the apple of contentment.

And were they married? Of course they were! And a grand wedding it was, I can tell you. It is a pity that you were not there; but though you were not, Christine's mother and sisters were, and, what is more, they sat with the other guests, though I believe they would rather have sat upon pins and needles.

"Never mind," said they. "We still have the apple of contentment at home, though we cannot taste of it." But no; they had nothing of the kind. The next morning it stood before the young Queen Christine's window, just as it had at her old home, for it belonged to her and to no one else in all the world. That was good for the King, for he needed a taste of it now and then as much as anybody else, and no one could pluck it for him but Christine.

Now, that is all of this story. What does it mean?

Can you not see?

Rub your spectacles and look again!

A Tree for the WILDERNESS

Jean Mundell   illustrated by Michael Johnston

The following fictional account is based on the events in Numbers 21:4-9. Although the author has written about an event, she has also used her story to describe one of God's provisions for the children of Israel—the acacia[1] tree. As you read, look for the reasons that the acacia tree was so useful to the Israelites on their journey in the wilderness. The author also uses her story to foreshadow another provision that God made for His people—the provision of His Son for a sacrifice.

Rachel loved to watch her father's fingers as they flew back and forth across the loom.[2]

Back and forth—
back and forth.

Up and down—
in and out.

In and out—up
and down.

The red and blue and purple threads grew into shapes of robed angels for the Tent.

She tapped her foot. It almost made her feel like singing.

Her poor brother, Obed, was struggling nearby on a smaller loom. His hands were all tangled up in the strings. She knew that someday Obed's work would be as beautiful as her father's, for all the men in their family had always been weavers, even when they lived in Egypt. But right now she liked to tease him.

"I sure wish I were a boy! My loom wouldn't look like that!"

She knew as soon as she saw the frown on her father's face that she shouldn't have said that.

Her father leaned over and quickly found the end of the string that would untangle poor Obed's loom.

"There, Obed, I think I see what your problem is. Rachel, I am sure you have something to do other than stand around and watch your brother and me. Why don't you go and find some acacia wood for your mother's supper fire?" He handed her a knife from his belt. "Here. Don't cut yourself."

That ended Rachel's happy weaving song! She was back in the wilderness. And all she could hear

---

[1]acacia (ə kā′ shə)—a tree with flowering branches
[2]loom—machine for weaving threads to make cloth

A Tree for the Wilderness   73

was the sad, sad song of the long, long journey.

As she turned away, she tried to hide the frown on her face. Her sandal came down harder with each step.

She passed the rows and rows of tents, all belonging to the family of Judah. She kicked a stone angrily. Why couldn't each family choose a spot of their own to set up their tent? Unless you counted the tents carefully, you would end up eating supper with someone else's family!

But then it wouldn't make any difference. Everyone would be eating the same thing—manna! There wasn't anything else to eat! That plain, white manna on the ground every morning! No matter how her mother fixed it, it tasted the same everyday. She comforted herself in knowing that she wasn't the only one to be tired of the manna.

She had heard people talk about the watermelons back in Egypt. They said they were so sweet and juicy! She probably would never get to taste one. They'd been walking around in the wilderness so long! When were they going to get to the place where they could live in a house and eat food grown in a garden?

As she looked up, she saw something that made her walk faster. It was the Tent. It always stood in the middle of the camp. The Cloud covered one end of it when they weren't traveling. All the rest was covered with a big, black-skinned blanket. It seemed like a big, black eye that watched her everywhere she went.

They said it was beautiful on the inside—furniture made of acacia wood covered with gold, but because she was a girl, she could only listen to what her brother and father had told her. Even they hadn't been in the inner rooms. Only the family of Levi could go there.

She shivered, and then that old, angry feeling came back. Why did the Lord allow them to wander in the wilderness? Did He want them to be unhappy?

Suddenly she remembered what she was supposed to be doing. She imagined herself weaving a beautiful piece of cloth on the loom. Instead, she was hunting for firewood.

By now she was outside the camp. There were acacia trees everywhere. Blossoms covered the trees like fluffy, yellow clouds, but they looked more like puffs of smoke to Rachel.

She hurried toward a small one.

It wouldn't be so hard to cut the branches from this one. Or perhaps the woodcutters had left some on the ground. It was hard to cut the branches from between the thorns on the leaves.

A couple of goats had already claimed this tree for their own. They seemed to love nibbling on the thorny leaves.

"Get out of here, you lazy creature! You're standing on the piece I need!"

She threatened the goat by pretending to kick it. Just then he moved, and Rachel's foot kicked the tree instead.

As she sat down holding her foot, she heard a voice. "What's wrong?"

Around the other side of the tree came a girl, who almost made Rachel forget her sore toe. She was very thin, and one leg seemed to be shorter than the other. She was a cripple. She hobbled toward Rachel, leaning on a crutch.

"Oh, you hurt your foot! I'm sorry! That wood is hard!"

"That's the truth!"

"But at least we don't have to worry about bugs when we pick up the wood. It's so hard no bug could dig his teeth into it!"

"I don't mind the bugs as much as trying to cut this hard old stuff!" Rachel rubbed her sore toe.

"But the wood from the acacia seems to burn forever! On cold nights we don't need to keep putting more sticks on the fire."

"The smoke always gets in my eyes when I sleep near enough to keep warm." She wondered if this silly girl on the crutch had any sense at all. Couldn't she see *any* of their difficulties? And her being crippled too!

"But acacia wood smoke smells so good," the girl was saying. "Something like the incense,[3] when the priest prays before the Holy Place."

---

[3]incense—substance that gives off a sweet smell when burned

"I wouldn't know! I've never been in the Holy Place!"

"No, neither have I. But I can think that this acacia tree that I touch every day has been made into furniture for the Tent, and it makes Jehovah seem very near." The girl touched the limb of the acacia. A light came into her eyes as she spoke. She looked earnest and sure of what she said.

Rachel couldn't understand this feeling; it made her uncomfortable.

"What are you doing out here walking under the acacia trees anyway?" Rachel asked.

"I'm watching the sheep. Look at their thick, beautiful coats! Won't they make lovely coverings for the Tent?" The girl picked up one of the small lambs as she spoke.

Rachel wished the girl would stop talking about the Tent! And why did she feel it was such a friendly place? Rachel wanted to say something to show her how miserable they were.

"Some of the lambs will be used for sacrifice." She pointed at the lamb resting in the girl's arms.

The girl sighed. "Yes, I know, but Jehovah has

chosen them to remind us that He will take our sin away."

Rachel knew the girl was right. But she would rather not be reminded of her sin.

Rachel reached up to cut off a branch from the acacia tree, but her knife fell out of her hand with a clatter. Curled around the limb of the tree was an ugly, orange snake!

"He almost bit me!" Rachel screamed, jumping back. Then as she turned quickly to run to the safety of the camp, she remembered that the girl was crippled. "Come on, you'll get bitten!"

The girl seemed not to hear. She was gathering her frightened sheep, scattered in all directions.

Rachel thought, "I'd better help her. She'll never get all those scared sheep to come!"

But the ugly snake was still staring fixedly at Rachel. It looked like a hot, burning fire. She gave up in fear and ran frantically toward the camp.

A Tree for the Wilderness 77

When Rachel had almost reached the tents, she stopped to catch her breath. There was a strange noise coming from the camp—loud crying, as though something terrible had happened.

But she didn't have time to wonder what it was, for right on the path in front of her was a whole nest of bright orange snakes, just like the one she had seen in the acacia tree! Heads swaying, they turned toward her.

Perhaps if she went in the back of the tents there wouldn't be any snakes there. She walked slowly around toward the back, trying to stay calm. If she only got back to her family, she would be safe, she thought. But even as she walked carefully along, those ugly, orange heads appeared around her as the snakes slithered closer. At last her nerve broke, and she ran for her tent. The snakes seemed more numerous now. In panic she leaped over them, stumbling and running frantically as she saw that they were crowding the path behind and before her.

At last she saw her tent, but just as she reached the entrance, an orange head shot out from the dust of the doorway. She jerked back, her teeth clamped together, but felt pinpricks of fire shoot through her leg and sudden flames of pain from the poison.

She called, "Papa! Papa!" Rachel spun for a moment, and then everything turned dark.

When she opened her eyes, she saw her father's face as though he were far away at the end of a dim cave. She heard him saying, "Look! Look, Rachel! Look up at the snake on the pole!" He had carried her back outside into the glaring light.

She blinked her dry eyes. Weakness and fever washed over her. A snake was the last thing she wanted to look at. She turned her head away.

"It's the only way, Rachel! Jehovah has promised that you will be healed if you look! Please, look up!"

She started to sit up, but she could not. She thought her head would burst. It ached so. And her leg felt as though it was weighed down with flaming rocks. She could feel nothing else. Only pain.

"No, Rachel, please do it God's way. Please! Look up, Rachel. Please!" His words pleading with her stung her conscience. She woke up a little more. She had been selfish—cruel even, and now somehow she sensed that she would die for it and deserved to die. In that same earnestness, Father was like the crippled girl. He was gently lifting her head. "Look, daughter. Don't despair of His forgiveness. Don't be condemned[4] forever."

---

[4]condemned—proven guilty and assigned a punishment

Suddenly she knew. She had always wanted to do things her way. Now there was nothing she could do but do it the way God wanted her to do it.

She saw through blurry and fading eyesight an orange acacia pole with an ugly snake made of brass curled around it. It was horrible! But then she understood it—horrible, like the slaying of the lambs. Like them, it meant something, a forgiveness, a taking away of sin. It was a symbol of death itself—another's death, not hers. In one instant she understood her own rebellion and the incredible forgiveness that God was giving her. It was as the prophets said, that God would bear man's sin and conquer it forever. The whole story of Jehovah's redemption[5] was on that pole.

And then she was weary.

But the pain stopped. Her father carried her inside to look at her wound, and she sat up. Her leg looked just like it always had—except for the two small fang marks that would always remind her of what had happened that day.

Rachel fell asleep while her father looked at her leg. After she rested, her mother brought her some manna cooked in goat's milk. It was soft and warm all the way through, and the milk felt good on her dry throat.

"Thank you," Rachel said.

[5]redemption—man's salvation

Her mother smiled and helped Rachel sit up to eat it. For a moment her mother said nothing, and Rachel sensed how frightened she had been during Rachel's brush with death. Why had Rachel been so ungrateful and tormented[6] everybody so? With a pang of guilt she thought of the crippled girl whose feelings she had wanted to hurt so badly that afternoon. "Have I changed so much from this afternoon?" she asked herself. "Or am I still the same person?"

"Look," her mother said. "The cloud has turned to fire." And Rachel looked out at the Tent with the shiny brass snake still hanging from the acacia pole. The acacia pole had been thrust up near the front entrance. She knew then that she really had been changed. Somehow, the Tent no longer seemed like something to avoid. Rachel knew and believed Jehovah and His promise of redemption.

Rachel looked back at the Tent, and there was her friend from the acacia tree! She had something in her arms. Of course, it was a lamb! So Jehovah had saved her from the snake. Rachel had to tell her! Tomorrow she would go to the acacia trees where the herds grazed and find her friend.

She would find a way to tell the crippled girl what Jehovah had done for her. His way seemed good now. At last she understood that His way was the way of redemption.

---

[6]tormented—caused pain; annoyed

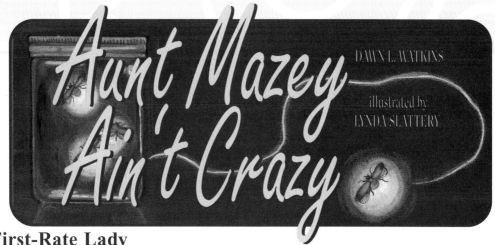

Aunt Mazey Ain't Crazy

DAWN L. WATKINS

illustrated by
LYNDA SLATTERY

First-Rate Lady

Just because Aunt Mazey was seventy-five years old was no reason to say she shouldn't keep lightning bugs in a jar on the window sill of the bathroom for a night light. There wasn't a kid in town that wasn't impressed with the ingenuity of that particular arrangement, but not everyone is as quick to recognize genius as kids are, apparently.

Aunt Mazey wasn't really my aunt. Neither was she the aunt or close relative of any of the two or three dozen children who ran by her place every day after school, helped her find the pictures that she said every stone had on it somewhere, and drank the root beer she made better than any store-bought I had ever tasted. In fact, we didn't know she was anyone's aunt at all. We just called her Aunt Mazey, because our parents did and because we all liked to pretend that she did belong to us somehow.

Her real name was Clara Letitia Mazedon Brannigan. We didn't know this full name or her exact age until they were printed in the papers after the hearing.[1] She had always been simply Aunt Mazey and was, we assumed, somewhere between twelve and one hundred years old. There was, however, nothing simple about Aunt Mazey.

"Aunt Mazey," said Taylor, my best friend, "will you help me with my spelling words?" Taylor asked her that every Wednesday.

"Think I'm a dictionary, do you?" She was repotting a blue violet by the kitchen window, the late afternoon sun making her wiry gray hair look almost white. "What are they, then? Make it quick, because I don't like to run down the battery on my memory."

"Okay," said Taylor. "Centurion, terrain, centennial, diamond, solitude, astronomer, liberty, extraordinary, generous, resolve."

---

[1] hearing—official meeting to listen to arguments

"Oh," she said turning from her work with a look of delight. "Those are first-rate words." Rarely was there a word on the list that Aunt Mazey did not declare first-rate, I noticed.

Taylor was always taken in by her enthusiasm. He glanced up from his paper with such a pleased look you would have thought he was responsible for inventing the words himself.

"Put *centurion* and *centennial* together," said Aunt Mazey. "They both come from the same word. So does *century*. They all have something to do with *one hundred*, which is what you both are going to get on this spelling lesson."

She put a few coffee grounds in the dirt. On his paper Taylor drew an arrow from *centennial* to the space above *terrain*.

"No," she said without even looking around from her work, "no arrow-drawing. Rewrite the words. *Centennial* first."

Taylor looked at me, and I just shrugged. Aunt Mazey did not always have to see you to know what you were doing.

"What does a Roman soldier have to do with one hundred?" I asked as Taylor was getting out a new sheet of paper to write on.

Aunt Mazey adjusted a comb in the back of her hair. "How many years are there in a century?" She seldom answered our questions directly.

"One hundred," I answered.

"Umm hmm," she said. "And how many soldiers do you suppose a centurion led?"

"One hundred?"

"One hundred." She put some little squares of potato on top of the dirt and set the flower back. "There was a centurion in the Bible who said to the Lord, 'For I am a man of authority, having soldiers under me.' Now, the next word was *terrain*, wasn't it? Let's put that with *resolve*."

"Why?" asked Taylor. "Do they come from the same word?"

"Oh, no," said Aunt Mazey, her blue eyes twinkling. "They just sound nice together, don't you think?"

Actually, neither Taylor nor I would have thought how words sounded together if it hadn't been for Aunt Mazey always pointing such things out to us.

"And let's put *diamond* and *generous* together," said Taylor. "Because they go together too."

"All right," she said, perfectly attuned to his logic. "Here," she said to me as she pulled a piece of paper out of my notebook. "You better rewrite your list too."

A half hour later Taylor and I were tramping through the late spring snow behind Aunt Mazey, searching for tracks.

"I know there was a fox out here last night," she said. "I looked for tracks this morning, but I couldn't find any. Still, I know the rascal was here."

"How do you know?" Taylor inquired.

"The chickens told me."

I took this to mean that the chickens had raised a ruckus in the night.

"Last night?" Taylor asked.

"No, this morning when I gathered the eggs." She might have been kidding, but you never could be sure.

We circled the henhouse and walked down to the woods twice. We didn't see any tracks.

"Hmmph," she said. "Well, I'll set out a few box traps and see what happens. Tomorrow. You boys get on home now. And mind you get those spelling words."

I arrived home just in time to wash and get to the supper table. Father said the blessing, after which there was the usual passing of serving dishes. I took the required amount of stewed tomatoes and no more. I took a lot of pickles.

"You can't live on pickles," said Mother, looking at my plate. She did not, however, pursue the topic.

"Did you know that *centurion* and *century* come from the same word?" I not only wanted to show that I knew an interesting thing but also to turn the talk as far from stewed tomatoes as possible.

"What's that you say?" Father said.

"They both come from a word meaning 'one hundred.' "

"Did you learn that in school today?" asked Mother.

"Aunt Mazey told us."

Across the table my older sister rolled her eyes. "Jon, you'd believe the sky was green if Aunt Mazey said it was so."

"Enough. Don't tease, Sylvia." Mother's voice clamped down on this particular branch of conversation. There was a brief lull[2] in the talk around the table.

"How *is* Aunt Mazey?" Mother said to me.

"Just fine," I told her. The question did strike me as odd, though, because Aunt Mazey was our nearest neighbor.

Mother said to Father, "I really should go over there more often. The poor old soul is probably lonely."

Father nodded as he buttered a piece of bread. He ate it in silence, apparently thinking over what Mother had said. At last he said, "How old is she by now anyway?"

"Well, past seventy, I'm sure. Jonathan, please eat a few more tomatoes." Mother was like that— she would be clean away from some topic and come right back to it so fast your head would spin.

The next afternoon Taylor and I reported to Aunt Mazey's as usual. The porch already had several kids on it and six buckets and spigots for tapping maple trees.

"Is it tapping time?" I asked.

"Not quite," came the familiar voice we loved. "But it's seeing-about-it time."

A cheer went up from the porch, and soon seven of us and Aunt Mazey started off to select the trees to be tapped for the season's maple syrup crop. There were still two or three inches of snow on the ground, but none of us—including the small old woman with us—cared. There was enough spring in the air that we were sure in our hearts that winter would not be back anymore this year.

Aunt Mazey studied each tree, looking for previous seasons' holes, pushing her thumbnail into the bark, and feeling the trunks with her un-gloved hand. Her hand looked surprisingly strong against the bark. Sometimes at the house, when she was holding a book or leaning against the porch post, her hands looked old and frail.

We tied red strings around the best trees and trooped joyfully back to the front porch to check the buckets for tightness. I saw as we passed the henhouse that a box trap had been set by the far corner in the hedge.

We found that all the wooden buckets were snug as the day they were made, the metal bands around the bottom having been securely drawn. We lined the buckets up at the edge of the porch against the day when Aunt Mazey would declare tapping time.

2lull—brief period of quiet or calm

"All right," she said the very next Friday, "tomorrow we get maple sap. Jonathan and Taylor, you'll be sure to come, won't you? I can't pound those spouts like I used to."

"Yes, ma'am," we said together. The other younger boys looked at us admiringly. By those few words, Aunt Mazey had raised our status[3] in the group immeasurably. I still had a slight edge on Taylor, though, because I lived closer to Aunt Mazey than anyone else.

Saturday morning came up in that clear, thin light of early spring, a wispy fog easily giving way to the day. Taylor and I were on the job in good time, sitting on the porch steps like two seasoned railroaders waiting for the train.

The other kids came and stayed down in the yard to look at the rabbits in the hutches. There was one big Norwegian rabbit that was bigger than Sam Swenson's hound dogs. His name was Cyclops because he was huge and was blind in one eye. We liked for Aunt Mazey to tell us the story of where the name came from, but she had to be in the mood to tell it.

At last Aunt Mazey came out, a black and red plaid wool shirt hanging nearly to her knees. She had a cardigan over her house dress and

---

[3]status—position or rank

apron. She wore laced leather boots that were nearly covered by her long skirt. On her head she wore a felt hat at a jaunty[4] angle. For a moment as she pulled the door closed, I could almost see the handsome woman my father said Mazey had once been.

Taylor and I stood up. We were nearly as tall as she now, and certainly heavier. I remember that morning because it was the first time that I really felt what it must be like to be a man, to be needed, and to be capable.

"Here we go," she said. There was a quality in her voice that made it seem as if we might be setting out for adventures in the Arctic. "Everybody have boots on? All right, then. Girls carry the spouts, and boys carry the buckets and lids."

We had far more crew than was needed, but somehow everyone was busy. It seemed to go against Aunt Mazey's fabric to see a person not usefully employed. "Sally, you go see that all the buckets have lids on, will you? And Jeannie and Bill, you look to see that every spout has a tight seal. And no dawdling."

Taylor and I bored the holes with a little hand auger[5] and pounded in the spigots. Six times we bored and pounded, and six times we felt that particular satisfaction that doing something well brings.

At last, the taps were done, checked, double-checked, and duly admired. There was nothing to do but wait now. Or so we thought.

Back at the house, Aunt Mazey said, "Now I need about four of you fellows to go in the shed and pull out the boiling kettle. Mind you don't roll yourselves flat with it."

Together, Taylor, Sam, Tweed, and I managed to drag the giant kettle out into the yard. We did run over Sam's toe, but he said it hardly hurt at all.

The great iron kettle sat like a vast[6] open money pouch on four spike legs just between the willow trees and the back path to the barn. It must have been as old as Aunt Mazey, for she said her father had used it to make syrup.

For many days after that we faithfully checked the buckets on the trees, emptying them more often than they really needed to be. And for more days than that we helped Aunt Mazey boil the sap down into syrup and soft sugar and a little hard sugar. Each person got a jar of syrup and a chunk of sugar for his labors.

---

[4]jaunty—perky, cheerful
[5]auger—tool for boring holes
[6]vast—very great in size or amount

What's Wrong?

Summer came all of a sudden. One day it was cool spring, and the very next it was that rich, yellow warm of summer. The fruit trees bloomed and faded into green, and the hay sprang up and got ripe almost as you watched it. Haying took up all my time then, and I hardly got to see Taylor, much less Aunt Mazey and the others. I heard there had been a strawberry expedition and a shortcake festival at Aunt Mazey's, but I couldn't stay awake through supper after pitching hay all day; so I hardly cared that I had missed the fun.

The Sunday after the hay was in, I sat in church between Father and Sylvia, looking at my calloused palms. Thus it was that I missed seeing Aunt Mazey come in. But the stir around me caused me to look up. Coming in beside Aunt Mazey was a handsome man in his late thirties, dressed to the teeth, as they say, and smiling like a cat. I didn't like the looks of him.

"Her nephew," said Mother on the way home. "Her late sister's only child. He's a big Elmira accountant, Liza Swenson says."

"Dresses like it," said Father. I thought I detected in his tone the same doubts I had about the fellow.

"How nice for Mazey to have some company," Mother went on.

"She has plenty of company," I said from the back seat. "We visit her all the time."

"Mother means adult company," said Sylvia beside me.

"Then don't you go over," I snapped, more angry that some slick newcomer was at Aunt Mazey's than at Sylvia's remark.

"Enough," said Mother. "Your sister's right. Aunt Mazey will be glad for a nice visit from her grown nephew."

I sat in the back and glowered.[7]

_____
[7]glowered—stared sullenly or angrily

Taylor and I walked by Aunt Mazey's the next few days, but seeing the white convertible in the driveway kept us from going up on the porch. The maple-syrup kettle still sat in the yard.

"I wish he'd go home," said Taylor.

"I wish he didn't smile all the time," I said.

Just then he came out on the porch. We hung back by the fence row, watching him. He dusted off the porch rail and half sat against it.

"Doesn't want to get those nice pants dirty," Taylor observed.

The man looked out over the yard. Even from our distance, I could see he was smiling.

"He's up to no good," I said. "Nobody grins like that all the time."

"Yeah," Taylor agreed. "Reckon he wants to come live with Aunt Mazey?"

I shrugged. Then Aunt Mazey came out on the porch. She said something, and he nodded and patted her on the shoulder. Aunt Mazey straightened up, and her face took on that handsome, chiseled[8] look I had seen a few times before when she was about to explain wherein one of us has failed. This time, however, she only stood there with that look for a moment and then went back into the house.

[8]chiseled—shaped as if from stone

"Wonder if we could ask Aunt Mazey to come out without getting him along," Taylor said.

I doubted it. "Hey," I said, "we could go up and tell her that we want to put the kettle back in the shed."

"Just us two?"

That was a good point. "Let's see if Sam and Tweed can help."

In an hour, the four of us stood on Mazey's porch. I knocked.

Aunt Mazey opened the door. She looked old to me. She smiled. "Hello, boys. What do you need?"

Taylor took up when I didn't say anything. "Want us to put your kettle back in the shed?"

She looked out toward the barn with a distant look I had never seen from her before. A little breeze caught a few strands of her hair and wisped them back from her face. "Yes," she said, "you might as well." She turned her gaze back to us, and for a moment her familiar smile shone forth. "Mind you don't roll yourselves over with it now." She nodded to us and then went back inside.

We struggled to get the kettle put away, and discovered that it was far easier to drag it out than in. At last it was done, and Taylor pulled the shed door shut. "Look," he said, "this latch is loose."

"Let's fix it," said Sam.

"Something's wrong with Aunt Mazey," I said.

"Like what?" said Taylor.

"How do you know?" said Tweed at the same time.

"I don't know exactly," I said. The answer served both questions. "I just know there's something wrong."

"Well, what makes you say that?" Taylor wanted to know.

"She looks different; didn't you think so?" I said.

None of them had noticed anything different.

"You think she's sick? Maybe that's why her nephew came." Tweed usually made better sense than that.

I said, "She was fine right up until the day he came."

"Well," said Taylor, "then maybe she got sick after that."

"Taylor! You're a genius."

Taylor didn't know how he had earned this title but seemed willing to accept it anyway.

"Why?" asked Tweed, sparing Taylor from having to ask himself.

"Because he's figured out the problem. The nephew is making Aunt Mazey sick."

We all considered this diagnosis[9] silently. It seemed logical enough. It also seemed that we were powerless to do anything about it. We stood around a while by the shed, not talking.

"Let's fix this latch," said Taylor at last. And so we did.

[9]diagnosis—conclusion drawn from studying a situation

There was an ice-cream social the next Saturday night. We made plans to have at least one bowl of every kind and to try every topping. My father said he was going to skip supper so that he could eat more ice cream. Even my mother said that she hoped Mrs. Swenson would bring that raspberry sauce she made. And we all hoped that Aunt Mazey would bring her pecan ice cream that had the sugar crumbles in it.

On Saturday afternoon, Father and I went to help set up tables at the community hall. We opened the doors and all the windows and pulled the ceiling fans on. When Father got through discussing the weather with Mr. Peters and Tweed's father, we set out the saw horses and laid the plywood over them. Then we covered the makeshift tables with wide, white paper—to keep the ladies happy, as Mr. Peters said.

By seven o'clock the hall was full of people and nearly four dozen ice-cream freezers. One whole table was lined with rows and rows of sauces and toppings on one side and pies and cakes on the other. But not only was Aunt Mazey's freezer not there, Aunt Mazey wasn't there either.

I went out back where Father and Mr. Peters were churning a big ten-quart freezer. I wanted to tell him that Aunt Mazey wasn't there. But he was talking to Mr. Peters.

"Well," said Mr. Peters, "she is getting pretty old to be living by herself. It might be the best thing."

"She's just going to make it worse by being so stubborn, though," said Father. "You know how independent she's always been." He paused to let Mr. Peters get to the crank and then stepped back. "She has enough money to do whatever she wants."

Father noticed me then and stopped talking.

"Are you talking about Aunt Mazey?" I demanded. I could hardly believe it. Aunt Mazey didn't have any money that I had ever heard of.

"Yes, son. But it's none of your business. Or mine either, I guess. So keep whatever you heard to yourself. Now then, go tell your mother the main freezer won't be ready for twenty minutes yet."

I went inside. Somehow the shine had gone out of the ice-cream social for me. Oh, the ice cream was good, of course. I just didn't enjoy things as much as I thought I was going to, is all.

Next morning Aunt Mazey was not at church. Nothing was said on the way home about her absence. I decided that no one would answer my questions if I asked them; so I didn't ask them. I chose to go the next morning and ask Aunt Mazey herself. It did occur to me that this approach might be a breach[10] of some social rule or other, but I ignored that thought.

It was nearly ten o'clock by the time I got my chores done and walked to Aunt Mazey's. The white convertible was gone. But Aunt Mazey's black Studebaker was pulled out of the barn and running.

Aunt Mazey came out of the house then, closing the door and locking it behind her. She had on a navy blue dress with white cuffs and collar. She also had on heeled black shoes and a small navy hat with a veil. As she came down the steps she saw me.

"Good morning, Jonathan." The smile was not the one I knew.

"Where are you going all dressed up?"

"I have to go into town," she said. "If I'm not back by dusk, will you come feed the rabbits?"

"Yes, ma'am." Her manner kept back all my other questions.

She nodded and came on down the steps. Pulling on a pair of white gloves, she got into the Studebaker. Aunt Mazey looked sad but beautiful. The Studebaker backed out of the drive slowly and turned onto the dirt road. I watched until the dust settled, and then I went back home.

No one was around but Sylvia. So I talked to her. "You should have seen how dressed up Aunt Mazey was just now. I've never seen her so dressed up."

---

[10]breach—breaking, as of a rule or contract

"Maybe she thinks that'll help her case," said Sylvia. Then she looked up, kind of startled.

"What do you mean, *case*?" I said.

"I'm not supposed to say anything," she said. "Forget I said anything."

"It's too late," I said. "You already did. Now finish it."

"I can't, Jon. Really."

"Is Aunt Mazey in some kind of trouble? Just tell me that."

"Not exactly trouble. No, she's not going to jail or anything. I mean, people can go to court without going to jail."

"Court!" I shouted, and Sylvia winced.[11]

"Now see!" she said. "You've tricked me into telling!"

I ran out the door and all the way to Taylor's house. I banged on the door until I nearly caved it in.

"Hey," said Taylor from the side porch, "I'm over here."

"Aunt Mazey had to go to court!" I waited for the shock to strike him. He just kept sitting there looking at me.

"Well?" I said.

"Well," he said, "I know. Dad and Mom were talking about it this morning. Her nephew wants her to sell the place and move into a home or something. She said she wasn't

going to, and he got a lawyer to make her."

"No!" I said. "We can't let this happen! We've got to help her."

"Just us two?" said Taylor.

He had a point. "Maybe Sam and Tweed can help. Yeah—in fact, Tweed's got a brother who could drive us into town."

It took some doing, but Tweed's brother finally agreed to take us into town in exchange for our doing his chores for a month. Nobody but Aunt Mazey would have survived such a bargain in my book. We got to the courthouse just after lunch.

"I'm hungry," Sam said.

"Just forget about that," I said. "You can eat later. Right now we have to figure out a way to see what's going on in there."

"Let's just go in," Taylor said.

"Are you kidding? They'll throw us out so fast our shoes will come off. No, we need a plan."

We thought and thought. I had almost despaired of finding a workable plan when Tweed said, "There's transom windows between the lobby and the courtroom. Maybe we could get up on something and look in those."

I was very glad to have Tweed as my friend right then.

---

[11] winced—moved or pulled back quickly

Amazing Miss Mazey

The operation of the plan was a little more difficult than we had expected. But with the goal so near, we weren't about to turn back. Tweed stood on the bench under the transom, and I stood on Tweed. Taylor and Sam stood guard at either end of the bench.

I could just barely see over the edge of the transom. "Can you stand up any straighter?" I said in a loud whisper down to Tweed.

"No."

We got down then, and Taylor took over for Tweed. That time I could see in without much strain. Aunt Mazey sat behind a big table off to the left. The nephew, in a navy blue suit, sat across the aisle. In the chairs behind I saw my parents! And Tweed's father, and Mr. Peters, and Taylor's mother and his grandmother.

"Hey," I whispered down, "everybody's folks are here."

"What else?" Taylor said.

A man was standing up beside Aunt Mazey. He was saying, "And my client[12] maintains that this competency[13] hearing is not only unnecessary but a violation[14] of her rights of privacy."

"This is a competency hearing," I reported, aghast.[15]

"What's that?" Sam said.

"It means they think Aunt Mazey is crazy."

"Aw," said Taylor, "Aunt Mazey ain't crazy."

The judge had white hair and gold-rimmed glasses. He said, "Mrs. Brannigan, this is just a hearing. I want you to understand that."

Aunt Mazey sat just as still as pond water, never saying a word. The man beside her said, "We understand, your honor."

The judge leaned back in his chair and looked over to the nephew. "Call your next witness."

"Carl Peters, please."

Mr. Peters, the banker, went up and sat down in the chair beside the judge's huge desk. He looked over at Aunt Mazey as if he might say something to her, but he didn't.

"What's going on now?" Tweed said.

---

[12]client—person who uses the services of a professional person
[13]competency—ability to function as is necessary or desired
[14]violation—disregarding; going against
[15]aghast—horrified

I reported what I had seen. Then I looked back in. "And what did she say she was going to do with this money?" the nephew's lawyer was asking.

"She didn't tell me," said Mr. Peters.

"Is it unusual for Mrs. Brannigan to draw that much money out at one time?"

"Well, I don't know what you mean by *unusual*," Mr. Peters said.

"Has she often drawn out that much money?"

"No."

"Has she ever drawn out that much money?"

"No."

"Didn't you think that it was unadvisable for her to do so?"

The man beside Aunt Mazey stood up. "I object. Calling for an opinion."

"Your honor," the other man said, "this man's business is money. He is an expert. I'm asking for his professional assessment."[16]

"Overruled," said the judge. "Answer the question, Mr. Peters."

Mr. Peters paused. "I told her it was her money and she could do whatever she liked. But I wouldn't have done it myself, no."

Taylor was getting shaky. I had to get down and let him rest.

"It doesn't sound good to me," I said.

"What can we do?" said Tweed.

"We need to talk to the judge," I said.

"What doesn't sound good?" Sam asked.

"Mr. Peters says Aunt Mazey didn't handle her money well."

"So?" Sam said.

"That's real important to grownups," Taylor put in.

We all knew that was so. We went outside to think, Taylor rubbing his shoulders. "Next time take your shoes off," he said.

The next time I manned the lookout, the nephew was up front. He had the same expression on his face that the know-it-all of the class always has right before he tells on you for something.

"And," he said, "she sleeps at odd hours day and night. She has all sorts of boxes stacked around the henhouse. Oh, I don't know. I hate to

say such things about my dear aunt. I just am concerned, you know, when I see such things. Why, there's a jar of insects in the bathroom!"

I felt my temper heating up. "I'm getting down," I said to Taylor. I told them what had been said. "We have to see that judge. That nephew is making everything sound backwards."

"When there's a break, we'll try to catch him," Tweed said.

Sam said, "Let's get an ice cream, quick. I have money."

This offer took first priority[17] briefly. We got ice cream.

---

[16]assessment—judgment; opinion
[17]priority—importance

A little later, I took my position on Taylor's shoulders again and peered in on the courtroom.

"Aunt Mazey's up front," I whispered down.

She sat by the judge's desk, her head up and her hands folded together like two small birds. She looked like a picture in one of those fancy ladies' magazines.

"What did you do with the money?" the nephew's lawyer asked.

Aunt Mazey did not answer.

"Mrs. Brannigan," said the judge, not unkindly, "you only hurt yourself by refusing to answer. Please answer the question."

She turned slightly in her chair and with the dignity of a queen said, "What do you do with your money, Sir?"

A little laugh ran through the room. "That's right, Mazey," said Tweed's father out loud.

The judge tapped his gavel, and silence followed. "Mrs. Brannigan, do not tempt me to find you in contempt."[18]

"I gave the money away," said Aunt Mazey.

The nephew came right up out of his chair. "All fifty thousand?" He caught himself and sat down again, embarrassed.

"All fifty thousand," she said calmly and coolly, looking directly at him.

"Aunt Mazey gave away fifty thousand dollars!" I reported to the group below me.

Tweed gave a low whistle. The figure seemed beyond comprehension, and we were impressed.

I looked back in. The judge was saying something to the bailiff[19] off to the side. The uniformed man nodded and went out.

"To whom did you give the money?" the nephew's lawyer wanted to know.

"That," said Aunt Mazey, "like everything else you've asked me today, is none of your business, young man."

"Mrs. Brannigan—"

"No, you see here. I'm no more incompetent than anyone else in this room. But because I'm seventy-five and rich and have a greedy, clever relative, I have to come in here and tell the whole town what time I go to bed and how many fireflies I keep in a jar."

"Jon," Tweed said.

"Shhhhh," I returned.

"Jon," said Taylor.

I drew my head back. "What?" And then I saw the bailiff, Tweed in one hand and Sam in the other.

"The judge would like to see you boys," he said.

---

[18]contempt—showing disrespect or disobedience to an authority in a court of law
[19]bailiff—one who keeps order in a courtroom

The walk through the crowd was most uncomfortable, as I could feel my father staring at me, first in shock and then in displeasure.

The four of us arrived before the judge's bench.

"Well," he said, leaning out to see us better. "I wonder what would prompt this fine collection of boys to hang from a transom window all afternoon? Hmm?"

None of us could think of anything to say. I could feel my father looking at me.

Finally, Taylor, as usual, spoke up. "We came to help Aunt Mazey." There was a hum and a buzz in the room.

"You did?" he said. "Why is that?"

"Because," Taylor went bravely on, "Aunt Mazey ain't crazy."

There was a laugh from the crowd. The judge banged his gavel.

I took courage from Taylor. "Right," I said. "You can't tell if a person is crazy by the questions that fellow has been asking."

"No?" said the judge, looking over at the nephew's lawyer with one edge of his mouth turning up just a little. "What questions should we ask then?"

I decided that I was already in enough trouble to last until I graduated from high school. So I went ahead and said all that I'd been thinking.

"If you want to find out what a person knows about reality, you don't ask about money. You should ask him about real things."

"Go on, counselor," said the judge to me.

"Well, you should ask about maple trees—they're real. Aunt Mazey can tell when a tree's been tapped and how often and when it can be tapped again. Or you should ask if the person knows how to understand the chickens or make pecan-crumble ice cream." I began to wonder if anyone would believe what I was saying. But the room was dead quiet, and I went on talking.

"I need to explain some things that Aunt Mazey's nephew said. She sleeps odd hours because she's watching for the fox that's after her chickens—which is also what all the boxes are for. She doesn't want to kill him, just catch him. And the lightning bugs are some we caught for her. And she said we'd saved her a lot of trouble because now she could have a night-light in the bathroom."

Again there was a slight laugh in the courtroom.

"Please don't send Aunt Mazey away," said Taylor in that innocent way of his. "I'll go back to getting a *D* in spelling again, and where will we go to hear stories about the Trojan War and stuff?"

Aunt Mazey looked at us with the oddest expression. I didn't know whether she would scold or cry. I plunged on to the end of what I had to say. "Aunt Mazey knows everything that's important, and if her nephew can't see that, he's crazy—not her."

To my astonishment, the audience broke into applause. Even the nephew's lawyer smiled. This time the judge rapped his gavel several times before there was quiet.

"You know, young man," he said, "I was thinking the same thing. All I needed was a little proof. Case dismissed." He banged the gavel once more, and the room came to life with laughing and clapping and bustling.

As Aunt Mazey stood up, the judge motioned for her to come near the desk. "Just for my own peace of

mind," he said, "what did you do with that money?"

Aunt Mazey regarded him silently for a moment. Then she said, "Very well. I'll tell you. I set up a college fund for the children."

Our eyes popped at that. The judge sat back surprised himself. "Why didn't you just say so?"

"I wasn't asked nicely," she said. To me then she said, "What about my rabbits? We'd better be getting home."

And so home we went, all of us. The next day our names were in the paper right along with Aunt Mazey's full name—Clara Letitia Mazedon Brannigan. "So *Mazey* is short for *Mazedon*," I said.

"Oh," said Taylor, coming to the heart of things offhandedly as usual. "I always thought it was short for *amazing*."

The Greater God

Sharon Woodruff
illustrated by Mary Ann Lumm

Ghosts and malign[1] spirits are often called "Good Brothers" by Chinese people who belong to pagan religions. The Chinese call the spirits this to appease[2] them and to protect themselves from bad luck. Christians who convert from religions that worship spirits often have to struggle against their old beliefs until they understand all that Christ has accomplished for them.

The Feast of the Good Brothers had always frightened ten-year-old Gwo Gwang Leo. And this night on the eve of the feast he lay on his mat with his eyes shut tightly in fear that if he opened them even a crack he would see dozens of malign ghosts floating in his room.

He had talked with his older brother, Lin Yi, about it before it had turned dark.

"Gwo Gwang, when will you stop being such a coward? No Chinese fears the Good Brothers. We give them a nice name and a feast, and we worship them so they will not hurt us," said Lin Yi.

"But what if one of the Good Brothers misses the feast; what if one does not see us paying them respect?"

[1]malign—evil
[2]appease—to make calm; to satisfy

100

"They'll see," said Lin Yi. "We don't have to worry. Your missionary friends are the ones who had better worry. They never try to please the Good Brothers. One day the spirits will get angry and bring bad luck to those American missionaries."

"Don't talk that way," cried Gwo Gwang, fearing that one of the ghosts might be listening and getting an idea.

Lin Yi continued his taunting.[3] "The Good Brothers may decide to hurt their little girl, little Mei Mei. Perhaps they will cast disease into her, or drown her, or cause her night terrors." He laughed. "Perhaps they hear us even now and go to accomplish their work."

"Stop it!" cried Gwo Gwang, horrified. He loved the little blue-eyed toddler from the faraway land called America.

"What? Is Gwo Gwang the coward going to stop me?"

Gwo Gwang balled up his fist to give Lin Yi a blow. But his good sense soon stopped him. Gwo Gwang had never yet won a fist fight with his older brother. If he hit his brother, Lin Yi would surely strike back—only much harder. Then Gwo Gwang would start crying. Lin Yi would run off laughing and tell all of the other children in the village of Shwei Nan what a coward young Gwo Gwang had been. It had happened many times before. Lin Yi delighted in continuing to torment his brother.

"Stop it! Stop! Stop!" screamed Gwo Gwang.

"What are you two fighting about?" Mrs. Leo entered the room, an irritated frown on her face.

"Gwo Gwang is being a coward again," said Lin Yi. And before Gwo Gwang could think of anything to say, Lin Yi blurted out a biased[4] version of the story. "First he tells me that the missionaries defy the Good Brothers. Then when I warn him of what will happen, he says he will fight me." Lin Yi smiled ruefully.[5] "Yet when I raise my hand to defend myself, he cries!"

"Go to your room, Lin Yi; it's time for bed," said their mother. Lin Yi marched off, very pleased with himself for his quick thinking.

Mrs. Leo sat down and studied her youngest son. Gwo Gwang quickly wiped away a tear.

"Ah, Gwo Gwang! My little Gwo Gwang! When will you learn to have some courage? When will you learn to speak up and defend yourself? I am afraid you are not a very clever boy, my son." This last thought she said more to herself than to Gwo Gwang.

Gwo Gwang could never explain it to her. How could one be courageous against the Good Brothers? It

---

[3]taunting—ridiculing or making fun of
[4]biased—preferring one opinion over another; prejudiced
[5]ruefully—causing one to feel pity or sorrow

was horrifying to even think of battling them. And yet he knew inside that he would always be battling them now. The missionaries had told him too much for him to cling to the mercies of the Good Brothers.

Gwo Gwang lay on his mat with the muscles of his face aching from keeping his eyes shut so tightly. He tried to plan the next day in an effort to keep his thoughts off the ghosts. He would have to help his mother prepare the food for the feast; that would take most of the morning and afternoon. Then he would be expected to stay and greet his aunts and uncles and cousins who would come. They would eat later in the afternoon. That was the part he hated the most. Perhaps when everyone had finished eating he could slip away unnoticed to the mission compound.[6] He wanted to make sure nothing happened to little Mei Mei. . . . Late in the night, an exhausted Gwo Gwang finally fell asleep.

[6]compound—group of buildings built for a special purpose

It was almost dusk the next day when Gwo Gwang knocked on the door of the mission compound.

"Why, hello, Gwo Gwang! Where have you been all day?" asked Mrs. Hart, the missionary's wife.

"At home. Today was a feast day," answered Gwo Gwang. As Mrs. Hart continued talking cheerfully, Gwo Gwang tried to hide his smile. It was so funny to hear the tall missionary speak Chinese. She said all the words in such a strange way. And sometimes she said a thought backwards. But of course he would never laugh at her, for that would be rude.

"I'll go get Gretchen. She's in her playpen in her room. I know she'll be glad to see you," and Mrs. Hart sailed out of the room to find Gretchen.

"Gr Chin," said Gwo Gwang to himself. "I wonder why Americans give their children such hard-to-pronounce names?" he thought. His own name for her, Mei Mei, was much prettier and easier to say.

"Here she is," said Mrs. Hart, reentering.

The little blue eyes sparkled when they saw Gwo Gwang, and the little arms stretched forward to be held by the boy.

"Gwa Gwa," cried the toddler.

"She's learning to say your name. Do you want to hold her?" asked Mrs. Hart.

"Yes, please," answered Gwo Gwang. After he had Mei Mei safely in his arms, he rubbed his light brown hand up and down her little arm. Can anything so white really be skin? Can eyes so blue really see? he thought. He was not the only person to be amazed at the fair American child. Whenever Mrs. Hart took Mei Mei out, village wives and even many of the men crowded around the remarkable little girl.

"I think next to her Daddy, Gretchen loves you the best," said Mrs. Hart fondly.

Gwo Gwang smiled. It was nice to have someone love you just the way you were. It was nice not to be called foolish or cowardly. He held the toddler a little tighter.

"Would you like a cookie?" asked Mrs. Hart.

"Yes, please," answered Gwo Gwang.

She brought out a plate full of cookies and set them in front of the boy. He dug into them, forgetting his manners.

"Why, Gwo Gwang, you go at those cookies as if you hadn't eaten all day," she said.

"I haven't," he admitted.

"Why not?" she asked.

"Today was the Feast of the Good Brothers. I am always afraid to eat the food prepared for the feast," he said, hanging his head and wondering if Mrs. Hart would think him foolish and cowardly.

After a long pause she spoke. "I'm going to fix you a sandwich. And then we can go outside where it's cooler and talk about it."

Gwo Gwang was still amazed at the strange foods Americans ate. Cookies he liked, but he wasn't very fond of sandwiches. They were either too slimy or too dry, never crisp, and always cold. However, at this point he was too hungry to refuse anything.

She came back a moment later. "Here, I'll take Gretchen, and you take the sandwich," she said, handing it to him. "Let's go sit out by the fish pond."

The fish pond was Gwo Gwang's favorite place on the compound. Tall palm trees surrounded it, and dozens of bright goldfish darted back and forth in its waters. Mrs. Hart put Gretchen down, and she immediately ran towards the pool, trying to grab a fish.

"No, no, Gretchen. That water is too deep for you," said Mrs. Hart, picking the toddler back up. "And besides, the fish don't want to come out of the water." She settled herself and then turned to Gwo Gwang. "Now, tell me about the 'Feast of the Good Brothers.'"

"The Good Brothers are ghosts and evil spirits who can bring us bad luck if we do not appease them," he began. "We fix them a great feast and set it out on a table so they can see it and take what they want of it."

"How do you know when a ghost has taken all he wants of the food?" asked Mrs. Hart.

"We light sticks of incense. When they finish burning, we know that the ghosts have eaten their fill. Whatever is left on the table is the food we may eat," he answered.

"Have you ever noticed any of the food disappearing as you wait for the incense to burn out?" she asked.

"No," he answered. "Yet I have seen their power, and I am afraid when they do not eat the food."

"Why?"

"I say to myself, 'I guess all of the Good Brothers have eaten at another feast.' But what if there is one late ghost who will see me eating his food? Won't he be angry? Won't he give me bad luck for taking his food?" Gwo Gwang raised his eyes to look at Mrs. Hart, his heart pounding at the thought.

She thought for a moment. "Gwo Gwang, do you remember three weeks ago when you asked the Lord Jesus to come into your life and save you?"

"Yes."

"Well, I want you to remember two things. First, the Lord promised never to leave us or forsake us.

Second, the Bible says, 'Greater is he that is in you, than he that is in the world.'"

"What does that mean?"

"The Lord Jesus is far greater than any ghost or demon. Before you were saved, you were under the power of the god of this world. But the Lord Jesus died for your sins on the cross. Now that Christ has bought you and lives in you, He is prepared to conquer any spirits who torment you," she answered.

"He has promised to protect me from the Good Brothers?" asked Gwo Gwang.

"Oh, yes!" she answered. "Our God is stronger than any ghost. Tomorrow I'll write that verse out

on a card for you. Then you can memorize it if you like."

That night as he lay on his mat, Gwo Gwang kept his eyes open for a long time. He thought again about Mrs. Hart's words: *The Lord Jesus is far greater than any ghost or demon.* "Now I need not be afraid," he thought.

The next morning his mother shook him awake from a peaceful sleep. "Today is not a feast day. You must get ready for school," she said, and left the room.

"Gwo Gwang," said Lin Yi in his taunting voice, "last night I saw the spirits outside your room!"

"If you saw the spirits, then you're the one who should be afraid.

I didn't see anything," Gwo Gwang answered boldly.

"How could you see when you're afraid to open your eyes?" asked Lin Yi, hoping to start a fight.

Gwo Gwang knew Lin Yi's strategy, and instead of answering him, Gwo Gwang dressed quickly and headed toward the mission compound. He wanted to get the verse card Mrs. Hart had promised to make. He walked through the back gate so that he could go by the fish pond. "I wonder if they have gardens and ponds in America," he thought.

Suddenly he stopped. Mei Mei was squatting at the edge of the pond, holding her hand out toward a darting fish. He could see her leaning further and further toward the water. Before he could call out to her, she fell forward into the water with a splash!

Gwo Gwang waited a moment, frozen in place. Mei Mei came up, coughing and sputtering, then disappeared under water again. He looked around wildly. Where was Mrs. Hart?

All of his thoughts came in a jumble: a Chinese should never touch a dead body—what if Mei Mei was already dead?—maybe the Good Brothers had willed Mei Mei's death because the Harts would not worship them—if Gwo Gwang tried to help, the Good Brothers might drown him for interfering.

Then Mrs. Hart's words came back to him: Jesus had said, "I will never leave you, nor forsake you." Jesus was greater than any ghost or demon.

These thoughts freed Gwo Gwang's muscles. His legs surged forward. He splashed through the water. He grabbed Mei Mei, lifted the little girl high, and called for the Harts as loudly as he could.

The moment the toddler's face was out of the water, she began to cough and gasp for air. Mr. and Mrs. Hart were instantly by the pond, helping him out.

"I don't know how this happened," said Mr. Hart. He stared at Gwo Gwang, shaking his head. "One minute Gretchen was standing by my wife in the kitchen, and the next minute she was gone!"

Mrs. Hart cradled the toddler close. "She's all right," she said. "She's breathing normally. Thank you, thank you, Gwo Gwang."

The shouting in the quiet morning had attracted many of the neighbors. The courtyard was swiftly filling with excited people.

"What happened?" asked Mrs. Leo, rushing in.

The crowd parted to let her see her son standing with the Harts and their little girl.

"You should be very proud of your son, Mrs. Leo," said Mrs. Hart. "He's a hero."

"My son?" asked Mrs. Leo.

"Yes. He saved our daughter's life," answered Mr. Hart.

"My Gwo Gwang?" Mrs. Leo looked at her son as though he were another person. "But he's usually so timid, so afraid," she blurted out.

"Well, he wasn't afraid today," said Mrs. Hart, looking at Gwo Gwang.

"I was very afraid at first," said Gwo Gwang as if in answer to Mrs. Hart's look. "But then I remembered what Mrs. Hart taught me. And the cross."

He looked from his mother to Mrs. Hart and down again. It was not courteous to be overbold in his speech before grownups. And yet he had spoken the truth.

"Jesus is greater than all the gods of this world," he said quietly. "This I know."

Nobody said anything for a moment. They knew Gwo Gwang was cowardly; yet here he was in defiance of the Good Brothers, a hero.

At last his mother's voice broke the quiet.

"Well, my brave son, it is time to come home and get ready for school again. You cannot go dripping wet." She bowed to Mrs. Hart. "You must come and visit us with your little Mei Mei," she said with great dignity. "I will look forward to drinking tea with you."

"Thank you. I will come soon," Mrs. Hart promised.

"We will talk about Jesus," said Mrs. Leo. She bowed again. As Gwo Gwang turned away, a knowing look of shared happiness passed between the missionary and her young convert.

Thanks to Gwo Gwang's courage, a door had opened for Mrs. Hart to witness to the women of the village!

Wind-Wolves

William D. Sargent
illustrated by Preston Gravely

Do you hear the cry as the pack goes by,
The wind-wolves hunting across the sky?
Hear them tongue it, keen and clear,
Hot on the flanks[1] of the flying deer!

Across the forest, mere, and plain,
Their hunting howl goes up again!
All night they'll follow the ghostly trail,
All night we'll hear their phantom wail,

For tonight the wind-wolf pack holds sway
From Pegasus Square to the Milky Way,
And the frightened bands of cloud-deer flee
In scattered groups of two or three.

[1]flanks—the sides of

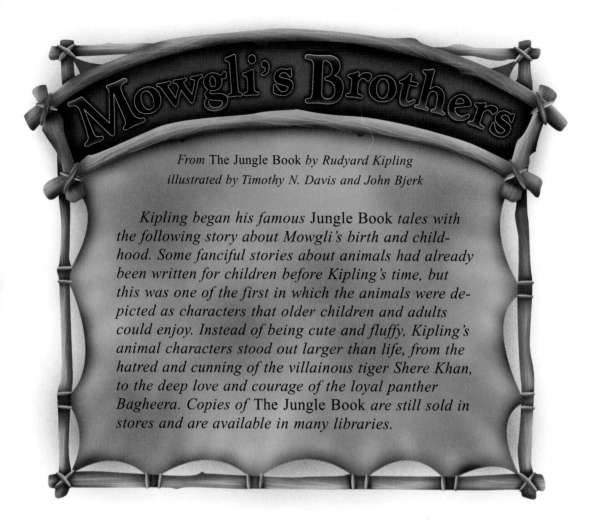

Mowgli's Brothers

From The Jungle Book *by Rudyard Kipling*
illustrated by Timothy N. Davis and John Bjerk

Kipling began his famous Jungle Book *tales with the following story about Mowgli's birth and childhood. Some fanciful stories about animals had already been written for children before Kipling's time, but this was one of the first in which the animals were depicted as characters that older children and adults could enjoy. Instead of being cute and fluffy, Kipling's animal characters stood out larger than life, from the hatred and cunning of the villainous tiger Shere Khan, to the deep love and courage of the loyal panther Bagheera. Copies of* The Jungle Book *are still sold in stores and are available in many libraries.*

The Law of the Jungle

It was seven o'clock of a very warm evening in the Seeonee Hills when Father Wolf woke up from his day's rest, scratched himself, yawned, and spread out his paws one after the other to get rid of the sleepy feeling in their tips. Mother Wolf lay with her big gray nose dropped across her four tumbling, squealing cubs, and the moon shone into the mouth of the cave where they all lived.

"Augrh!" said Father Wolf. "It is time to hunt again." He was going to spring downhill when a little shadow with a bushy tail crossed the threshold[1] and whined: "Good hunting go with you, O Chief of the Wolves. And good hunting and strong white teeth go with the noble children that they may never forget the hungry in this world."

---

[1]threshold—the floor or ground at an entrance or doorway

110

It was the jackal—Tabaqui, the Dish-licker—and the wolves of India despise Tabaqui because he runs about making mischief, and telling tales, and eating rags and pieces of leather from the village rubbish heaps. But they are afraid of him too, because Tabaqui, more than anyone else in the jungle, is apt to go mad, and then he forgets that he was ever afraid of anyone, and runs through the forest biting everything in his way. Even the tiger runs and hides when little Tabaqui goes mad, for madness is the most disgraceful thing that can overtake a wild creature. We call it hydrophobia,[2] but they call it *dewanee*—the madness—and run.

"Enter, then, and look," said Father Wolf stiffly, "but there is no food here."

"For a wolf, no," said Tabaqui, "but for so mean[3] a person as myself a dry bone is a good feast. Who are we, the Gidur-log [the jackal people], to pick and choose?" He scuttled to the back of the cave, where he found the bone of a buck with some meat on it, and sat cracking the end merrily.

"All thanks for this good meal," he said, licking his lips. "How beautiful are the noble children! How large are their eyes! And so young too! Indeed, indeed, I might have remembered that the children of kings are men from the beginning."

Now, Tabaqui knew as well as anyone else that there is nothing so harmful as to compliment children to their faces. It pleased him to see Mother and Father Wolf look uncomfortable.

Tabaqui sat still, rejoicing in the mischief that he had made, and then he said spitefully:

"Shere Khan, the Big One, has shifted his hunting grounds. He will hunt among these hills for the next moon,[4] so he has told me."

Shere Khan was the tiger who lived near the Waingunga River, twenty miles away.

"He has no right!" Father Wolf began angrily—"By the Law of the Jungle he has no right to change his quarters without due warning. He will frighten every head of game within ten miles, and I—I have to hunt for two, these days."

"His mother did not call him Lungri [the Lame One] for nothing," said Mother Wolf quietly. "He has been lame in one foot from his birth. That is why he has only killed cattle. Now the villagers of the Waingunga are angry with him, and he has come here to make *our* villagers angry. They will scour[5] the jungle for him when he is far away, and we and our children must run when the grass is

---

[2]hydrophobia—rabies
[3]mean—common; low in status
[4]moon—a month
[5]scour—to search thoroughly

set alight. Indeed, we are very grateful to Shere Khan!"

"Shall I tell him of your gratitude?" said Tabaqui.

"Out!" snapped Father Wolf. "Out and hunt with thy master. Thou hast done harm enough for one night."

"I go," said Tabaqui quietly. "Ye can hear Shere Khan below in the thickets. I might have saved myself the message."

Father Wolf listened, and below in the valley that ran down to a little river he heard the dry, angry, snarly, singsong whine of a tiger who has caught nothing and does not care if all the jungle knows it.

"The fool!" said Father Wolf. "To begin a night's work with that noise! Does he think that our bucks are like his fat Waingunga bullocks?"

"H'sh. It is neither bullock nor buck he hunts tonight," said Mother Wolf. "It is Man." The whine had changed to a sort of humming purr that seemed to come from every quarter of the compass. It was the noise that bewilders woodcutters and gypsies sleeping in the open, and makes them run sometimes into the very mouth of the tiger.

"Man!" said Father Wolf, showing all his white teeth. "Faugh! Are there not enough beetles and frogs in the tanks that he must eat Man, and on our ground too!"

The Law of the Jungle, which never orders anything without a reason, forbids every beast to eat Man except when he is killing to show his children how to kill, and then he must hunt outside the hunting grounds of his pack or tribe. The real reason for this is that man-killing means, sooner or later, the arrival of men on elephants, with guns, and hundreds of men with gongs and rockets and torches. Then everybody in the jungle suffers. The reason the beasts give among themselves is that Man is the weakest and most defenseless of all living things, and it is unsportsmanlike to touch him. They say too—and it is true—that man-eaters become mangy,[6] and lose their fur.

The purr grew louder, and ended in the full-throated "Aaarh!" of the tiger's charge.

Then there was a howl—an untigerish howl—from Shere Khan. "He has missed," said Mother Wolf. "What is it?"

Father Wolf ran out a few paces and heard Shere Khan muttering and mumbling savagely as he tumbled about in the scrub.

"The fool has had no more sense than to jump at a woodcutter's campfire, and has burned his feet," said Father Wolf with a grunt. "Tabaqui is with him."

"Something is coming uphill," said Mother Wolf, twitching one ear. "Get ready."

The bushes rustled a little in the thicket, and Father Wolf dropped with his haunches under him, ready for his leap. Then, if you had been watching, you would have seen the most wonderful thing in the world—the wolf checked in midspring. He made his bound before he saw what it was he was jumping at, and then he tried to stop himself. The result was that he shot up straight into the air for four or five feet, landing almost where he left ground.

"Man!" he snapped. "A man's cub. Look!"

Directly in front of him, holding on by a low branch, stood a brown baby who could just walk—as soft and as dimpled a little atom as ever came to a wolf's cave at night. He looked up into Father Wolf's face and laughed.

---

[6]mangy—having bare or dirty spots

"Is that a man's cub?" said Mother Wolf. "I have never seen one. Bring it here."

A wolf accustomed to moving his own cubs can, if necessary, mouth an egg without breaking it, and though Father Wolf's jaws closed right on the child's back not a tooth even scratched the skin as he laid it down among the cubs.

"How little! and—how bold!" said Mother Wolf softly. The baby was pushing his way between the cubs to get close to the warm hide. "Ahai! And so this is a man's cub. Now, was there ever a wolf that could boast of a man's cub among her children?"

"I have heard now and again of such a thing, but never in our Pack or in my time," said Father Wolf. "He is altogether without hair, and I could kill him with a touch of my foot. But see, he looks up and is not afraid."

The moonlight was blocked out of the mouth of the cave, for Shere Khan's great square head and shoulders were thrust into the entrance. Tabaqui, behind him, was squeaking: "My lord, my lord, it went in here!"

"Shere Khan does us great honor," said Father Wolf, but his eyes were very angry. "What does Shere Khan need?"

"My quarry.[7] A man's cub went this way," said Shere Khan. "Its parents have run off. Give it to me."

Shere Khan had jumped at a woodcutter's campfire, as Father Wolf had said, and was furious from the pain of his burned feet. But Father Wolf knew that the mouth of the cave was too narrow for a tiger to come in by. Even where he was, Shere Khan's shoulders and forepaws were cramped for want of room, as a man's would be if he tried to fight in a barrel.

"The Wolves are a free people," said Father Wolf. "They take orders from the Head of the Pack, and not from any striped cattle-killer. The man's cub is ours—to kill if we choose."

"Ye choose and ye do not choose! What talk is this of choosing? By the bull that I killed, am I to stand nosing into your dog's den for my fair dues? It is I, Shere Khan, who speaks!"

The tiger's roar filled the cave with thunder. Mother Wolf shook herself clear of the cubs and sprang forward, her eyes, like two green moons in the darkness, facing the blazing eyes of Shere Khan.

"And it is I, Raksha, who answers. The man's cub is mine, Lungri—mine to me! He shall not be killed. He shall live to run with the Pack and to hunt with the Pack; and in the end, look you, hunter of little cubs—frog-eater—fish-killer—he

---

[7]quarry—a person or animal that is hunted; prey

shall hunt thee! Now get hence, or by the Sambhur that I killed (I eat no starved cattle), back thou goest to thy mother, burned beast of the jungle, lamer than ever thou camest into the world! Go!"

Father Wolf looked on amazed. He had almost forgotten the days when he won Mother Wolf in fair fight from five other wolves when she hunted in the lead of the Pack not for compliment's sake. Shere Khan might have faced Father Wolf, but he could not stand up against Mother Wolf, for he knew that where he was she had all the advantage of the ground, and would fight to the death. So he backed out of the cave mouth growling, and when he was clear he shouted:

"Each dog barks in his own yard! We will see what the Pack will say to this fostering[8] of man-cubs. The cub is mine, and to my teeth he will come in the end, O bushtailed thieves!"

---

[8]fostering—raising; bringing up

Mother Wolf threw herself down panting among the cubs, and Father Wolf said to her gravely:

"Shere Khan speaks this much truth. The cub must be shown to the Pack. Wilt thou still keep him, Mother?"

"Keep him!" she gasped. "He came by night, alone and very hungry; yet he was not afraid! Look, he has pushed one of my babes to one side already. And that lame butcher would have killed him and would have run off to the Waingunga while the villagers here hunted through all our lairs in revenge! Keep him! Assuredly I will keep him. Lie still, little frog. O thou Mowgli—for Mowgli the Frog I will call thee— the time will come when thou wilt hunt Shere Khan as he has hunted thee."

"But what will our Pack say?" said Father Wolf.

The Law of the Jungle lays down very clearly that any wolf may, when he marries, withdraw from the Pack he belongs to. But as soon as his cubs are old enough to stand on their feet he must bring them to the Pack Council, which is generally held once a month at full moon, in order that the other wolves may identify them. After that inspection the cubs are free to run where they please, and until they have killed their first buck no excuse is accepted if a grown wolf of the Pack kills one of them. The punishment is death where the murderer can be found; and if you think for a minute you will see that this must be so.

Man's Cub

Father Wolf waited till his cubs could run a little, and then on the night of the Pack Meeting took them and Mowgli and Mother Wolf to the Council Rock—a hilltop covered with stones and boulders where a hundred wolves could hide. Akela, the great gray Lone Wolf, who led all the Pack by strength and cunning,[9] lay out at full length on his rock, and below him sat forty or more wolves of every size and color, from badger-colored veterans[10] who could handle a buck alone to young black three-year-olds who thought they could.

---

[9]cunning—slyness or cleverness
[10]veterans—those who are experienced

The Lone Wolf had led them for a year now. He had fallen twice into a wolf trap in his youth, and once he had been beaten and left for dead; so he knew the manners and customs of men. There was very little talking at the Rock. The cubs tumbled over each other in the center of the circle where their mothers and fathers sat, and now and again a senior wolf would go quietly up to a cub, look at him carefully, and return to his place on noiseless feet. Sometimes a mother would push her cub far out into the moonlight to be sure that he had not been overlooked. Akela from his rock would cry: "Ye know the Law—ye know the Law. Look well, O Wolves!" And the anxious mothers would take up the call: "Look—look well, O Wolves!"

At last—and Mother Wolf's neck bristles lifted as the time came—Father Wolf pushed "Mowgli the Frog," as they called him, into the center, where he sat laughing and playing with some pebbles that glistened in the moonlight.

Akela never raised his head from his paws, but went on with the monotonous[11] cry: "Look well!" A muffled roar came up from behind the rocks—the voice of Shere Khan crying: "The cub is mine. Give him to me. What have the Free People to do with a man's cub?" Akela never even twitched his ears. All he said was: "Look well, O Wolves! What

have the Free People to do with the orders of any save the Free People? Look well!"

There was a chorus of deep growls, and a young wolf in his fourth year flung back Shere Khan's question to Akela: "What have the Free People to do with a man's cub?" Now, the Law of the Jungle lays down that if there is any dispute[12] as to the right of a cub to be accepted by the Pack, he must be spoken for by at least two members of the Pack who are not his father and mother.

"Who speaks for this cub?" said Akela. "Among the Free People who speaks?" There was no answer, and Mother Wolf got ready for what she knew would be her last fight, if things came to fighting.

Then the only other creature who is allowed at the Pack Council—Baloo, the sleepy brown bear who teaches the wolf cubs the Law of the Jungle: old Baloo, who can come and go where he pleases because he eats only nuts and roots and honey—rose up on his hind quarters and grunted.

"The man's cub—the man's cub?" he said. "I speak for the man's cub. There is no harm in a man's cub. I have no gift of words, but I speak the truth. Let him run with the Pack, and be entered with the others. I myself will teach him."

---

[11]monotonous—never changing; dull
[12]dispute—quarrel or disagreement

118

"We need yet another," said Akela. "Baloo has spoken, and he is our teacher for the young cubs. Who speaks besides Baloo?"

A black shadow dropped down into the circle. It was Bagheera the Black Panther, inky black all over, but with the panther markings showing up in certain lights like the pattern of watered silk. Everybody knew Bagheera, and nobody cared to cross his path; for he was as cunning as Tabaqui, as bold as the wild buffalo, and as reckless as the wounded elephant. But he had a voice as soft as wild honey dripping from a tree, and a skin softer than down.

"O Akela, and ye the Free People," he purred, "I have no right in your assembly,[13] but the Law of the Jungle says that if there is a doubt which is not a killing matter in regard to a new cub, the life of that cub may be bought at a price. And the Law does not say who may or may not pay that price. Am I right?"

"Good! Good!" said the young wolves, who are always hungry. "Listen to Bagheera. The cub can be bought for a price. It is the Law."

Bagheera faced the pack. "Knowing that I have no right to speak here, I ask your leave."

"Speak then," cried twenty voices.

"To kill a cub is shame. Besides, he may make better sport for you when he is grown. Baloo has spoken in his behalf. Now to Baloo's word I will add one bull, and a fat one, newly killed, not half a mile from here, if ye will accept the man's cub according to the Law. Is it difficult?"

[13]assembly—a group gathered together for a special purpose

There was a clamor of scores of voices, saying: "What matter? He will die in the winter rains. He will scorch in the sun. What harm can a frog do us? Let him run with the Pack. Where is the bull, Bagheera? Let him be accepted." And then came Akela's bay, crying: "Look well—look well, O Wolves!"

Mowgli was still deeply interested in the pebbles, and he did not notice when the wolves came and looked at him one by one. At last they all went down the hill for the dead bull, and only Akela, Bagheera, Baloo, and Mowgli's own wolves were left. Shere Khan roared still in the night, for he was very angry that Mowgli had not been handed over to him.

"Ay, roar well," said Bagheera, under his whiskers, "for the time will come when this thing will make thee roar to another tune, or I know nothing of man."

"It was well done," said Akela. "Men and their cubs are very wise. He may be a help in time."

"Truly, a help in time of need; for none can hope to lead the Pack forever," said Bagheera.

Akela said nothing. He was thinking of the time that comes to every leader of every pack when his strength goes from him and he gets feebler and feebler,

till at last he is killed by the wolves and a new leader comes up—to be killed in his turn.

"Take him away," he said to Father Wolf, "and train him as befits one of the Free People." And that is how Mowgli was entered into the Seeonee Wolf Pack for the price of a bull and on Baloo's good word.

Now you must be content to skip ten or eleven whole years, and only guess at all the wonderful life that Mowgli led among the wolves, because if it were written out it would fill ever so many books. He grew up with the cubs, though they, of course, were grown wolves almost before he was a child. And Father Wolf taught him his business, and the meaning of things in the jungle, till every rustle in the grass, every breath of the warm night air, every note of the owls above his head, every scratch of a bat's claws as it roosted for a while in a tree, and every splash of every little fish jumping in a pool meant just as much to him as the work of his office means to a business man.

When he was not learning he sat out in the sun and slept, and ate and went to sleep again. When he felt dirty or hot he swam in the forest pools; and when he wanted honey (Baloo the bear told him that honey and nuts were just as pleasant to eat as raw meat) he climbed up for it, and Bagheera the panther showed him how to do it. Bagheera would lie out on a branch and call, "Come along, Little Brother," and at first Mowgli would cling like the sloth, but afterward he would fling himself through the branches almost as boldly as the gray ape. He took his place at the Council Rock, too, when the Pack met, and there he discovered that if he stared hard at any wolf, the

wolf would be forced to drop his eyes, and so he used to stare for fun.

At other times he would pick the long thorns out of the pads[14] of his friends, for wolves suffer terribly from thorns and burrs in their coats. He would go down the hillside into the cultivated[15] lands by night, and look very curiously at the villagers in their huts, but he had a mistrust of men because Bagheera showed him a square box with a drop gate so cunningly hidden in the jungle that he nearly walked into it, and told him that it was a trap. He loved better than anything else to go with Bagheera into the dark warm heart of the forest, to sleep all through the drowsy day, and at night see how Bagheera did his killing. Bagheera killed right and left as he felt hungry, and so did Mowgli—with one exception. As soon as he was old enough to understand things, Bagheera told him that he must never touch cattle because he had been bought into the Pack at the price of a bull's life.

"All the jungle is thine," said Bagheera, "and thou canst kill everything that thou art strong enough to kill; but for the sake of the bull that bought thee thou must never kill or eat any cattle young or old. That is the Law of the Jungle."

---

[14]pads—small cushionlike parts on the bottoms of the feet of certain animals
[15]cultivated—prepared and tended soil to grow plants

Mowgli obeyed faithfully.

And he grew and grew strong as a boy must grow who does not know that he is learning any lessons, and who has nothing in the world to think of except things to eat.

Mother Wolf told him once or twice that Shere Khan was not a creature to be trusted, and that some day he must kill Shere Khan. But though a young wolf would have remembered that advice every hour, Mowgli forgot it because he was only a boy—though he would have called himself a wolf if he had been able to speak in any human tongue.

Shere Khan was always crossing his path in the jungle, for as Akela grew older and feebler the lame tiger had come to be great friends with the younger wolves of the Pack, who followed him for scraps, a thing Akela would never have allowed if he had dared to push his authority to the proper bounds. Then Shere Khan would flatter them and wonder that such fine young hunters were content to be led by a dying wolf and a man's cub. "They tell me," Shere Khan would say, "that at Council ye dare not look him between the eyes," and the young wolves would growl and bristle.

Bagheera, who had eyes and ears everywhere, knew something of this, and once or twice he told Mowgli in so many words that Shere Khan would kill him some day. Mowgli would laugh and answer: "I have the Pack and I have thee; and Baloo, though he is so lazy, might strike a blow or two for my sake. Why should I be afraid?"

It was one very warm day that a new notion came to Bagheera—born of something that he had heard. Perhaps Sahi the Porcupine had told him; but he said to Mowgli when they were deep in the jungle, as the boy lay with his head on Bagheera's beautiful black skin, "Little Brother, how often have I told thee that Shere Khan is thy enemy?"

"As many times as there are nuts on that palm," said Mowgli, who, naturally, could not count. "What of it? I am sleepy, Bagheera, and Shere Khan is all long tail and loud talk— like Mor the Peacock."

"But this is no time for sleeping. Baloo knows it; I know it; the Pack know it; and even the foolish, foolish deer know. Tabaqui has told thee too."

"Ho! Ho!" said Mowgli. "Tabaqui came to me not long ago with some rude talk that I was man's cub and not fit to dig pignuts. But I caught Tabaqui by the tail and swung

him twice against a palm tree to teach him better manners."

"That was foolishness, for though Tabaqui is a mischief-maker, he would have told thee of something that concerned thee closely. Open those eyes, Little Brother. Shere Khan dare not kill thee in the jungle. But remember, Akela is very old, and soon the day comes when he cannot kill his buck, and then he will be leader no more. Many of the wolves that looked thee over when thou wast brought to the Council first are old too, and the young wolves believe, as Shere Khan has taught them, that a man-cub has no place with the Pack. In a little time thou wilt be a man."

"And what is a man that he should not run with his brother?" said Mowgli. "I was born in the jungle. I have obeyed the Law of the Jungle, and there is no wolf of ours from whose paws I have not pulled a thorn. Surely they are my brothers."

Bagheera stretched himself at full length and half shut his eyes. "Little Brother," said he, "feel under my jaw."

Mowgli put up his strong brown hand, and just under Bagheera's silky chin, where the giant rolling muscles were all hid by the glossy hair, he came upon a little bald spot.

"There is no one in the jungle that knows that I, Bagheera, carry that mark—the mark of the collar; and yet, Little Brother, I was born among men, and it was among men that my mother died—in the cages of the king's palace at Oodeypore. It was because of this that I paid the price for thee at the Council when thou wast a little cub. Yes, I too was born among men. I had never seen the jungle. They fed me behind bars from an iron pan till one night I felt that I was Bagheera—the Panther— and no man's plaything, and I broke the silly lock with one blow of my paw and came away. And because I had learned the ways of men, I became more terrible in the jungle than Shere Khan. Is it not so?"

"Yes," said Mowgli, "all the jungle fears Bagheera—all except Mowgli."

"Oh, thou art a man's cub," said the Black Panther very tenderly. "And even as I returned to my jungle, so thou must go back to men at last—to the men who are thy brothers—if thou art not killed in the council."

"But why—but why should any wish to kill me?" said Mowgli.

"Look at me," said Bagheera. And Mowgli looked at him steadily between the eyes. The big panther turned his head away in half a minute.

"That is why," he said, shifting his paw on the leaves. "Not even I can look thee between the eyes, and I was

born among men, and I love thee, Little Brother. The others, they hate thee because their eyes cannot meet thine; because thou art wise; because thou hast pulled out thorns from their feet—because thou art a man."

"I did not know these things," said Mowgli sullenly,[16] and he frowned under his heavy black eyebrows.

[16]sullenly—silently and angrily; glumly

it!" said Bagheera, leaping up. "Go thou down quickly to the men's huts in the valley, and take some of the Red Flower which they grow there, so that when the time comes thou mayest have even a stronger friend than I or Baloo or those of the Pack that love thee. Get the Red Flower."

By Red Flower Bagheera meant fire, only no creature in the jungle will call fire by its proper name. Every beast lives in deadly fear of it, and invents a hundred ways of describing it.

"The Red Flower?" said Mowgli. "That grows outside their huts in the twilight. I will get some."

"There speaks the man's cub," said Bagheera proudly. "Remember that it grows in little pots. Get one swiftly, and keep it by thee for time of need."

"Good!" said Mowgli. "I go. But art thou sure, O my Bagheera—" he slipped his arm around the splendid neck and looked deep into the big eyes—"art thou sure that all this is Shere Khan's doing?"

"By the Broken Lock that freed me, I am sure, Little Brother."

"Then, by the Bull that bought me, I will pay Shere Khan full tale for this, and it may be a little over," said Mowgli, and he bounded away.

"That is a man. That is all a man," said Bagheera to himself, lying down again. "Oh, Shere Khan, never was a blacker hunting than that frog hunt of thine ten years ago!"

"What is the Law of the Jungle? Strike first and then give tongue. By thy very carelessness they know that thou art a man. But be wise. It is in my heart that when Akela misses his next kill—and at each hunt it costs him more to pin the buck—the Pack will turn against him and against thee. They will hold a jungle Council at the Rock, and then—and then—I have

Mowgli's Brothers 125

The Red Flower

Mowgli was far and far through the forest, running hard, and his heart was hot in him. He came to the cave as the evening mist rose, and drew breath, and looked down the valley. The cubs were out, but Mother Wolf, at the back of the cave, knew by his breathing that something was troubling her frog.

"What is it, Son?" she said.

"Some bat's chatter of Shere Khan," he called back. "I hunt among the plowed fields tonight," and he plunged downward through the bushes, to the stream at the bottom of the valley. There he checked, for he heard the yell of the Pack hunting, heard the bellow of a hunted Sambhur, and the snort as the buck turned at bay. Then there were wicked, bitter howls from the young wolves: "Akela! Akela! Let the Lone Wolf show his strength. Room for the leader of the Pack! Spring, Akela!"

The Lone Wolf must have sprung and missed his hold, for Mowgli heard the snap of his teeth and then a yelp as the Sambhur knocked him over with his forefoot.

He did not wait for anything more, but dashed on; and the yells grew fainter behind him as he ran into the croplands where the villagers lived.

126

"Bagheera spoke truth," he panted, as he nestled down in some cattle fodder[17] by the window of a hut. "Tomorrow is one day both for Akela and for me."

Then he pressed his face close to the window and watched the fire on the hearth. He saw the husbandman's[18] wife get up and feed it in the night with black lumps. And when the morning came and the mists were all white and cold, he saw the man's child pick up a wicker[19] pot plastered inside with earth, fill it with lumps of red-hot charcoal, put it under his blanket, and go out to tend the cows in the byre.[20]

"Is that all?" said Mowgli. "If a cub can do it, there is nothing to fear." So he strode round the corner and met the boy, took the pot from his hand, and disappeared into the mist while the boy howled with fear.

"They are very like me," said Mowgli, blowing into the pot as he had seen the woman do. "This thing will die if I do not give it things to eat"; and he dropped twigs and dried bark on the red stuff. Halfway up the hill he met Bagheera with the morning dew shining like moonstones on his coat.

"Akela has missed," said the Panther. "They would have killed him last night, but they needed thee also. They were looking for thee on the hill."

"I was among the plowed lands. I am ready. See!" Mowgli held up the fire pot.

"Good! Now, I have seen men thrust a dry branch into that stuff, and presently the Red Flower blossomed at the end of it. Art thou not afraid?"

"No. Why should I fear? I remember now—if it is not a dream—

---

[17]fodder—chopped corn stalks, hay, and other dry food for farm animals
[18]husbandman—a farmer
[19]wicker—material made of thin twigs or branches that bend easily
[20]byre—barn

how, before I was a Wolf, I lay beside the Red Flower, and it was warm and pleasant."

All that day Mowgli sat in the cave tending his fire pot and dipping dry branches into it to see how they looked. He found a branch that satisfied him, and in the evening when Tabaqui came to the cave and told him rudely enough that he was wanted at the Council Rock, he laughed till Tabaqui ran away. Then Mowgli went to the Council, still laughing.

Akela the Lone Wolf lay by the side of his rock as a sign that the leadership of the Pack was open, and Shere Khan with his following of scrap-fed wolves walked to and fro openly being flattered. Bagheera lay close to Mowgli, and the fire pot was between Mowgli's knees. When they were all gathered together, Shere Khan began to speak—a thing he would never have dared to do when Akela was in his prime.[21]

"He has no right," whispered Bagheera. "Say so. He is a dog's son. He will be frightened."

Mowgli sprang to his feet. "Free People," he cried, "does Shere Khan lead the Pack? What has a tiger to do with our leadership?"

"Seeing that the leadership is yet open, and being asked to speak—" Shere Khan began.

"By whom?" said Mowgli. "Are we all jackals, to fawn[22] on this cattle butcher? The leadership of the Pack is with the Pack alone."

There were yells of "Silence, thou man's cub!" "Silence, thou man's cub!" "Let him speak. He has kept our Law"; and at last the seniors of the Pack thundered: "Let the Dead Wolf speak." When a leader of the Pack has missed his kill, he is called the Dead Wolf as long as he lives, which is not long.

Akela raised his old head wearily:

"Free People, and ye too, jackals of Shere Khan, for twelve seasons I have led ye to and from the kill, and in all that time not one has been trapped or maimed. Now I have missed my kill. Ye know how that plot was made. Ye know how ye brought me up to an untried buck to make my weakness known. It was cleverly done. Your right is to kill me here on the Council Rock, now. Therefore, I ask, who comes to make an end of the Lone Wolf? For it is my right, by the Law of the Jungle, that ye come one by one."

There was a long hush, for no single wolf cared to fight Akela to the death. Then Shere Khan roared: "Bah! What have we to do with this toothless fool? He is doomed to die! It is the man-cub who has lived too long. Free People, he was my meat from the first. Give him to me. I am

---

[21]prime—the best or highest stage or condition
[22]fawn—to flatter

128

weary of this man-wolf folly. He has troubled the jungle for ten seasons. Give me the man-cub, or I will hunt here always and not give you one bone. He is a man, a man's child, and from the marrow[23] of my bones I hate him!"

Then more than half the Pack yelled: "A man! A man! What has a man to do with us? Let him go to his own place."

"And turn all the people of the villages against us?" clamored Shere Khan. "No, give him to me. He is a man, and none of us can look him between the eyes."

Akela lifted his head again and said, "He has eaten our food. He has slept with us. He has driven game for us. He has broken no word of the Law of the Jungle."

"Also, I paid for him with a bull when he was accepted. The worth of a bull is little, but Bagheera's honor is something that he will perhaps fight for," said Bagheera in his gentlest voice.

"A bull paid ten years ago!" the Pack snarled. "What do we care for bones ten years old?"

"Or for a pledge?" said Bagheera, his white teeth bared under his lip. "Well are ye called the Free People!"

"No man's cub can run with the people of the jungle," howled Shere Khan. "Give him to me!"

"He is our brother in all but blood," Akela went on, "and ye would kill him here! In truth, I have lived too long. Some of ye are eaters of cattle, and of others I have heard that, under Shere Khan's teaching, ye go by dark night and snatch children from the villagers' doorsteps. Therefore I know ye to be cowards, and it is to cowards I speak. It is certain that I must die, and my life is of no worth, or I would offer that in the man-cub's place. But for the sake of the Honor of the Pack—a little matter that by being without a leader ye have forgotten—I promise that if ye let the man-cub go to his own place, I will not, when my time comes to die, bare one tooth against ye. I will die without fighting. That will at least save the Pack three lives. More I cannot do; but if ye will, I can save ye the shame that comes of killing a brother against whom there is no fault—a brother spoken for and bought into the Pack according to the Law of the Jungle."

"He is a man—a man—a man!" snarled the Pack. And most of the wolves began to gather round Shere Khan, whose tail was beginning to switch.

"Now the business is in thy hands," said Bagheera to Mowgli. "We can do no more except fight."

---

[23]marrow—the soft material inside bones

Mowgli stood upright—the fire pot in his hands. Then he stretched out his arms, and yawned in the face of the Council; but he was furious with rage and sorrow, for, wolflike, the wolves had never told him how they hated him. "Listen you!" he cried. "There is no need for this dog's jabber. Ye have told me so often tonight that I am a man (and indeed I would have been a wolf with you to my life's end) that I feel your words are true. So I do not call ye my brothers any more, but sag [dogs], as a man should. What ye will do, and what ye will not do, is not yours to say. That matter is with me; and that ye may see the matter more plainly, I, the man, have brought here a little of the Red Flower which ye, dogs, fear."

He flung the fire pot on the ground, and some of the red coals lit a tuft of dried moss that flared up, as all the Council drew back in terror before the leaping flames.

Mowgli thrust his dead branch into the fire till the twigs lit and crackled, and whirled it above his head among the cowering wolves.

"Thou art the master," said Bagheera in an undertone. "Save Akela from the death. He was ever thy friend."

Akela, the grim old wolf who had never asked for mercy in his life, gave one piteous look at Mowgli as the boy stood in the lights of the blazing branch that made the shadows jump and quiver.

"Good!" said Mowgli, staring round slowly. "I see that ye are dogs. I go from you to my own people—if they be my own people. The jungle is shut to me, and I must forget your talk and your companionship. But I will be more merciful than ye are. Because I was all but your brother in blood, I promise that when I am a man among men I will not betray ye to men as ye have betrayed me." He kicked the fire with his foot, and the sparks flew up. "There shall be no war between any of the Pack. But there is a debt to pay before I go." He strode forward to where Shere Khan sat blinking stupidly at the flames, and caught him by the tuft on his chin. Bagheera followed in case of accidents. "Up, dog!" Mowgli cried. "Up, when a man speaks, or I will set thy coat ablaze!"

Shere Khan's ears lay flat back on his head, and he shut his eyes, for the blazing branch was very near.

"This cattle-killer said he would kill me in the Council because he had not killed me when I was a cub. Thus and thus, then, do we beat dogs when we are men. Stir a whisker, Lungri, and I ram the Red Flower down thy gullet!"[24] He beat Shere Khan over the head with the branch, and the tiger whimpered and whined in an agony of fear.

"Pah! singed jungle cat—go now! But remember when next I come to the Council Rock, as a man should come, it will be with Shere Khan's hide on my head. For the rest, Akela goes free to live as he pleases. Ye will not kill him, because that is not my will. Nor do I think that ye will sit here any longer, lolling out your tongues as though ye were somebodies, instead of dogs whom I drive out—thus! Go!"

[24]gullet—throat

The fire was burning furiously at the end of the branch, and Mowgli struck right and left round the circle, and the wolves ran howling with the sparks burning their fur. At last there were only Akela, Bagheera, and perhaps ten wolves that had taken Mowgli's part. Then something began to hurt Mowgli inside him, as he had never been hurt in his life before, and he caught his breath and sobbed, and tears ran down his face.

"What is it? What is it?" he said. "I do not wish to leave the jungle, and I do not know what this is. Am I dying, Bagheera?"

"No, Little Brother. That is only tears such as men use," said Bagheera. "Now I know thou art a man, and a man's cub no longer. The jungle is shut indeed to thee henceforward. Let them fall, Mowgli. They are only tears."

So Mowgli sat and cried as though his heart would break; and he had never cried in all his life before.

"Now," he said, "I will go to men. But first I must say farewell to my mother." And he went to the cave where she lived with Father Wolf, and he cried on her coat, while the four cubs howled miserably.

"Ye will not forget me?" said Mowgli.

"Never while we can follow a trail," said the cubs. "Come to the foot of the hill when thou art a man, and we will talk to thee; and we will come into the croplands to play with thee by night."

"Come soon!" said Father Wolf. "Oh, wise little frog, come again soon; for we be old, thy mother and I."

"Come soon," said Mother Wolf, "little son of mine. For, listen, child of man, I loved thee more than ever I loved my cubs."

"I will surely come," said Mowgli. "And when I come it will be to lay out Shere Khan's hide upon the Council Rock. Do not forget me! Tell them in the jungle never to forget me!"

The dawn was beginning to break when Mowgli went down the hillside alone, to meet those mysterious things that are called men.

Character

Morgan Reed Persun

Revelation of Character

In literature, the reader comes to know characters in many of the same ways that he gets to know people in real life. Just like real people, story characters can be divided into heroes and villains, into those that we like or those that we dislike, into people we understand and have compassion on and those whom we don't trust. Of course, an author has a few extra ways to reveal characters to us because he's in control of the characters and the story.

Consider "Mowgli's Brothers" as an example of good and bad characters. They were revealed to us in five different ways.

◆ **Appearance**—The appearance of Tabaqui—the small, slinky form of the jackal—told the reader that Tabaqui was a mean character. His small stature[1] was a mirror of his smallness at heart. On the other hand, Bagheera the panther, with his beauty and big, rolling muscles, suggested both strength and honesty. Illustrators of most books use the physical traits that the author suggests about characters. Their pictures illuminate[2] what the author

---

[1]stature—height; build
[2]illuminate—to make understandable

has said and help the reader to know what the different characters look like and how they play their own parts in the story as villains or heroes.

◆ **Actions of the Character**—Even when Tabaqui was cringing and flattering the wolf cubs or Shere Khan, he was betraying himself to the reader. In spreading gossip, speaking flattery, and delivering messages for Shere Khan, Tabaqui showed himself to be a deceiver, a coward, and a beggar. On the other hand, by purchasing Mowgli's life, Bagheera proved himself a hero from the start.

◆ **What the Character Says**—Tabaqui gleefully reported all of Shere Khan's doings to Mother and Father Wolf, and when they reacted in anger and worry to having their hunting grounds invaded, Tabaqui's answer revealed him as a tattletale and mischief maker. His question, "Shall I tell him of your gratitude?" was a threat to tattle on the wolves. It revealed that he would use Shere Khan's power for his own pleasure in making trouble.

But Bagheera's speech revealed his love for Mowgli. He often called Mowgli "Little Brother," and he told

Mowgli that he loved him. Unlike Tabaqui, Bagheera never wasted his words on flattery. He only said what was true and necessary, and so he showed us that he was honest and brave.

◆ **What Other Characters Say—**
" 'Ho! Ho!' said Mowgli. 'Tabaqui came to me not long ago with some rude talk that I was man's cub and not fit to dig pignuts. But I caught Tabaqui by the tail and swung him twice against a palm tree to teach him better manners.' " Mowgli's words revealed his low opinion of Tabaqui and his belief that the jackal was nothing more than a cowardly troublemaker. Earlier in the story, Father Wolf told Tabaqui to get out of the cave and go hunt with his "master," Shere Khan. By his words, Father Wolf showed his own belief that Tabaqui was nothing more than a slave and a follower of the tiger. Readers pick up clues about a character from what other characters say.

◆ **What the Author Tells Us**—The narrator of "Mowgli's Brothers" gave us a clear idea of Tabaqui right from the start, simply by telling us why everybody both loathed[3] and feared the jackal. An author has the choice sometimes to tell the reader directly about a character. Kipling did this in the paragraph where Tabaqui came to the mouth of the cave.

It was the jackal—Tabaqui, the Dish-licker—and the wolves of India despise Tabaqui . . . but they are afraid of him too, because Tabaqui, more than anyone else in the jungle, is apt to go mad, and then he forgets that he was ever afraid of anyone.'

Character and Incident

In most literature, the action in the story rises from the characters themselves. Consider Shere Khan and Mowgli. Shere Khan was vicious, cruel, and crafty, and he hated man. Mowgli, a man's cub, had been raised under the stern code of the wolves—to be brave, straightforward, loyal, and faithful. It was natural for these two charac-

---

[3]loathed—despised; hated

ters to clash. Shere Khan's traits[4] showed that he would attempt to kill Mowgli, and Mowgli's traits made him fight against Shere Khan without fear.

Characters often determine what will happen in a story. We expected that Shere Khan and Mowgli would clash with each other because we understood them. Likewise, we understood why Bagheera helped Mowgli and why Mowgli ordered that Akela be spared.

When a story has believable and strong characters that interact with each other, we say that the story has a strong *unity* of character and incident. The term *unity* means that the characters and incidents are united or associated together. Not every story has a strong unity of character and action. Examples of stories that do would be "Mowgli's Brothers" and "Listening to Katey," in which the brother's wild imagination let us know that he would never get the money together in time. Katey's quiet and industrious[5] spirit showed us that somehow she would earn the money to go to the amusement park.

Readers enjoy stories that have a unity of character and incident. A strong unity is one more thing to look for and enjoy in good writing.

---

[4]traits—special features or qualities
[5]industrious—working hard; diligent

VICTORIES

The Granddaddy of All Frogs

Milly Howard
illustrated by Bruce Day

In a Pickle

The old pickup bounced along the dirt road that threaded through Sawmill Cut and plunged downward toward Raeburn's Cove. Two boys rode in the back, legs dangling over the edge of the truck bed. They were brothers, mountain bred, thin, and sun-darkened, as much a part of the hills as the trees that lined the Cut. The one was long and stretched with

138

the lanky growth of a budding teenager. The other, born late to their parents, was a towheaded,[1] bright-eyed boy of six years. He chattered along happily, jumping from subject to subject. From time to time he would touch the bib pocket of his faded overalls as if to make sure that whatever caused the pocket to bulge was still there. Occasionally, he would interrupt himself to say, "Right, Luke?" or to interject another "Why?" question into his monologue.[2] Luke Clanton answered absently, his thoughts on the county fair in Raeburn's Cove and the Tarketts, who he knew would be there.

"Hey, wake up, Luke!"

A sharp dig in the ribs brought Luke's attention back to Jason. "What?" he asked blankly.

"Bet you're thinking about Elton and Tigh again," Jason said, peering from under his shock of pale hair. "If they ask for trouble this time, they're gonna get it. We'll pound 'em into bacon. We'll tan their hides. We'll fix 'em good, won't we, Luke?"

Luke groaned. Jason was most of his trouble with the Tarketts. Ma had said once that Jason would tear into a mama bear without thinking twice and probably would come out of the fray at least as well off as the bear. There weren't any bears at school, but there certainly were Tarketts.

Seven, at last count. And Luke had been sent home more than once for finishing a fight that Jason had started.

One more fight, Pa had said last time, and Luke could forget that set of adventure books he wanted to order from Emmett's Dry Goods. Luke got his love of reading from his ma. Though nothing pleased Pa more than seeing the two boys' heads bent over a book, he meant for the fighting to stop.

Refusing to give Luke permission to get the books he had saved so hard for was the hardest punishment Pa could deal out.

Jason didn't get off easy either. Luke glanced down at Jason and grinned. Not much stopped Jase, though. A born scrapper,[3] Granny always said. Needs a good example, a good testimony. How to be a good example and still keep from getting squashed by the Tarketts was something that Luke hadn't figured out yet. He wished he had. He sure wanted those books.

"We're here," Jason shouted, squirming around. Luke grabbed him around the waist as the pickup rattled over the covered bridge that spanned Possum Creek.

"You want to get dunked good? Sit back down, Jase!"

---

[1]towheaded—very pale blond
[2]monologue—a long speech by one person
[3]scrapper—a person who gets into fights easily

As soon as the truck stopped behind the exhibits, Jason leaped down. "I'm gonna show the Colonel my granddaddy frog," he announced, proudly patting the huge mound in his bib pocket as he started across the lot. "Granddaddy's the sure winner of the frog contest."

"Hold on, Son," Mr. Clanton called. He turned to Luke. "Luke, you keep up with Jase until Ma gets her things all laid out here."

"Can't Arie?" Luke asked.

Fifteen-year-old Arie shook her head gently, trying not to disturb her grown-up coil of golden braids. "I have to help Ma this morning, Luke. Maybe this afternoon."

"Come on, Luke," Jason said impatiently.

"No trouble now, boys. This is your ma's day to shine," their father called.

The two boys climbed over the barrier of boxes and crates that cluttered the back of the exhibit booths and crossed over to the fairway. Jason's mouth was going a mile a minute as usual when Tigh and Elton Tarkett stepped out in front of them and blocked their way. Three of the Tarkett cousins moved in behind the boys, grinning. They were set for a spell of fun.

"Whatcha got there, Jase?" Elton drawled, motioning toward Jason's bib pocket.

"I tole you it'd happen someday. Looks like he's finally got too big for his britches," Tigh said. He reached for Jason. "Let's see what's puffing you up so."

"You touch my frog, and . . ."

Luke grabbed Jason by the collar before the boy launched himself at Tigh. "Pa said no trouble," Luke reminded Jason, and hauled him into the alley beside the shooting gallery. "Let's go!"

Whooping, the Tarkett boys followed. It was hard enough to shake the Tarketts alone, but dragging a reluctant, arguing brother made it almost impossible. A few quick turns and a sudden dash through the livestock barn helped. When the owner of a hefty cow brandished[4] a pitchfork at the Tarketts, Luke and Jason escaped out the other door. Luke climbed over a wagon and leaped down onto the fairway. Half a leap behind, Jason tripped and sprawled into the dust. "Luke!"

Luke turned back and helped Jason up. "We lost 'em, Luke," Jason announced triumphantly, brushing off his overalls. As his hand touched the bib pocket, a look of horror crossed his face. Gingerly,[5] he patted the flat pocket. "Luke! Granddaddy Frog! I—I squashed him flat!"

"Aw, Jase," Luke said, carefully raising the flap of Jason's pocket. "Why'd you have to put him in there, anyway?"

---

[4]brandished—waved about as a weapon
[5]gingerly—very carefully

"I thought it was safe," Jason replied, near tears. He stood still as Luke eased the pocket open.

"Relax," Luke said. "He's not there. You must have lost him back a ways. Come on, let's go look."

They found the stunned frog huddled under a table two alleys back, near the ladies' cooking exhibits. "You'd better find a safer place to keep this frog if you plan on having one to enter in the contest," Luke warned. "If he hadn't been the fattest frog this side of Blackmoor Crag and near knocked out of his wits in the bargain, he'd be long gone by now."

He left Jason crooning[6] to the confused frog and checked the fairway in both directions. There was no sign of the Tarketts, but he waited a

[6]crooning—singing in a soft voice

few minutes to make sure. When he turned around, Jason was standing beside him.

"Where's the frog?" Luke asked. "I hid him good," Jason announced proudly. "See if you can find him."

Luke glanced around but could see nothing out of the ordinary. The booths that housed the ladies' cooking exhibit stretched along the fairway. The tables in the booths fairly groaned under their load of cakes and pies and jars of canned fruits and vegetables, preserves, and pickles. Nothing seemed to be out of place.

"Give up?"

"Uh-huh. Where is he?"

"In one of Granny's pickle jars."

"Pickle jars?"

Jason grinned. "Yep. She had some quart jars under the table. I just stuffed Granddaddy into one and screwed on the lid."

When Luke stopped laughing, he asked, "So where did you put the jar?"

"I left it under the table."

Luke bent over to look. "It's gone."

"But I put it right there," Jason insisted, pointing to the empty jars.

"I bet Granny picked it up and put it with the others. If she finds that frog in one of her pickle jars, we'd be better off with those Tarketts!"

Quickly Luke and Jason began inspecting the jars of pickles. As they reached the far side of the table, Granny came around the corner, beaming. With her was the lady judge from Coverton City. When Granny saw the boys, she shooed them away.

"Away with you two, now! Miz Aletha here is goin' to choose twixt my pickles and Carrie Folton's." Dismissing the boys, she picked up the nearest jar and turned back to the tall, thin woman behind her. "This is the best batch of pickles I ever did put up, Miz Aletha. Just look at that color!"

Miss Aletha adjusted her spectacles and held the jar up to the light to judge the color. "Nice green," she said grudgingly, pursing her lips. Frowning, she added, "Odd shape."

"Why, they do look a little funny," Granny said, puzzled. "Whatever could have happened? I sliced them just like I always do."

Miss Aletha rotated the jar.

"She's got him!" Jason hissed.

Luke saw Granddaddy a quarter turn before Miss Aletha did. The huge frog was stuffed into the quart jar, his eyeballs magnified by the curve of the glass. Miss Aletha held the jar closer to inspect the strange shape of the pickles and came eyeball to eyeball with Granddaddy. She let out a shriek and dropped the jar.

On the Move

The jar hit the edge of the table on the way down and shattered. Granddaddy Frog exploded into action. His first leap took him right smack into the middle of Addie Wilson's prizewinning blueberry pie. Then, down the tables and up and across the top of Coralee Trask's brand-new, lace-edged apron he scrambled. Splattering blueberry juice with every leap, Granddaddy Frog headed for wide-open spaces.

Jason and Luke were right behind. Besides the need to catch Granddaddy, it was downright unhealthy to remain behind in the shambles Granddaddy had made of the ladies' exhibits. They reached the fairway just in time to see a green blur shoot across right in front of the Tarkett boys.

"Uh-oh," Luke groaned.

"Lookit that frawg!" one of the cousins yelped. The boys swung around in one fluid movement and dashed after the hapless frog. Halfway down the fairway, Tigh made a flying tackle for Granddaddy. He missed and thudded into the dust. Plowing ground every inch of the way, he slid under the fence into the greased-pig contest. With seven boys after a frog and fifteen men after a greased pig, the contest degenerated[7] into a free-for-all. In less than ten minutes, all seven boys had been unceremoniously dumped back over the fence.

By the time they struggled to their feet, Granddaddy Frog was long gone. The two groups of boys watched each other warily as they tried to clean mud from their overalls.

Giving up on the mud, Tigh wiped a dirty hand across his face and asked, "Where'd you find that whopper of a frog, anyway?"

Jase sniffled. "In Bleek Bog."

Even Elton was impressed. "You go in that bog all by yourself?"

"Uh-huh."

"He's a whopper all right." Elton looked at Jase uneasily. "Never seen you cry. Frog's not worth crying over."

"Yeah, you're no crybaby, Jase," one of the cousins added. "Come on; you're a scrapper."

Luke stood beside Jason. "He was counting on winning that contest real bad. Not much hope of finding that frog now."

[7]degenerated—became something lower; got worse

144

A series of shrill shrieks came from the outskirts of the fair. Tigh's lean face broke into a grin. "Well, somebody found him!"

The seven boys raced in the direction of the screams. Granddaddy Frog was on the move again. The boys caught a glimpse of him as he charged across a cotton-candy stand. He emerged on the other side enveloped in a pink cloud, heading toward the corrals where the riders had gathered for the relay race.

The Colonel didn't believe in real horseracing. To burn off excess energy and try the spirit of the mountain horses, he had initiated[8] a horseback relay race from the fair to Laurel Heights and back. It was a thundering, no-holds-barred, wildcat race to the finish. More than one feud[9] had begun or ended on the finish line.

The boys headed for Old Man Travers, who leaned against the rail beside his mule, watching the riders milling about at the starting line. He blinked as a fuzzy pink-and-green ball whizzed over his shoulder and landed on the mule's neck.

Snorting wildly, the mule yanked back on the halter and whirled. Screeching, it charged through the pack of riders and onto the trail. The startled riders, thinking someone had taken a head start, whooped and galloped after the mule. Old Man Travers stood frozen on the spot,

eyes round as scuppernong grapes. The boys climbed the corral fence beside him and watched in amazement.

"Lookit that!" The Tarketts bent over with laughter, slapping their legs or each others' backs. "Just lookit 'em go!"

Jason beat the corral fence angrily. "Come back here, you fool frog! Come back here!"

Luke leaned his head on the top rail and sighed. Pa would never believe this one. Down the trail, the riders hit a straight stretch. Leaning close, they tried for every ounce of speed they could get from their horses. The mule, still in front, seesawed wildly back and forth, tossing his head in an effort to dislodge the clinging frog.

Exhausted from laughing, the Tarkett boys hung over the fence and watched until the animals disappeared into the woods, the frog still clinging to the mule's neck.

"I think he's stuck," Tigh said, awestruck.[10]

"Whoo!" One of the cousins slid weakly to the ground. "I never seen anything so funny in my life."

Elton grinned at Jason. "Some frog," he said solemnly. Jason was too distraught[11] to even answer.

---

[8]initiated—started
[9]feud—a long, bitter quarrel between two people or groups
[10]awestruck—amazed
[11]distraught—upset

The boys waited near the finish line for nearly two hours before the race was over. It took another hour before the mule came back. It trudged toward them, head hanging down. Sure enough, Granddaddy Frog was stuck in the mule's straggly mane.

Elton gently disengaged[12] the frog and handed it carefully to Jason. Seeing Luke's astonished look, Elton frowned and stepped back, thrusting his hands deep into the pockets of his overalls. "Don't get the wrong

[12]disengaged—untangled

146

The buildings were made of wood and tarpaper, but the winter air and summer heat made the occupants[8] miserable. There were central mess halls, recreation halls, and laundry/restroom facilities at the camp.

Some camps allowed the prisoners to come and go in nearby towns. Others were securely secluded.[9] Many *Nisei* in the camps were allowed to find work outside the camps on farms, on the railroads, and in factories. They earned some money and also showed their loyalty to the United States by contributing[10] to the war.

Many believed that God had appointed government and that citizens should obey government officials if they did not contradict what God commands. Some *Nisei* took the evacuation order to court, but most did not resist violently. They tried to prove their innocence by their conduct.

By 1945 the enemy was defeated. The Japanese Americans were no longer considered suspects by the government, and the *Issei* and *Nisei* were allowed to leave the relocation camps.

[8]occupants—people who are living in a place
[9]secluded—kept apart from everything else
[10]contributing—supplying; donating

Readjusting to normal life was not easy. Many Americans still regarded the Japanese Americans with suspicion. Jobs were hard to find because of their ancestry. Some *Nisei* did not return to where they previously lived. Others returned and found their properties ruined. Some moved away to start over; others made the most of the ruins.

The Constitution of the United States guarantees all of its citizens certain rights. But this promise is only as strong as those in office.[11] If the United States government does not uphold the Constitution, its people will suffer.

When the war was over, the *Nisei* formed several citizens' leagues. They kept informed about the government and kept the government informed about them. The *Nisei* learned that personal freedoms sometimes depend upon personal involvement. They wanted to understand current events and ideas in the United States government.

Japanese Americans now include *Sansei* (san-say) and *Yonsei* (yon-say)—third and fourth generation Japanese Americans. Time is not the only factor that distinguishes them from the *Issei* and *Nisei*. A vast change in the country's acceptance of them has taken place. They hold prominent[12] positions in industry, education, and government. American citizens now treat the *Nisei* and their descendants as what they are—fellow American citizens.

[11]"in office"—referring to those in governmental positions
[12]prominent—important

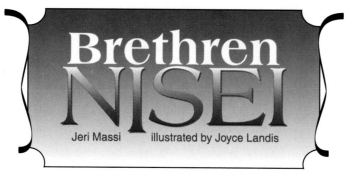

Brethren NISEI

Jeri Massi   illustrated by Joyce Landis

Although certain senators and statesmen opposed any type of legal or civil action[1] against the Nisei, action was taken against them to "relocate" them away from the West Coast. The following story takes place shortly before the relocation begins. Although this was a time of great suffering for Japanese Americans, as you read this story consider the advice that Pastor Blaine gives to his son, Rick.

Not Afraid

He was working on the *J*. The top of it was a little higher than his head, and the lowest part of it was at his belt. But the bricks resisted a cleaning. He swished the fluid in his bucket of paint thinner and scrubbed the drenched rag anew against the outside wall of the storefront church, trying to wipe out the scar of that hideous red *J* and the letters that followed it.

Behind him, a delivery truck squealed its brakes, and two eggs smashed the wall, not far from his face. The truck roared away, leaving Rick with a thumping heart.

Then, suddenly resolute,[2] he resumed his scrubbing. The delivery truck had probably been loaded with men looking for trouble, but at the sight of his sandy hair and blue eyes, they had left him alone.

Though only eleven, Rick Blaine thought like a soldier, figuring where danger was, deducing[3] when troubles would come. He knew that trucks didn't deliver on Sundays. A company driver had probably "borrowed" his weekday truck that morning to scout for victims.

His father came down the front steps, alerted by the squealing brakes from the truck. His voice arrested Rick's thoughts.

"Are you all right, Son?"

Rick nodded and blinked back tears as he scrubbed. They weren't tears of fright, but of rage. He would have died before anybody scared him away from that wall. Just cleaning it was a blow against them all—all the world that was threatening the people he'd grown up with.

His father came down the step. "Are you angry, Rick? Do you hate them?"

---

[1] civil action—people within a community acting without authority of the law
[2] resolute—firm; determined
[3] deducing—concluding from known facts

154

"No!" But he couldn't look up. "Well—I don't know! Aren't you angry? Look at what they did to our church!"

And he stepped back from the wall to take in again the hideous red letters and broken windows that now marred[4] the once neat little church.

"What will they do to Seto?" he asked. "And to the rest?"

Pastor Blaine put his hand on his son's shoulder. "Nothing that God doesn't permit. Nothing can happen to the *Nisei* Christians that God doesn't permit and control for His purposes. Come inside."

The interior of the tiny church had not been damaged—not yet. By instinct, Rick strode up the center aisle and stood by the front right-hand chair. It was Michael's chair— *had been* Michael's chair. Even now in the late part of the mild San Francisco winter, Rick had to remind himself that Michael would not be returning and that the flow of letters from Hawaii would never be renewed.

His left hand fingered the back of the cold folding chair. He could accept this part of the war. Both Michael and Rick had been raised not to fear death, and weeks before Michael had left to serve in the navy, he had explained to Rick that he might not come back.

As always, Rick had understood his older brother's advice. Now,

---

[4]marred—damaged

three months after the news of the attack on Pearl Harbor, Rick sorrowed, but without bitterness. It was, after all, war, and he thought like a soldier. But now it seemed like his own world had gone crazy.

The door of the church opened, admitting Deacon Metamura and Seto, his son. Both were pale and tightlipped.

"It was good of you to come, Dan," the deacon said huskily, as he wrung the pastor's hand in both of his. Rick was surprised. Usually the Japanese adults, even the *Nisei,* were reserved with his father. They would call Dan Blaine "Pastor" and shake hands stiffly and politely.

Deacon Metamura, his tan Adam's apple bobbing up and down over his tight white collar, suddenly broke down and embraced his pastor. "What have we done, Dan? Nothing. Nothing!" And he wept. Seto looked pained. His anguished[5] eyes met Rick's.

"Was there more violence, Metamura?" Pastor Blaine asked.

The deacon stepped back, sniffed a little, and blinked tears from the brown eyes behind the owlish glasses. "Only threats, Pastor, but so many!" He composed himself. "I should not despair. Did you not hear about the Wednesday night service?"

On Wednesdays Pastor Blaine held prayer meeting at the main church in Mountain View, while the Deacon conducted a service for the *Nisei* at the mission church here in the city of San Francisco.

"I didn't go home until midnight," Metamura continued. "Something happened as we prayed, Pastor. It was as though—How do I say it? The Savior saw our anguish and fear, and He was ready to meet us here. The time seemed scarcely to pass, and we could not bear to tear ourselves away from His presence— it was so painful to leave."

Deacon Metamura sat down heavily on a folding chair. "Before all this, I told myself I was a man of prayer, and then Wednesday came, and I see I am not truly what I thought I was. I have never found Him so close as I did in the hour that I lost everything I had on this earth." He lifted his hands helplessly and dropped them, unable to explain more.

Rick knew that Dr. Metamura had been financially ruined in the last few months. Yet he looked wistfully at the Japanese American. For himself, Rick usually found prayer meetings long and hard. The deacon's words bit into him. He longed to be in a prayer meeting like that. Until the night they'd learned that Michael had died, he had never felt the Lord's presence unusually close. But that night he had, when his dad

---

[5]anguished—feeling very great pain or suffering of body or mind

had prayed for strength and courage. Now he saw that somebody else had felt the Lord's presence too.

"Get the hymnbooks, please, boys," Pastor Blaine said.

"Did you see the word on the wall?" Rick whispered to Seto as they trotted up the aisle.

Seto, almost the picture of his father in starched white collar and round glasses, nodded. "A word cannot hurt us," he said stolidly.[6] "I'm as American as they are, Rick. Red paint cannot change that."

"Did anything happen at school?" Rick asked.

The muscles in Seto's tan face tightened. "Monday. A group of us *Nisei* were ambushed.[7] With rocks. My mother will not let me go back. She won't leave the house at all."

And he let out his breath as a sign that he would joyfully have gone back to face his tormentors. But then his sparkling black eyes looked pained again.

"My older brother Matsu—he sent word. He has been out in the Pacific, you know. He still grieves for you and your family, Rick . . . Ricky-san."

Rick smiled. "Ricky-san" had long been a joking nickname for Rick, but in these tense days few people called him that. Seto's older brother Matsu was an American serviceman like Michael had been, enlisting before the *Nisei* had been banned[8] from serving in combat

---

[6]stolidly—showing no emotion
[7]ambushed—attacked from a hidden position
[8]banned—forbidden by law or decree

zones. He also had been at Pearl Harbor when the merciless Japanese fighters had strafed[9] and bombed the base, killing almost twenty-five hundred Americans, including Rick's older brother.

Matsu had an office job as an interpreter, so he had been a half-mile from the docks that morning, working on code breaking for Intelligence. His college education in math and logic and his mastery of both Japanese and English had secured him a high position as an enlisted man. For now, he was better off than his family back in San Francisco. Matsu had a job and would be served in stores and restaurants in Hawaii, unlike his family or the rest of the second generation Japanese people who lived on the West Coast. For them, life had become a nightmare of survival.

Deacon Metamura, a medical doctor, had had his license to practice medicine suspended. These days he couldn't even cash checks. Yet as Rick and Seto came with the stacks of hymnbooks, Seto's father was saying, "My wife sends a casserole for the food collection, Pastor. It is in the back room. She cannot come today, but she would not forget the fishermen. Please distribute it. We would keep it quiet."

The fishermen had lost their fishing licenses. Because they had been poor to start with, they were the worst off now.

By now more of the *Nisei* were filing in, all of them stiff and starched for church. They smiled politely at the boys. Some of them bowed a little as they took the hymnbooks and found chairs.

"Look, here is Sasaki Oshiro," Rick heard Deacon Metamura say.

Pastor Blaine's eyes widened. Oshiro bowed to him gravely[10] and took a seat. He was a Buddhist priest, and he had never cared for a word of Christianity before. Rick watched as at least a dozen new people filed in, all grave and polite. A dozen! The church might continue for a year before a dozen new people crossed its threshold. Yet today they had come.

"They are not afraid to come!" the deacon whispered. "In here, they are not afraid. It is the spirit of Christ. You must preach well, Pastor."

"I don't know if I can," Rick's father whispered. "I don't know what's going to happen."

"Good! Forget the war! Forget the politics! Preach Christ. He works best when we are weak. Preach!"

---

[9]strafed—fired at with machine guns from airplanes flying close to the ground
[10]gravely—very seriously; solemnly

The Right Response

It was time to start. The tiny missionary church to the *Nisei* was packed. Rick slid into Michael's old chair.

Pastor Blaine was so flustered that he forgot to have a hymn or even take an offering. He preached.

"If it wasn't a taste of revival, I don't know what it was," Pastor Blaine said later as he, Rick, and Rick's mom sat around the dinner table. "So many were saved—at least ten. The Buddhist priest, Oshiro, he came forward too. I've never felt the Lord's power so much." He let out his breath with a sigh. Now that he and Rick were back home, they both felt weak and drained from the tense morning in the city. After the *Nisei* service, they had rushed to the main church for Pastor Blaine to preach there.

Rick's heart was soaring. He had never yet seen a devout[11] Buddhist saved from among the *Nisei*. And now Oshiro had gotten saved, and more than that, the *Nisei* congregation had seemed encouraged after the service—emboldened. Rick had never felt so close to a group of people, so much like a friend.

"Son," his father's voice recalled him. "It's good to feel uplifted, but it's not over yet. The hard times haven't ended for the *Nisei*."

"But they have so much faith, Dad!"

"I know. I just want to warn you. You were angry this morning at the vandals[12] and egg throwers. And now you're happy because you were assured from God. But you have to be assured *all the time,* even when people call the *Nisei* 'tojos'[13] and

---

[11]devout—deeply religious
[12]vandals—those who deliberately damage another's property
[13]tojos—an informal name for Japanese persons, used as an insult

'Japs.' Don't defend the *Nisei* because they're Americans. We help them because we are all loved by Christ. Every saved *Nisei* has been redeemed and given to Christ, just like you. If you defend them on any other grounds, you'll be outnumbered."

Rick nodded, but he didn't understand. The *Nisei* were Americans. Why did they have to suffer for what Japan did?

It was the next day at school when he understood better.

"You love those tojos, don't you Blaine?" Allen Sarsen said when they were on the track field. "*Love 'em, don't you?*"

Other boys were coming up, looking hard and cold. Rick had never fought before, but suddenly he knew he was going to. They would make him.

"Those people are innocent," he began, his throat feeling tight. "Innocent Americans."

"No Jap is innocent. A Jap's a Jap. Look what they did at Pearl Harbor," a big blond boy said. "And your dad's preachin' at them, isn't he? *My* dad says he's gonna' stop that."

"Christ died for all—" he began, but the big kid pulled him up by his shirt.

"Shut up! He didn't die for Japs!"

"He did!" Rick cried. All his fear fled as he understood it. "He died for them, and you can't change it!"

Next thing he knew, he was on his back on the ground. He didn't know what they would do, but suddenly someone was standing over him, screaming.

"Leave him alone! Leave him alone!" It was Sam O'Donnell. O'Donnell stood as high as the tall blond boy and was unafraid. "His

brother *died* at Pearl Harbor," Sam screamed. "Leave him alone! Mind your own business!"

Sam was an eighth grader, and so his defense shamed the sixth-grade boys. They walked away. Without even looking at Rick, the older boy walked away too.

Shaking, Rick stood up. He had been spared, he told himself, but he understood what his dad had meant. His first duty to the *Nisei* was as a Christian brother.

He meant to tell his parents about the fight, but when he got home, his father was standing in the kitchen with the same look on his face as when Pearl Harbor had been attacked and Michael had died. Mom was at the table.

"What is it?" Rick asked.

"The *Nisei*," his father said. "They're being moved—taken away."

"Where?"

"I-I don't know." He glanced at his wife. "I've got to go to Metamura—see what I can do to help."

She nodded mutely.[14]

"Can I go?" Rick asked.

"No, Son. I don't know what the situation will be like. Take care of your mother for me." And he was gone.

Rick thought it would be a long wait, but his dad was back in an hour and a half.

He sat at the table that Rick was setting and shook his head.

"Nothing," he said. "Nothing. All the *Issei* and *Nisei* are suspect for spying activities and will be re-located. They'll be moved out in the next few days."

"But where will they go?" Rick asked. "Prison?"

[14]mutely—choosing not to speak

"Relocation camps eventually. For now, most of them are going to temporary housing, but nobody knows where. At least, the *Nisei* don't know."

"Are they frightened?" Mrs. Blaine asked.

"Metamura's not. He's keeping them calm and as cheerful as possible. And he's witnessing." But Pastor Blaine shook his head.

"Our church is gone, then," Rick said.

The words roused[15] his father. "No, Son, no. Not gone, just moved. The *Nisei* Christians have a job to do, and they're doing it—witnessing to and serving the other *Nisei*."

"But how can the government do this?"

"Because government is divinely appointed, Rick, but it isn't divine. It makes mistakes. In time the *Nisei* will prove themselves. In time this war will end. It's like a long, dark journey, and we're the only ones with light. We can't be angry or bitter. Even this is in God's hands, and He has His purpose."

"It's a long, dark journey," Rick lamented.[16]

"But we have light, Son. Do you believe that?"

And somewhere, somehow, Rick did believe it. For the second time that day he realized that they had to deal with the *Nisei* on spiritual grounds. His mind roved[17] back to Sunday and the power of God he had seen, and he answered, "Yes, Dad, I believe it."

---

[15]roused—caused to become active or alert
[16]lamented—mourned
[17]roved—wandered

ATLAS

If you wanted to find out how two places are alike or how they are different, what would you do? Let's say that the two places you wish to compare and contrast are Japan and California. You could read books about each of these places. You could read encyclopedia articles about them or find information in an almanac. You could read travel brochures and magazine articles. Perhaps through all of these sources you could find the information you need to make your comparison. There is another source, however, that may have just what you need—a world atlas.

World atlases contain maps that tell us many things about places around the world. Most atlases also contain charts and graphs that give us even more information. Some atlases have more maps and information than others. You must choose the atlas that has the information you need.

Map Information

An atlas will help us find the location of Japan and California. We can see from a world map that Japan is a group of islands that form a country. These islands are located near the eastern coast of Asia. Although hundreds of tiny islands are included in the country of Japan, the four major islands are Hokkaido, Honshu, Shikoku, and Kyushu.

California is a part of the United States and is located on the western coast of the North American continent. Although separated by the Pacific Ocean, Japan and California are located at about the same latitude, or distance from the equator.

From topographical[1] maps such as these, we can see that Japan is very mountainous. California has many mountains also, but it has great, wide valleys as well.

[1]topographical—having the physical features of a place or region

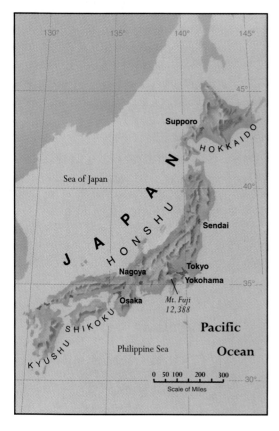

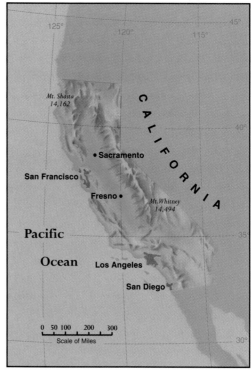

Precipitation[2] maps show the reader the average rainfall of different places. They would indicate that Japan has a very wet climate, while most of California has a very dry climate. As you may have realized, some parts of southern California even contain desert land.

[2]precipitation—the amount of water that falls from the sky and reaches the ground

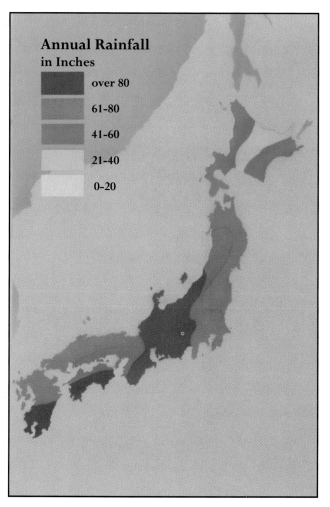

Annual Rainfall
in Inches

- over 80
- 61–80
- 41–60
- 21–40
- 0–20

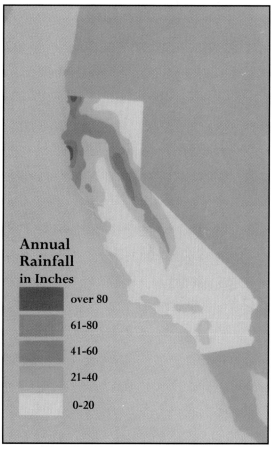

Annual Rainfall in Inches

- over 80
- 61–80
- 41–60
- 21–40
- 0–20

Product and land-use maps would tell us that the highland areas of both places are often covered with forests. Japan's small valleys are used mainly for rice farming, while California's wide valleys contain cattle ranches, fruit and vegetable farms, and other agricultural[3] concerns. Many Japanese and California cities are large and full of industries. Population[4] maps such as those found in an atlas show us that Japan is much more densely[5] populated than California. Notice that there are over 250 people per square mile in most areas of Japan. California's map shows that most of California has fewer than twenty-five people per square mile.

Atlases often have many other maps that give information about such subjects as the average temperatures, kinds of soils, and natural resources of each place. Others give information about the people who live in those places. Such maps may show their languages, their literacy[6] rate, their religion, and their birth and death rates.

[3]agricultural—having to do with farms or farming
[4]population—the number of people who live in a certain place
[5]densely—closely packed together
[6]literacy—the ability to read and write

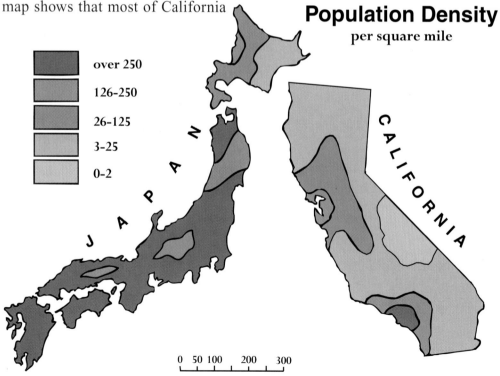

Population Density
per square mile

over 250

126-250

26-125

3-25

0-2

JAPAN

CALIFORNIA

0 50 100 200 300

Chart and Graph Information

Charts and graphs often accompany the maps in an atlas. These help us to make many more comparisons between Japan and California. We can compare their total populations, their land areas, and many other details. A diagram may be included to show land elevations or mountains' heights. From this diagram we can learn that Japan's highest mountain, Fuji, is not as tall as California's highest, Mount Whitney.

Much more information awaits our discovery in an atlas. This one book can be a valuable reference tool for learning about any place in the world.

High Mountains of the World

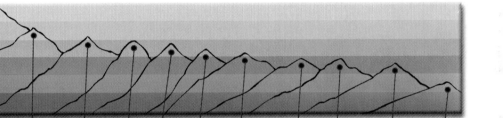

Thousands of Feet

Mt. Everest 29,028
Mt. Aconcagua 22,835
Mt. McKinley 20,320
Mt. Kilimanjaro 19,340
Mt. Elbrus 18,510
Mt. Vinson Massif 16,860
Mt. Blanc 15,771
Mt. Whitney 14,494
Pikes Peak 14,110
Mt. Fuji 12,388
Mt. Kosciusko 7,316

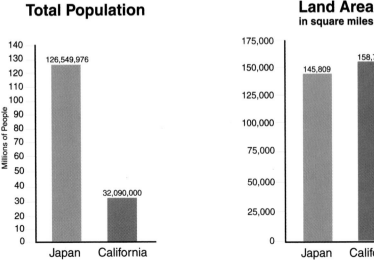

Total Population

Millions of People

126,549,976 — Japan
32,090,000 — California

Land Area
in square miles

145,809 — Japan
158,706 — California

A Ride to HONOR

Dawn L. Watkins ▪ illustrated by Preston Gravely

Riding Out a Riddle

The winter sun seemed more white than yellow. And it seemed to carry almost no heat.

There had been no winter rabbits today, no tracks of highland deer. The small light left fell upon empty snow as far as she could see. As she stood on the top of the iced ridge, Innera unstrung her bow and put it through the sling at her side.

Her cheeks now burned with the cold and in her fur-lined boots, her toes began to feel numb. Her thoughts went ahead of her to the fire her grandmother would have going. The cave they owned was small, but always warm.

From the west, not far, came the crack of a tree limb, giving way probably, Innera thought, to the weight of ice and snow. And then, Innera was sure, a faint cry. She stopped and held her breath. On a gust of wind it came again, barely. She turned toward the sound, waiting. Time passed in silence. Innera wiggled her toes and opened and clenched her hands. Then, at last, a cry came to her again through the darkening cold.

Innera hesitated. But in a moment she walked west. She went straight in the direction of the sound, though it never came again. She guessed that no more than five hundred yards should bring her to whoever had made it.

She stopped again. Far enough, she decided. And then, like a thought that comes for an instant and flits away, she registered a dark shape lying among the straight black trees. She leaned into the dusk to make it out. It seemed to move, but she could not be sure. Another minute and she would not be able to see it at all. She willed herself forward.

The shape stirred, changed. She was almost upon it when she recognized the shield on the ground beside the shape, brilliant even in the gloom. She knelt in the snow. "Your Grace," she said. "What has happened?"

His answer was a ragged cough, then, "I am not the king. I carry—" The dark mound of cloak and helmet fell silent.

Innera leaped up and looked about. A little way off she made out a horse. "Come," she said. Immediately the horse stepped forward, with a light chink of a martingale[1] against a breastplate. The animal stopped beside her and nudged her.

The man stirred. She knelt again. "Can you get on your horse?" He seemed to nod. Innera took his arm across her shoulder and helped him lever to a half stand. In a moment the man made a stumble toward the horse and caught the stirrup in his hand. He rested a fleeting moment and then with a groan, put his foot in the stirrup and heaved himself onto the horse.

And then he slumped over the neck of his mount.

Innera steadied him. She drew his hands under the horse's neck and wrapped them with the reins to keep him from falling. She swept up the

---

[1] martingale—a strap between a horse's girth and nosepiece used to steady the head

shield from the snow. Then taking the bridle she was off, east and then north, struggling to keep a good pace in the dark.

She made the cave entrance with no breath to call for her grandmother. She made the last steps toward the light stumbling. Her grandmother was already waiting. "I heard the horse coming," she said.

Innera let her burden slide from the horse and freed her other hand from the strap of the shield. The old woman gazed at the hammered brass. But Innera, between breaths, said, "He's not the king."

Together they got him to the fire and laid him on blankets. The grandmother loosened the cloak of the soldier and took off his helmet.

Innera shook from exhaustion. "Is he hurt?"

"Hurt or frozen." The old woman glanced at the helmet. "He is a captain of the Cordus guard."

Her grandmother brought water and broth. But the man was beyond the help of food and warmth. He opened his eyes unseeing. "A wedding ring. An eagle's wing. Watch and see—The Towers Three," he whispered. "Take the message to the guards of Cordus." He gave a long sigh, then, and closed his eyes.

Innera sank back. For the first time she felt the fire. She could only

gaze upon this soldier. His boots were well made but worn. The cuffs of his leather gantlets[2] were polished but scarred. His face had a week's beard at least.

"Who is he?" Innera said. "Why is he alone? And why does he carry the king's shield?" Her head jerked up. "Maybe he killed the king!"

Her grandmother got the cloak and spread it over the soldier. She stood up, staring at the shield. "I don't think so," she said after so long a time that Innera started. "Perhaps he has the shield because the king sent him ahead and wanted him to be believed."

"But," Innera said, "what was that he said? What did he mean?"

The old woman stared into the fire. "I don't know."

Innera picked up the shield. The tracery of silver and copper glinted in the firelight. The umbo[3] was embossed with the royal coat of arms. She turned it so her grandmother could see.

Her grandmother nodded.

Innera said, "What are we going to do?"

Her grandmother nodded again. "Come morning, we will see. Now let us see to you and the horse."

---

[2]gantlets—protective gloves
[3]umbo—a raised knob on a shield

At first light, Innera found her grandmother still sitting beside the captain. She tried again to waken him, to get him to take a sip of water. But he did not stir.

Innera looked through the gear she had so hastily taken off the horse the night before. The armor was like the man's—worn but well polished. In the side pouch were the captain's campaign medals[4] and a document under a king's seal.

She held the document up. "Look."

Her grandmother took the paper and studied it. "It is for the commander of the Cordus guard. The seal is unbroken. Put it back."

Innera put away the medals and the letter and closed the smooth leather pouch.

"Innera," said her grandmother. Something in the tone made Innera rise and wait without answering. "Wars far off may seem to have nothing to do with us. And our lives are little touched by kings. But this event has come into our house for a purpose. We must do right regarding it."

Innera only nodded. Everyone knew the wisdom of Calla of Dider and respected it.

Her grandmother glanced at the soldier and back to Innera. "This man is dying. And among all my remedies there is nothing to prevent it."

[4]campaign medals—awards given for military accomplishments

Innera felt a pang of sorrow, though she did not even know the man's name. "Oh," she said.

"He is an honorable man, I think, calling out with his last words the mission he was charged with. And though his king is not our king, we must see his message on. The King of Kapnos is a true king."

Innera drew in a breath. "Cordus is a hundred miles from here. It would take weeks, maybe a month to get there in this season."

"Nevertheless, Innera, grand-daughter of Biden and daughter of Artios, you are able to do this thing." And it was true. Her grand-father had taught her to navigate by a hundred different signs. Her grand-mother had taught her how to find the food and medicine in every sprouting thing. And she feared no animals, and none feared her.

Innera felt a surge of courage at the mention of her heritage. For hun-dreds of years her people had held to their honor and their compassion as others held to land and titles. "All right," she said, "at your word, Grandmother."

"But," Calla said, "always take care. Good unguarded is good lost."

Less than an hour later, Innera was riding steadily under the winter sun toward Cordus. She had taken only the barest of gear for the horse, as a fully armored one travels slowly. She herself was clad in leather and

fur, and she wore the captain's hel-met. From a leather strap on the saddle hung the king's shield. In the pouch was only the document. The medals were to be buried with the captain. Perhaps by now her grand-mother had chosen a spot among the trees to lay his body and reverently pile stone upon stone, a lasting and proper burial for a soldier who dies in winter.

By nightfall, Innera had covered much frozen ground. She removed her helmet and searched in the fading light for a place to rest. Through the bare trees at a little distance wavered a curl of smoke. She urged the horse on. Shortly the small hut from which the smoke came was visible as well. She clicked her tongue to get one last burst of energy from her mount.

The door opened. A bearded man looked out upon her. From behind him, about at his knees, two children also gazed at her.

"Your pardon, sir. I am Innera, daughter of Artios and granddaugh-ter of Biden. I would—"

The door swung fully open. "The daughter of Artios is welcome here. Come in." He nodded to an older boy by the fire. "See to the horse, my lad."

The man told her he had been once rescued from drowning by her father and that he was grateful in-deed to be able to make some small repayment on that debt.

"I am Reudh. This is my wife. And my children. We are honored to have you enter under our roof."

The meal that followed the introductions was simple but stout, eaten amid much talk of her father and his kindness long ago.

"And what, then, brings you out alone in winter, if it is not bold to ask?" He looked at her from under his brushy eyebrows. He smiled and his red beard moved up a little on his chest.

"I am finishing a journey for a soldier who died in the attempt."

The man glanced at his wife. "A soldier? Not of Kapnos?"

"Well, yes. A Cordus captain."

A breath exploded from the man, like a cork popping out of a bottle. "Dider owes Kapnos nothing. It is not a good errand you have chosen."

Innera did not look away. "You are my father's friend and my host. I would not seem to contradict you at your own table. I can only say that my grandmother, Calla, says that this is to be done. And so I am doing it."

Reudh's mouth twitched. "Calla is wise. Of course. But perhaps she does not know that Kapnos, for all its conquerings, is not ruling here."

Again Innera paused to consider her answer. "Grandmother knows many things that I do not. I find it best to follow her advice."

Reudh cocked his head and raised his chin. "Well. As you say then. But it is a far and dangerous way to go to help those who have done *you* no service."

Late in the night, Innera awoke with a little niggling[5] fear she had not felt before. What if this were a bad errand? She wished indeed that she were beside her own fire at home, listening to the wind from the ridge.

In the morning, she thanked her hosts, and after a moment's hesitation reined her horse toward Cordus.

She rode with deliberate speed all day, pondering what could be meant by the riddle of a dying man.

At the end of the second day, Innera chose a hollow to find a place for herself and the horse. In the gathering dusk she saw that the hollow opened onto a meadow. And it seemed to her that the meadow was a perfect circle. Round as a ring, she thought. "A wedding ring!" she said and the horse lifted his head to look at her. She pondered the coincidence.

Light fell across the mouth of a cave at the other side of the meadow. Ice framed the entrance, shining rainbow lights as the sun went down. She crossed the meadow and ventured in. Thin slits in the ceiling, sealed with clear ice, let the last of the light in. "This will do," she told her horse. "It is the loveliest place in the world, I think. Wouldn't Grandmother love this!"

---

[5]niggling—troublesome

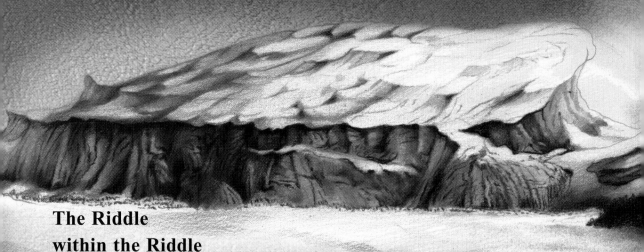

The Riddle
within the Riddle

Something told her to awake. It
was nearly dawn. The fire was long
since out. She ate a small piece of the
meat from the leather bag of provisions her grandmother had sent. She
wrote "Thank you" in the soft ground
of the cave's entrance—in case it belonged to someone—and rode to the
top of the mountain and looked ahead.

A range of low mountains fanned
to the north and southeast before
her, their tops snow-covered and
their feet gray granite. The sun came
fully over the east ridges and
splashed across the mountains. Amid
the gray and white of them, glints of
brass shone. "Ah!" she said, as the
fully lit view now showed itself like
nothing so much as an outspread
wing, the tip pointing north.

"An eagle's wing." Despite the
milder day, her breath still hung in
the air as she spoke. "It is no coincidence this time." She sat for a full
minute, deciding. If the riddle were
indeed a map, then she would have
to veer away from Cordus, which
was northeast. Her sense of the mo-

ment told her to follow the riddle
even so. "Well," she said to the
horse, "since we are responsible for
this mission, we are also free to
make the choices, aren't we?"

A sound, very faint even to her,
made Innera look back the way she
had come. She sat listening. Nothing
more, not even a bird, broke the stillness. She adjusted her position in the
saddle and moved on, occasionally
looking behind her.

Some minutes later, she pulled
the horse up and turned it full about.
"Step forward, whoever you are, and
slowly."

From a short distance, a boy
emerged from a stand of trees. He
was raggedly dressed, but he carried
a fine longbow.

"Who are you?" Innera demanded.
He shook his head.
"What do you want then?"
He pointed to her horse.
"It is not mine to give away."
Still he stood silent in the snow.
Innera listened, but she could not
hear any other people anywhere.

174

"Are you out here alone?"

He did not give any sign of an answer.

"Can you speak?"

He nodded.

"Speak then."

"We need food."

"We?"

He was silent again.

She pulled the leather bag of provisions away from the saddle and held it out to him. "This is not much, but it is something at least."

He regarded her as a rabbit might regard a hunter. He moved as if to come forward, but did not. He never took his eyes from her.

She dropped the bag. "I leave it then. And welcome." She drew up the reins to leave.

"Wait," he said. She lowered her hands to the pommel.[6] "Thank you." She nodded. Then he said, "Travel the bottom of the mountains. This high up will be a trap for you."

"How?"

But his sparse words were now gone altogether. But there was something in the way he came forward to pick up the bag then that made her believe he was telling the truth.

She travelled as hard as the weather allowed along the feet of the mountains for two days. She sought the land for late berries and edible barks and took game where she found it. Where the mountains turned, Innera glanced east and then reined the horse along the rest of the eagle's wing. It was almost another three days before the last scalloped edge of granite passed behind her.

"A wedding ring. An eagle's wing. Watch and see—The Towers Three." The horse snorted and bobbed its head under the constraint[7] of waiting to go on. "Yes, my friend," she said, "I know. But the riddle seems to have run out. I'm watching, but there are no towers, are there?" She urged the horse on, travelling until the light ran out.

She travelled north three days, crossing a narrow river. The land

---

[6]pommel—the raised front of a saddle
[7]constraint—restraint; restriction

was flat and silent all around. Two days more she trekked over the wasteland. In a gathering of an afternoon, she pulled up the horse to rest. In the stillness, she heard from far, far off, the sound of falling water. She judged it to be a day's ride at least. She chose to stay on the plains for the night, though it was not yet sundown. A little fish from a partly frozen stream there made for cold catching but warm eating.

"Now think," she said to the horse browsing on brush still showing amid the winter harshness. "If 'The Towers Three' means not Cordus, then what?" The horse snatched dried leaves from a branch. She patted his neck. "You are a very good horse for riding, but not much of one for riddling."

Before sunup, she was riding hard toward the rush of water. It was exactly north, in keeping with the tip of the "eagle's wing." She stopped only once, at noon, determined to make the falls by night. In all the king's army there was not a soldier who could have outpaced her that day.

Suddenly the landscape gave way to a gorge, as though the earth had only moments before gaped open and away. Innera dismounted and walked to the edge. Below in the last of the sun sparkled a lake. She drew in her breath at its beauty and immensity. To the west, water plunged from the rim of the gorge to the lake, boiling and spraying, churning as though some giant hand swished itself clean there.

But even amid all the thunder of the water, Innera thought she heard singing. She focused her listening, and then she was sure. Somewhere behind the falls, a man was singing. She scanned the gorge until she made out a rough trail leading down to the falls. She assessed the daylight left and mounted her horse.

It was full dark when she reached the thunderous base of the falls. The singing had stopped much before, but she arrived at its source without a falter.[8] Some way into a comfortable cave directly behind the falls, with a high fire going, sat an elderly man and woman. They were eating a steaming stew from deep bowls.

Innera stepped into the circle of light. "Hello!"

The old man looked up and rose to his feet in one movement. He was alert but not alarmed. His wife turned more slowly and did not get up.

"Hello, yourself," the man said. "Come near."

Innera liked his easy manner and his wife's calm countenance. "I am Innera, daughter of Artios and granddaughter of Biden. I have ridden thirteen days on behalf of the king of this country."

"Indeed," said the old man. He nodded at her helmet. "Are you a captain, then?"

Innera reached up to the helmet as though noticing it for the first time. "No, sir. I am but a girl completing a captain's mission."

The woman rose then and went to Innera. "Come," she said. She put an arm around Innera's shoulders and drew her closer to the fire. "For now you are but a girl in need of food and rest. Just look at you."

Innera wondered how she must look after thirteen days of hard riding and sleeping on the ground. But the smell and look of the stew sent almost all else from her mind. "My horse—my horse needs tending—" She turned toward the entrance.

The old man had already gone to see to the horse. He touched the shield and looked back at Innera, but he did not question her.

The woman filled her a bowl. "Where are you going, in this winter, by yourself?"

"I was going to Cordus, but now I am not entirely sure."

The old man returned to the fire. "Where have you come from?"

"Dider."

"My!" said the woman. "You came by way of the Brass Mountains then?"

"If that is what those beautiful hills spread out like a wing are called, I did."

"And were you not robbed?"

Innera thought of the ragged boy. "No."

"It's a wonder. Those mountains are full of fugitives and thieves."

"Wife," said the man, "we should let her eat."

---

[8] falter—unsteady movement

Innera woke in the early morning, fur beneath her and fur around her. She lay still for a moment, relishing the comfort. Then she remembered her mission and unwrapped herself.

"There she is," said the old man. "The girl who carries the shield of a king and masters a captain's horse. These guard horses are trained not to obey any but the one who owns them. You are, I see, no common girl."

"I thank you for taking me in. But I must see this duty through."

"Thank you for your loyalty to this duty," said the man. "I serve any who serve our king. If the king's Watch of the Sea may help you, you have but to say."

"This is a sea?"

"Windermere. The sea of Kapnos. Out of which flows the Valor River."

Innera stared at him. "You are the watchman! Watch and *seal!*"

The old man tipped up his head. "What's that?"

"A wedding ring. An eagle's wing—"

"Watch and see—The Towers Three!" he finished with her.

"The captain's last words. I think they are a map to where I must take the message he was carrying."

"Aye, you have unlocked a riddle, and now the riddle will unlock something for you."

"What?" she asked.

"Watch and see. You have a map of ground and a map of government there. Come, I have ferried a Cordus guard or two before. And I will ferry you over as well. You are almost where you want to be."

Innera, the old man, and the horse passed over the narrow end of

178

the Windermere on a sturdy flatboat. As they neared the shore, a triplet of stone turrets[9] arched against the sky from across a wide plain. The old man nodded toward the towers. "An easy morning's ride," he said.

She disembarked.[10] She turned to thank him again. He said, "Come this way on your return to tell us the end of your story, and that will be thanks enough. You will find me here at mainday and somewhat after every day."

[9]turrets—towers
[10]disembarked—left and went on shore

She nodded and smiled. "I will see you again." Then she mounted and set off at a trot. "A map of ground." That meaning was clear enough. But what is a map of government? She could not make it out.

In two hours the walls of the fortress were directly before her. A massive stone edifice, the fortress seemed to grow larger even as she looked at it. A guard addressed her from a parapet[11] above the outer gates. "Rein up, rider."

"I have a message for the Cordus guard from their king."

"Answer me this. What sign has fidelity?"

Innera considered her answer. Fidelity is loyalty, faithfulness, she thought. What sign means faithfulness? Suddenly, it came to her. "A wedding ring."

The gate swung open.

She passed under the parapet to a second set of gates. A soldier there said, "Rein up, rider. Answer me this. What sign has freedom?"

She smiled. "An eagle's wing."

He opened the gate. She passed through it and was immediately confronted by the captain of the guard. He glanced at her helmet and said, "Rein up, rider. Answer me this. What sign has faith?"

"Watch and see."

The captain shouted behind him, "Open the gates!"

The captain led her through the third set of gates. She slid off her horse and removed her helmet. "This horse and this helmet belonged to a captain of your country. I return them and bring a message." A guard stepped forward and took them. "And this is the shield he carried. A king's shield." All about stared at it. No one stepped forward to take it.

"And the message?" said the captain.

Innera took the document from the pouch.

"Who are you?" he said.

"Innera, granddaughter of Biden and daughter of Artios, of Dider."

The captain of the guard said, "You came all the way from the mountains of Dider? By yourself?"

Innera nodded.

"Innera of Dider, will you yet serve us in one more thing?"

Again she nodded.

He led her up into the fortress to an inner courtyard. There were several soldiers and a young man only slightly beyond her in years who seemed to command them all. Behind him on the wall was a tapestry of the very fortress she stood in. The three towers each bore a word: *fidelity, freedom, faith.* At the bottom was woven the motto "The Towers Three of Governing."

---

[11]parapet (păr´ ə pĭt)—low wall built to protect soldiers

The captain told this young man Innera's story and then stepped back. Innera held forth the document. The young man, in a fine mesh mail, received it with the dignity and bearing of a man many years older. He smiled warmly at her, and she blushed.

"I thank you for this service," he said. He opened the document. For some moments he gave no sign. Then he slowly folded it back together. He looked at the men around him, particularly at the captain. "My father has died in battle. He is borne home at funeral pace to the capital Cordus. Let us go there at once."

Every soldier knelt on one knee, and the captain said, "The king is dead. Long live the king." Innera gazed around her and then at the young man with no small amazement.

The young king looked immeasurably sad, but his voice was clear and firm. "For your faithful service to a king not yours, for your courageous acts on his behalf, I, son of Gher of Kapnos, present you with the Circle Meadow through which you passed to come here."

Innera opened her mouth to refuse, but he went on. "I give you also the horse on which you came."

With a grace she did not know she had, Innera bowed her head slightly. "Thank you, Your Majesty."

"And from this day forward, Innera of Dider shall be known in Cordus as Lady Enna with all the rights and privileges of a citizen of Cordus." The young man hesitated, as though he had to speak with great effort. "I hope we may meet again in better times, Lady Enna."

Innera said, "As do I, Your Grace." She respectfully held out the shield. He took it from her as though it were far heavier than it was. He gave her the smallest smile. Then he motioned to a guard and left the company.

The guard bowed to Innera and stood ready to accompany her home. When she understood, she said, "I thank you and your new king. But I am able to go alone. I would not have you so far from the burial of your old king."

As she rode back toward Windermere, she thought of how she would tell the old watchman and his wife and her grandmother the end of her story. For she had no way of knowing that it was only just the beginning of it.

STICKBALL

Virginia Schonborg
illustrated by Dyke Habegger

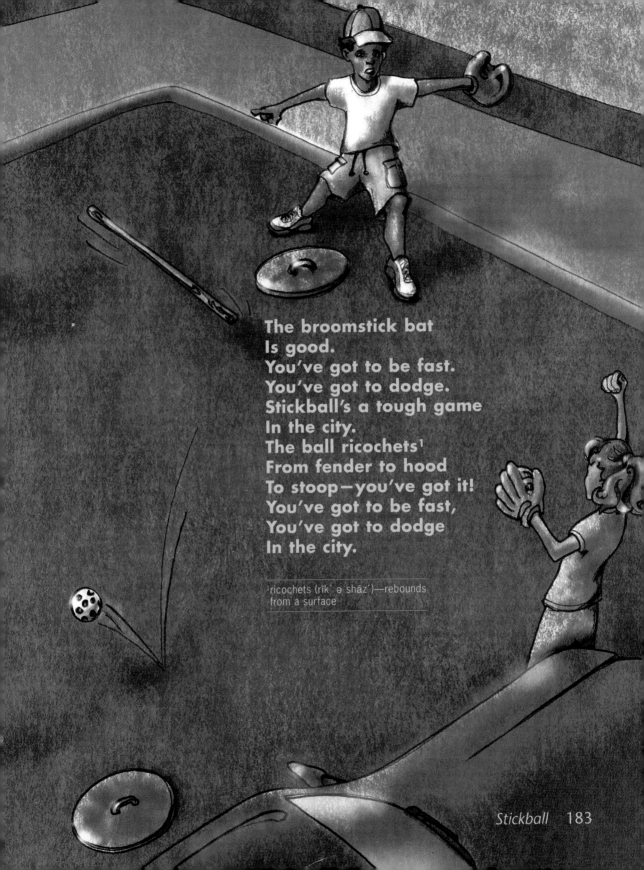

The broomstick bat
Is good.
You've got to be fast.
You've got to dodge.
Stickball's a tough game
In the city.
The ball ricochets[1]
From fender to hood
To stoop—you've got it!
You've got to be fast,
You've got to dodge
In the city.

[1]ricochets (rĭk´ ə shāz´)—rebounds
 from a surface

THE SECRET PITCH

Earl Chapin
illustrated by Eden Anderson

Somebody said something the other day about "one of the greatest games of organized baseball." Well, whatever that game was like, it couldn't compare with what you can see in unorganized baseball.

Take the game, for instance, which decided the junior boys' championship of Montrose and was pitched by a girl. What was a girl doing in a boys' league? Well, our baseball was not only unorganized, it was disorganized. And there was only one Sissy Wyatt.

The name is spelled with an *S*, not a *C*, and maybe that is what got Sissy going. In the Wyatt family there were lots of boys but only one

girl, and as the last of the troupe,[1] she was called Sister. You know what happens to a name like that. Pretty soon everyone in the neighborhood called her Sissy. When she grew to understand what the name meant, she always seemed to be going out of her way to prove she wasn't one.

It got so that we boys of the South Side couldn't have a game of baseball or football or shinny without Sissy getting right into the middle of it. At first her brother Jim, who is my age, used to pick her up and toss her off the field. After a few years he couldn't do that.

---

[1]troupe—group; usually referring to traveling
  performers

Sissy grew up fast and tall, with knobby knees and sharp elbows. She had dark red hair, which she conquered with two pigtails that stuck out on either side of her freckled face. She looked formidable,[2] and she was.

Sissy was sharp, too, and that made things all the more difficult. She got the local paper route and had more money to spend than any of us. That's how she got on the ball team. She owned the catcher's mitt, the chest protector, and the baseballs.

In practice we let Sissy play shortstop. We needed players, anyway. Besides, she was really good, and I admit it. We wouldn't let her play regular games, but she was always with us, and her whooping and yelling were embarrassing. In fact, our opposition called us the Sissies! If we tried to shush her, she threatened to take her catcher's mitt, chest protector, and baseballs and go home.

To make matters worse, in time she imagined herself to be a pitcher. She bought a book on how to pitch, and she practiced. It was weird. She had just one delivery, which she called a fork ball. Somehow her hand was just big enough to get her first and second fingers on either side of the ball. The batter never knew where it was going. Neither did Sissy.

We never let her pitch to us, and to that I ascribed[3] the fact that our South Side Scrappers got through the season uninjured. We proudly announced that we were the Junior Champs of Montrose and promptly received a challenge from a team we'd never heard about, the North End Nuggets. They said *they* were the champs and challenged us to a showdown. We asked if they would agree to a couple of basic rules— nobody over fourteen should be on the team, and all members should come from the immediate neighborhood. The Nuggets crossed their hearts and hoped to die, and we took them at their word. Well, not exactly. We went over and scouted their practice. They were a pretty seedy[4]-looking outfit, so our team agreed to a seven-inning championship game on their field.

I'm the manager of the Scrappers, and I saw too late that we had been swindled. I'd never seen half the Nuggets that were working out on the field when we arrived for the game. If some of those boys were only fourteen, they must have been eating an awful lot of vitamins.

What could we do? We had a good crowd that had paid admission, and we wanted our split of the gate in order to buy a chest protector and get rid of Sissy. Besides, the

---

[2]formidable—causing dread or fear
[3]ascribed—gave credit for
[4]seedy—shabby; inferior

Scrappers never walked out on anything.

I thought we just might pull the game out of the fire at that, because Fats Walker, our pitcher, was the best pitcher this side of high school.

We went to bat and fanned out in order. The boy who was throwing for the Nuggets must have been a relative of someone in the Baseball Hall of Fame.

Fats rose to the occasion and retired the Nuggets without a score, but not so easily as they had retired us.

That Nuggets pitcher was mean. He dusted off Paul Jass so close that Paul got rattled and struck at balls and the shadow of a bird crossing the diamond. Our side was down again.

It was a cool day for August, but Fats Walker was perspiring profusely[5] as he fogged them in. He was good, too, but I could see he was outdoing himself. The Nuggets got a scratch hit, executed a nice bunt, got a sacrifice and a single. At the end of the third inning the score was 2 to 0.

In the fourth, Fats began to come unraveled. I kept my eye on Bill Brady, our other pitcher, who was playing in left field. The Nuggets had two on when Fats put one across the corner that was hard to hit. But the batter was one of those overgrown fourteen-year olds. He got the ball on the end of his bat and lofted it into the outfield. Bill Brady saw it coming, started to run back, changed his calculations on the arc of the ball, and plunged back again, his arms outstretched. The ball sailed between his outstretched arms and hit Bill square on the noggin. While our outfielder-pitcher measured his length on the grass, the three Nuggets streaked for home. We helped Bill to the bench.

You have no idea of the troubles of a manager. Fats dragged himself up, looking like a limp dishrag. "I'm woofed," he said. "I can hardly reach the plate."

"But we haven't any more pitchers!" I cried.

"Let me pitch!"

I winced at that shrill voice. I'd been hearing it from the bench since the game started. "You!" I snorted at Sissy. "You've only got one pitch, and you can't hit the plate—" I stopped, suddenly thinking of the beanballs we had been suffering, and evil flowered in my heart. "It would serve 'em right," I muttered.

"I can too," shrilled Sissy. "I've got two pitches. And I've got a secret one too."

I looked at the boys. I think some of them had caught my idea. And anyway, we had no choice.

---

[5]profusely—more than is normal; excessively

"All right," I said. "You pitch."

"Girls are against the rules," the Nuggets cried.

"What rules?" I demanded. I had them there.

They went into a huddle and conceded.[6] Actually I could see they thought it was very funny.

Sissy started the last of the fifth with the score 5 to 0 against us. Her first pitch got stuck in the screen about twelve feet above the plate. On her next pitch the batter just topped the ball. It dribbled out to the plate. Sissy fielded it, and one was out.

The next batter was the Nuggets' tough pitcher. Sissy stuck out the tip of her tongue, and I could tell that she was going to throw her fork ball again. The ball floated up as big as a barn. You could count every stitch in it. The pitcher took a clout that would have knocked it right through the sound barrier. But just as he swung, the ball fell away. The bat met nothing but air.

The pitcher spun around like a top and went to the ground. When the Nuggets got him untangled, they claimed he had dislocated a vertebra and fractured his collarbone. That was an exaggeration. One thing was

sure, though, the pitcher was out of the game.

The Nuggets were so unnerved[7] by this disaster that the third man up fanned ingloriously.[8]

---

[6]conceded—admitted that something is true, often without wanting to
[7]unnerved—without poise or confidence
[8]ingloriously—without dignity or honor

With that hotshot pitcher out of the way, the future looked a little less glum. We Scrappers and our rooters came to life, and we had two on before the new pitcher struck out a batter. The next one up was Sissy. The Nuggets' pitcher should have taken a clue from what had happened already, but he had to show his contempt for girls. He tossed up a nice, fat patsy.[9] Sissy swung at it like Babe Ruth at his best. The ball was still rising when it disappeared over the fence.

That didn't end the inning. The score was tied by the time the Nuggets got three away.

I was feeling pretty complacent[10] when Sissy took to the mound again, but you can never trust a girl. She threw four wide pitches, and the batter took his base.

Sissy threw another great drop. It struck the ground in front of the plate, and before the catcher could get it, the runner had advanced to second. Sissy threw the ball again. The batter missed it, and so did the catcher. The runner was on third.

"Tell her to try her other pitch!" I yelled to our catcher.

Sissy's pigtails were sticking straight out. She reared back and threw the ball up in the air. The arc couldn't have been more perfect! The ball dropped down cleanly in the strike zone. The batter just stood there with his mouth open. Sissy fi-

nally struck him out and then put two away to retire the Nuggets.

We opened the seventh and last inning by breaking the tie. With the score 6 to 5, all we had to do was hang on. But, oh, brother! I mean, oh, sister! The first man hit a looper that creased the second baseman's head.

Then, advancing to the plate, swinging three bats, came one of those overgrown fourteen-year olds. He had hit safely every time.

Sissy prepared to throw a knuckle ball, but it slipped prematurely[11] from her fingers. The batter grinned and lowered his head to let the overthrow pass. But as the ball neared the plate, it took a drop and struck with a sodden thump on the head of the guy in the batter's box.

The next man smacked a perfect bounce to third for a force-out, and the next one fanned.

Sissy's eyes brightened. She smiled a smile of triumph. But pride goeth before a fall. She tossed a real blooper. Nick had to run out in front of the plate to catch it. She threw another. Nick jumped back to get it. Sissy tried another, but it was a ball. She had lost the range on the next pitch, and the man walked.

Two out, and the bases loaded! A great quiet settled over the diamond.

[9]patsy—something or someone easily taken advantage of
[10]complacent—pleased with oneself; contented
[11]prematurely—too early

188

Sissy was trying hard, and her drop was breaking more crazily than ever. The batter decided if he just waited, the odds would be in his favor. He was right. He stood there until the count was three and two.

"Tell her to throw that dark one!" I yelled. I was instructing the catcher, but you could hear me all over the diamond. Sissy motioned for a conference. She stood with her hands on her hips, talking vehemently,[12] her pigtails bobbing. I could see that Nick didn't believe her. But finally he gave up and took his position.

"Please," I muttered, "let it be a double curve!"

Sissy went into an awesome wind-up and let loose. The ball was like a bullet, straight down the middle, and so fast I don't think Babe Ruth could have hit it. Only after the ball whanged into the catcher's mitt did the batter show a slight twitch of reflex movement. "Why didn't you throw that one before?" I chortled.[13]

"Oh," she said innocently, "I was saving that for an emergency."

That's the way it is with girls. But we could teach her.

"Next year you can be our starting pitcher," I said.

Sissy drew herself up primly.[14] "I have decided," she announced, "that it's unladylike to play baseball."

Maybe it was for the best. I don't know if we could have stood a whole year of Sissy's pitching.

[12]vehemently—forcefully; strongly emotional
[13]chortled—chuckling in a snorting way
[14]primly—showing proper manners

The Secret Pitch 189

AMERICA'S FAVORITE PASTIME

Amy Miller

The Beginnings of Baseball

In 1744 John Newbery published a book called *A Little Pretty Pocket Book*. In it was the following verse under the title "*B* is for Baseball":

> The Ball once struck off
> Away flies the Boy
> To the next destin'd[1] Post
> And then Home with Joy.

Now, anyone who knows anything about baseball knows that that boy wasn't running home to lunch. He was running to home base on a baseball field to score for his team. *Home* is one of the most common baseball terms. We sometimes talk about being "home free" when we're not even talking about baseball.

Baseball started in the 1700s with a game called *town ball*. Town ball is believed to have developed from the games *rounders* and *cricket,* which were popular in England. Town ball was an informal game played by the men of a town, often with twenty to fifty men and boys on the field trying to catch the ball that was hit by a four-inch flat bat.

The rules for town ball continued to evolve[2] until the number of players on the field had dwindled down to nine and bases were added, thus changing the name to baseball.

---

[1]destined—determined or established ahead of time
[2]evolve—to develop gradually

Changes in Baseball

After 1860, many rules and practices were established that have remained until the present day. For instance, the pitcher was originally allowed to run as he delivered his pitch. In 1858 the regulation changed so as to forbid even a step while pitching. Then, in 1863, he was allowed as many steps as he wanted, and finally in 1884, he was confined to one step in the delivery of the pitch. It wasn't until 1864 that the rules stated that a runner must touch each base as he ran from base to base. The year 1865 was an important year in that the first slide to steal a base was taken and the first batting averages were calculated.

Understanding Batting Average

$$\text{Batting Average} = \frac{\text{number of hits}}{\text{number of times at bat}}$$

hits	at bats	Batting Average
200	1000	.200
219	662	.331
206	645	.319

In 1879, a pitcher could pitch nine balls before the batter could walk. But, 1879 also saw the regulation stating that three strikes was an "out." In 1893, the pitching distance was established at 60 feet, 6 inches as it remains today. One regulation that has been dropped over the years is the umpire's ability to fine a coach or player $25 for using vulgar language.

The People of Baseball

During this time of growth and change in baseball, women and African-Americans were forced to form leagues of their own. The first African-American teams, known as Negro leagues, were formed in the early 1900s. Many of these players batted, pitched, and played just as well as, or better than, their counterparts.[3] In recognition of these excellent players, many of their names have been added to the Baseball Hall of Fame.

The day when an African-American man was first permitted to play in the official league was a signal of great changes in the history of sports. In 1946, Jackie Robinson became the first African American to sign a contract with a major league team. Robinson proved to be worthy of his hire, when in his first season, he won the International League batting title and became the best second baseman in the League. In his second season, he won the "Rookie of the Year" title and held a respectable .296 batting average. Then in 1949, Robinson was named the Most Valuable Player in the National League. This courageous front-runner certainly entered with a bang, doing much to help erase prejudices of the day and paving the way for other African-Americans, as well as

---

[3]counterparts—those that are exactly alike or closely resemble another

Jackie Robinson was the first African-American to sign a contract with a major baseball team.

players of other races, to enter the major leagues.

Though women have belonged to leagues of their own, the integration[4] of men and women on teams has been sparse. For about forty years, women's leagues ran strong and were so competitive that they occasionally had men playing with them as a start on the road to the major leagues, or at least the minor leagues. Even though many women participate in softball leagues, there is still an effort to allow the first female into the major leagues.

Records Set in Baseball

Lest the stars of recent days outshine the stars of the past, remember that some records set in the early years have not yet been broken. For instance, Ty Cobb is still considered by some as the greatest baseball player ever, an opinion held more than ninety years after he batted an all-time high of .420 in 1911. In 1894, when baseball was still in its very early stages, a man named Hugh Duffy batted a .440 season. However, no one was able to lead in batting averages for as many seasons as Ty Cobb, who ended his career with a .367 batting average. During his distinguished career, Cobb went over .400 three times—a very significant accomplishment that has rarely been matched. The last person to have even one season of batting over .400 was Ted Williams in 1941.

However, Ty Cobb is not only known for his sky-high batting averages but he also ranked first in runs scored for seventy-three years. Cobb stole home plate more than any other player ever. Anyone who has stolen a base before knows that home plate is guarded more carefully than any other base, since that's where the

---

[4]integration—the act or process of making something open to all groups

runs are scored. You might say that Ty Cobb was a very daring player!

Ricky Henderson, who wasn't even born when Ty Cobb retired from baseball, broke the seventy-three-year-old record in 2001 when he scored the 2,246th run of his career. The forty-two-year-old Henderson has also held the record for stolen bases since 1991. However, in 2001 his career total of 1,395 stolen bases only included eight *home plate* steals. Compare that to Cobb who once stole home eight times in a single season!

Though there are many who set incredible records, the best known is Babe Ruth. "The Babe," as some called him, broke all home run records and set a standard that no one could challenge for over thirty years. As you can imagine, many have since tried to break it, but when Babe hit sixty home runs in the 1927 season, no one could imagine even coming close! It wasn't until 1961 that Roger Maris hit sixty-one home runs in a season. Then, another thirty-seven years lapsed[5] before anyone broke that record. In 1998, Mark McGwire hit his sixty-second home run on September 8, setting a new record. Sammy Sosa wasn't far

Ty Cobb is known for his high batting averages and stolen bases.

behind with his sixty-second home run on September 13.

McGwire and Sosa ran a close race and even tied at one point, but McGwire stayed ahead, setting a new incredible record. At season's end, McGwire cashed in with seventy homers and Sosa with sixty-six. 1998 was an exciting year for baseball fans!

However, McGwire's record would not stand for long. Barry Bonds challenged the record and ended the 2001 season with 73 home runs. The thirty-seven-year-old record was broken and then beaten again only three years later.

There are other record-breaking feats that have nothing to do with official baseball statistics. Anyone who collects baseball cards knows that many factors go into determining the worth of a single card. Some factors that make a card valuable are, of course, the player on the card and the condition of the card. One card has become known as "the Mona Lisa of baseball cards." Honus Wagner played for the Pittsburgh Pirates from 1897-1917 and continued as a coach in the years following. In those days, baseball cards were sold on the covers of

---

[5]lapsed—passed by

tobacco pouches. Wagner didn't like this idea one bit. He did not want young people to buy tobacco in order to get baseball cards, so he did not give the tobacco company permission to sell his card. In fact, some say he even paid the company the money they would have made had they sold them. However, by some mistake approximately fifty cards slipped through and were sold. These fifty or so cards of Wagner are among the most valuable.

As one of the first to be inducted to the Baseball Hall of Fame, Wagner had a distinguished record as a player, but the story behind the cards has drawn additional interest. One of those fifty cards, because of its rarity, has continued to be worth the most money of any baseball card. The card of a man who earned only $2,000 in a year recently sold for over one million dollars. Hang on to those baseball cards!

With a long and exciting history like this, no wonder baseball has continued to be the favorite of millions around the world. Whether in someone's back yard, in a neighborhood field, or in a major league stadium, baseball is truly America's "favorite pastime."

Baseball "greats" with home run records include Babe Ruth, Mark McGwire, and Barry Bonds.

Rest in Hope: The Michael Weathers Story

a testimony by John Weathers
with Eileen M. Berry

One Saturday afternoon in October, my twelve-year-old son Michael and I went deer hunting on a friend's farm near Woodruff, South Carolina. The weather that afternoon was perfect for hunting—a beautiful seventy-degree day with no rain—and the wind was still. It seemed that everything was just right. We didn't realize when we started out that something would go wrong—something that would change our lives in a marvelous way.

We chose spots along the creek to watch for deer. After Michael was situated in his deer stand, I climbed another tree about two hundred yards to his right. As darkness began to fall, I suddenly heard a gunshot. "All right! Michael got a deer!" I thought, smiling to myself.

But then I heard a sound I'll never forget. "Daddy!" Michael was calling to me for help.

I left my gun, scrambled down, and ran toward his tree, feeling as if it were taking forever to get there. My glasses began to fog up. I pulled them off and kept running.

As it turned out, Michael had propped his 20-gauge shotgun against the rail of the deer stand beside him and had fallen asleep. He jerked awake, and his foot hit the gun, causing it to fall. When the gun struck the side floor of the deer stand, the quick jar pushed the firing pin into the shell, and the gun went off right next to his left thigh. Miraculously, he had been able to climb down by himself. When I reached Michael, he was lying on the ground. He was still conscious, but he was bleeding. When I waved my fingers in front of his face, he just stared. I quickly realized that he was in shock and needed medical attention as soon as possible.

I looked up into the trees. "Please, God, have mercy on him," I prayed silently. "If you have something very special in life for him to do, please keep him alive." I thought of the verse in II Kings where the Lord opened the eyes of Elisha's servant so that he could see the angels that surrounded them. I prayed that the Lord would let His guardian angels work overtime while I was gone. "I love you, Michael," I said. "I'm going to get help, and I'll come back as soon as I can." I rushed away, thinking as I ran that I didn't know what condition I would find him in when I got back. That was the hard part.

I ran to the farmhouse as fast as I could. No one was home, but God had prepared the way. One of the doors was unlocked, so I went in and used the phone to call 911. "What's the address of the house?" the operator asked me. I didn't know. Fumbling around on the counter, I found a letter that had the address of the home. It was then that I remembered I had left my glasses in the woods! I couldn't read the address. As a feeling of desperation rose inside of me, I heard the operator say, "Sir, it's all right. We've had time to trace your call." Relief washed over me.

I went out and stood in the road to wait for the rescue squad. "I wish I could go back to Michael," I thought. "But I'm the only one who knows where he is. I have to lead the rescue crew to him. Lord, please let him be alive when we find him in the woods." Thankfully, I heard the squad coming just a few minutes later. As I guided them to the spot where I had left Michael, I feared the worst. "Lord, please let him be alive."

When we reached the spot, hope surged through me. Michael was sitting up! "Thank you, Lord." He was still alive, although very weak from loss of blood. The rescue squad ran to him with their stretcher.

"Lord, please help us to get him to the ambulance." The Lord answered that prayer as well, and as the ambulance sped up the road, I prayed, "Lord, help us get him to the hospital—please." We were able to get Michael to Spartanburg Regional Hospital in a matter of minutes. The Lord answered each one of my prayers through the whole ordeal.

Michael was rushed to the emergency room. My wife and my

two other children met me in a little room to wait. We waited all through that long night. As the hours passed, friends from our church and friends we work with at Bob Jones University came and went. Many of them offered to pray with us. The Lord used those prayers to encourage us through that difficult waiting time. Every now and then, the nurse and doctors would come in to give us updates. At one point, the head surgeon told us, "We'll try to save his leg, but right now we need to save his life." We continued praying.

Michael went through seven hours of surgery. Finally, at 4:30 the following morning, the doctor came in. "Michael's going to make it," he said, "but we'll still have to watch his leg. We're not sure how much damage has been done." You can imagine our joy and thankfulness.

Michael had received five units of blood during surgery, and he received three more later on. He had three different operations, and he was in the hospital for several more weeks. The muscle on his outside lower leg had died due to lack of oxygen, and the dead tissue had to be removed. But the Lord gave us a special provision. During his recovery, Michael was able to receive the treatment of a vacuum pump that kept his wounds moist and stimulated[1] tissue growth. This treatment allowed his wounds to heal and scar without skin grafts.[2] Finally, just before Thanksgiving, he was able to come home. He continued to use the vacuum pump, but he was able to attend school for half-days. In January he went back to school full-time.

For six more months Michael continued to go to physical therapy every three weeks. His wounds have scarred over completely, and he can participate in most normal activities of a boy his age. But several nerves and muscles were damaged in his left leg, and as a result, he has not regained complete feeling in his foot. He will have to wear a plastic brace the rest of his life. We thank God that he is still with us.

One special verse that has helped me is Psalm 16:9: *"Therefore my heart is glad, and my glory rejoiceth: my flesh also shall rest in hope."* I praise the Lord for His abundant love, mercy, and grace that He has shown our family through this experience. He has truly enabled us to say that our flesh can rest in hope.

---

[1]stimulated—temporarily made more active
[2]grafts—body tissue removed and attached to a different place

Interview with
Michael Weathers

Eileen M. Berry

Interviewer: What special things did your friends do for you after you had your accident?

Weathers: A lot of my friends came to visit me in the hospital. And a lot of people sent me cards; the cards filled a whole wall in my hospital room! I couldn't really read them while I was there, but I had fun reading them after I came home. Sometimes I still like to get them out and read them before I go to bed at night.

When I first came back to school, there were posters all over the walls welcoming me back. Someone brought a giant cookie to class.

Interviewer: How has your life changed since the accident?

Weathers: Right after I came back to school, I was in a wheelchair for a while, then on crutches. I had to take my vacuum machine with me everywhere I went. It was very heavy, so someone always had to help me carry it. Now I just have to wear a brace on my leg. It goes down underneath my foot, so my shoes have to be a little wider.

Sometimes if I stand for a long time, my leg swells, and I have shooting pains now and then. My foot feels like it is always asleep. But I can still play soccer. I got to go to sports camp and for a week of camp at The *Wilds* last summer. And I can still play the piano—it didn't mess up my pedal foot.

I'd still like to go hunting again, but not with a gun. Maybe a crossbow.

Michael (far right) with his family.

Interviewer: What did you learn about God as a result of your experience?

Weathers: That He *does* answer prayer. I'm able to go to school now, and we prayed for that. Also, I've learned that everything that happens to me is for my good and for God's glory.

Interviewer: As you think about what you learned through your accident, what would you tell other students your age?

Weathers: I'd tell them that God has something planned for your life. In the hospital, I had good and bad days, and it was hard to see that. But now, looking back, I can see that what happened to me wasn't so bad. Now I thank God for letting me go through that, and I thank God for my family too.

The Proud-Minded Princess

A folktale dramatized by Dawn L. Watkins
illustrated by Justin Gerard and John Bjerk

Dramatis Personae[1]

Etain, *Princess of Castle Wydyr*
Her father, *the King of Wydyr*
Her mother, *the Queen of Wydyr*
Her nurse
Two county kings, *suitors[2] to Etain*
Gwydion, *the King of Golud*
A beggar/singer

A nobleman and noblewoman
A coachman
Branwen, *a cook in Castle Golud*
Serving maids and women
A stableboy
Princes, princesses, nobles, and
 noblewomen

ACT 1

The Castle Wydyr in Ireland long ago.

Scene 1

Curtain rises on Etain in a lavish[3] room, having her hair braided by her nurse.

ETAIN: Is this not the worst of cruelties, Nurse? Banishment would be kinder! I will not be traded like a horse at auction!

NURSE: I beseech[4] my mistress, be not so angry. Your hair has come undone again, and soon the King and Queen—

ETAIN: Let it be undone—for I am.

NURSE: Mistress—Etain—do I not know you from a little girl? All

will yet be well. The King only wants—

ETAIN: (*Rising, striding away*) What do you know of such things? Did your father want to be rid of you as mine does?

NURSE: My lord, the king—your father—is not cruel, Mistress. He offers you a choice among the great county kings, all rich and lordly men.

---

[1] dramatis personae—Latin for "cast of characters"
[2] suitors—men who seek the affection of a woman
[3] lavish—extravagant; abundantly furnished
[4] beseech—beg

ETAIN: Choice! That is no choice! A choice would be to say I will or will not marry! But to be told you *will* marry and then to pick among doddering,[5] whiskered fools is slavery. I am not a slave! (*She pulls the tiara from her head and hurls it down.*) Nor princess either, if it means I must live like a slave!

As the nurse hurries to pick up the hammered gold band, the King and Queen of Wydyr enter.

KING OF WYDYR: What's this? (*He picks up the gold tiara.*) So, Etain, you throw down my love and your honor so hastily?

QUEEN OF WYDYR: Etain, compose[6] yourself.

ETAIN: Would I were a song, Mother, that I could be composed at will. But I am a girl.

KING OF WYDYR: And out of tune again, I see.

QUEEN OF WYDYR: Come, the suitors are waiting to meet you.

ETAIN: Why call them suitors when none will suit me?

KING OF WYDYR: Daughter! Enough. You will choose one of these kings, and there is an end

[5]doddering—old and feeble
[6]compose—1. to make calm or controlled; 2. to write; create, especially music

on it. (*to Nurse*) Show in the suitors to this wild and ungrateful child of mine. (*to Etain*) I command you to obey me, Etain of Wydyr. Return this to its proper place. (*He hands her the tiara. Etain hesitates and then puts it on.*)

The first king enters. He is old but lavishly dressed.

FIRST KING: (*to King of Wydyr*) If I am to take this daughter of yours, I must speak of her dowry[7] first. I am—

ETAIN: Good morning, your lordship. I apologize for your having to come so far in your finery for nothing.

FIRST KING: Do not speak so lowly of yourself, Princess. You are a king's daughter. You are not nothing.

ETAIN: I am to you, for that is all you will have from me.

QUEEN OF WYDYR: Etain! Your manners!

ETAIN: Your pardon. Nothing is all you will have from me, *sir.*

FIRST KING: (*to Queen of Wydyr*) Fine manners cannot disguise a proud heart.

ETAIN: Nor fine clothes a cold heart, *sir.*

FIRST KING: (*to King of Wydyr*) I am too old to have such a willful wife. I wish you well in finding a match for this one! (*He exits.*)

KING OF WYDYR: Your Grace, I implore[8] you! (*turns to Etain*) Comport[9] yourself like a princess! That king was more wealthy than ten kings together!

ETAIN: Bring in the next, Father. I will see if he is to my taste.

Enter second king. He is not quite as old as the first king and not quite as well dressed.

SECOND KING: Princess! You are even more beautiful than I was told! Would you permit me to say—

ETAIN: Good-bye? Indeed I would, and speed you well.

SECOND KING: Princess, I have much to offer you. Will you but hear me? (*He brings a huge ruby ring from his pocket.*) I heard you had a taste for rubies.

ETAIN: (*taking the ring from him*) Perhaps whoever told you that should have also told you that no ring is so beautiful that I would be willing to wear it through my nose! You cannot buy me with a thousand ruby rings! (*She tosses the ring out the door.*) Take your gifts and go—I have no taste for them, or you! (*As he turns to go, she gives him a shove.*)

---

[7]dowry—money or property brought by a bride to the man she is going to marry
[8]implore—to beg; plead with
[9]comport—to behave in a particular manner

The second king hastily leaves, picking up the ring on the way. The third king enters as the second exits. He is young and handsome and dressed well but not flashily.

ETAIN: *(looking suddenly at the third king and liking what she sees)* Is this then the third verse of the same song?

KING OF GOLUD: I do not hear any music here, my lady.

ETAIN: Nor shall you, my lord. I am not disposed[10] to be tuned as my father wishes. It is no fault of yours. I simply do not want to marry on command. So let us part company then while we are still friends.

KING OF GOLUD: Are we friends? Well, that is something to start with. I had heard from my predecessors[11] that you had no friends.

ETAIN: *(stung to her own defense)* How could you hear anything of me, being deaf to music as you said?

KING OF GOLUD: Are you now saying that you are willing to be tuned? I thought there was no music here because you refused to sing.

ETAIN: I warn you, friend, you do not want a war with me. I have the arsenal[12] to win against any king. *(She thumps him on the side of the head with a bolster[13] from a chair.)*

KING OF GOLUD: I warn you, friend—I never go to war but that I win. *(He takes the bolster from her and throws it back on the chair. Without taking his eyes from her, he addresses her father.)* It seems your daughter is not inclined[14] to marry, sir. I thank you for your invitation and your hospitality. I will now take my leave. *(bowing)* Princess, Your Majesties. *(He exits.)*

KING OF WYDYR: Sullen and blind! You have turned away the best the world could offer! I do not recognize you for any daughter of mine. I shall marry you to the very next beggar that happens by!

The lights go down as all exit.

10disposed—of a certain frame of mind
11predecessors—those who went before
12arsenal—stock of weapons
13bolster—a long, narrow pillow or cushion
14inclined—having a preference

Scene 2

The Nurse and Etain come in alone again. As the scene progresses, a man can be heard singing.

ETAIN: Where is my mother?

NURSE: In her chambers,[15] my lady. She is crying too much to come out.

ETAIN: Well, you will not see me cry. Father can do as he pleases with me.

NURSE: There is yet time to send for the King of Golud to return, Mistress. He was to my eye a match for you.

A man's singing can be heard quite well now, although the words are still indistinct.[16]

ETAIN: It no longer matters what he was. My life is—listen! Do you hear that?

NURSE: What a lovely voice!

ETAIN: *(going to the window)* I've never heard such fine singing. It beguiles[17] me from all my troubles. Listen! How it lifts my heart!

The voice sings a now audible verse.

SINGER: *"No prisoner of the heart am I; No stranger to the road.*

[15]chambers—rooms
[16]indistinct—not clearly understood
[17]beguiles—distracts; amuses

So long as I have voice to sing,
I have no weary load.
Away with me, my dearest love;
Away with me tonight.
Though poor we be, we shall be free;
Our lives be fair and bright."

NURSE: Come away from the window, my Etain. The night air—

ETAIN: *(calling out the window)* Singer!

SINGER: *(from offstage)* Here, my lady, under a starless sky, until you appeared.

ETAIN: I will pay you to sing again.

SINGER: You are too kind to a wandering beggar, my lady.

ETAIN: You do not know me then. Here.

She takes coins from her pocket and throws them out the window. The singer sings the same verse again. As he comes to the end of the song, the King of Wydyr enters.

KING OF WYDYR: *(to the nurse)* Go bid that man to come inside. Tell him tonight he takes a wife.

NURSE: Your Majesty!

ETAIN: Father!

KING OF WYDYR: Go! *(Nurse exits.)* Now, my ungrateful daughter, collect what you will take with you.

ETAIN: But, Father, I beg you!

KING OF WYDYR: Yes, you will beg. Your beggar husband will teach you how.

ETAIN: Please, Father. I have changed my mind. I will marry the King of Golud. I will!

KING OF WYDYR: I'll not humiliate myself again, Daughter. You spurned all the kings you ever will. Now get ready. *(He exits.)*

ETAIN: *(to herself)* So be it then! This beggar will be no match for me. I'll have him gone in seconds.

Enter the nurse and the beggar. He is raggedly dressed, with long scraggly hair. He is stooped and dirty.

ETAIN: You're filthy!

BEGGAR: And you are beautiful.

ETAIN: Impertinent![18]

BEGGAR: Arrogant!

ETAIN: How dare you speak to me like that!

BEGGAR: As you dare to speak to me.

ETAIN: You are insufferable![19] I am the Princess of Wydyr. You will address me appropriately!

The King and Queen of Wydyr enter. The Queen carries a handkerchief, but she only dabs her eyes occasionally with it.

KING OF WYDYR: In a few minutes, he will appropriately

---

[18]impertinent—rude; disrespectful; insulting
[19]insufferable—difficult to endure; unbearable

address you as wife. *(to the beggar)* My good man, will you have my daughter to be your wife?

BEGGAR: Sire, I find her most beautiful, more beautiful than the stars. But her tongue is too sharp, and her heart is too high for me. What would I do with such a wife?

KING OF WYDYR: I realize what I am asking of you. But I ask it still.

ETAIN: What you ask of him! What about me? You want to send me out to marry this?

KING OF WYDYR: This is the very man you deserve, but you are too proud to see it. *(to the*

perhaps, but surely she can learn to be a happy woman.

ETAIN: No! I will not marry this . . . this vagabond![20] You cannot make me!

KING OF WYDYR: I can and I will. Send for the priest! *(The Queen weeps into her handkerchief.)*

BEGGAR: Sire, if I may. I think I would like to marry your daughter. But she looks too far above me in station.[21] If she were to wear the clothes of one of your serving maids, it would be better to my liking.

KING OF WYDYR: Well thought, my good man. *(to the nurse)* Bring some of the clothes the kitchen maids have cast away.

ETAIN: *(beginning to cry)* Father, please do not punish me more. If I must be married to this beggar, then let me at least have my lovely dresses to go with me!

KING OF WYDYR: And still your pride speaks. Say no more. We will have a pauper's[22] wedding here tonight. *(to the nurse)* Take her away.

Curtain falls.

beggar)* So will you take her and teach her to be a good wife?

BEGGAR: Why would your lordship want his daughter to marry me?

KING OF WYDYR: A man of your ways could teach her what I cannot. She cannot be a princess,

---

[20]vagabond—a homeless, wandering person
[21]station—social position; rank
[22]pauper—one who is very poor

ACT II

At the Cottage Rigor in Avalon Wood.

Scene 1

Curtain rises on a humble cottage. The beggar and Etain approach the cottage. Etain is in a serving maid's clothes. She carries a bundle.

BEGGAR: So, my new wife, we are home at last. This is Cottage Rigor.

ETAIN: *(obviously worn out with the trip)* What! This is where you expect me to live? I cannot live here! I will not go in there!

BEGGAR: Suit yourself then. Here is a bench by the door to sleep on. Or sleep on the ground if you wish. My dog used to sleep well enough on the ground.

ETAIN: I am the Princess of Wydyr! I will not sleep upon the ground!

BEGGAR: You *were* the Princess of Wydyr. Now you are my wife, and you may sleep where you please.

ETAIN: Where are the servants? Where is my supper? You have kept me walking all this day. My feet are worn out, and my head is aching. I say, where are your servants? They should be in attendance, watching for us.

She drops down upon the ground with her bundle in a temper. Her husband ignores her pouting.

BEGGAR: *(taking up her two hands and holding them in front of her face)* These are your servants. I will help you train them. As for

208

supper—that would be my question to you, Wife. Where is my supper?

ETAIN: *(pulling away and snatching up her bundle)* I am going home! You cannot make me stay here and be a slave to you.

BEGGAR: Go then. Do you remember the way, some twenty winding miles? And it is but an hour until dusk. Mind the beasts tonight. *(He goes inside.)*

ETAIN: You are the only beast I see around here! OOOH! *(She picks up the little bench and throws it at the cottage.)* I'm hungry! Do you hear?

When there is no response, she begins to look for something to eat. She looks in a basket by the door.

What's this? Bread? *(She gives a little scream and drops the loaf.)* Moldy and full of ants!

She looks around the outside of the cottage. She finds some apples.

Ah! Apples! *(picking one up and then dropping it in horror)* Rotten. Spoiled and rotten!

BEGGAR: *(from inside the cottage)* Somewhat like my wife!

ETAIN: Come out here and give me something to eat!

BEGGAR: Come inside and get something to eat.

ETAIN: No!

BEGGAR: Well, if my house and my food are not to your taste, then that is how it is. Good night, sweet wife. I love you well.

ETAIN: In faith, you lie! What love is this to starve your wife and leave her in the cold? *(She rights the bench and sits on it. Then she pulls it up to the cottage so she can lean against the wall. As she tries to get comfortable, the beggar sings his song. She curls up on the bench and falls asleep.)*

BEGGAR: *(looking out the door)* Poor thing. She finally fell asleep. *(He goes out and looks at her.)* My poor and beautiful wife, a warm fire and soft bed could be yours, but you shall have to learn that on your own.

He gets a blanket and puts it over her; then he pulls an awning out over her. As he does these things, he sings the refrain[23] *of the song again. With one last look, he goes inside.*

The lights dim slightly.

Scene 2

When the lights come back up, bird-song sound effects tell that it is a new morning. The beggar comes outside with a basket.

BEGGAR: Good morning, feathered singers. Did you see what a beautiful, spirited wife I have? She sleeps outside like a soldier. But she shall be a sweet wife, too, you wait and see. For there is great gentleness under this stub-

bornness, I know. *(He whistles to himself as he settles beside the bench and takes some bread and cheese from the basket.)*

ETAIN: *(throwing off the blanket)* Where am I? What place is this?

BEGGAR: Hear, little birds? That is my new wife. We must teach her to be happy! *(to Etain)* Why, it is your new home, Wife. How did you sleep?

ETAIN: *(awaking sleepily)* How did I get this blanket? And this shelter? I fell asleep with nothing.

BEGGAR: Someone must have looked after you. Do you have friends roundabout here? I must admit there are many things I do not know about you!

ETAIN: Why did you marry me then?

BEGGAR: So that I would have time to find them out.

ETAIN: What kind of man are you?

BEGGAR: What kind of man? A kind man. The kind of man who sees you for what you are.

ETAIN: Do not insult me.

BEGGAR: I meant it kindly.

ETAIN: How do you live?

BEGGAR: As honorably as I can.

ETAIN: I meant how do you make a living?

BEGGAR: By serving others.

---

[23]refrain—a phrase repeated several times in a poem or song; chorus

ETAIN: You mean by singing?

BEGGAR: No. I sing because I am happy. Would you like some breakfast? *(He offers the basket. She hesitates, then accepts.)*

ETAIN: What service then do you do that provides you a living? If this is what you believe to be a living.

BEGGAR: Whatever is required. After breakfast, I will show you how to gather herbs and berries and how to make a stew that hunters love. These are things you will need to know if you are to live with me.

ETAIN: What makes you think I am staying? *(She starts to take her first bite.)*

BEGGAR: Why would you not? Everything you could want is here before you.

ETAIN: And you called me arrogant!

BEGGAR: So you remember what I say to you. There's a good sign.

ETAIN: *(standing up and throwing down the basket)* Don't look for signs from me. I will never love you.

BEGGAR: Nevertheless, I love you, sweet wife. Have you had enough to eat? One bite a day! You will be an easy wife to keep, I see! Let's get to work then. *(When Etain does not move, he takes her hand and pulls her along. She follows reluctantly.)* Now here is wood to be stacked.

ETAIN: You surely do not expect me to touch that wood, do you?

BEGGAR: If you want to be warm at night and have hot food, I do. But, as I said before, you can stay outside and eat spoiled apples to your heart's content.

ETAIN: What else?

BEGGAR: The cottage needs to be cleaned. And food prepared against the winter. Fall is nearly full upon us.

ETAIN: *(beginning to stack wood)* I never thought I would come to this.

BEGGAR: It is a wonder how one's life is always turning out better than one expects, isn't it? Well, I am off to hunt. A kiss good-bye, sweet wife?

ETAIN: *(rising up with a stick of wood in her hand)* I'll knock you soundly in the head!

BEGGAR: *(laughing)* A block of wood to a block of wood. You'll have kindling yet. *(He exits. She throws down the wood and goes inside. The lights dim.)*

Scene 3

When the lights come up again, Etain can be heard whistling the tune of the beggar's song faintly. Leaves are falling. As Etain comes out of the cottage, sweeping, a well-dressed nobleman comes by with his wife. Etain has on an apron now and a kerchief on her head.

NOBLEMAN: Goodwife! Attend!

ETAIN: Are you talking to me?

NOBLEMAN: Indeed. Is your husband about?

ETAIN: I don't have—no, he is not.

NOBLEMAN: I require assistance.

ETAIN: I am sorry.

NOBLEMAN: Go and get your husband.

ETAIN: Who do you think you are talk—I don't know where he went.

NOBLEMAN: I am lord of this woods. You will do as I say.

ETAIN: *(throwing down her broom)* I have no idea where he is. Send one of your servants.

NOBLEWOMAN: See here, woman. You are one of the servants. Now go as my husband told you.

Just as Etain is about to argue more, the beggar returns from his hunt. He carries a rabbit on a leather strap over his shoulder. He bows.

BEGGAR: Good day, your lordship. Your ladyship. How may I serve you?

NOBLEMAN: I was inquiring[24] of your wife for some assistance. She seems not to understand her place.

BEGGAR: My wife is new to this life, my lord. I beg your indulgence[25] with her. What can a humble man such as myself do for you?

NOBLEMAN: Our carriage has lost a wheel. My servants have stayed with the carriage and its con-

---

[24]inquiring—asking
[25]indulgence—tolerance; generosity
[26]oblivious—inattentive; unaware

tents. Until it is repaired, my wife needs a place to rest.

BEGGAR: Our honor, your lordship. Please, what would you? What can we offer you?

NOBLEMAN: That bench there.

Since Etain is nearest the bench, all eyes turn on her. She seems oblivious[26] at first, and then she realizes she is expected to get the bench. She ungraciously hauls it forward. The noblewoman sits down and arranges her great skirts.

BEGGAR: If I may ask, your lordship, how you are come this way into Avalon?

NOBLEMAN: His Royal Highness, the King of Golud, is to be married in a fortnight. I am at His Majesty's service.

ETAIN: Ah!

The others look at her, somewhat surprised and curious.

NOBLEWOMAN: And what is this sound, goodwife?

ETAIN: That might have been my wedding.

The nobleman and noblewoman burst into laughter.

BEGGAR: Your Worships. It is true. My wife was once a princess.

NOBLEMAN: *(still laughing)* Wife, we have stumbled into a house of crazy people! Perhaps we should keep walking.

BEGGAR: Please, Your Graces, if you will. Look at my wife. Could any but a princess be so beautiful?

NOBLEWOMAN: You are a most generous man, to think and speak so well of your wife. Perhaps, my husband, this man is not crazy—just beset by love. *(The nobility laugh again.)*

ETAIN: He may be many things, but he is not crazy.

BEGGAR: Why, Etain, thank you. This is a good sign!

ETAIN: *(tearing off her apron and kerchief and throwing them at the beggar)* I told you not to look for signs from me! You rude, rough no-account! I will not love you!

NOBLEMAN: Your wife is shrill and shabby for a princess, goodman. How do you stand it? I will tell you how you may have a little peace, if you like.

BEGGAR: Your grace need not bother about me. I am a happy man now. And I will yet be happy.

NOBLEWOMAN: Hear that, you shrew?[27] This is possibly the only man in the world who could love you, with that disposition[28] of yours!

NOBLEMAN: Hear me, goodman. The Castle Golud is in great preparation for the next two weeks. Many more serving women are needed in the kitchens. Lend your wife to us for the duration,[29] and I promise to return her to you with her temper mended.

ETAIN: No! I will not be sold a second time into slavery! This is bad enough.

BEGGAR: Perhaps it would make her more appreciative of me to be away from me.

NOBLEWOMAN: I should hope something would!

BEGGAR: I accept your worship's favor with thanks.

A coachman enters at a trot. He stops and bows before the nobility.

COACHMAN: Your coach is repaired, my lord, and waits upon your pleasure.

NOBLEMAN: Then we will be going. Come, my dear. And you, goodwife—follow us.

ETAIN: I will not!

NOBLEMAN: Coachman, bring that woman.

The coachman takes her by the arm.

ETAIN: Take your hand off me! Husband, what say you?

BEGGAR: *(after a moment's pause)* Take her away.

Curtain falls.

---

[27]shrew—an ill-tempered woman
[28]disposition—a person's usual mood
[29]duration—length of time

ACT III

In the beautiful Castle Golud near the mountains.

Scene I

The curtain rises on the great hall of Castle Golud. Etain, more ragged than ever, is polishing silver. Her overseer, Branwen the cook, is dusting the table.

BRANWEN: Day after tomorrow, it will be. So much we have done. And so much still to do. I doubt we will see our beds again twixt now and then!

ETAIN: I never knew how much work royalty[30] caused.

BRANWEN: Well, and how would you, child? But 'tis no trouble to serve King Gwydion of Golud. No finer man 'midst peasants or princes breathes this earth's air.

---

[30]royalty—kings, queens, and other members of a royal family

The Proud-Minded Princess 215

ETAIN: I met him once.

BRANWEN: Oh, and sure you did. Met him at your palace, no doubt?

ETAIN: Yes.

BRANWEN: His lordship who brought you here told us you were a bit touched in the head. But since you've naught said but three words since you came, I had no way of judging.

ETAIN: I'm not crazy.

BRANWEN: I don't think so myself. You're just a dreamer, as they say. No harm in that.

A serving girl enters with a platter of pastries.

SERVING GIRL: Branwen, are these passable for the nobles' tables?

BRANWEN: They look even and light. I will come by and by and taste one. Every dish must be exactly to the king's taste, or we'll not be putting it out to anyone. On the king's wedding day even the stablehands will eat like royalty!

ETAIN: Does everyone love this king so?

BRANWEN: Anyone who knows aught[31] of him at all. How can we help it? He is wise and kind and good.

SERVING GIRL: And handsome.

BRANWEN: Be off with you! Speaking of the king that way! Though it be true enough, it's not for us to be saying. (*She swats, laughing, at the parting girl.*)

ETAIN: Who is he marrying?

BRANWEN: We none of us have heard. But surely she is some wise and beautiful and kind someone herself. She would have to be—for the king of this land has never done an unwise thing in all his reign.[32]

ETAIN: I hope she realizes what she has.

BRANWEN: Well, and who would not!

ETAIN: Me.

BRANWEN: What?

ETAIN: I had happiness within my reach twice, and twice I let it slip.

BRANWEN: Meaning what, my dear?

ETAIN: A rich man asked me to marry him, and I refused for stubbornness. And then a poor man married me for love, and I refused to love him back for pride. He used to sing to me.

BRANWEN: And what was it made you think you had a right to be so proud as to lose two good men as that?

---

[31]aught—anything
[32]reign—the period of time that a monarch rules

ETAIN: I cannot even think now what I was thinking. I wanted to make my own choice. Now I see the choice I had in my power was to be happy or not to be happy.

A serving girl enters again.

SERVING GIRL: Branwen, the pudding kettles are starting to bubble.

BRANWEN: I'm coming. Etain, can you not get the poor man back? Perhaps he still would sing to you.

ETAIN: Perhaps.

BRANWEN: When you finish with the silver, trim all the candles to exactly the same height as the goblets.

Branwen exits; Etain continues to work, but she cries as she works. Presently, King Gwydion appears in the hall.

KING OF GOLUD: Serving woman, a word with you.

ETAIN: *(Recognizing him, she drops into a curtsy and stays there.)* Yes, my lord.

KING OF GOLUD: You have not been here long, I take it? Since I have not seen you in here before?

ETAIN: No, my lord. Not quite a fortnight.

KING OF GOLUD: I do not know how you were trained, but in my house it is permissible to stand and look at me when I speak to you. What is your name?

ETAIN: *(standing and looking up shyly)* Your pardon, my lord. I am Etain.

KING OF GOLUD: Now tell me why it is that one of my servants is crying when all the rest of the house is full of laughing and joy?

ETAIN: I—I miss my husband.

KING OF GOLUD: Indeed! Well, we shall send for him! Where is he?

ETAIN: In the Woods of Avalon, in a cottage near the lake. But please make no effort on my account.[33]

KING OF GOLUD: It is no effort. He shall be sent for and then you shall be happy. I want no single cloud on my wedding day.

ETAIN: Your Majesty is most kind. I promise not to rain on your joy any more.

The king goes out, and Etain goes back to work with more energy. She exits carrying candles, humming the beggar's tune. The lights dim.

---

[33]"on my account"—for me; because of me

Scene 2

The lights come back up on the hall. Etain and Branwen come in, followed by serving girls carrying trays of candlesticks and candles. They arrange the table as they talk.

BRANWEN: Oh, time is so short now! Girls, we must be out of here by dusk with everything in place.

ETAIN: Has anyone seen the bride yet?

BRANWEN: No, nor heard of her coming either.

SERVING GIRL: Will we get a glimpse of her, do you think?

BRANWEN: You all have worked so hard and well, I think I can get you into nooks here and there to have a peep at all the glory!

The serving girls giggle and whisper to each other.

BRANWEN: Yes, girls, I am sure she is the finest flower in all of Ireland. Now see to the work at hand. There's time enough for speculating later.

A stableboy enters.

BOY: Branwen, I have a message from my master.

BRANWEN: Out with it then.

BOY: He has had no word of the Princess's arrival and wants not to leave the gates. He asks that food be sent to him and the outriders[34] who have sat mounted and waiting since morning.

BRANWEN: Done. Girls, go take baskets of bread and meat to the gates. But come straight back! This is no day for dawdling!

ETAIN: If only kings and princes knew how their every move affects so many. All morning men have sat on horseback waiting for the princess. Now others must carry food to them.

BRANWEN: And no trouble it is to them, so the king asks it. She will be their queen, and for the love of their king, they serve her too. *(Suddenly Branwen claps her hands twice and calls loudly.)* Time it is now! Lay the tables!

Serving girls enter with dishes and silver goblets and linen napkins. They work like a precision[35] team and have the table laid perfectly in quick time. Branwen sings an Irish song as they work. When the work is done, they all cheer and go into the kitchen, including Etain, who is beginning to get into the spirit of things. Lights dim.

---

[34]outriders—riders who go before
[35]precision—exact; accurate

Scene 3

The lights come back full. The princes and nobles begin to come in, dressed in their finest clothes. There is light music from somewhere. Soon the king himself enters, resplendent[36] in his regalia.[37] He walks among the nobles, smiling and greeting them. The men bow, and the women curtsy to him. Branwen, in better clothes now, enters with serving girls carry-ing platters of food. They put the platters on the tables and then curtsy to the king.

KING OF GOLUD: Lords, ladies, friends of the court of Golud, I welcome you here tonight! I want to share my joy with you. Let us sit to eat!

The nobles and ladies take their places at the table. The king takes the center chair, leaving the one to his left empty.

---

[36]resplendent—splendid; brilliant
[37]regalia—the emblems and symbols of royalty; fancy clothing

KING OF GOLUD: I know you want to know when the lady, the love of my life, will be here. Soon, I promise. And when you see her, you will know why I chose her. We will have no need for the stars and the moon once she is here!

Everyone cheers and wishes the king all happiness with his bride.

KING OF GOLUD: But, as you who know me well will understand, I must have everyone in

the house happy today, so there be not one dark cloud over this event. So if you will indulge me one moment, I must attend to a matter with Branwen.

Branwen steps forward from her station near the door of the kitchen.

BRANWEN: *(in a deep curtsy)* My good lord, my king, what is amiss at your table?

KING OF GOLUD: Branwen, please, rise. The tables are more splendid and generous than a hundred kings could want. It is with Etain that I must speak. Please send her in.

Branwen curtsies again and goes out.

KING OF GOLUD: You see, my lords, and ladies, it seems that one of my serving women misses her husband. And we cannot have such sorrow if we can help it. Ah, here she comes.

Etain, obviously terribly embarrassed by her ragged condition, comes just inside the hall and drops into a full curtsy.

KING OF GOLUD: Etain, I tried my best to find your husband. I sent riders to the cottage you described. But they found the cottage empty and all the wood around. I'm sorry, but I failed my promise to you. Can you yet find it in your heart to be happy this one night for my sake anyway?

ETAIN: Your Grace, I am so undeserving of your notice, I can hardly speak. Of course, I will be happy for you. I am happy for you. And for the lady so honored to be your wife.

KING OF GOLUD: You say then that to be my wife would be an honor?

ETAIN: *(still not looking up)* Of course, Your Majesty. The honor of her life.

KING OF GOLUD: Was your marriage the honor of your life?

ETAIN: It was, Your Grace, but I was too proud to see it.

KING OF GOLUD: Then you wish me to seek your husband still? And if I find him, bring him here?

ETAIN: If it so please Your Majesty, it would so please me.

KING OF GOLUD: This is a good sign, Etain. Musicians, the music I asked for.

Music swells. The king sings the beggar's song. As he finishes the first line, Etain looks up. He leaves the table singing and takes her by the hand and finishes the song.

ETAIN: You! It was you all along!

KING OF GOLUD: It is I, Etain. The riders could not find your husband for he it was who sent them. Lords and ladies, I introduce to you my bride, Etain of Castle Wydyr.

The nobles and noblewomen rise from their chairs and curtsy and bow. As they do, the King and Queen of Wydyr enter, followed by the nurse.

KING OF GOLUD: And her parents, their majesties the King and Queen of Wydyr, by whose devices[38] I got this beautiful woman to marry me.

Etain hugs them both and the nurse.

KING OF GOLUD: Attend, Branwen. The feast will begin in earnest now that all is happiness as far as I can reach. Etain, your nurse has brought wedding finery for you. I bid you go and put it on.

Etain runs to him and kisses him.

KING OF GOLUD: My friends, this is a good sign! *(Everyone laughs.)* King of Wydyr, and your queen, please take your honored places at my table. *(taking Etain's hand and putting it in the nurse's)* Nurse, take her away. *(Etain and the nurse turn to go out.)* But—*(they turn back)* bring her right back!

The king picks up the refrain for his song, and all join in as the curtain falls.

---

[38]devices—plans, schemes, or tricks

Setting

Morgan Reed Persun

Of Time and Place

One of the most important jobs of a storywriter is to make it seem as if his story really happened, to draw the reader into believing—for the little while he is reading—that he is participating in a real event. How do fiction writers do that?

The answer is *detail*. Writers who give specific descriptions of place and time in their stories help the reader see and experience what the characters experience.

Sometimes only a little detail is needed to bring the reader in. "The Secret Pitch" sets the time and place by simply telling us that "it was a cool day for August" and the game is baseball. The writer assumes that everyone will fill in for himself, from his own experience, the appearance of a ball field.

Even the lighthearted poem, "Stickball," has telling details of place: "In the city"; "From fender to hood / To stoop." How different the poem of the city ball game would be without those details.

Other writers spend a great deal of time making the geography, the weather, the times of day and year, the architectural designs, and so on, clear. In "A Ride to Honor" the description of the places and the time of year get as much attention as the action and the characters.

Setting as Part of the Whole

Details of time and place are the *setting* of a story. It takes in all the geography of a story, whether it is a ball field in a short story or all the places mentioned in a whole novel. It also encompasses[1] all the time of the story. Short fiction generally takes place in a short time. "The Secret Pitch" is set for the most part on one afternoon. There are a few references to times past, but only as a way to introduce Sissy and the speaker. "A Ride to Honor" covers about two weeks. Novels usually cover much longer or more varied times.

---

[1]encompasses—includes

Setting influences both plot and character. All three function together. For example, in "A Ride to Honor," Innera doesn't at first want to make the journey in the winter. The setting has an impact on Innera—it tests her character. It also has an effect on the plot—how different would this story have been set in the lush summertime? It is almost a character itself, providing the main opponent to Innera's goal. Such developed settings are called *integral*[2] *settings.*

When setting is only briefly described and mainly just there to orient the reader (as in "The Secret Pitch"), it is called a *backdrop setting.* Would you call the setting in "Stickball" an integral or a backdrop setting?

Setting as Symbol

Often in fiction, writers use settings to underline a theme or represent an idea. A place can stand for something besides itself—it becomes a *symbol.* In "A Ride to

[2]integral—essential

Honor," the round meadow is a symbol of fidelity, of faithfulness to duty and purpose. The cold represents opposition to doing one's duty. The Windermere Sea represents a test of faith. Innera must cross with the watchman, not knowing exactly where she is or what the second meaning of her riddle is.

However it is used in a story, setting must make the reader feel at home in the made-up world—or at least feel comfortable. If he can't get his bearings, he will not be able to follow the plot or care about the character. But if he has enough details of time and place to be convinced to "live" in the fictional world awhile, then the writer has done his job, and the reader is in for a very good ride indeed.

VENTURES

3

Jeri Massi

illustrated by Del Thompson
and John Bjerk

ANTARCTICA

ARCTIC EXPEDITION

Drew Thompson stood against the rail of the *Gloria,* unconscious of the wooden bar digging into his stomach, his binoculars fixed on the iced landscape. Clear, subzero air stirred the frosted bits of hair sticking out from under the rim of his knit cap. He had made the best adjustments possible on the focus of the binoculars while down in the cabin. Out on deck his heavily gloved hands were too clumsy to work the dials.

The diesel craft moved with its own choppy rhythm through the narrow channel of open water. Days before, a navy icebreaker had come through, splitting the narrow channel in McMurdo Sound so that the summer supply ships could get through. But Uncle Jim's neat little *Gloria* could have managed her way unaided down to Ross Sea from the U.S. station McMurdo. She had already banged through icy water a few weeks ago when coming into the Sound, and the ice chunks had not even slowed her speed of twelve knots.

His observations were interrupted by a slam of the door against the bulkhead behind him. It was Derrick, up for a breath of air. "Alaska was prettier," Derrick said, coming up alongside his twin brother. "Maybe not prettier, but more alive, somehow."

Drew nodded briefly. It was too cold to talk much. The temperature had read 25 degrees Fahrenheit when they had left the station fifteen hours earlier, in a morning that had known no dawn, following a night that had known no darkness. But out on the water the cold was deeper and more penetrating. Right around zero, he guessed. This was Antarctic summer. In winter the temperature might go down to a hundred below.

Sunlight poured like a host of stagelights around them, reflecting off the ice and the thin slits of water. The two boys gave easily with the rocking deck, accustomed to the rolling of the sturdy little icebreaker. Already, both of them had accompanied their uncle on expeditions[1] to Alaska and the North Pole.

After getting a little fresh air and inspecting the ice shelf that was the only shore, Derrick went below. Months of isolation[2] on the expeditions had taught the teenager a painstaking craftsmanship. In the cabin that he and Drew shared, he was patiently chipping away at a wood carving of a moose that Drew had photographed in Alaska. The photograph hung on the bookrack where they kept their Bibles, maps, and travel brochures. Every now and then, Derrick would squint at the photograph and then return to his patient chipping and carving.

Meanwhile, Drew stayed topside, breathing in the thin, chill air and watching the landscape. People said Antarctica was dead—hostile.[3] Maybe, Drew told himself. It wasn't friendly to man, but it wasn't unfriendly. A man had to come to terms with the cold weather and shifting spells of daylight and darkness. But the land was anything but dead.

Along the Ross Ice Shelf, he spotted seals sunning themselves. His fingers itched for his camera, which was down in the cabin with Derrick. But he resisted the urge to get it. The seals were far away, and he had plenty of group pictures of seals picked up on the other trips. He had only three rolls of film in his luggage to use up. One photograph had to be good enough to win the national photography contest he was entering.

[1]expeditions—long trips, usually for exploring or studying something
[2]isolation—the condition of being separated from others
[3]hostile—unfriendly or unfavorable to health or well-being

A gloved fist banged on a portal[4] behind Drew. That would be Uncle Jim, giving the signal for mess. In twenty-four-hour daylight, they no longer called their meals anything else but mess. If Drew or Derrick felt like eating instant pancakes, Uncle Jim whipped them up, but if they felt more like having something from the dehydrated[5] packs or the canned foods, he was just as obliging. Once they had enjoyed five straight meals of chili. They had been working up on deck and on the wharves,[6] loading up the *Gloria* for travel, and they had all agreed that the canned chili was the most warming of all their food and the least obnoxious to the taste-buds. Eating out of cans had taken some getting used to.

"What is it today?" Drew asked as he swung himself down into the narrow galley that Uncle Jim kept shipshape.

Derrick had already squeezed to the back of the little table that they shared for their meals. The galley was cramped—Bunsen burners right by the table, and the few cupboards packed to bursting with canned foods. Still wearing most of their woolen outerwear and rubber jump-suits, they huddled to eat around the cramped table.

"Potatoes!" Uncle Jim exclaimed. "Fried 'em myself!"

[4]portal—doorway
[5]dehydrated—having water taken from it for preservation
[6]wharves—landing places or piers at which ships may tie up and load or unload

230

Drew wrinkled his nose, expecting the reconstituted,[7] dehydrated stuff that passed for potatoes aboard ship; then he gasped when his uncle slid a plate of the real thing in front of him.

"Told you they were fried potatoes," Uncle Jim said.

"Where'd we get these?"

Derrick grinned, and Uncle Jim said, "That brother of yours picked 'em up somehow when we were back at McMurdo. Don't ask me how."

Drew looked at Derrick, who shrugged with his slow, easy shrug. "Got to talking with one of the cooks out there," he said simply. "Told the guy how much we like French fries, and here they are. I was saving them for a celebration when you get that award-winning picture—"

"Only I talked him out of three or four of the little ones," Uncle Jim interrupted. "Sort of a pre-celebration."

Uncle Jim prayed over the meal. Afterward they ate in silence, wolfing down tinned beef and sardines with the fried potatoes. Happily, there were no women to tell them how to behave.

Of course, not having Mom nearby didn't stop them from attending to important things. One thing that these wilderness excursions[8] had taught Drew was to accept responsibility even when nobody was there to tell him what to do. If he didn't spend time alone with the Lord while on a wilderness trek,[9] Uncle Jim might not realize it as quickly as Mom would have. Nobody would be there to tell him to read his Bible. On the first excursion to Alaska he had given in to temptations to spend all his time studying the land and the new people.

But then he had realized that nobody could have ever *made* him be a Christian anyway—not on the inside. It was a decision between him and God. Realizing that had made him realize what he was giving up by ignoring his Bible and prayers. Though he was thankful for a godly mother and for Uncle Jim, now he understood that nobody else could have a relationship with the Lord *for* him. For some reason, knowing that he was expected to commune[10] with God on his own had made God seem nearer. And, really, there was no better place to be alone with the Lord than in the great snowy regions of the earth, where the very bigness and wildness of everything showed a man how he depended on God.

Since Derrick had provided the potatoes, Drew offered to do the simple cleaning up that followed. He had finished and was snooping through the cans looking for chili for

---

[7]reconstituted—put back in its original form by adding water
[8]excursions—short trips; outings
[9]trek—a difficult trip
[10]commune—to talk closely with, have a relationship with

the next mess, when the report of a rifle brought him out of the cupboard, tense and ready.

"Come up, Drew; come up!" Uncle Jim called from topside. Drew swung himself up through the galley. The chilly breeze slapped his face, and he buttoned his wool shirt and zipped up the rest of his rubber jumpsuit as he came out on deck.

"There's a stranded party on the shelf," Uncle Jim said as Drew came out. His uncle nodded across the widening expanse of water. A summer thaw and several icebreakers had loosened up this part of the widening sea, releasing the frozen water from its bonds. In the distance, a fire burned on the shore. Drew couldn't make out any other shape in the water that would give evidence of a damaged or sinking boat.

Uncle Jim took Drew's binoculars. "Now why would they be out in these waters with no pickup?" he asked himself, squinting through the binoculars. "Wonder if they were after something. They've got a toboggan[11] with them—no, two. Hmm. Well, we can't leave 'em there. Make ready to go in and get them. Tell Derrick to get my cabin ready for visitors. I'll bunk with you two."

Drew obeyed. A rescue would mean heading back up the Sound to the base, postponing the trip to Cape Crozier and Uncle Jim's study of the Adélie penguins. It would also post-pone Drew's chances of a good picture for the contest. But that didn't matter. There would still be time to get the pictures and then get to a base in time to send the pictures in.

The *Gloria* swung round and came in toward land, chugging sturdily as great bits of ice crashed off her bow. A group of seals farther up the shelf flipped into the water at the sight and sound of the smoking and belching monster, her bright red mast and stacks looking somehow rusty against the dazzling pure whiteness of the Antarctic snow and sunshine.

Derrick came up from below. He didn't resent the fact that Uncle Jim always automatically chose Drew for important jobs like rescue and handling the most delicate photographic and scientific equipment. In a crisis Drew thought fast and moved fast. Derrick was slower and more deliberate[12] in everything he did.

At the moment, while Drew made ready to lower the small dory for rescue, Derrick helped him at the ropes between snatching glimpses of the party on the ice shelf.

As the ship came within hailing distance of the party, Uncle Jim leaned out to halloo them and wave.

"I'll watch the *Gloria,* Uncle," Derrick offered.

---

[11]toboggan—a long, narrow sled without runners, made of thin boards curved up at the front
[12]deliberate—not hurried or quick; careful; cautious

Their uncle gave a brief nod and waved to the group of four men standing on the ice shelf before a roaring fire. Derrick disappeared down below.

"Now where'd he go?" Uncle Jim asked, irritated. "Oh well, we'll manage it. That boy's a dreamer. Come on, Drew." They lowered the dory and clambered down the ladder, easily dropping into the rowboat as the swells brought both ship and small boat together.

After a stretch of a hundred yards or so, they landed on the shelf and were helped ashore by the sorriest-looking bunch Drew had ever seen.

"I'm Tyce," one thin and wind-burned man said, his breath coming out sour from between his unshaven lips. "How many be on your ship, and where you headed to, friend?"

"Private science expedition," Uncle Jim told him. "Just come down from McMurdo to take a look at some penguins farther out. There are three of us for this short stint,[13] but my boat there will hold all of us. Come aboard."

One of the men had stood with his back to the rescuers, and when he turned around there was a long, smooth rifle in his hand that he swung smoothly in Uncle Jim's direction, stopping it at chest level.

"Ah, no," Tyce said to Uncle Jim. "We ain't going up to the base, I'm afraid. Nor are you, man, nor are you."

---

[13]stint—a certain period of work

POTATOES AND PIPES

Drew's first thought was for his twin, and he glanced at the ship in time to see Derrick's figure disappear again below decks. For one breathless instant the man held the gun on Uncle Jim, but at last Drew realized he wasn't going to fire.

"We're going to load up our goods and tents and go," the man

named Tyce said. "But we'll trade you the rest of our camp for your boat—as fair a deal as I can offer you, man. These here fuel cans we been burning, our toboggans, air mattresses, and some food."

"At least give us the tents. You know we'll die of exposure[14] without cover," Uncle Jim cut in. "There are no boats due here for weeks!"

"It's the Antarctic, mate," Tyce said. "A hard cruel place, and every man takes his chance here."

Uncle Jim started forward angrily, but the man with the rifle brought it up instantly.

"Why maroon[15] us?" Drew asked.

"Ah, that's our business—" But Drew's eye had fallen on the canvas-covered bales stacked behind the other two men.

"You've been poaching[16] seal," he said quickly. Uncle Jim's hand restrained him.

"You're a smart kid, but you talk too fast," Tyce said. "Hey, you two, load the stuff. Let's leave these men to their haven."

"My other nephew—" Uncle Jim began. "Don't hurt him!

"Oh, no, I'm not so rough a man. We'll be glad to deliver him to your

[14]exposure—the condition of being subjected to harsh weather
[15]maroon—to leave a person helpless and alone on a deserted shore or island
[16]poaching—hunting illegally

He was a small man, and weeks on the ice had weakened him. He dropped his gun in the face of the last blast, shielding himself from flying bits of ice, and Derrick gave the revolver a kick into the water. "That's enough!" a loud voice barked. It was Uncle Jim, holding the .30-06 rifle. Derrick rolled clear. Drew kept Tyce pinned.

Uncle Jim pointed it at the dory. "Bring it back, boys; you can't travel fast enough to outdistance this." So the two men rowed back.

Once they were landed, he rounded them up into a circle and sent Derrick to bring back their tents, bales of skins, and some food.

"There," he said when Derrick had brought the goods. "You can stay here snug as you please for another night. We'll give you your tents and camp gear back and call our friends up at McMurdo to give you all a ride home. Come on, boys."

"Wait a second," Derrick said, pulling a knobby leather packet out of his rubber jumpsuit. "I brought Drew's camera so he can win that contest." He picked up the discarded cannon and handed it to Drew. "There, sling it on your shoulder like the big-game hunter. That's right. Here, set the timer so you can say you took the picture."

Drew set the timer so that the picture could qualify as his own. While Derrick held the camera on his hands like a tripod, Drew stood in front of Tyce and his men with the cannon over one shoulder and gave a grin. The four poachers glowered[26] in the background.

"Now that that's over, could we please go back to the *Gloria*?" Uncle Jim asked.

"Sure," Derrick said. They retreated carefully, then boarded the dory, taking both the rifle and the remaining cannon with them. When Drew reached up to scratch his face, he realized he was bleeding.

"From the cannon exploding," Derrick explained. "I got out of the way in time."

"Could have been a lot worse," Drew observed.

"You *could* have lost your eyes," Uncle Jim said gloomily. "Anybody that would use that crazy contraption—well, at least it's over, and no one's hurt. I will say that I've never seen surprise like those poachers showed when you let loose. They thought for sure you had a gun up there, and they must have figured you had buckshot, too, when that spray of ice hit them. Not enough 'oomph' behind it to do any more than scratch, though." He looked approvingly at Derrick. By his uncle's expression, Drew could see that Uncle Jim was revising his opinion of the quieter, more deliberate boy. There was plenty to be said for careful planning.

Derrick didn't seem to notice his uncle's expression as they tied up at the *Gloria*. "Now to clean those pipes," he said. "Then to find the penguins. Then the base, so we can send off the award-winning picture."

"Any potatoes left?" Uncle Jim asked hopefully.

"Three big ones."

"Let's celebrate early," Drew suggested.

"Sounds good to me."

Uncle Jim glanced at his watch. "Hey! Six A.M.! Good morning, everybody!"

Derrick laughed as he swung off the ladder. "Time for a new day."

"You can say that again," Uncle Jim agreed as they went below.

[26]glowered—stared sullenly or angrily

SUNRISE

Emily Dickinson

I'll tell you how the Sun rose –
A Ribbon at a time –
The Steeples swam in Amethyst[1] –
The news, like Squirrels, ran –
The Hills untied their Bonnets –
The Bobolinks[2] – begun –
Then I said softly to myself –
"That must have been the Sun!"

---

[1]amethyst—the shade of a purple or violet form of
 quartz used as a gemstone
[2]bobolink—an American songbird with black, white, and
 tan feathers

Weaver of Light

Louise D. Nicholas
illustrated by Preston Gravely

Day arrives, and weaves
Her early purple threads
With lavender, then leaves
Her loom for golds and reds.
She picks up thistle blue
At noon, and amber-white,
'Til somewhat after two,
To blend with coming night,
She draws magenta yarns
Of light across our hay,
And lastly past our barns
Twines indigo with gray.

Ornan the Jebusite

Becky Davis

illustrated by Del Thompson and John Bjerk

This story is a fictional account based on I Chronicles 21. It is told as Ornan might recount the events, giving details to help you feel as if you were there when the biblical event actually occurred.

The Unseen God

The sun had not even risen to its peak yet, but Ornan wiped beads of sweat off his brow and ran his hand impatiently through his thick, curly hair. He snapped the whip again and yelled at the oxen to move faster in their tedious[1] work of pulling the thresher.

Jeconiah, who was winnowing[2] the grain, looked up. "Father! Someone is approaching. It looks like the man of God."

Ornan's dark, heavy eyebrows squinted together as he strained to see the man trudging up the hill. "Yes, it is, Jeconiah," Ornan said. "It is the prophet Gad. And we must show him hospitality. A blessed relief from the heat!" He laughed wearily. By late afternoon or evening, when they would most likely be able to return to their work, the sun would have lost much of its anger.

Ornan ran to offer his arm to the elderly prophet. Such a visit was not unheard-of in Jerusalem, but Ornan had never been blessed by one, nor had he ever expected to be. He was not an Israelite. "What brings you here, O man of God?" he asked.

The prophet's voice was strong, though his face was lined with age. "I have come out of a special curiosity—to hear the story of the foreigner who lives with such abundance among our people. I pray you, tell me how it came to be that you, a Jebusite, still live here in the city that was taken from your people so many years ago."

"I would be honored to, my lord." Ornan bowed his head in reverence. "But first, come into the house, I pray you, out of the heat of the day. Come, and my wife will fix you some meat."

Ornan and Gad entered the little house where a small, pretty woman busied herself with her spinning. As soon as her husband let her know that this was the man of God, she hurried to prepare a feast. Her eyes did not focus on her work, but her deft[3] hands moved unerringly.

---

[1]tedious—long and tiring
[2]winnowing—separating the grain from the chaff
[3]deft—quick and skillful

Ornan brought oil to anoint the prophet's head. He quickly removed Gad's sandals and washed his feet with water. "Your God has blessed me in allowing me to live as a free man here in the city of my birth," he said with a wry smile, "but He has not blessed me with servants. With a capable wife, though, and four strong sons, I should not complain."

"You have promised to tell me how this came to be," Gad gently reminded him. "There are many Jebusite women in Jerusalem, I regret to say, but I believe you are the only man of that clan who has been allowed to remain."

"And this was not by chance. My story is an interesting one—my wife and sons have heard it many times. But I think they would not be loath[4] to hear it again." And while the family ate, Ornan talked.

"When I was a child, the Israelites had conquered almost all the land in Canaan. Stories about their greatness—even about their killing giants of the Philistines—I had heard many of these. In my great city of Jerusalem I had even heard stories of a neighboring city, Jericho, that once had belonged to Canaanites. But by then, supposedly because of the strength of their God, Jericho belonged to the Hebrews.

"No one in the fortress of Jerusalem even bothered to worry about the Israelites. For three hun-

dred years, ever since the great Joshua had conquered all the surrounding land and Jericho had fallen, still no one had conquered the walled land we called Jerusalem. Even though they lived all around Jerusalem, they were afraid to try to take it. Of course they wanted it—it would have made a perfect capital, since it was right in the middle of their land, up on a hill, surrounded with strong walls. But it was those strong walls that made even the greatest king afraid to try to take it. It was an impregnable[5] fortress. I have heard that the very sight of the walls made the Israelites quake with fear.

"I had lived my whole life inside those strong walls, with my father, my mother, my grandmother . . . and my uncle. My father and mother were quiet people. They worshiped the gods faithfully, but not boisterously[6] and boastingly as my uncle did. More and more I found that it was my uncle I turned to and modeled my life after.

"My uncle was wicked and vile in all his doings. He spat out the names of the very gods he professed to worship and laughed uproariously as he did so. He engaged in wickedness of all types and encouraged me to do the same. He told me stories

---

[4]loath—unwilling
[5]impregnable—unable to be broken into
[6]boisterously—loudly; noisily

244

that were so horrible that they made my hair stand on end. But I always asked for more.

"Of course my uncle scoffed at the Israelite God. 'Some god, a god they cannot even see,' he would sneer. And he would put on a funny face and imitate them: 'Oh, our God is greater than even gods of gold or silver.' Then he would say, 'I tell you, I could make a greater god than theirs out of the ashes of wood that are left after I have cooked my supper.' And he would spit into the fire.

"He hated their God, and he hated them, mostly because they claimed to be holy and said that they would not participate in any of the wicked things that our people did. They said that there was only one God, and He was the only one they should serve. But there were stories that many of the Israelites were starting to worship our idols of wood and clay even as they went through the motions of worshiping Jehovah. This made my uncle despise them even more.

"My parents had taught me to fear every god to keep from offending any god, so I feared the Israelite God too. But I worshiped my uncle at least as much as I worshiped any of the stone gods that sat in the place of prominence[7] in our home. He bravely stood in defiance of everything anyone held sacred, and I wanted to do the same. I wanted to be able to spit into the fire.

[7]prominence—importance

"Now, as you know, it came about that David, who had been the king of Judah, reigning in Hebron, found that the people wanted him to be king of all of Israel and Judah. I remember distinctly that it was when I was twelve years old that he decided that Jerusalem was the city he wanted as his capital.

"He came against our city with a whole host of Israelites. With them around him, he yelled up to us, 'Listen to my words, O ye Jebusites. This city shall be the Lord's to glorify Him. For who are these uncircumcised Canaanites? They are a people who hate the Lord and who hate all that is right.'

"But the ruler of the Jebusites himself leaned over the huge wall and scorned him. 'You think your God can protect you?' he yelled. 'You will never come in here! The blind and the lame can protect this city!' And for proof, he placed some blind and lame people along the wall. How well I remember—my grandmother was one of them. My uncle wanted to fight the Israelites and kill as many of them as he possibly could, but the king felt confident that if we just stayed inside our fortress, they would soon grow weary and leave. There they were, encamped on a hill that I could see from the wall. I watched them often, wondering if they were praying to that strange, invisible God of theirs. In truth, I felt some fear in my heart, for I wondered if they would march around the walls until they came crashing down at their feet, as their ancestors supposedly had done to Jericho. I felt some fear, but mostly I felt hatred for a people and a God who wanted to upset my way of life.

"My mother and father, the pragmatic[8] souls who wanted to worship every god to keep from offending any god—something

---

[8]pragmatic—interested only in the desired result of an action rather than in the correctness of the action

happened to them after they heard David speak. They acted different. My uncle said it was just fear and that they would get over it soon. How well I remember his words of encouragement: 'This God cannot conquer the mighty Jerusalem! What god could possibly be stronger than our great city?' And I agreed. Of course I agreed, for I agreed with everything my uncle said.

"But they *were* afraid. For they knew that this man David was different from the king who had gone before him. This man had slain mighty Philistines, even a giant! He had a power that other men did not have. So that very night, when most of the people in the city were comfortably asleep in their beds without a care, my father and mother paid the watchman to let them sneak out of the huge city gates to the camp of the Israelites. They took me with them, even though I fought to stay in Jerusalem with my uncle. My father was a strong man, and for some reason, they cared enough about me to make me leave. Thus they saved my life.

" 'Who are these approaching?' an Israelite guard hissed as we trudged up the hill to the camp. 'You are spies!'

" 'Nay, we are not spies,' my father said, 'but only a family who begs for mercy from the same God who showed mercy to Rahab the harlot in the city of Jericho.' The guard narrowed his eyes suspiciously, but it must have been the mention of Rahab that made him allow us to enter camp. He awakened one of the other soldiers to stand guard over us until the dawn.

"My parents got little enough sleep that night, I know, and I had no desire to sleep either. I stared at the horizon, at my beloved city. My twelve-year-old mind was logical enough to know that I would probably never be allowed to live there as a free citizen again. If the Israelites were defeated, as surely they would be, both my parents and I would be killed as traitors. And if the Israelites somehow conquered the city, as they seemed to be so determined to do, we would surely be slaves for the rest of our days. That was a chance my parents were willing to take. And I was furious with them for doing it. I couldn't imagine living the rest of my life as a slave for a people that I hated. My uncle's words rang in my ears—I knew how he would scoff at us for leaving. But surely he knew how little I wished to be sitting on that hill. . . .

"I decided to wait for an opportunity to escape. I determined to agree with my uncle that this God could not possibly conquer our great city. Any god you could not see had to be a sham,[9] a hoax.

---

[9]sham—something that is not real; a fake

"When morning came, the messenger of the king came with word that we could stay in David's camp. He told us that he didn't understand the orders he'd been given but that we were not to be treated as spies.

"My parents both breathed a prayer of thankfulness, but I could not tell which god it was they were praying it to.

"As soon as an opportunity presented itself, my father spoke to the guard. He didn't ask him the questions *I* would have asked—about the strengths and weaknesses of David's army. 'Tell me,' he said, 'about the history of your people. Tell me the stories of how your God has worked miracles for you.'

"I still remember that guard's name—it was Jeconiah. Oh, how his eyes lighted up at my father's question. I imagine now that being out there for battle, he had missed the opportunities to tell those stories to his little ones at home. He delighted to tell us. In fact, he told them with such enthusiasm and emotion that I found myself getting interested in them too. He had a story of the great Flood, just as we did. Even though it was quite different, the points of similarity made me wonder if perhaps our two stories had come from the same source.

"Then we heard of the great father of the Israelites, Abraham, who had been called by their God from a far land. Jeconiah said that Jehovah had talked to Abraham and told him, so many hundreds of years ago, that this very land would belong to him and to his descendants. Tears came to Jeconiah's eyes as he told us the story of Joseph in the land of Egypt—how their God had prepared the relief from famine, even through the harsh cruelty of Joseph's own brothers.

"But he became especially excited when he told the stories of Moses. His voice grew intense. 'Just as the Israelites reached the Red Sea, the Egyptian Pharaoh decided that he *wouldn't* let them go—he was going to get them back! And he sent his men out, hundreds of swift chariots, chasing that flock of people in the wilderness. Oh, but the Lord Jehovah is mighty to save! He opened up a path in the middle of the sea for His people to walk across on dry ground!' And Jeconiah sat back, looking up into the sky, overwhelmed by the story that he had probably told a hundred times.

"I realized that this story was even more exciting to me than the story of the River Jordan that I had heard before. Perhaps it was because it was being told by a man who really believed it and honored the God who had done it. That day may have been the beginning of a new way of thinking for me.

"My parents wanted to see how the God of the Israelites would help them win this battle. And I did too. I never dared to make my way back to Jerusalem. Perhaps my cowardly childishness decided I would rather be a living slave than a dead hero. And my curiosity compelled[10] me to watch how the God who had supposedly accomplished so many miracles in the past would now accomplish this one.

---

[10]compelled—forced someone to do something

Merciful Deliverance

"The next day my father said to Jeconiah, 'I have a word to say to your king. I think I can help him.' I knew not what it was he might say, for I knew that my lowly father was not privy to[11] any secrets of the city.

"But when my father emerged from the king's tent, he told us. 'I told the king where the water shaft is,' he said simply, 'and I gave him information about what to do when he enters the city.'

"I groaned inwardly—the water shaft was the secret passageway by which water was brought into Jerusalem. It was the only vulnerable[12] spot in the city.

" 'In return,' my father continued, 'he has offered us our freedom when he has conquered Jerusalem.'

"Before long two spies came back into camp with news for the king. 'We have investigated the water shaft, and it is as the Jebusite says. We can enter the city through it.'

"I wondered, why hadn't the people of Jerusalem placed some guards at the entrance of the water shaft? It was as if they didn't care, as if their gods would protect them, perhaps.

[11]privy to—aware of
[12]vulnerable—exposed to attack

250

"All the Israelites rejoiced while the king retired to pray to his unseen God. While he prayed, I thought. I realized that no matter how many men entered the water shaft, they would have to exit one at a time. If only someone were waiting at the proper place inside the city, they would easily be killed . . . .

"David came back out of his tent and asked his men, 'Who is willing to climb the water shaft to take the city? That man will be captain of my army.'

"One young man stepped forward immediately. 'I will do it.'

"He was a man that I had noticed before. I had heard his loud, boastful talk of how he could conquer the city of Jerusalem single-handedly. I knew he must be eager to be the captain of the army—he seemed like one who would enjoy telling others what to do. I didn't really like him, and yet . . . he was brave enough to be the first to enter the water shaft. His name was Joab.

"Several other men volunteered to go with him. They all showed so much faith—either in this man or in the God he professed to serve. Maybe both. But they did not seem afraid to die in their attempt to conquer my city. That very night they sneaked through the water shaft into Jerusalem. I know that they had very

little trouble taking the city because none of the people expected to be attacked, especially not from the inside!

"I thought of my uncle . . . and I felt strange. I compared that man that I had adored to the guard, Jeconiah. I compared the stories my uncle had told with the stories I had heard from the lips of this Israelite. And though part of me longed to indulge[13] once again in the wickedness my uncle had encouraged in me, another voice called me away from that. I felt torn inside, and I threw myself down on the grass and cried.

"Hardly anybody escaped the swords of the Israelites. Some people were able to run away and hide in neighboring cities, but even many of them never returned. I never saw my uncle again.

"I was in a daze for weeks afterwards, even as the Israelites entered the conquered city and changed its whole appearance. Most of them began to call it 'the city of David.' Some of them called it 'the city of God.'

"They tore down shrines[14] to our Canaanite gods and goddesses; they destroyed our temples and our high places. Every wooden god was cast into the fire and burned. The stone gods were broken to pieces, and the gods of silver and gold were melted down. The Israelites built new altars to offer praise to their God for the deliverance into their hands of this marvelous city that their forefathers had not had the faith to conquer. I scoffed inwardly. As far as I could tell, it was only because of my parents that the Jews had accomplished anything.

"Part of me still hated the unseen God of the Israelites. But, with my parents, I trembled at the purity of these people. At that time, because the king was living in close communion with the word of his God, those who did not obey the law of God were severely punished. And it was a firm law.

"My parents wanted to do all that they could to fit in with this new way of life. Even though they did not then truly know the one true God, they trembled at His power, and they offered sacrifices to Him every day and honored Him with their mouths. They studied the Law and even began to teach me about this new God. I read enough of the Hebrew law to see that in a Hebrew land, if the child does not respect his father and mother, he is to be stoned to death. So for the sake of expediency,[15] I obeyed my parents. I prayed to the God of the Israelites, and I offered sacrifices to Him, but

---

[13]indulge—to allow oneself to have something that is desired but not needed
[14]shrines—temples; places of worship
[15]expediency—effectiveness in achieving a desired end; self-serving

252

part of my heart still clung to the old Jerusalem, to the wickedness that had been almost all I had ever known before the Israelites had come. No, I never said anything to my parents about it. But it was still in my heart.

"Time passed, and I took Adah to be my wife. All her family was dead, and the sight was gone from her eyes, but she was pretty, and she was deft, so I married her. As it turned out, she loved and worshiped the God of the Israelites, and she taught me about Him. Through her teaching, I came to accept something that I had never wanted to admit before—that the God of this people really was more than the gods of wood and stone. Her stories reminded me of the ones the guard, Jeconiah, told us on the hill that day. Then one day this God of hers became my God too—my one and only God. She helped me to understand that He has worked in mighty ways, not only for the reward of His people but also for their punishment.

"In fact," Ornan sighed, "Adah fears that the Israelites are overdue for judgment because of the wickedness that they have indulged in of late. I have seen evidences of it too. Some of them now worship gods of wood and stone, the very ones that they destroyed when they took this city. Even King David seems not to walk as closely with the Lord as he once did."

The old prophet nodded his head slowly. "I thank you for taking the time to tell your story. And I regret to say that you and your dear wife have been quite perceptive. The Lord does indeed intend to punish this land for the sin of its king."

Ornan bowed his head, and when he raised it, tears glistened in his eyes. "When?"

"I am on my way even now to inform the king." The prophet rose. "But I trust that we shall meet again." His dark, piercing eyes searched Ornan's soul as he grasped his shoulders.

"Yes. I trust so."

Ornan shaded his eyes from the setting sun as he watched the prophet trudge down the hill. He did not sleep that night.

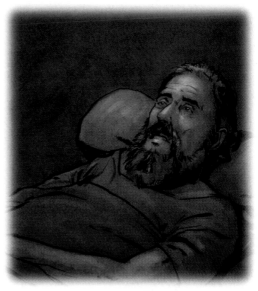

News of the pestilence[16] spread quickly. Though it had not struck Jerusalem yet, it had struck all around, and thousands of people were killed the first day. Everyone went about in sackcloth and ashes, petitioning[17] the God of heaven to relieve them of this terror. But the second day was no better. Thousands more died. People blamed the king for his sin of numbering the people.

The wheat could not be left on the threshing floor to rot, so Ornan and his sons still had to work. But even as he worked, Ornan wept and prayed. So the first and second days passed.

The third day as Ornan was working and praying, he heard a terrible gasp and a yell. "Jeconiah, what is it?" he called in terror.

"Father! An angel of the Lord! There!" And Jeconiah ran to hide, his three brothers close behind him. The angel stood with sword drawn. The bright light blinded Ornan's sight as he ran to follow his sons to the safety of the house. There they hid, trembling in terror at the sight they had seen.

When Ornan finally had the courage to look out of his house, he saw a royal procession coming up the hill. It was King David himself! Ornan ran outside and bowed before the king. "Why has my lord come here?" he asked, trembling, although he thought he knew the reason.

King David looked very old. "The Lord has sent me," he said.

[16]pestilence—plague
[17]petitioning—making a formal request

"The angel of the Lord is here. The prophet Gad told me that I must build an altar to the Lord so that the plague[18] will be halted."

Ornan's voice caught in his throat. "Oh, please, my lord, take the threshing floor to use for your altar. Take it, and take these oxen. Please. Offer them as a sacrifice to God. And here. Use these threshing instruments to burn on the altar. And wheat, here, for the meal offering. I give it all. Please, my lord."

"Nay." The king shook his head. "I cannot take it. I cannot offer anything to the Lord that is not my own. Let me buy it, I pray."

Ornan saw his king's determination. "Very well." He watched through something of a haze as King David counted out the money into his hand. "Is that enough?"

"More than enough, my lord." Ornan bowed. "And may God be pleased with your sacrifice."

"He is all-loving and all-forgiving." The king's voice broke, and tears glistened in his eyes. "Though I have failed Him, oh, so many times, still He will accept the sacrifices of a broken and contrite[19] heart."

David trudged wearily to the threshing floor and built his altar. Ornan stood back with the servants, watching and praying as David prayed aloud to the Lord, crying with tears that the Lord might spare the people. Suddenly a flame of fire struck from heaven and consumed the sacrifice. The angel of the Lord put his sword back into its sheath.

"He has heard me!" David shouted through his tears. "He has heard my prayers!"

"Praise be to God!" Ornan whispered. "Praise His holy name. And may His people return to Him."

---

[18]plague—a very serious disease that spreads rapidly from person to person
[19]contrite—repentant

We don't know the reason that the Lord chose to honor the threshing floor of a Jebusite as the place that David was to build his altar. But that very place was also the site on which David's son, Solomon, later built the temple, where Jews for hundreds of years came to worship the Lord.

Bible Reference Tools

Tammie Jacobs

Suppose that after reading the story "Ornan the Jebusite" you want to know what the Bible says about Ornan or what a threshing floor looked like or why threshing floors were built on high hills. Perhaps you want to find out about all the different kinds of sacrifices or if Ornan had another name. Where could you find this information?

Tools for Bible Study

Five of the most commonly used Bible study tools are Bible concordances, Bible commentaries, Bible dictionaries, Bible encyclopedias, and Bible atlases.

A **concordance** is an alphabetical list of keywords that are found in the Scriptures.
• Lists all the verses that contain a given word.
• Located in the back of some Bibles.
• Available in separate volumes and on computer software.

```
ORNAN (or'-nan) See ARAUNAH. A Jebusite prince.
  threshingfloor of O the Jebusite ......... 1Chr 21:15    771
  threshingfloor of O the Jebusite ......... 1Chr 21:18    771
  O tuned back, and saw the angel ........ 1Chr 21:20    771
  Now O was threshing wheat ............... 1Chr 21:20    771
  And as David came to O, O ............... 1Chr 21:21    771
  Then David said to O, Grant me ........ 1Chr 21:22    771
  O said unto David, Take it to ............. 1Chr 21:23    771
  And king David said to O, Nay .......... 1Chr 21:24    771
  So David gave to O for the place ....... 1Chr 21:25    771
  threshingfloor of O the Jebusite ......... 1Chr 21:28    771
  threshingfloor of O the Jebusite ......... 2Chr 3:1      771

ORPAH (or'-pah) Daughter-in-law of Naomi.
  the name of the one was O ................ Ruth 1:4      6204
  O kissed her mother in law ............... Ruth 1:14     6204

ORPHANS
  We are o and fatherless, our ............. Lam. 5:3      3490
```

Bible commentaries contain explanations of verses of Scripture.
• Include maps, details of Bible customs, and cross-references.
• Organized usually in the order of book, chapter, and verse.

> **24** By refusing to present an "offering that costs me nothing," David confirmed the truth that God takes no pleasure in the man who yields only what involves no sacrifice. He requires of his followers a totally surrendered life (Rom. 12:1; cf. Luke 21:1-3).
>
> **25** So David bought "the site"—*hammāqôm,* which may have included the whole area of Mount Moriah—for 240 ounces of gold (cf. NIV mb.). This was worth about one hundred thousand dollars, on a standard of about 1 ounce to four hundred dollars (cf. comment on 19:6). Second Samuel 24:24 notes a much smaller amount, 20 ounces of silver, for the threshing floor itself (NBCrev. p. 380).
>
> **26** God's answer of "fire from heaven on the altar" publicly attested his acceptance, both of the king's repentance and of the altar site (note similar miracles: in the past, in reference to the tabernacle, Lev. 9:24; and yet to be revealed, in Solomon's temple, 2 Chron. 7:1).
>
> **27** Furthermore the angel's sword was sheathed and the plague ceased (2 Sam. 24:25).
>
> **29** On the tabernacle's contemporaneous location at Gibeon, see the comment on 16:39.

There are several kinds of **Bible dictionaries.**

- Some give simple definitions of words found in Scripture; they provide teaching about the use of a word in Scripture.
- Others give Bible references where a word may be found or an explanation of the meaning(s) of a word in the original language.
- Some are similar to the encyclopedias, providing details beyond a simple definition.

THRESHING FLOOR (Heb. goren, "even"). A level and hard-beaten plot in the open air (Judg. 6:37; 2 Sam. 6:6), on which sheaves of grain were threshed (Isa. 21:10; Jer. 51:33; Mic. 4:12; Matt. 3:12). The top of a rock was a favorite spot for this purpose; on this the sheaves were spread out and sometimes beaten with flails—a method practiced especially with the lighter grains, such as fitches or cummin (Isa. 28:27)— but more commonly by oxen. The oxen were either yoked side by side and driven around over the grain, or were yoked to a drag (Lat. *tibulum* or *trahea*), consisting of a board or a block of wood, with stones or pieces of iron fastened to the lower surface to make it rough. This was dragged over the grain, beating out the kernels.

The threshing floors were watched all night to guard against theft of the grain (Ruth 3:3-6. 14); they were often of considerable value, and frequently named in connection with a wine press (Deut. 16:13; 2 Kings 6:27; Hos. 9:2; Joel 2:24), since grain, wine, and oil were the more important products of the soil. They were sometimes given specific names, such as that of Nacon (2 Sam. 6:6) or Chidon (1 Chron. 13:9),

---

Bible encyclopedias function much like standard encyclopedias.

- Include pictures, maps, diagrams.
- Organized alphabetically or by topic.
- Published in single-volume or multivolume works.
- Provide more in-depth explanations of topics.

JERUSALEM

Shalem"; cf. its initial Biblical designation, Moses' writing of Genesis, c. 1450 B.C., as "Salem" (Gen. 14:18; cf. Ps 76:2). שלם, q.v., signifies : complete, : prosperous, : peaceful: (cf. Heb. 7:2), though it may also have been the name of a "prospering" Canaanite deity, Shalem. The name was not originally Heb. in any event.

The choice of Jerusalem's location seems to have been dictated by factors of defense and of water. The latter was supplied from the Gihon spring in the Kidron Valley below and to the E (2 Chron 32:30), from which a supply tunnel angled upward to within the city; *see* below. Correspondingly, the E walls, which were once thought to have run along the eastern edge of the crest, and hence to have restricted the city to a width of about 100 yards, are now known, at least from 1800 B.C. onward, to have lain some 50 yards farther E, two-thirds of the way down the slope, which was crowded with houses. The wide northern wall, over 20 ft. in thickness, has not yet been fully exposed, but its area has been closely pinpointed by K. Kenyon's excavations. They demonstrate that occupation prior to the 10th cent. B.C. began at a point 100 yards S of the present S wall of Jerusalem (op. cit., p. 26). The city then extended about one-quarter m. southward. Its western wall lay on the summit of the ridge, along its W side. Its total area, thought to have been less than which is still not uncharac- of Canaan's towns), is now to have been almost eleven. ally, its elevation, while less than Moriah or Gareb, was not such as to impair its security, fire power being limited as it was in those days.

2. Jebusite vs. Israel, to 1003 B.C. Midway in the Late Bronze Age (1600-1200 B.C.) Scripture, in its

records of Joshua's wars at the time of the conquest (1406-1400 B.C.) identifies a certain Adoni-zedek as "king of Jerusalem" (Josh. 10:1). This Amorite, indeed, headed up the confederacy of southern Canaanitish kings that opposed Joshua; and he lost his life, following their defeat at Bethhoron (10:23, 26; 12:10). But Jerusalem itself seems to have escaped unscathed.

A decade or so later, after the death of Joshua, Jerusalem was captured by the tribe of Judah (Judg. 1:1, 8,) only to be reoccupied by the Canaanitish Jebusites (Judg 1:21). The eighteenth dynasty Egyp. Amarna tablets include letters from an Abdi-Hipa (a Hurrian, or Horite, name), king of *Urusalim* or *Bethshalem*, to the pharaoh Akhenaten (prob. 1379-1361, CAH rev., *Chronology*, p. 19). They speak of the former's need for Egyp. mercenary troops in view of the threatening presence of the Habiru (q.v.), possibly the Hebrews. At the time of the Benjaminite outrage early in the 14th cent. (cf. Judg 20:28: Aaron's grandson was still high priest), Jerusalem is thus disparagingly described as "the city of foreigners" (19:12), "this city of the Jebusites" (v. 11), though actually its moral standards could not have been worse than those of the Heb. Benjaminites to its N (vv. 18, 22, 25). It remained Jebusite until David's final victory and conquest in 1003 (Josh 15:63; 1 Chron 11:5).

During the period of the judges the city carried the corresponding name of יבוס, Jebus (Judg 19:10-11; 1 Chron 11:4). It was at this point, in the 14th cent. that the Jebusites constructed a series of stone filled platforms down the hilly slope to the wall on the E side of the city; cf. Jerusalem's designation as, "by the valley of the son of Hinnom unto the side [ASVmg., 'shoulder'] of the Jebusite southward" (Josh 15:8;

This excerpt comes from a forty-four page entry on Jerusalem. This is a much more in-depth description than a dictionary would contain.

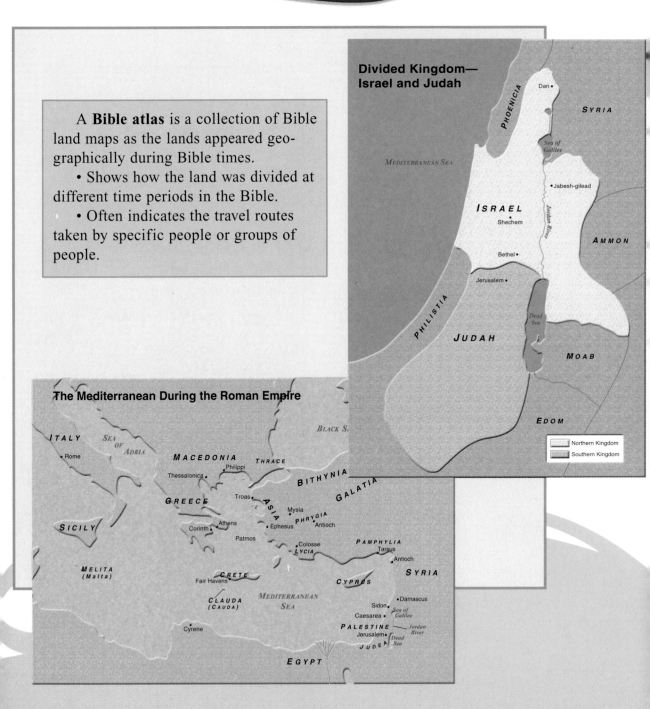

A **Bible atlas** is a collection of Bible land maps as the lands appeared geographically during Bible times.
• Shows how the land was divided at different time periods in the Bible.
• Often indicates the travel routes taken by specific people or groups of people.

Divided Kingdom—Israel and Judah

Northern Kingdom
Southern Kingdom

PHOENICIA
Dan •
SYRIA
Sea of Galilee
MEDITERRANEAN SEA
• Jabesh-gilead
ISRAEL
Shechem •
Jordan River
AMMON
Bethel •
Jerusalem •
Dead Sea
PHILISTIA
JUDAH
MOAB
EDOM

The Mediterranean During the Roman Empire

ITALY
SEA OF ADRIA
• Rome
MACEDONIA
THRACE
BLACK S.
Philippi •
Thessalonica •
BITHYNIA
GALATIA
GREECE
Troas •
ASIA
Mysia •
PHRYGIA
Antioch •
Athens •
Ephesus •
Corinth •
Patmos •
Colosse •
LYCIA
PAMPHYLIA
Tarsus
SICILY
Antioch •
CRETE
CYPRUS
SYRIA
MELITA (Malta)
Fair Havens •
MEDITERRANEAN SEA
Damascus •
Sidon •
Sea of Galilee
CLAUDA (CAUDA)
Caesarea •
Cyrene •
PALESTINE
Jordan River
Jerusalem •
Dead Sea
JUDEA
EGYPT

Using the Tools

If a library is organized using the Dewey decimal system, you will find Bible reference books in the 220 section of the library. The shelves will contain commentaries, Bible concordances, Bible atlases, Bible encyclopedias, and Bible dictionaries. The tools are usually arranged in alphabetical order or in canonical order, which is the order of the sixty-six books of the Bible officially accepted as Holy Scripture.

Which tool would be best for finding out Ornan's other name?

ORNAN (or'-nan) See *ARAUNAH. A Jebusite prince.*		
threshingfloor of *O* the Jebusite 1Chr 21:15	771
threshingfloor of *O* the Jebusite 1Chr 21:18	771
O tuned back, and saw the angel 1Chr 21:20	771
Now *O* was threshing wheat 1Chr 21:20	771
And as David came to *O, O* 1Chr 21:21	771
Then David said to *O,* Grant me 1Chr 21:22	771
O said unto David, Take it to 1Chr 21:23	771
And king David said to *O,* Nay 1Chr 21:24	771
So David gave to *O* for the place 1Chr 21:25	771
threshingfloor of *O* the Jebusite 1Chr 21:28	771
threshingfloor of *O* the Jebusite 2Chr 3:1	771

What if you wanted to know more about a threshing floor and why God might have chosen to use such a place for such an important event? Where would you look?

THRESHING FLOOR (Heb. goren, "even"). A level and hard-beaten plot in the open air (Judg. 6:37; 2 Sam. 6:6), on which sheaves of grain were threshed (Isa. 21:10; Jer. 51:33; Mic. 4:12; Matt. 3:12). The top of a rock was a favorite spot for this purpose; on this the sheaves were spread out and sometimes beaten with flails—a method practiced especially with the lighter grains, such as fitches or cummin (Isa. 28:27)— but more commonly by oxen. The oxen were either yoked side by side and driven around over the grain, or were yoked to a drag (Lat. *tibulum* or *trahea*), consisting of a board or a block of wood, with stones or pieces of iron fastened to the lower surface to make it rough. This was dragged over the grain, beating out the kernels.

The threshing floors were watched all night to guard against theft of the grain (Ruth 3:3-6. 14); they were often of considerable value, and frequently named in connection with a wine press (Deut. 16:13; 2 Kings 6:27; Hos. 9:2; Joel 2:24), since grain, wine, and oil were the more important products of the soil. They were sometimes given specific names, such as that of Nacon (2 Sam. 6:6) or Chidon (1 Chron.

Where would you look to find out more about Ornan? Hint: A good place to start would be to find out all the places he is mentioned in the Bible. Which reference tool would be best for finding all the verses where Ornan is mentioned?

ORNAN (or'-nan) See *ARAUNAH. A Jebusite prince.*		
threshingfloor of *O* the Jebusite 1Chr 21:15	771
threshingfloor of *O* the Jebusite 1Chr 21:18	771
O tuned back, and saw the angel 1Chr 21:20	771
Now *O* was threshing wheat 1Chr 21:20	771
And as David came to *O, O* 1Chr 21:21	771
Then David said to *O,* Grant me 1Chr 21:22	771
O said unto David, Take it to 1Chr 21:23	771
And king David said to *O,* Nay 1Chr 21:24	771
So David gave to *O* for the place 1Chr 21:25	771
threshingfloor of *O* the Jebusite 1Chr 21:28	771
threshingfloor of *O* the Jebusite 2Chr 3:1	771

Where would you look to find out what the fire from heaven meant when God consumed David's sacrifice?

26 God's answer of "fire from heaven on the altar" publicly attested his acceptance, both of the king's repentance and of the altar site (note similar miracles: in the past, in reference to the tabernacle, Lev. 9:24; and yet to be revealed, in Solomon's temple, 2 Chron. 7:1).

27 Furthermore the angel's sword was sheathed and the plague ceased (2 Sam. 24:25).

29 On the tabernacle's contemporaneous location at Gibeon, see the comment on 16:39.

Using different reference tools can help you understand the Bible better, but you need to remember that imperfect men have written these books. The Bible is its own most accurate tool.

SHIPWRECKED!

from The Swiss Family Robinson
by Johann Wyss,
adapted by Amy Miller
illustrated by MaryAnn Lumm

Johann David Wyss, a Swiss pastor who lived from 1743 to 1818, wrote The Swiss Family Robinson to entertain and instruct his own four sons. Wyss got his idea for this book from reading Daniel Defoe's book, Robinson Crusoe. First written in German, the story about the Swiss family has been translated into English and other languages many times. Even though some of the English translators changed parts of the book, they could not change the message. As you read, you will see how this truly is a story written by a father for his sons.

Fixed on the Rock

The seventh day of the raging storm brought despair to all on board the tossing ship. Sailors and passengers alike had but one cry left, pleading for mercy from God and each commending his soul to his Maker.

My children stood clinging to their mother, trembling with fear in our little cabin, and I endeavored to cheer them by saying, "My children, God can save us if it is His will; if not, we must resign[1] ourselves to what He judges is best for us. To die will be to meet again in a better world, where partings are unknown."

My poor wife on this wiped her tears and became calm, to give courage to her boys. Yet I could scarcely control my own grief, even while attempting to comfort my family.

Together, we knelt in prayer to the Almighty, pleading, yet confident in His will. The cry, "Land! Land!" from above interrupted the prayers of my children with a sound of frantic hope. Almost immediately, though, we felt a shock so violent that I feared the ship had struck on a rock, and should immediately fall to pieces.

My fears were confirmed when the despairing cry came from above, "We are all lost! Lower the boats!"

"Lost!" I exclaimed. "Keep courage!" I shouted back to my fearful children and brave wife as I ran above to see what deliverance might be left.

Wave after wave knocked me about as I witnessed the departure of the last boat, lowered in haste over the side of the ship. Cry and plead as I might, the sound of my voice could not be heard above the crashing waves; and I realized that even if they had heard me, it would be impossible for them to turn back.

As I gathered my strength to bear this news to my family, I observed that the ship was not in so dangerous a position as I had first thought. With renewed hope, I entered the cabin.

"Take courage, my children," I announced. The children eagerly looked at me with worried faces. "All hope is not lost. The ship is fixed between the rocks, and this little place of refuge[2] is high above the water. Tomorrow, if the wind and waves subside,[3] we may be able to reach the land."

The hopefulness of childhood enabled my boys to receive this news with transports[4] of joy. They passed all at once from despair to unbounded confidence. But my wife could see my hidden anxiety in spite of my calmness. Yet, while I saw this clearly, I

---

[1]resign—to give up
[2]refuge—a place where one can go for protection
[3]subside—to sink to a lower or more normal level
[4]transports—strong emotions

knew by her manner that her confidence in God was still unshaken, and this gave me renewed courage.

She immediately went to search in the steward's room for provisions and met with such success that a plentiful supper was quickly prepared for us.

"Let us take food," she said. "Nourishment for the body gives strength to the spirit, and we may have a very disturbed night."

And so it truly proved. The night passed in prayerful watchfulness, the storm undiminished[5] in its fury. While the younger boys slept, Fritz, his mother, and I fashioned swimming belts by tying empty flasks together with handkerchiefs. With this accomplished, we tied the belts around my wife and the younger boys who could not swim, should we be forced to leave the safety of the boat.

However, the night passed without further trouble. As the morning advanced the wind lulled, the sky cleared, and with joyful eyes we gazed at the brilliant colors that glowed in the east as the sun rose, foretelling a bright day.

All during that day, the boys and their mother searched the entire ship, bringing their treasures forward, creating such a store of provisions, that I feared we would not be able to take them all. In the meantime, I plotted a way to build some sort of vessel in which to carry my family to the safety of land. As I puzzled over

what to do, Jack piped in, "Can we not sail in tubs? I have often done so on the pond at home."

Spurred on by this thought, four large empty casks were recovered from the lower decks where they floated in the water. Encouraged that they were indeed watertight, I set about to saw them apart through the middle.

A long flexible plank served to fasten the eight half-casks together. With two more long planks along each side, I had formed a narrow boat divided into eight compartments. Upon lowering the heavy tub-boat into the water by means of a lever, I realized that even a calm sea could present danger in capsizing[6] so unsteady a vessel. So, after the manner of native islanders of whom I had read, I attached a long bar across each end with empty flasks fastened on each side. The balance achieved was enough to excite each of the boys, so that they nearly bounded into the craft immediately. However, I pointed out the setting sun, making them see that the longed-after journey would have to wait until the light of the next day. So, once again, my wife prepared a sumptuous[7] meal from the ship's stores, and we rested peacefully after a long day of hard work.

---

[5]undiminished—not diminished or lessened
[6]capsizing—turning bottom side up; overturning
[7]sumptuous—suggesting great expense; lavish

to think about than that kid. Ever since she'd overheard the new game warden talking about the problems he was having lately with poachers,[2] she'd spent every spare minute in the Pines.

Not that it would help any, as far as Dad was concerned. An aching sense of loss quivered inside her, and with it came the bitterness, so dark and strong that she could almost taste it. Poachers! How she hated them, the way they came sneaking into these beautiful woods. It was bad enough that they shot the animals and spoiled the precious wilderness. But now Dad had been crippled because of them. Even though the police said that the stray bullet was an accident, it didn't change anything. The doctors didn't think he'd ever walk again. And it would be months before he could

even come home. The Pine Barrens had lost its best game warden, and she had lost more than anyone knew.

She bit her lip hard to make herself stop thinking about Dad and grabbed for Charcoal's red collar. "We're going to find those poachers, boy," she whispered brokenly into one of his cocked ears. "And we'll find that quisling too."

Her father had suspected that someone in their small town was helping some of the poachers operate by keeping them informed of the game warden's plans. To anyone who loved the Pines, that man was worse than a traitor.[3] Dad had called him a quisling.

Chris slowed her pace as she caught sight of a small peaked roof

---

[2]poachers—those who hunt illegally
[3]traitor—a person who betrays his or her country, a cause, or an idea

half-hidden in the forest. That must be the old piney cabin she had heard about. She crept through the underbrush, leaving Charcoal behind. He was still a young dog, and she wasn't sure how he'd react if she took him near the cabin. At least he'd been trained well enough to wait for her on the path.

The tiny cabin seemed to be lost in the tall bushes that crowded against its dark, unpainted walls. If it weren't for the trampled weeds and tire tracks in the sandy clearing behind it, she would have thought that it was another of the ruined buildings so common in the Pines. Chris slipped along one splintery wall of the cabin and reached a dirty back porch that was propped up by cement blocks. Anxiously she gazed across it. How could she tell who lived here? Poachers would have rifles and hunting equipment, but all of that was probably inside.

A sound reached her, and she froze. It was a dry, whispering sound, like nothing she could identify. It seemed to be coming from under the gray tarpaulin[4] that had been dropped on the porch. Cautiously Chris edged toward it and lifted one corner. She had time for only one glance before she heard the thump of footsteps from inside the cabin. She ducked back around the corner into the bushes as the cabin door creaked open.

Someone stepped onto the porch, which shuddered under his weight. He must be a big man. She could hear the heavy rasp of his breathing, and then the popping sound of a can being opened. She listened to the gurgle of his drinking as she crawled away through the sheltering bushes.

Her heart lifted as she thought about what she had seen. Snakes! It had been a mistake to think that the poachers were after deer. A glance into that cage had changed her mind. Those pine snakes and corn snakes were endangered species in New Jersey, and it was illegal to trap them. But poachers could sell them to pet stores in New York and make a lot of money. When she reached the path, Charcoal jumped up and licked her face. She hugged him. "I think we've got 'em, boy. Let's get going." Maybe she still had time to talk to the game warden before dark if she could catch him at home.

After a long hike they left the path and turned down a narrow gravel road. Chris was pulling her bike out of its hiding place in the bushes when a brown pickup truck roared past. Through the dusty haze she glimpsed the bald head of Tom Crockett, the jeweler. As she pedaled toward the game warden's house, she wondered briefly what the jeweler was doing this far out in the Pines, but she forgot about him when she arrived at the game warden's house.

---

[4]tarpaulin—waterproof canvas cover

The game warden listened attentively to her report, and Chris hurried home through the twilight with growing excitement. When she burst into the kitchen, her mother looked up from the carrots she was peeling. "Now where have you been? I expected you to have supper started by the time I got home."

Chris hardly listened. "Oh, Mom!" Chris wanted to throw her arms around the tall, thin woman, even though her mother wasn't the hugging kind. "Mom, I think I've caught some poachers in the Pines. I talked to the warden, and he said he'd check on them."

Her mother pushed a lock of gray hair off her forehead and shook her head. "I've told you I don't like you wandering around in those woods. And you've brought that dog into the house again." She sent a disapproving glance toward Charcoal, who was sprawled happily on the worn linoleum. "He's got fleas and who knows what else. Please take that dog outside."

Silently Chris took Charcoal out onto the porch. She shouldn't have said anything about those poachers, anyway. It had just reminded her mother of what had happened to Dad.

Later that evening when the warden phoned, she wished she hadn't told him about the poachers either. The warden had driven out to the cabin and found a tall man there, all right. But the man said that he and his teenage son were tourists visiting the Pine Barrens for a few weeks. The cage on the back porch was empty. They claimed that they kept it for their little terrier to travel in.

Chris sighed with dismay as she hung up the phone. Slowly she finished drying the dishes, puzzling over the warden's report. What had happened to those snakes, anyway? The tall man wouldn't have let them go; he must have moved them to another place.

By the next afternoon, she had stopped thinking about poachers: Charcoal was missing. He sometimes disappeared on an overnight prowl, but he never failed to return by sunrise. Chris trudged up and down the gravel road beside her house, gazing into the forest that suddenly looked dark and impassable. If only she could go and look for him! But where to start? He might be anywhere in hundreds of square miles of wilderness. He could be hurt; he could be in terrible trouble.

"Hey, what's going on? You look as if you lost your best friend." Tim Branson's voice spoke from behind her.

Chris didn't even feel like telling the kid to get lost. "He *is* my best friend," she said miserably. "It's Charcoal. He's been out all night and hasn't come back."

"My dog stayed out three nights once," Tim said cheerfully. "And he was O.K."

"Yes, but the Pines are different." Chris started to explain, but the sight of a dark shadow in the trees stopped her. "Charcoal!" she cried. "Oh, what's the matter?" His legs were caked with mud from exploring the cedar swamps—that was nothing new—but the black dog was not his usual joyous self. He limped toward her, wagging his tail in piteously slow circles.

"Charcoal, how could you?" She stared at the dozens of white-tipped porcupine quills sticking out of his muzzle. The dog rubbed the side of his face on the ground and whined. "Silly dog, don't you know enough to leave porcupines alone?" Chris groaned. She could see that the barbed ends of those quills were deeply embedded. "Now what are we going to do?

Mother will never let me take you to a vet." She bent over him, worrying. Vets cost too much money, and Mom didn't like Charcoal, anyway.

Tim knelt beside Chris and reached toward Charcoal's head.

"Don't do that," she warned hastily. "He hates for people to handle him, except me."

But Charcoal was standing still, allowing Tim to turn his head gently as he examined the quills. "Have you got a pair of pliers?" he asked finally.

"Yes, but—"

"Good. I think we can take care of these."

Chris ran for the pliers, and Tim set to work. It seemed like a long time before Tim got the last quill out, but Charcoal endured it with only a few whimpers. He licked Chris's face happily when Tim was finished.

"How did you know what to do?" she asked, hugging Charcoal thankfully.

"I've watched Dad do it; he's a vet." The boy stood up and faced her with a pleading grin. "Hey, you sure know a lot about the Pine Barrens; will you show me around? I really like it here."

It was a return favor that he was asking, but Chris didn't mind, not after what he'd done for Charcoal. Besides, the kid acted pretty old for his age. He might not be such a pest after all. "Sure," she agreed. "I'll show you the fire tower first—it's fun to climb."

It was during their hike up to the fire tower that she first noticed Tim's limp. When he stumped slowly up the metal steps of the tall orange structure, it was obvious that he had one stiff leg. Trying not to stare, Chris leaned over the railing at the top while she waited for him.

Tim pulled himself up the last step and stood next to her without saying anything for once. Together they gazed at the billowing green forest below, with its spidery network of sandy white roads. Suddenly he exclaimed, "Don't you love it, living here?"

She glanced at him in surprise. "Yes," she admitted softly. "I do love it. If only—" She made herself stop.

"If only what?"

"Well, my dad got hurt in an accident a couple of months ago, and it's not the same without him." Slowly she added, "In fact, sometimes I hate it, because if he hadn't been a game warden trying to protect the Pines, he'd never have been crippled. Yeah. Sometimes I hate it."

Forgetting about the boy beside her, she muttered, "And I almost hate God sometimes too."

"Why?" His question startled her.

"He let it happen, didn't He?" she demanded fiercely. "He's supposed to be so powerful, but He let my dad get shot. I don't think His love's so great, either, if that's what it is."

Tim's voice was calm. "God doesn't make mistakes." He took a deep breath and asked suddenly. "Chris, do you know about Jesus, how He died for your sins?"

"Yes," she said, wondering why he had asked. "I accepted Him as my Savior a long time ago."

The boy's face brightened. "Then how can you say God doesn't love you? He punished His Son for your sake."

Chris answered impatiently. "This is different. You don't understand how it feels to have something taken away from you like I have. Dad will never be the same again. Let's forget it, O.K.?" To her relief, he let the subject drop, and they started down the fire tower together.

No Mistakes

For the next two days, Chris was kept too busy by her mother to do anything about the poachers. In her spare minutes she showed Tim the main trails through their part of the Pines and a few of her favorite places, like the hidden rock where the turtles sunned. He learned quickly and soon could identify most of the animal tracks that she pointed out.

On her next trip to the grocery store, Chris met a tiny blonde woman who stopped her with a smile. "You must be Chris. I'm Tim's mother. He talks about you all the time." The woman chattered on, just like Tim did when he was excited. "I hope he isn't a nuisance,[5] but I'm glad he's found a friend. He's had such a rough time. Did he tell you about the car accident and his leg and all those operations?"

Seeing the surprise on Chris's face, she added, "No, I guess he wouldn't have said anything. Well, you've really been good for him. I appreciate it."

She moved away with a friendly nod, but her words raised a question that haunted Chris for the rest of the day. How could Tim feel so sure about God's love when something like that had happened to him?

She ventured to ask him about it the next morning on their way to ex-

[5]nuisance—someone or something that annoys or is not convenient; a bother

plore a cranberry bog. Her question didn't seem to bother him. "I guess it's part of His plan for my life," he said simply.

Chris felt like shaking him. "How can you say that?" she demanded. "It's cruel of God to let your leg get smashed like that."

"Nope." He shook his head. "You've got to look at it from another angle. Remember Joseph in the Bible, how everything seemed to go wrong for him?"

Chris nodded. Joseph was one of Dad's favorite characters.

"Well, after the car accident I felt pretty sorry for myself. But then I decided that I wanted to be like Joseph." Tim straightened his narrow shoulders. "I asked God to help me trust Him like Joseph did. He changed the way I felt about my leg." He glanced up at her. "God says to 'trust in the Lord with all thine heart and lean not unto thine own understanding.' He showed me that it was better to wait on Him. And just waiting has helped me to trust Him more."

Chris saw the confidence in his blue eyes, and she felt a stir of longing. What would it be like to trust God like that? Abruptly she switched to another subject. "I've been hunting some poachers," she announced. "Pretty soon I'm going to catch them

too." Tim looked so intrigued[6] that she went on to explain how her father had suspected that somebody in town was giving inside information to the poachers.

"Why, that guy's a traitor," exclaimed Tim hotly.

Chris nodded in agreement. "My dad said there's a name for a man like that. He calls him a quisling."

"A quisling." Tim repeated the word approvingly. "That's a good name for a traitor. Sounds sort of slippery and slimy."

Chris went on to tell him about the old cabin and the snakes that had disappeared. He flushed red. "Chris, I've got to—"

"O.K., O.K.," she interrupted him with a smile. "I know you're dying to find out where it is. I'd planned to go back again, anyway. How about tomorrow afternoon?"

He agreed immediately, but he had a troubled look on his face. She remembered it the next day when he didn't meet her by the crooked oak tree as they had planned. After waiting there for a long half an hour, she trotted down to his house.

Tim's mother smiled at her from the doorway. "He left over an hour ago, all excited. Said something about a cabin and a surprise for

---

[6]intrigued—caught the interest or increased the curiosity of; fascinated

you." Her blue eyes darkened. "Is anything wrong?"

"No," Chris said hastily. "I think I know where he is."

She shared her worry with Charcoal as he trotted along beside her through the pine forest. "He probably went hunting for that cabin. I sure hope he didn't get himself lost on the way."

When they finally reached it, the old piney cabin looked dark and un-friendly, as if it had gathered all the afternoon shadows to itself. She left Charcoal by a clump of turkey-beard grass and crept through the bushes. As she care-fully set each foot

down, she noticed tracks in the sand that were not her own. The tracks looked like small sneakered feet and had an odd feature—a slight furrow in the sand at the tip of one foot. Was that made by a dragging foot? They must be Tim's tracks. For some reason he had tried to sneak up to the cabin too. Where was he now?

She checked the small clearing behind the cabin. The weeds had been recently trampled.

There were fresh tire tracks in the sand. The cabin seemed to be deserted, though, and its dusty windows were blank. She stepped across the empty porch and through the back door, which hung carelessly ajar. The single room inside was bare.

Alarm pounded through her. Quickly she retreated to the sandy clearing and studied the maze of tracks once more. It looked as if a car or a truck had pulled in and backed out. Two cages had left the imprint of their sharp corners in the sand while they waited to be loaded. Someone heavy, wearing boots, had walked here, and so had a lighter person. But there was no sign of Tim.

Unless . . . ? She gazed at a shapeless imprint left in the sand by some kind of bundle. Had Tim been tied up there while they cleared out the cabin? She stared at the imprint, and her mind filled with terrifying pictures. The poachers had caught Tim trying to spy on them. They had loaded him on the truck and dumped him into some cedar swamp. . . . It was her fault, too, with all her talk about catching poachers. Maybe she would never see him again.

Chris sat down on the porch steps with a thump. Something inside her ached unbearably. How could God let this happen?

God doesn't make mistakes. Tim's voice was so clear in her memory that she gave a start. She shook her head, but the high, boyish voice rang through her mind. *I asked God to help me trust Him.* Chris sprang to her feet, arguing with herself. She didn't have the kind of faith that Tim had. And anyway, how could she expect God to help her, especially after all the things she'd said about Him since Dad's accident?

She buried her face in her hands. Suddenly she was talking to God for the first time in months. "Lord, you know how awful I've been. But You saved me, and Your Word says You still love me, and I need to trust You—now." She added in a choked whisper, "Please help me; I've got to find Tim."

For a moment Chris stood still; then she shook back her hair and eyed the tracks in the sand with new determination. It looked as if the poachers had loaded up in a hurry. But where were they going, and what had they done with Tim? The quiet woods seemed to mock her questions, and she fought back a creeping sense of despair. "Lord, I'm going to start trusting You now. Show me what I need to do," she exclaimed.

Chris whistled for Charcoal. While he plunged through the bushes to join her, she gazed thoughtfully at the place where Tim's body had left an imprint. What was that odd scratching in the sand beside it?

"Charcoal, sit," she commanded. She knelt by the smudged markings in the sand. Was that the outline of an airplane? If it was, then Tim had left her a message: the poachers were going to fly out of the Pines. And Tim was still alive. At least he had been.

She headed back to the path, calling for Charcoal. Taggert Road. They had to be going there. It was the only road anywhere nearby that was wide enough, and it had one straight stretch that was just long enough for a small plane to use for a runway. She raced down a shortcut trail, wondering if she would get there in time. But even in her hurry she was conscious that the bitterness inside her had disappeared, and in its place was a comforting sense that she wasn't alone anymore.

As she splashed across a creek beside the far end of Taggert Road, the sound of an engine warming up confirmed her conclusion that the poachers were using an airplane. She was too late. By the time Chris reached the trees at the edge of the road, the plane was already rolling past her, taxiing[7] for takeoff.

---

[7]taxiing—moving slowly over the surface of the ground or water before taking off or landing

She stood there, panting, and watched helplessly. The little plane rushed down the length of the gravel road. It was getting closer and closer to the end of the straightaway,[8] where the road made its turn by the creek. After endless seconds the plane lifted off, but it still was dangerously low. Chris leaned forward in alarm. Would it clear those trees in front of it? The plane's nose

pulled up, and the roar of its engines sounded frantic in her ears. At last it began climbing. Not enough, she thought. It's going to crash. She began to run.

The plane hit the dark wall of trees with an agonizing screech of metal against wood. The engine died. The wings tore off, the tail crumpled, and the plane's body fell through splintered branches to the ground.

Minutes later Chris reached the wingless, twisted hulk. In the dead silence she could hear her own heart pounding. And then a groan.

She jumped for the pilot's door and wrenched it open. The tall man staggered out with a dazed look on his face. Still groaning, he allowed her to lead him away from the plane. As she turned back, she saw a thread of black smoke curling up from below the engine. The odor of gasoline hung heavily in the air like a warning.

She ducked back into the cockpit and found the man's son, but no one else. The teenager was unconscious. Hastily she yanked up the metal flap to release his seat belt and tried to lift him out of the plane. His limp body was heavier than anything she'd ever tried to carry. Anxiously she glanced at the smoke. Now it was a thick black column fed by an orange flame. She had to get him out before the flame reached the gas tank. With a desperate effort she heaved the boy clear of the plane and struggled with him to the trees.

Beside her, Charcoal pranced and whined, but she ignored him. All she could think of was Tim. Why wasn't he in the plane? She ran to throw handfuls of white forest sand onto

[8]straightaway—the straight part of a road or track

the fire. Charcoal was a nuisance, nudging at her. He turned and dashed toward the rear of the plane, barking in excited yips.

"Yes, they've probably got snakes back there, Charcoal," Chris muttered distractedly. "I've got to put this fire out." But she stepped over to take a quick look through the door of the baggage compartment. Half-hidden under a tangle of boots, cages, and supplies, she saw a brown sneaker. She dived toward it. "Tim!" He was tied hand and foot, and his mouth was taped shut, but the blindfold had slipped off, and his blue eyes were sparkling at her.

She grabbed his bound hands and dragged him to safety, laughing with relief. "Wait there; I'll be right back." She hurried to throw more sand on the smoking engine. At last the flames seemed to be dying down.

She heard the welcome clatter of a car on the road and turned toward it. The game warden's truck braked to a halt, scattering gravel, and two men leaped out. She ran to meet them.

"Thought I heard a plane go down," the warden said as she rapidly explained. The other man checked on the poachers while the game warden cut Tim's ropes and removed the tape.

"I found that quisling, Chris," Tim burst out. "He's Tom Crockett. That's why I had to come out to the cabin—to make sure. They've got snakes in the plane too."

The game warden was already leaning into the plane. "Whew, what a load. No wonder they went down. Look at all this stuff." He lifted out a cage of snakes.

Tim hoisted himself to a sitting position, and his words tumbled out in a rush. "Chris, I've got to tell you something. I'm the one who let those snakes out of the cage at the old cabin—I followed you there. I thought it was mean of them to trap them, and I didn't know you were going to call the game warden."

Before she could say anything, he hurried on. "See, I heard a guy say something about Tom Crockett in the grocery store, and it made me pretty sure that he was the man your dad wanted to catch. So when I knew he was going to warn the poachers, I went out to the cabin too." His face fell. "Only they caught me, and then I didn't know what to do. But I prayed a lot."

Chris understood what he meant. "I found your message."

His eyes lit up. "The airplane? I knew the Lord would show it to you. Hey, Chris, He made it turn out O.K. in spite of me. No mistakes—right?"

"No mistakes," Chris agreed. She blinked away happy tears and grinned at him. "I'm learning about that."

A Visit with a Mystery Writer: Gloria Repp

Eileen M. Berry

Interviewer: How long have you been writing mysteries?

Repp: About fifteen years.

Interviewer: What first caused you to become interested in mystery writing?

Repp: I've always liked to read anything, and especially mysteries. I wanted to write for children, and I knew that children like mysteries. Writing mysteries is kind of like putting a puzzle together, only even more fun because you actually get to make the puzzle yourself.

Interviewer: Do you have a favorite place to be when writing?

Repp: I have a big old brown chair at home where I like to sit. It has a table next to it where I can set all my stuff. I also write at a computer sometimes, but I like to do my rough draft in longhand. Somehow I can think better with a pencil in my hand rather than staring at a screen.

Interviewer: How much planning do you do before you start writing a mystery?

Repp: Oh, I do a *lot*. I get my character in mind first—I even have a character sketch form that I fill out for my main character and all the other major characters. For example, in "The Quisling Hunt," I decide what the main character's exterior and interior characteristics will be—everything from age and hair color to how the character reacts when other people cry. I make sure I have a clear understanding of the main character's spiritual condition and what the problem is. The character's main problem must intersect[1] with the mystery.

Interviewer: How much of the mystery do you plan ahead of time, and how do you keep track of all those clues and details as you write?

Repp: I plan the mystery itself, starting at the end. It's easier to plan the events leading up to the crisis[2] if I already know how it will turn out.

I make a notebook for each of my books while I'm still in the planning stages. I put all my ideas in there— character sketches, articles I've read on my topic, notes I've taken from research material or written to myself as I think about the book. Sometimes I even glue in little scraps of paper or napkins that I've jotted ideas on. I also make a lot of charts to help me keep track of the plot and the spiritual growth of the characters.

Interviewer: Do you ever change the plan as you're writing?

Repp: Sometimes. But I don't usually change the way the mystery turns out, just the minor details.

Interviewer: Do you draw your characters and plots from imagination, real life, or a combination of the two?

Repp: A combination of the two, plus research that I've done on the

---

[1]intersect—to come together or cross
[2]crisis—the turning point in a story; the highest point
 of intensity

topic. Once I got an idea for the criminals in a mystery from an article I read while waiting in the dentist's office.

Interviewer: What is the average length of time it takes you to write a mystery novel?

Repp: About two years, from the start of the planning stage to the end of the writing.

Interviewer: What do you find most challenging about writing a mystery?

Repp: Two things. First, keeping it from being trite[3] or stereotypical[4]— you know, having the criminal be the guy with the scar on his face who drives the black van. The plot and characters have to be unique. The other thing is making the characterization[5] and spiritual growth of the characters convincing.

Interviewer: In your opinion, what makes a mystery worth reading?

Repp: The interaction of the *character* with the plot. It has to be more than a superficial,[6] plot-driven story.

Interviewer: Do you have a favorite mystery or a favorite mystery author?

Repp: Phyllis Whitney is my favorite author of children's mysteries. I read a book of hers on writing for children, and it got me interested in reading some of her fiction. I like her mysteries because they focus on a character with a problem, not just a suspenseful plot.

Interviewer: What advice would you give young writers who would like to write mysteries?

Repp: Of course they should read widely. And they should analyze[7] while they read. Note the characterization, and if it is a mystery, try to figure it out as you go along. Think about why you liked the book when you finish it.

---

[3]trite—lacking interest because of overuse or familiarity
[4]stereotypical—a fixed view of something which doesn't allow individuality
[5]characterization—the way an author represents a character in writing
[6]superficial—only presenting the obvious; shallow
[7]analyze—to examine very carefully

Gloria Repp has also written several missionary stories.

Yeoman Knight

Dawn L. Watkins

illustrated by Chris Koelle
and John Bjerk

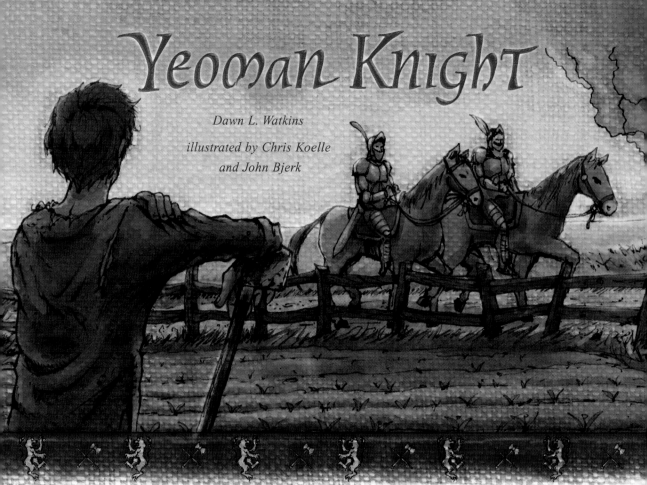

Courage, Wit, and Duty

The knights flashed past on their horses, their armor glinting in the late afternoon sun. Geoffrey leaned on his wooden hoe, watching the plumes on the shiny helmets until he could not see them any longer.

"That's what I'm going to be," he said to the boy next to him. "A knight in the service of the king."

The other boy laughed as though he had seen a jester at the fair. "And what will you use for armor?" he asked.

Geoffrey looked down at his tattered yeoman's[1] leggings and his poorly shod feet. "Courage," he said, looking up again brightly.

"And what will you use for a helmet?" his companion continued.

"My wits," Geoffrey answered unabashed.[2]

The other yeoman boy shook his head. "And what, Sir Geoffrey, will you use for a steed?"[3]

Geoffrey straightened his shoulders. His handsome face, tanned and

---

[1] yeoman—a commoner who works the land
[2] unabashed—not embarrassed
[3] steed—horse

286

smooth, was smudged with dirt from the field. "Duty, my friend. Duty spurred by loyalty."

Before the other boy could make any answer, Geoffrey shouldered the worn hoe and strode away toward the road the knights had taken to the west.

The sun was going down, and as Geoffrey walked along, he thought briefly of the supper he had left behind.

"Well, no matter," he said to himself. "A knight learns to do without supper and sleep, if he is to be any kind of a knight at all."

He stopped at a brook to wash his face and hands, thinking that perhaps he should find a good place to rest, but as he turned to go deeper into the woods, he heard riders coming on the road. He could make out three riders, their horses trotting easily. Suddenly two more riders, one on each side of the road, raced out from the trees. Before he could blink, these two riders knocked one of the first three from his horse.

Geoffrey burst forward, yelling as he did when he chased the wild boars to the hunters. The two riders whirled in surprise, but the yeoman was already upon them, brandishing[4] his hoe. The robbers' horses reared, throwing one robber to the ground. The second lashed at Geoffrey with his club, but Geoffrey ducked neatly

and sprang up, charging the man with his hoe handle.

"Oooghf," the robber said, as he slipped sideways on his mount, the hoe handle in his ribs.

The free horse whinnied and galloped away. The fallen robber pulled himself up behind his off-balanced companion, and on one snorting horse they escaped.

Geoffrey turned back to the riders behind him. "Anyone hurt?"

"No, young fellow," said an older man dressed in a rich blue riding cape. A younger man, the one who had been knocked from his horse, was dusting off his velvet cap.

"Wretches!"[5] said the young man, putting the cap on his head. "They had the advantage, certainly, taking us by surprise."

"We are grateful to you," said the older man. "What reward do you require?"

"Why, none, sir," said Geoffrey, surprised.

The third rider put back a cape hood and spoke for the first time. "Surely you are no mere yeoman, sir."

Geoffrey looked up in amazement. The speaker was a beautiful girl about his own age with thickly braided bronze hair.

---

[4]brandishing—waving about as a weapon
[5]wretches—evil or wicked persons

"I used to be a yeoman," he said, suddenly shy. "I am starting a new life."

The old man smiled. "And a good start it is too. I am the duke of Arandale. This is my daughter, Brith. And this is Tanlin, a scholar who joined us earlier today. And you are?"

"Geoffrey, Your Grace." He bowed low. Had he been trained all his life in court manners, he could not have made a more proper answer.

"Then, Geoffrey," said the duke, "ride on with us to Glennon Inn and let me buy your supper."

Geoffrey, whose hunger had now outrun his modesty, agreed happily.

"And bring your lance," said the duke. "We may need it yet again."

Everyone laughed. Geoffrey got up behind Tanlin, and away they rode toward Glennon, the hoe making a long, dark silhouette against the falling evening.

"Have more venison,"[6] said the duke later. Geoffrey would have liked to, but he had eaten more already than he had ever believed he could. The inn's fire blazed heartily at the other end of the room, and a man played a lilting tune on a pipe while everyone ate.

Brith sat quietly by her father, her hair more beautiful in the firelight than it had been under the setting sun. The former yeoman stole only occasional glances at her. But somehow, each time, she happened to be looking at him.

Tanlin, growing a little weary of the attention shown to the ragged farmer, said, "Your Grace, I must compliment you on your choice of inns. This is the finest I've seen in this country."

"You are much traveled then?" asked the duke.

"I've been to France and Spain, and sailed some on the open sea."

"Indeed," said the duke, "travel educates a man, does it not?"

Tanlin turned a rather snobbish gaze to Geoffrey. "Have you done any traveling?"

For a moment, there was only the snapping of the fire and the high, thin music of the pipe to be heard. Brith looked at her father, who was looking disapprovingly at Tanlin. Anyone could see the boy was poor, and only someone bent on embarrassing him would have asked such a question.

Geoffrey put down his cup and smiled at Tanlin unwounded. "I have traveled more today than ever I have in my life—as you count travel. But there are other kinds of travel, and in those I am experienced enough."

Both the duke and Brith looked toward Geoffrey, the duke in mild but pleased surprise and Brith with open admiration.

"And what ways might those be?" said the scholar, not to be bested by some farmer.

---

[6]venison—the meat of a deer

"Well," said the boy, "I have traveled much through conversation. I have talked with wise men and poor men and men who have learned from experience. I have been where they have been by careful listening. I have done such traveling even today with my lord the duke and you."

"Well said," replied the duke, and Brith nodded.

"A rather common travel," said the scholar, taking refuge in rudeness.

"And," Geoffrey continued, "I have been to ports and palaces everywhere and nowhere—"

"Nowhere?" Tanlin broke in.

"By imagination." Geoffrey looked past Tanlin, as if to one of those places he had often traveled to when he worked in the fields.

The scholar laughed aloud.

"Tell me about one of the ports of nowhere," said the pretty Brith, and Tanlin stopped laughing.

After supper, Geoffrey thanked his host and made ready to leave the inn.

"Hold a moment," said the duke. "Would your new life include any service to a duke?"

"Sir?"

"Would your plans allow you to serve me for a while?"

"I would gladly serve you, sir, were I fit. But I have much to learn and no means with which to serve."

"You have courage and wit and good sense. These things are means enough. What training and materials you lack, I can give you. What do you say?"

"Thank you, my good lord," he answered, bowing.

At Arandale Manor, Geoffrey received a handsome pair of leggings and a stiff linen shirt with wide shoulders and full sleeves. All of the duke's servants were dressed well, Geoffrey noticed as he looked around.

"Now you be sure to bring this to me when it gets dirty," said the old woman who had given him the shirt. "The duke won't have his servants smudged up like ploughboys."

Geoffrey winced at her words.

"What's your job to be here?" she asked.

"Stable boy, I think."

"Pah!" she said with a short shake of her head. "You'll be coming up here twice a day to get your shirt washed. Here"—she tossed him another shirt—"wear one and then the other and don't be coming to me saying you don't have a clean shirt."

Geoffrey laughed a little. "Thank you," he said, and left.

He was assigned his duties and was happy to learn that he already knew how to do much of the work. So he could do his work and still take notice of how the guard mounted their horses, carried their weapons, and put on their gear. He even had time some late afternoons to look at the coats of arms along the walls of the armory.

"Hello, boy," said the white-bearded man who kept the armory.

"Here again, are you? Let's see what you remember."

Geoffrey came up boldly, sure of his memory.

"Now then," said the man, "who bears the long bow and arrows on a field of gules?"[7]

"The duke of Wilcom."

"Who bears a silver deer on an azure[8] field?" The man turned as he spoke to look at the banner on the stone wall.

"The prince of Barlanty."

"Well done, my boy. Now," the old gentleman continued, "who bears the gold dove over three trees?"

Geoffrey could not remember having learned that one. He quickly swept his gaze around the armory, but he could not find the banner. "I don't know," he said at last.

"Well, of course you don't," said the man, chuckling. "I made it up to see what you would say."

Under orders from the duke, Geoffrey was taught courtly manners and the rules of speaking to the nobility. There were so many rules, and so many exceptions, that Geoffrey began to wonder if he were not after all more suited to the plough.

Before sunrise Geoffrey would muck[9] out the stables and curry[10] the

---

[7]gules—vertical lines that indicate the color red on a coat of arms
[8]azure—light to medium blue
[9]muck—to clean the dirt or manure from
[10]curry—to groom with a special comb

great horses that the duke's guard rode. They were massive iron-gray horses, capable of carrying a man in full armor at a gallop. But as Geoffrey brushed them they stood docile[11] as kittens, snorting now and then as if to thank him for his efforts.

"Good morning, boy," said the captain of the guard as he strode into the stables. "Up before all but the nightwatch again, are you? I fear the horses don't even wake as early as you."

"I have much to learn," the boy answered. "I want to finish my work so I can watch the horsemen and practice fencing."

The captain, a large man with a close-cropped black beard, merely chuckled. "Boy, you had best be content with polishing the armor—do not plan to wear any." And saying, "Ho, ho," he walked on, slapping the rump of the horse Geoffrey was standing beside.

Geoffrey took hold of the horse's halter and pulled the great head down. "I will be a knight," he said to the horse. The horse tossed his head and nickered.

"Geoffrey! Geoffrey, my lad." It was the duke himself come to the stables.

"Yes, my lord," answered the boy from a deep bow.

"Tell the captain I want my best hunting horses made ready. I've promised some of my guests a boar hunt, and this morning the air feels right for it."

"Yes, it does," said Geoffrey before he remembered that he should make no answer unless asked a question.

The duke ignored the breach of courtly rules. "Do you know about boar[12] hunts?"

"I was once employed by a man who had me run the boars far more often than plough the fields."

"Indeed. Then you shall surely come with us today. See that six of my light horses are well harnessed and waiting by morning bells." He turned to leave but stopped. "And get yourself a leather chestpiece from the armory." Then he went on, calling for a page to get down the spears and daggers.

Geoffrey flew to his work, and by morning bells, six perfectly equipped horses stood in the court-yard, pawing the cobbles and bobbing their heads. The duke came out in his riding gear, followed by four noblemen and one noblewoman.

"Well done," the duke said to Geoffrey, who held the bridle as the duke mounted. "Go on ahead now and stay with the captain."

---

[11]docile—easy to handle or train
[12]boar—a wild pig with a thick coat of dark bristles

The boy ran forward toward the wood, and the handsome company rode at a walk behind. The men carried spears and daggers and wore strung bows over their shoulders. The lady wore a longbow over her left shoulder and a leather quiver of arrows on her belt. She rode easily, a light veil drifting out and back from her cap in the early morning breeze.

The runners fanned out as they entered the wood. Geoffrey paused a moment in the stillness, looking keenly around. He saw a rough swath[13] off to the left, and experience told him a boar was probably at the end of it. He trotted away from the path at a diagonal for several

---

[13]swath—a strip cut through grass or trees, as if by a mower

yards and then straight across to it. Out again at a diagonal he ran and then straight across, always brightly alert and listening.

When the duke entered the wood, he saw his young servant and said to one of his companions, "See that boy there? He knows how to roust[14] up a boar without endangering himself or us too much." The other man looked at Geoffrey and nodded.

The seventh time Geoffrey ran toward the swath, he saw the large, dark form of a sleeping boar. He stopped short, trying to see which way the animal was turned. It was headed away from the riders. Geoffrey signaled to the duke that he had come upon a boar. The riders halted some way back and readied their weapons.

Geoffrey devoted his full attention to the boar. He circled to the right and stamped the ground and yelled loudly. The animal grunted once and slightly lifted its head. Geoffrey yelled again and ran farther around toward the head. The surprised boar shoved its weighty bulk up and began to swing his head back and forth.

"Yah! Yah!" Geoffrey hollered. Another servant had come in on the other side. The boar, distracted, lunged first at Geoffrey and then at the man on the left. Both sprang back out of easy range.

The duke and his party made an uneven circle within twenty yards. "Lady Gwendolyn shoots first," cried the duke. The lady, her bow at the ready, waited for the runners to turn the boar. Geoffrey glanced swiftly up to see whether the hunters were prepared. He caught a brief glimpse of the woman before he had to look back to the animal.

"Now!" he yelled to his companion. They charged forward together. The boar, confused, pulled back and suddenly wheeled around. As he did, an arrow came humming from the lady's bow. It struck him behind the shoulder and stayed in. The boar roared once before a spear took him. He quivered briefly and fell dead.

A cheer went up from the whole party. "Excellent!" shouted the duke. "Splendid!" said two of the other men together. "Let's have another," said a third.

By the end of the day, a tired company went home with four fine boars borne on poles before them. The duke, breaking a rule of court himself, let Geoffrey ride with him as a reward for his skillful work of the day.

---

[14]roust—to wake; stir up

Test of a Loyal Heart

The next week there was a huge feast at the castle. The duke had invited dozens of noblemen and their ladies to the opening banquet and to the week of games and contests after. The whole castle was scoured and swept, aired and shook out, lit with torches and hung with tapestries and colorful swags of velvet. The manor servants were dressed in blue and gold, and every window held a laurel wreath.

Geoffrey in all his days and in all his imagination had never seen such brightsome splendor. He gazed into the interior halls from the kitchen, his eyes adazzle. Behind him in the kitchen, puddings and sauces bubbled over the fires and sent thick, sweet smells through the whole house.

Outside, whole wild boars turned slowly over open fires, nearly roasted now. They had been put upon the spits two days ago, basted with honey and herbs, and smoked well over green wood. Two or three times a day, Geoffrey passed by to see how things developed.

Officers of the guard burnished[15] their greaves[16] and breastplates and oiled the joints of their kneepieces and pauldrons.[17] Geoffrey watched them intently, wishing he were among them.

As it was, he polished the leather chestpiece that the duke had allowed him to keep. He shined it until it was almost brighter than the metal of the armor. Brith came to him on an afternoon as he buffed the leather for yet the thirtieth time.

"Good day, Geoffrey," she said. She smiled like a field of daisies, he thought.

He stood up and bowed to her. "Good day, Lady Brith."

She looked down briefly at the leather. "Will you be playing in the games?"

"I think not," he said, hoping his disappointment did not show.

"Did you ask Father?"

"No, my lady."

"You needn't fear him. He likes you."

Geoffrey blushed. "To ask a special favor from your father the duke would not be suitable. Favors are not asked for, but given. He would think me rude."

Brith drew a silk scarf from her sleeve. "Should you decide to ask," she said, "I would like you to tie my scarf to the bridle of your horse." She laid the bright blue scarf down and left without more words.

Geoffrey was left in a quandary.[18] The honor of the scarf dismayed him. Only proven knights and gallant men were worthy of such things. He wanted desperately to ask the duke for permission to join the games. He considered long and hard. At last,

---

[15]burnished—polished
[16]greaves—armor that covers the leg below the knee
[17]pauldrons—armor that covers the shoulder
[18]quandary—a perplexing situation

there was to be seen and what pleasure to be enjoyed for a week!

Soon, just as he had thought, the duke on his way to the falcon keep turned through the gate where Geoffrey was standing. He nodded to the boy.

Geoffrey summoned up his voice but could not use it. The duke hesitated. "Something, my lad?"

The moment of opportunity hung in the air like a fragile bubble, shimmering and brief.

"No, my good lord," said Geoffrey, and the moment was gone forever. He thought of the scarf in his pocket. "Your pardon, sir; there is something."

"Well?" said the duke, looking keenly down at this boy he liked.

Geoffrey drew out the scarf admiringly and held it out. "Sir, your daughter . . ."

"Yes?"

"Your daughter left this in the stable earlier. It is not my place to return it. I thought perhaps, if you would be so good, sir, you might give it to her."

"Very well," said the duke.

Geoffrey bowed and stepped back.

against his better judgment, he went to where he knew the duke would be sure to pass.

As he waited by the gate, two serving women went by. "You'd think the king was coming," said one.

"Never have there been such preparations in this place. Did you see those wonderful imported tablecloths?" said the other.

"Oh, yes, and the gold platters for the goose!" Their voices could not be heard after they turned the corner. Geoffrey thought his heart would burst with excitement. What splendor

The duke said, "I want you to tend the stables during the festival here. Keep all the horses as you keep mine, and I will be well pleased."

"Yes, Your Grace," said the boy.

"I will see to it that your meals are brought to you," the old man said.

Geoffrey's heart fell. He had nourished a hope that he could attend the banquet. What then had all those lessons in courtly manners been for? The tears threatened, but he mastered them. "Yes, sir," he said.

"Come not to the house unless you are sent for," the duke said, and went away.

The cheery lights faded, and the great halls lost their color in Geoffrey's mind. The sweet smells turned repugnant,[19] and the wreaths seemed now black circles of some poisonous weeds. The yeoman returned to the stables and sat down on the cobbles before the door. Had not the desire to be a knight still been deep in his heart, he would have let a tear or two escape him. Instead he made an intense study of the stones and straw around him.

From this dismal reverie,[20] he was pulled by a deep voice. "Are you Geoffrey? Geoffrey of boar-hunting fame?"

Geoffrey looked up to see he was being addressed by a nobleman. He stood up, brushed himself off, and answered. "I am Geoffrey, sir."

"I am Lady Gwendolyn's husband. She tells me you are the best runner she has ever seen in the field."

"The lady is too kind, sir," said the lad.

"And you are well-mannered, as well, I see. At any rate, I've come to ask you to work for me."

Geoffrey could not conceal his surprise. "I am in the service of His Grace the duke, sir, thank you."

"Ah," said the nobleman, "you must give this more thought. I will treat you well—not keep you in the stable during festival."

Geoffrey hesitated only a moment. "With respect, sir, the duke treats me well and gives me more than ever I had. I cannot leave his service; it would be most disloyal of me."

"I hear you aspire[21] to be a knight."

Geoffrey felt his ears get red, but he made no answer, nor did he have to, since he had not been asked a question.

"I can help you," the man continued. "I have the king's ear."

"You are kind to offer," said Geoffrey. "But were I to leave the duke after he has been only kind to me, I would not be worthy to be a knight."

---

[19]repugnant—repulsive; disgusting
[20]reverie—daydream
[21]aspire—to have a great ambition; strive toward

296

"I would give you yet another chance," said the nobleman. "I will make you captain of all the hunts at my manor. What do you say?"

"Sir, you are generous. But my service is here. If my lord requires me to keep the stable, I shall keep the stable as though it were the king's treasure room and count myself honored to serve so gracious a master." Geoffrey's face in this last had assumed the same handsome determination it had that day some time ago when he had left the field.

The nobleman only smiled and nodded. He said nothing further, leaving Geoffrey to his work at the stable.

The guests began to arrive, lords and ladies with brightly garbed entourages[22] on well-trimmed and high-stepping horses. Some of the ladies' horses had tiny bells braided into their manes, and these mounts made a shimmering little music as they came.

Geoffrey found pleasure in unharnessing the grand horses and in wiping the dust from the silver-and-leather saddles. There was so much to do to attend to all these horses that Geoffrey almost forgot that he was not going to see the celebration in the manor.

[22]entourages (ŏn´ tŏŏ räzh´ ĕz)—groups of attendants or friends following someone

On the afternoon before the banquet, there was suddenly a stir and a bustle in the stables, uncommon in even these uncommon times. Geoffrey ran out to the main stable to see what had happened. The captain, dressed in his best, was proudly leading a black horse covered with a purple silk. From two leather-and-gold straps hung a diamond-shaped medal, engraved with words and set with gems. It was the most magnificent sight the boy had ever seen.

"Whose horse is this?" he asked another stableman who was sharing the vantage point of the same tack rail with him.

"Why, the king's!" was the incredulous[23] answer.

Geoffrey stared in wonder. Ah! The king had indeed come. If only he could catch sight of him. But what chance would there be of that? When the shining horse had been closed in his special stall and Geoffrey could not see anything but grooms running here and there, he went back to his work with only a little less pleasure than before.

Late that evening, from his window over the stable, Geoffrey could hear the lovely pipe and string music and see the warm light given off by the fireplaces and the torches. He even thought he could smell the rich meats and sauces and the bubbling, thick puddings. He strained to gather all he could with his senses, and his quick imagination supplied the rest.

He imagined himself seated by Lady Brith, dressed in fine clothes, and eating some of the boar he had helped to bring down. It was so real to him that when his meal was brought by one of the manor servants, he almost said that he had already eaten. The smell of real food, however, quickly changed his opinion. He got up, put on his clean shirt, and ate his small plate of food alone.

Sometime later, one of the officers of the guard appeared in the stable. "His lordship sends for you," he said. "Go directly to the banquet hall. Another servant will meet you and show you in."

Geoffrey ran out, nearly knocking the officer off his feet. He ran all the way to the hall and stopped briefly to catch his breath. He collected himself and entered the side outer hall. A servant somewhat older than himself motioned for him to come along. Geoffrey followed.

They passed through a bustling of serving women and cooks. They went on past the neatly dressed serving men and right up to the huge double doors, all carved with scenes of hunting and feasting. Here they paused as the servant said something to the man at the door. The man nodded and swung open the door.

---

[23]incredulous—shocked and unbelieving

For a moment, Geoffrey was nearly blinded by the lights within. Every iron bracket held a magnificent glowing torch. Two huge fireplaces, larger than whole houses Geoffrey had known, blazed up with fires that looked as though they would never die out. The air was filled with the mingling aromas of garlands of wild flowers, basted meats, and rich spices. The tables were covered with blue and gold tablecloths and set with more gold and silver pieces than the boy had believed existed in the world.

He followed the servant in a daze and arrived after no small walk be-fore the duke. Geoffrey by great ef-fort remembered his manners. He bowed and said, "At your service, my good lord."

The duke smiled. He turned to the man beside him who wore a vel-vet of deep purple. "This is the boy, Your Majesty," the duke said.

Geoffrey gasped audibly. He bowed, twice, but could not think of what to say. So he said nothing.

The king looked kindly at the boy. "It is told me you want to be a knight. Is that so?"

"Yes, Your Majesty," Geoffrey answered, barely above a whisper.

"I have heard of your courage with robbers and of your wit with haughty scholars and wild boars. How may I know you are loyal?"

"Pardon, Your Majesty," said the duke. "I can tell you of that."

"Say on, then," said the king.

"I have learned that my daughter encouraged this boy to ask a favor of me. He graciously refused without giving offense anywhere. Then I told him to keep the stables when I had let him believe he would be allowed to see the feast. He obeyed without a word or look of displeasure."

"He is well-mannered to be sure—but is not loyalty more than proper speech?" asked the king.

"That is so, Your Majesty," said the duke. "So I tested his heart. I sent my friend, Lord John, to lure[24] the boy away from my service with promises of position and plenty."

The king turned to Lord John, who sat with the Lady Gwendolyn farther down the same table. "What answer did you receive, John?"

"Right gladly would I have kept my promises to the lad," Lord John replied, "but he said he could not leave the service of so kind a lord. He said that he would keep the duke's stable as if it were your grace's treasure room and count it an honor to do so, Your Majesty."

There was a general murmur of approval around the table.

"Well answered," said the king. "Geoffrey, I have your master's leave to ask you a question."

Geoffrey, still amazed at what he had just heard about the events of the day which he had counted so miserable, waited.

"Will you leave the duke of Arandale to train at my palace to be a knight?"

Geoffrey felt his face redden and looked quickly to the duke. The duke nodded his permission.

Geoffrey turned back to the king. "I will, Your Grace."

The king looked pleased and leaned back in his chair. The duke said, "Come, lad; my daughter has kept a place for you at her table. In the morning we will talk a bit further."

"Perhaps he would like to join the games tomorrow," said the king.

"Certainly, Your Majesty," said the duke.

Geoffrey bowed his best bows, first to the king and then to the duke. He stepped back without turning, but he could not keep from smiling.

As Geoffrey took his seat, the duke called for more music and more venison and more light. The former yeoman looked about him. And for the first time in his life, the reality was greater than his dream.

---

[24]lure—to attract; tempt

Plot

Morgan Reed Persun

What is a Plot?

When you tell your friends something that happened to you, you usually tell it like a story. You tell what happened first, and then next, and then after that. You know intuitively[1] that events follow in order, that a story has a beginning, a middle, and an end.

Sometimes a *plot* is defined simply as a series of events in order from beginning to end. But a plot is more than an order of events, more than an outline of a story. E. M. Forster, who writes novels for adults, once explained plot like this: " 'The king died, and then the queen died' is a story. 'The king died, and then the queen died of grief' is a plot."

Do you see the difference? The first example gives two events in order; the second example shows how the first event *caused* the second. A plot, then, is an order that shows how events link to each other, causing the next thing to happen, and the next, until at last a defining outcome occurs and the story ends.

You could think of plot as a line of dominoes, the first event tipping into the next, causing the second to topple the third and so on until they all fall. The writer, like the person who sets up dominoes, arranges things so that they finish falling right where he wants them to. He chooses how many events he will use, what sequence they will be in, and what pattern they will make when they are all toppled.

Where Plots Start

Just as dominoes placed in a row hit one against the next, so elements[2] in a story "hit" against

---

[1]intuitively—knowing or sensing something without needing to ask
[2]elements—basic parts of something

other elements. When ideas, characters, or events "hit" against each other in a story, we call it *conflict*. It is very hard to talk about plot without talking about conflict. Conflict creates action, and without action, there is no plot.

For example, you might keep reading about a boy who wants a horse and just goes out and buys one, *if* you like the descriptions of the horse or you want a horse yourself and want to see how much the boy paid for his horse. But you are much more likely to keep reading if the boy has an opportunity to earn a horse but then his father gets sick, and the boy has to work at home and so gives up his job in town, and—you get the idea. There has to be a struggle in order for there to be a real plot.

Plots rise out of many kinds of conflict. Some stories are about one character against another. In "The Squire's Bride," the squire and the poor farmer's daughter have such a conflict. Others are about characters struggling against some force larger than themselves. The story "Antarctica" pits Drew, Derrick, and their uncle against the cold and danger of an ice shelf; the fight is against nature. Other plots show characters struggling against God. Gwo Gwang in "The Greater God" must strive to

trust God in spite of what he has been taught about bad spirits. Still other stories show a character struggling against himself. The Bible presents many narratives about real people who must overcome something in themselves. For example, Esther overcomes fear to stand up for her people.

How Plots Progress

Most short stories, such as are in this book, follow a *dramatic plot structure*. A dramatic plot structure begins with an *introduction* that shows the setting and the main character or characters. It then arrives at the *inciting*[3] *incident,* a moment in the story after which nothing will ever be the same as it was in the introduction. From the inciting incident, the tension increases as the story unfolds in the *rising action*. The event of highest interest, the point at which the action comes to a deciding moment, is called the *crisis*. The story then quickly proceeds through events of less tension—the *falling action*—and resolves in the *denouement*.[4] *Denouement* comes from a French word; it means "unraveling." How is that an appropriate word for the last part of the plot? (Denouement plays

---

[3]inciting—putting into motion
[4]denouement (dā´noo män´)—the ending or resolution of a plot

INTRODUCTION RISING ACTION CRISIS FALLING ACTION

INCITING INCIDENT

DENOUEMENT

out what happens after the crisis; it "pulls the last strings" of the plot.)

In "Listening to Katey," the author first lets you get to know Pete and Katey and how they live and that they want to go to Kingdom by the Sea. Then she introduces the event that changes everything about their summer. The inciting incident is when their father says, "You can earn the money yourselves." The rising action consists of Pete and Ike trying to

make a fast dollar and Katey working steadily along. The crisis occurs when Ike and Pete have an accident trying to trap rabbits. The falling action starts with Ike literally falling into a hole and continues to the denouement in which Katey offers to lend the older boys money.

Plots for books, or much larger stories, can sometimes follow other kinds of plots. The Laura Ingalls Wilder books, for example, such as *Little House on the Prairie,* progress through *episodes.* Each chapter of such a book seems a short story in itself, and not all the events affect events that follow. But all the chapters together give the reader a full idea of how life on the frontier was and show how families had to work together to survive. Such plots are called *episodic.*

What Makes a Good Plot?

Plots can be based on real life, as in "The Greater God." Or they can imitate (seem close to) real life, as in "Aunt Mazey Ain't Crazy." Or they can be completely imaginary, such as in "Yeoman Knight." But whatever the plot is based on, it must be believable.

In funny or fanciful stories, the world of the characters may seem like the real world yet it is imaginary. For example, the places in "A Ride to Honor" cannot be found in any atlas of Earth. Nowhere in our world would you find, for example, Cordus of Kapnos or Brass Mountains. But the action in the story abides by the rule of the fanciful setting, and the characters respond as we expect them to. So although the story is entirely imaginary, it is—within its own boundaries—believable.

Good plots also make themes memorable. In "Listening to Katey," Pete's many attempts to make money quickly may make the reader laugh. But in the end, when such schemes all fail and he has to borrow money from his little sister, the events of the plot point to the theme—the value of hard work.

The end of the plot is really what creates the meaning of the story.

Suppose, for example, that "Listening to Katey" ended with the rabbit trapping bringing lots of money. What would the story say then? It would say that get-rich-quick schemes are better than working steadily and responsibly toward a goal, which is not a true or valuable message. Good plots end in ways that support good themes.

But perhaps the mark of a good plot easiest to see is its ability to move from point to point, keeping the reader wondering what will happen next. In "Mowgli's Brothers," Kipling uses a plot that does it all. It abides by the rules established in the setting, it makes the themes of courage and doing the right thing easy to see, and it most certainly keeps the reader turning the pages.

The next time you find yourself being swept along in a story, take a moment to see how the author has arranged the "dominoes" and what pattern they have made when the story is over. And then you will see how the author used plot to make his story say what it does.

EXTRAVAGANZAS 4

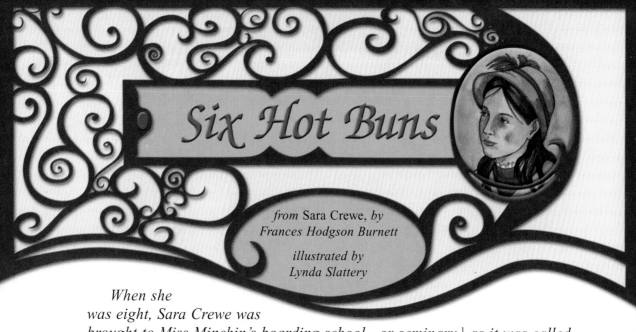

Six Hot Buns

from Sara Crewe, *by*
Frances Hodgson Burnett

illustrated by
Lynda Slattery

*When she
was eight, Sara Crewe was
brought to Miss Minchin's boarding school—or seminary,[1] as it was called—
and her father returned to India to finish serving as an officer there. For two
and a half years, Sara was well treated and became a star pupil. Then word
came that Captain Crewe had died and his fortune had been lost. From that
day onward, Sara took her place as the lowest servant at Miss Minchin's. She
was made to sleep in a bare and unheated attic and sent about the streets of
London in ragged clothes to run daily errands. Neglected, mistreated by everybody, and made to feel that she belonged to nobody, Sara fought despair by
telling herself that she was a princess who had been driven out—a princess in
rags. She continued to read and educate herself when she could and to treat
all people with courtesy and grace as a princess would. The following chapters
from her story tell of Sara's inner nobility and of the sudden changes she
found one day in her attic bedroom. Sara's story also appears in an expanded
form in the novel* A Little Princess.

One of the Populace

It was a dreadful afternoon. For
several days it had rained continu-
ously; the streets were chilly and
sloppy; there was mud everywhere—
sticky London mud—and over everything a pall[2] of fog and drizzle. Of
course there were several long and
tiresome errands to be done—there
always were on days like this—and
Sara went out again and again, until
her shabby clothes were damp
through. The old feathers on her for-
lorn hat were more bedraggled[3] and
absurd than ever, and her downtrod-

[1]seminary—private school for girls
[2]pall—a covering
[3]bedraggled—drooping; shabby

306

Pleasure in Improbabilities

It was dark when she reached the square in which Miss Minchin's Select Seminary was situated; the lamps were lighted, and in most of the windows gleams of light were to be seen. It always interested Sara to catch glimpses of the rooms before the shutters were closed. She liked to imagine things about people who sat before the fires in the houses or who bent over books at the tables. There was, for instance, the Large Family opposite. She called these people the Large Family—not because they were large, for indeed most of them were little, but because there were so many of them. There were eight children in the Large Family, and a stout, rosy mother, and a stout, rosy father, and a stout, rosy grandmamma, and any number of servants. The eight children were always either being taken out to walk, or to ride in perambulators,[9] by comfortable nurses; or they were going to drive with their mamma; or they were flying to the door in the evening to kiss their papa, and dance around him and drag off his overcoat and look for packages in the pocket of it; or they were crowding about the nursery windows and looking out and pushing each other and laughing—in fact, they were always doing something which seemed enjoyable and suited to the tastes of a large family.

Next door to the Large Family lived the Maiden Lady, who had a companion and two parrots, and a King Charles spaniel; but Sara was not so very fond of her because she did nothing in particular but talk to the parrots and drive out with the spaniel. The most interesting person of all lived next door to Miss Minchin herself. Sara called him the Indian Gentleman. He was an elderly gentleman who was said to have lived in the East Indies and to be immensely rich and to have something the matter with his liver—in fact, it had been rumored that he had no liver at all, and was much inconvenienced by the fact. At any rate, he was very yellow and he did not look happy; and when he went out to his carriage, he was almost always wrapped up in shawls and overcoats, as if he were cold. He had a native servant who looked even colder than himself, and he had a monkey who looked colder than the native servant. Sara had seen the monkey sitting on a table, in the sun, in the parlor window, and he always wore such a mournful expression that she sympathized with him deeply.

---

[9]perambulator—a baby carriage

"I daresay," she used sometimes to remark to herself, "he is thinking all the time of coconut trees and of swinging by his tail under a tropical sun. He might have had a family dependent on him, too, poor thing!"

The native servant, whom she called the Lascar, looked mournful too, but he was evidently very faithful to his master.

"Perhaps he saved his master's life in the Sepoy rebellion," she thought. "They look as if they might have had all sorts of adventures. I wish I could speak to the Lascar. I remember a little Hindustani."[10]

And one day she actually did speak to him, and his start at the sound of his own language expressed a great deal of surprise and delight. He was waiting for his master to come out to the carriage, and Sara, who was going on an errand as usual, stopped and spoke a few words. She had a special gift for languages and had remembered enough Hindustani to make herself understood by him. When his master came out, the Lascar spoke to him quickly, and the Indian Gentleman turned and looked at her curiously. And afterward the

Lascar always greeted her with salaams[11] of the most profound[12] description. And occasionally they exchanged a few words. She learned that it was true that the Sahib[13] was very rich, that he was ill, and also that he had no wife nor children and that England did not agree with the monkey.

"He must be as lonely as I am," thought Sara. "Being rich does not seem to make him happy."

That evening, as she passed the windows, the Lascar was closing the shutters, and she caught a glimpse of the room inside. There was a bright fire glowing in the grate,[14] and the Indian Gentleman was sitting before it in a luxurious chair. The room was richly furnished and looked delightfully comfortable, but the Indian Gentleman sat with his head resting on his hand and looked as lonely and as unhappy as ever.

"Poor man!" said Sara; "I wonder what *you* are supposing?"

---

[10]Hindustani—a group of Indian dialects
[11]salaams—respectful greetings; low bows
[12]profound—felt very deeply
[13]Sahib—term used in India to address a European man
[14]grate—a framework of bars to cover an opening

When she went into the house, she met Miss Minchin in the hall.

"Where have you been wasting your time?" said Miss Minchin. "You've been out for hours!"

"It was so wet and muddy," Sara answered. "It was hard to walk because my shoes were so bad and slipped about so."

"Make no excuses," said Miss Minchin, "and tell no falsehoods."

Sara went downstairs to the kitchen.

"Why didn't you stay all night?" said the cook.

"Here are the things," said Sara, and laid her purchases on the table.

The cook looked over them, grumbling. She was in a very bad temper indeed.

"May I have something to eat?" Sara asked rather faintly.

"Tea's over and done with," was the answer. "Did you expect me to keep it hot for you?"

Sara was silent a second.

"I had no dinner," she said, and her voice was quite low. She made it low because she was afraid it would tremble.

"There's some bread in the pantry," said the cook. "That's all you'll get this time of day."

Sara went and found the bread. It was old and hard and dry. The cook was in too bad a humor to give her anything to eat with it. She had just been scolded by Miss Minchin, and it was always safe and easy to vent[15] her own spite on Sara.

Really it was hard for the child to climb the three long flights of stairs leading to her garret.[16] She often found them long and steep when she was tired, but tonight it seemed as if she would never reach the top. Several times a lump rose in her throat, and she was obliged to stop and rest.

"I can't pretend anything more tonight," she said wearily to herself. "I'm sure I can't. I'll eat my bread and drink some water and then go to sleep, and perhaps a dream will come and pretend for me. I wonder what dreams are."

Yes, when she reached the top landing, there were tears in her eyes, and she did not feel like a princess—only like a tired, hungry, lonely child.

"If my papa had lived," she said, "they would not have treated me like this. If my papa had lived, he would have taken care of me."

Then she turned the handle and opened the garret door.

Can you imagine it—can you believe it? I find it hard to believe myself. And Sara found it impossible. For the first few moments she thought something strange had happened to her eyes—to her mind—that the dream had come before she had time to fall asleep.

---

[15]vent—to let out; express
[16]garret—an attic room, usually under a sloping roof

"Oh!" she exclaimed breathlessly. "Oh! It isn't true! I know, I know it isn't true!" And she slipped into the room and closed the door and locked it, and stood with her back against it, staring straight before her.

Do you wonder? In the grate, which had been empty and rusty and cold when she left it, but which now was blackened and polished up quite respectably, there was a glowing, blazing fire. On the hob[17] was a little brass kettle, hissing and boiling; spread upon the floor was a warm, thick rug; before the fire was a folding chair, unfolded and with cushions on it; by the chair was a small folding table, unfolded, covered with a white cloth, and upon it were spread small covered dishes, a cup and saucer, and a teapot; on the bed were new, warm coverings, a curious wadded silk robe, and some books. The little, cold, miserable room seemed changed into fairyland. It was actually warm and glowing.

"It *is* enchanted!" said Sara. "Or *I* am enchanted. I only *think* I see it all; but if I can only keep on thinking it, I don't care—I don't care—if only I can keep it up!"

She was afraid to move, for fear it would melt away. She stood with her back against the door and looked and looked. But soon she began to feel warm, and then she moved forward.

"A fire that I only *thought* I saw surely wouldn't *feel* warm," she said. "It feels real—real."

She went to it and knelt before it. She touched the chair, the table; she lifted the cover of one of the dishes. There was something hot and savory[18] in it—something delicious. The teapot had tea in it, ready for the boiling water from the little kettle; one plate had toast on it, another, muffins.

"It is real," said Sara. "The fire is real enough to warm me; I can sit in the chair; the things are real enough to eat."

It was like a fairy story come true—it was heavenly. She went to the bed and touched the blankets and the wrap. They were real too. She opened one book, and on the title page was written in a strange hand, "To the Little Girl in the Attic."

Suddenly—was it a strange thing for her to do?—Sara put her face down on the odd, foreign-looking quilted robe and burst into tears.

"I don't know who it is," she said, "but somebody cares about me a little—somebody is my friend."

Somehow that thought warmed her more than the fire. She had never had a friend since those happy, luxurious days when she had had everything; and those days seemed such a long way off—so far away as

---

[17]hob—a shelf inside a fireplace
[18]savory—appetizing to the taste or smell

318

to be only dreams—during these last years at Miss Minchin's.

She really cried more at this strange thought of having a friend, even though an unknown one, than she had cried over many of her worst troubles. But these tears seemed different from the others, for when she had wiped them away they did not seem to leave her eyes and her heart hot and smarting.

And then, imagine if you can, what the rest of the evening was like. The delicious comfort of taking off the damp clothes and putting on the soft, warm, quilted robe before the glowing fire, of slipping her cold feet into the luscious wool-lined slippers she found near her chair. And then the hot tea and savory dishes, the cushioned chair and the books!

It was just like Sara that, once having found the things real, she should give herself up to the enjoyment of them to the very utmost. She had lived such a life of imagining, and had found her pleasure so long in improbabilities,[19] that she was quite equal to accepting any wonderful thing that happened. After she was quite warm, and had eaten her supper and enjoyed herself for an hour or so, it had almost ceased to be surprising to her that such fairy-like surroundings should be hers. As to finding out who had done all this, she knew that it was out of the question. She did not know a human soul by whom it could seem in the least degree probable that it could have been done. "There is nobody," she said to herself, "nobody."

And when she fell asleep beneath the soft white blanket, she dreamed all night of a magnificent person, and talked to him in Hindustani, and made salaams to him.

---

[19]improbabilities—things that are not likely to happen

Although Sara accepts the mysterious quality of her gift, she will soon find out who is responsible for it. She will discover that there is someone who cares and has been looking for her for a long time. But the change in Sara's circumstances does not change her desire to behave in every way as a princess.

THE CHRISTMAS STORY

A choral reading from Luke 1:26-38, Matthew 1:18-25, and Luke 2:1-20,
arranged by Christa G. Habegger
illustrated by Johanna Ehnis

Readers:

Reader One: Gabriel
Reader Two: Angel
Reader Three: Angel of the Lord
Reader Four: Mary
Chorus One: light voices
Chorus Two: dark voices

Key:

/	slight pause
//	complete pause
⌣	continuation of the voice so that the thought is continued to the next line

All: And in the sixth month /
the angel Gabriel was sent from God ⌣
unto a city of Galilee, ⌣ named Nazareth, //
To a virgin espoused[1] to a man ⌣
whose name was Joseph, /
of the house of David; //
and the virgin's name was Mary. //
And the angel came in unto her, ⌣ and said,

Reader One: Hail, / thou that art highly favoured, //
the Lord is with thee: /
blessed art thou among women.

Chorus One: And when she saw him, /
she was troubled at his saying, /
and cast[2] in her mind ⌣
what manner of salutation this should be. //
And the angel said unto her,

---

[1]espoused—married or promised in marriage
[2]cast—searched or looked for

Reader One: Fear not, ⌣ Mary: //
for thou hast found favour with God. //
And, ⌣ behold, // thou shalt conceive in thy womb, /
and bring forth a son, //
and shalt call his name JESUS. //
He shall be great, /
and shall be called the Son of the Highest: //
and the Lord God shall give unto him ⌣
the throne of his father David: //
And he shall reign ⌣
over the house of Jacob for ever; //
and of his kingdom there shall be no end.

Chorus One: Then said Mary unto the angel,

Reader Four: How shall this be, ⌣
seeing I know not a man?

Chorus One: And the angel answered and said unto her,

Reader One: The Holy Ghost ⌣
shall come upon thee, //
and the power of the Highest ⌣
shall overshadow thee: //
therefore / also that holy thing ⌣
which shall be born of thee /
shall be called the Son of God. //
And, ⌣ behold, / thy cousin Elisabeth, //
she hath also conceived a son in her old age: //
and this is the sixth month with her, /
who was called barren.[3] //
For with God / nothing shall be impossible. //

Chorus One: And Mary said,

Reader Four: Behold the handmaid of the Lord; //
be it unto me according to thy word. //

---

[3]barren—not able to bear children

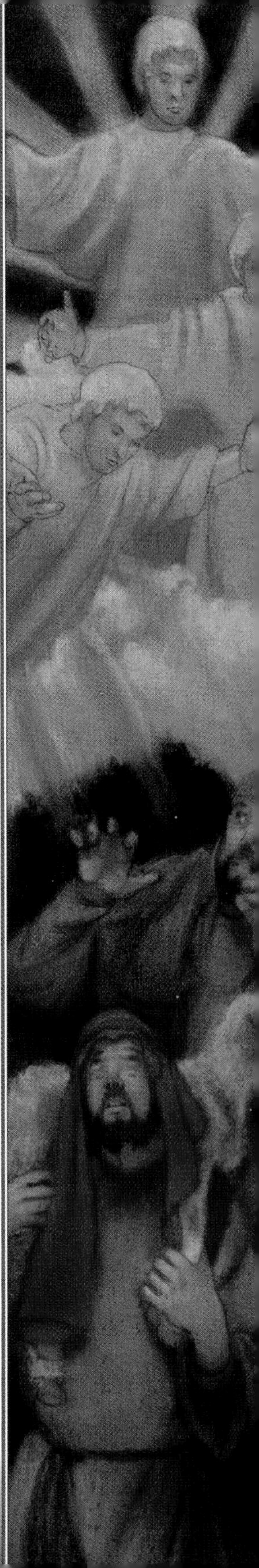

The Christmas Story

All: And the angel departed from her. //
Now the birth of Jesus Christ was on this wise: //
When as his mother Mary was espoused to Joseph, /
before they came together, //
she was found with child / of the Holy Ghost. /

Chorus Two: Then Joseph her husband, /
being a just man, / and not willing ⌣
to make her a publick example, //
was minded to put her away privily.[4] //
But while he thought on these things, //
behold, ⌣ the angel of the Lord ⌣
appeared unto him in a dream, ⌣ saying,

Reader Two: Joseph, / thou son of David, //
fear not to take unto thee Mary thy wife: //
for that which is conceived in her ⌣
is of the Holy Ghost. //
And she shall bring forth a son, /
and thou shalt call his name JESUS: //
for he shall save his people from their sins.

All: Now all this was done, /
that it might be fulfilled ⌣
which was spoken of the Lord ⌣
by the prophet, ⌣ saying,

Reader Two: Behold, / a virgin shall be with child, /
and shall bring forth a son, //
and they shall call his name Emmanuel, //
which being interpreted is, / God with us.

Chorus Two: Then Joseph /
being raised from sleep /
did as the angel of the Lord had bidden him, //
and took unto him his wife: //
And knew her not /
till she had brought forth her firstborn son:

All: and he called his name / JESUS. //

[4]privily—privately

And it came to pass in those days, /
that there went out a decree ⌣
from Caesar Augustus, //
that all the world should be taxed.

Chorus One: (And this taxing was first made ⌣
when Cyrenius was governor of Syria.)

All: And all went to be taxed, /
every one into his own city. //
And Joseph also went up from Galilee, ⌣
out of the city of Nazareth, /
into Judaea, / unto the city of David, ⌣
which is called Bethlehem;

Chorus One: (because he was of the house and lineage of David:)

All: To be taxed with Mary /
his espoused wife, /
being great with child.

Chorus One: And so it was, /
that, ⌣ while they were there, //
the days were accomplished that ⌣
she should be delivered. //
And she brought forth her firstborn son, /
and wrapped him in swaddling clothes, /
and laid him in a manger; //
because there was no room for them in the inn.

Chorus Two: And there were in the same country /
shepherds abiding in the field, //
keeping watch over their flock by night. //
And, ⌣ lo, / the angel of the Lord ⌣
came upon them, / and the glory of the Lord ⌣
shone round about them: //
and they were sore afraid. //
And the angel said unto them,

Reader Three: Fear not: // for, ⌣ behold, /
I bring you good tidings of great joy, /
which shall be to all people. //

The Christmas Story

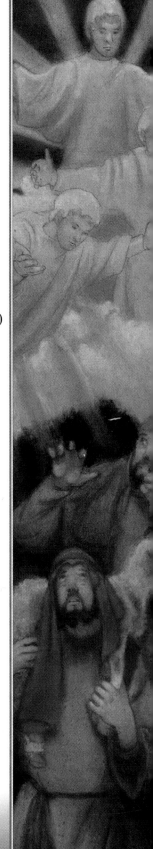

For unto you is born this day ⌣
in the city of David / a Saviour, /
which is Christ the Lord. //
And this shall be a sign unto you; //
Ye shall find the babe ⌣
wrapped in swaddling clothes, /
lying in a manger.

All: And suddenly / there was with the angel ⌣
a multitude of the heavenly host /
praising God, ⌣ and saying, //
Glory to God in the highest, //
and on earth / peace, //
good will toward men. //
And it came to pass, /
as the angels were gone away from them into heaven, //
the shepherds said one to another,

Chorus Two: Let us now go even unto Bethlehem, /
and see this thing which is come to pass, /
which the Lord hath made known unto us.

All: And they came with haste, /
and found Mary, / and Joseph, /
and the babe lying in a manger.

Chorus Two: And when they had seen it, //
they made known abroad the saying ⌣
which was told them concerning this child.

All: And all they that heard it wondered ⌣
at those things which were told them by the shepherds.

Reader Four: But Mary kept all these things, //
and pondered them in her heart.

All: And the shepherds returned, //
glorifying and praising God for all the things ⌣
that they had heard and seen, //
as it was told unto them.

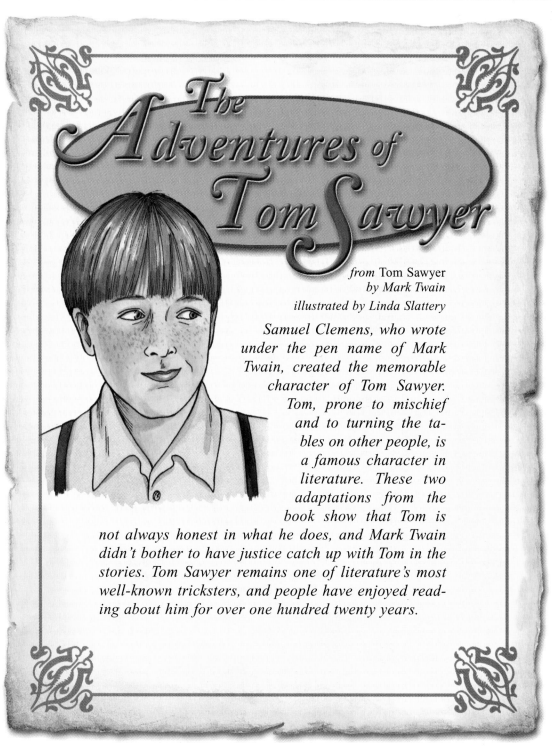

The Adventures of Tom Sawyer

from Tom Sawyer
by Mark Twain
illustrated by Linda Slattery

Samuel Clemens, who wrote under the pen name of Mark Twain, created the memorable character of Tom Sawyer. Tom, prone to mischief and to turning the tables on other people, is a famous character in literature. These two adaptations from the book show that Tom is not always honest in what he does, and Mark Twain didn't bother to have justice catch up with Tom in the stories. Tom Sawyer remains one of literature's most well-known tricksters, and people have enjoyed reading about him for over one hundred twenty years.

The Glorious Whitewasher

Saturday morning was come, and all the summer world was bright and fresh, and brimming with life. There was a song in every heart; and if the heart was young, the music issued at the lips. There was cheer in every face and spring in every step. The locust trees were in bloom, and the fragrance of the blossoms filled the air. Cardiff Hill, beyond the village and above it, was green with vegetation, and it lay just far enough away to seem a Delectable[1] Land, dreamy, reposeful, and inviting.

Tom appeared on the sidewalk with a bucket of whitewash and a long-handled brush. He surveyed the fence, and all gladness left him and a deep melancholy[2] settled down upon his spirit. Thirty yards of board fence nine feet high. Life to him seemed hollow, and existence but a burden. Sighing, he dipped his brush and passed it along the topmost plank; repeated the operation; did it again; compared the insignificant whitewashed streak with the far-reaching continent of unwhitewashed fence, and sat down on a tree-box discouraged. Jim came skipping out

---

[1]delectable—pleasing; delightful
[2]melancholy—sadness; gloominess

The Cat and the Painkiller

This story occurs later in Mark Twain's novel. You will see that Tom's tricks extend to his own family, and he often takes advantage of Aunt Polly's sentimentality[10] and innocence.

Tom's mind found a new and weighty matter to interest itself. Becky Thatcher had stopped coming to school. Tom began to find himself hanging around her father's house, nights, feeling very miserable. She was ill. What if she should die! There was grief in the thought.

The charm of life was gone; there was nothing but dreariness left. He put his hoop away, and his bat; there was no joy in them anymore. His aunt was concerned. She began to try all manner of remedies on him.

Aunt Polly was one of those people who believe all the newfangled methods of producing health or mending it. She was an experimenter in these things. When something fresh in this line came out, she was eager, right away, to try it, not on herself, for she was never ailing, but on anybody else that came handy.

She never observed that her health journals of the current month usually upset everything they had recommended the month before. She was as simple-hearted and honest as the day was long, and so she was an easy victim. She gathered together her quack[11] magazines and her quack medicines, and thus armed, went about on her pale horse, figuratively speaking. But she never suspected she was not an angel of healing in disguise to her suffering neighbors.

The water treatment was new, now, and Tom's low condition was a windfall[12] to her. She had him out at daylight every morning, stood him up in the woodshed, and drowned him with a deluge[13] of cold water; then she scrubbed him down with a towel like a file, and so brought him to; then she rolled him up in a wet sheet and put him away under blankets till she sweated him clean.

Yet in spite of this, the boy grew more and more pale and dejected. She added hot baths, shower baths, and plunges. The boy remained as dismal as a hearse. She began to assist the water with a slim oatmeal diet and blister plasters. She measured his ability to hold things as she would have measured a jug's, and filled him up every day with quack cure-alls.

Tom had become indifferent to suffering by this time. This phase

---

[10]sentimentality—the quality of being easily moved by emotions
[11]quack—lacking qualified medical information
[12]windfall—a great opportunity
[13]deluge—flood

filled the old lady's heart with concern. She heard of Painkiller for the first time. She ordered a lot at once. She tasted it and was filled with gratitude. It was simply fire in liquid form. She dropped the water treatment and everything else and pinned her faith to Painkiller. She gave Tom a teaspoonful and watched with the deepest anxiety for the result.

Her troubles were instantly at rest, her soul at peace again, for the indifference was broken up. The boy could not have shown a wilder, heartier reaction, if she had built a fire under him. She determined to dose him with it every day.

Tom felt that it was time to wake up. This sort of life was getting to have too little pity and too much unpleasant variety to it. So he thought over various plans for escape, and finally decided upon claiming to be fond of Painkiller. He asked for it so often that he became a nuisance, and his aunt ended by telling him to help himself and quit bothering her. If it had been Sid, she would have had no misgivings, but since it was Tom, she watched the bottle secretly. She found that the medicine in the bottle did really grow less as some was taken out each day. It did not occur to her that the boy was curing the health of a crack in the sitting room floor by pouring his daily dose of Painkiller into it.

One day Tom was in the act of dosing the crack when his aunt's yellow cat came along, purring, eyeing the teaspoon hopefully and begging for a taste. Tom spoke to the cat.

"Don't ask for it unless you want it, Peter."

But Peter indicated that he did want it.

"You'd better make sure."

Peter was sure.

"Now you've asked for it, and I'll give it to you because there ain't anything mean about *me;* but if you find you don't like it, you mustn't blame anybody but your own self."

Peter was agreeable, so Tom pried his mouth open and poured down the Painkiller.

Peter sprang a couple of yards in the air, and then delivered a war whoop and set off round and round the room, banging against furniture, upsetting flowerpots, and making general havoc.[14] Next he rose on his hind feet and pranced around in a frenzy, with his head over his shoulder and his voice proclaiming his happiness. Then he went tearing around the house again, spreading chaos and destruction in his path.

Aunt Polly entered in time to see him throw a few double somersaults, deliver a final mighty hurrah, and sail through the open window, carrying the rest of the flowerpots with

---

[14]havoc—disorder

him. The old lady stood petrified[15] with astonishment, peering over her glasses; Tom lay on the floor, rolling with laughter.

"Tom, what on earth ails that cat? I never did see anything like it. What *did* make him act so?"

"Why, Aunt Polly, cats always act so when they're having a good time."

"They do, do they?" There was something in her tone that made Tom worry. The old lady was bending down. Too late he saw her "drift." The handle of the telltale teaspoon was visible under the rocking chair. Aunt Polly took it, held it up. Tom winced, and dropped his eyes. Aunt Polly raised him by the usual handle—his ear—and cracked his head soundly with her thimble.

"Now sir, what did you want to treat that poor dumb beast so, for?"

"I done it out of pity for him—because he hadn't any aunt."

"Hadn't any aunt!—you numbskull. What has that got to do with it?"

"Heaps. Because if he'd a had one, she'd a burnt him out herself! She'd a roasted his insides out of him without any more feeling than if he was a human!"

Aunt Polly felt a sudden pang of remorse.[16] This was putting things in a new light; what was cruelty to a cat *might* be cruelty to a boy too. She began to soften; she felt sorry. Her eyes watered a little, and she put her hand on Tom's head and gently spoke.

"I was meaning for the best, Tom. And Tom, it *did* do you good."

Tom looked up in her face, with just a small twinkle peeping through his gravity.[17]

"I know you was meaning for the best, Auntie, and so was I with Peter. It done *him* good too. I never see him get around so since—"

"Oh, go 'long with you, Tom, before you aggravate me again. And you try and see if you can't be a good boy, for once, and you needn't take any more medicine."

---

[15]petrified—dazed or paralyzed
[16]remorse—regret
[17]gravity—seriousness

THERE IS A FOUNTAIN

William Cowper

There is a fountain filled with blood
Drawn from Immanuel's veins;
And sinners, plunged[1] beneath that flood,
Lose all their guilty stains.

The dying thief rejoiced to see
That fountain in his day;
And there may I, though vile[2] as he,
Wash all my sins away.

E'er since by faith I saw the stream
Thy flowing wounds supply,
Redeeming[3] love has been my theme,
And shall be till I die.

When this poor lisping,[4] stammering tongue
Lies silent in the grave,
Then in a nobler, sweeter song,
I'll sing Thy power to save.

---

[1]plunged—thrust
[2]vile—grossly evil
[3]redeeming—rescuing or paying for
[4]lisping—speaking with difficulty in pronouncing words

Devices of Style

Morgan Reed Persun

Authors appeal to their readers by painting pictures with words. Words that make a story more enjoyable and picturesque[1] are called *devices of style*.

One common device of style is *imagery*, a group of words appealing to one or more of the five senses. For example, in "The Glorious Whitewasher," Mark Twain writes, "The locust trees were in bloom and the fragrance of the blossoms filled the air. Cardiff Hill, beyond the village and above it, was green with vegetation." Twain appeals to the senses of sight and smell. Another time in "The Cat and the Painkiller" the author uses an image that appeals to the reader's sense of touch when he writes that Aunt Polly "drowned him with a deluge of cold water; then she scrubbed him down with a towel like a file, and so brought him to; then she rolled him up in a wet sheet and put him away under blankets till she sweated him clean." The reader almost feels the cold water, the rough towel, and the heavy blankets.

Another tool that writers use is exaggeration, or *hyperbole*.[2] Sometimes writers use this device for humor. For instance, when Mark Twain compares Aunt Polly's towel to a file, he uses exaggeration. No towel is as rough as a file would be, but the comparison makes Aunt Polly's method of drying off the boy seem humorous. Other writers, however, often use exaggeration or hyperbole to convey[3] serious messages or ideas difficult to express

---

[1]picturesque—interesting or very attractive
[2]hyperbole (hī pûr´ bə lē)—exaggeration
[3]convey—to communicate

directly. For example, in the hymn, "There Is a Fountain," the poet makes use of overstatement in the following verse:

> *When this poor lisping, stammering*
>   *tongue*
> *Lies silent in the grave,*
> *Then in a nobler, sweeter song,*
> *I'll sing Thy power to save.*

The reader probably realizes that the poet did not lisp or stammer. The poet overstates, for emphasis, his inability, saying that his best speech is but stuttering compared to what it ought to be in order to praise God. He uses hyperbole, not to condemn his ability, but rather to emphasize how much greater God is.

Another tool of style is *allusion.* An allusion is a reference to another well-known piece of writing or a famous event. Many pieces of literature refer to the Bible. For centuries writers have referred to the parables of Jesus and other parts of Scripture. However, Christian writers are most inclined to use allusions to the Bible. In "There is a Fountain," the poet refers to the "dying thief." This phrase is an allusion, or reference, to the thief who repented on the cross. By using allusion, the writer has said in two words how encompassing and free Christ's love is.

Authors allude to all kinds of writing. In "The Glorious Whitewasher," Mark Twain says that Cardiff Hill beyond the village looks like a "Delectable Land." This description is an allusion to *The Pilgrim's Progress,* in which the two pilgrims see the Delectable Mountains on their way to the Celestial City. The apostle Paul alludes to other writings of his day in his speech on Mars Hill. By using those allusions, he increases his credibility[4] with his learned audience.

Authors have many tools for creating word pictures for their readers. These are just three. Whether in funny stories or serious literature, devices of style can help you enjoy and remember what authors have to say.

---

[4]credibility—believability

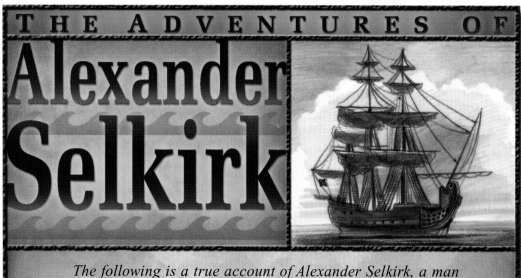

THE ADVENTURES OF Alexander Selkirk

The following is a true account of Alexander Selkirk, a man whose temper had ruined his life while he was still young. Disciplined and barred from his church—or kirk, as the Scottish called it—for brawling during the services and rebelling against his parents, he became a seaman. He cared little that he had broken his mother's heart and that few people could get along with him. You will see from this account how God in mercy brought Selkirk to the end of himself and enabled him to repent and come back to the Lord. Selkirk's story is interesting for another reason. Daniel Defoe used it years later as the background material for his famous novel, Robinson Crusoe.

illustrated by Preston Gravely

Untamed Spirit

In those days the greed of France and Spain to rule the world and crowd England out of the South Seas made the relations of England with those countries none of the friendliest, and the British government commissioned[1] private vessels to make war on the boats of the enemy wherever they might overtake them on the high seas. Of such sort was the *Cinque Ports,* and she had sailed along the rich gold coast of Spanish America, now and again running down some Spanish galleon, and meeting with sundry and divers[2] adventures. Her commander was one Captain Straddling, a cross-grained, quarrelsome fellow. He had serving

[1]commissioned—giving someone the power or right to do something
[2]divers (dī´ vərz)—various

under him as sailing master of the vessel, a certain hotheaded, independent young Scotchman, by name Alexander Selkirk, or Selcraig, as it is more properly written. He was the son of a well-to-do tanner and shoe-maker of Largo in Fifeshire and a follower of the sea from his youth. Now Selkirk was an expert and able seaman, but from the start of the voyage he got on none too well with Straddling. Straddling was an insolent[3] bully. Right and left it was hot tongue and heavy fist wherever Straddling appeared on deck. Month after month, Selkirk held his temper in check—Straddling was his superior officer, and he had a sailor's wish and training to obey. Yet now and again when Straddling rode his high horse, there was an outburst from Selkirk that threatened the gathering of a terrific storm.

As they sailed day after day and month after month, the *Cinque Ports* grew leaky and altogether unsea-worthy, so Captain Straddling found himself forced at last to put in for fresh water and repairs at the island of Juan Fernandez, some four hun-dred miles off the coast of Chile. Juan Fernandez was lonely, wild, and uninhabited. It was off the beaten track of commerce and was rarely visited by vessels of any kind. During the three weeks or so that they lay to in the chief bay of the island, the differences between

Straddling and Selkirk grew daily worse, until at last on the very day when the vessel was getting under way, an angry discussion arose. Hotter and hotter it grew. Selkirk's temper took such furious fire, he burst out the door of the Captain's cabin and rushed up the companion-way, shouting:

"Let me off this crazy vessel! Put me ashore, I say! I'll sail not a day longer under such an obstinate[4] mule!"

The Captain followed onto the deck, bestowing upon him a string of like forceful compliments and bawl-ing out:

"Down with the pinnace![5] Take him ashore! Off with the mutinous[6] hound! He's turned out o' service!"

While the sailors swarmed to the small boat, Selkirk calmed himself sufficiently to gather together his belongings, and, having piled these into the pinnace, he was over the side of the galley and being rowed off to the shore almost before he knew it.

He saw before him a wild, luxuriant, and yet savage coast. Mountains towered above, and over all rose the craggy peak of El Yunque (the Anvil) of which no man knew whether or no it would one day belch forth fire and overwhelm all

---

[3]insolent—rude and disrespectful
[4]obstinate—stubborn
[5]pinnace—a small sailing boat
[6]mutinous—rebellious

that lay at its base with a mighty stream of lava. Yet Selkirk's spirit, at that moment, was as wild and untamed as that savage shore, and the fire within him was smoldering, ready to flame, like volcanic fires of the earth. To such a state of mind the shore was inviting rather than forbidding. Anger and defiance buoyed[7] him up. He held his head high, and his eyes were glowing. Straddling himself had command of the small boat, and the moment its keel grated on the sand, Selkirk sprang lightly ashore, standing by with the utmost unconcern while the Captain gave orders concerning the unloading of his luggage.

The matter was carried through with the greatest dispatch, and the sailors were soon bidding their comrade a sorrowful farewell, while Straddling sat in the boat and in surly fashion called them to make haste and be off. And there alone on the shore he stood, Alexander Selkirk, alone, all alone!

In a trice[8] with a sudden revulsion[9] of feeling, it came over him what he had done. Anger and defiance were dead. The scales had

---

[7]buoyed—raised; supported in spirits
[8]trice—moment; instant
[9]revulsion—a strong change in feeling; disgust

340

fallen from his eyes. He knew what he had done. To stay alone on a savage shore—to hear no human voice—to see no human face—for years, perhaps forever! He raised his voice in a cry that was almost a shriek, stretched out his arms toward his comrades, and rushed to the very edge of the water.

"Come back! Come back! Come back!" he cried. The wind carried his voice away, and yet it seemed to him he heard from the stern of the pinnace where the Captain sat, a sound of mocking laughter. Even while it echoed in his ears, the men in the small boat boarded the larger vessel. All sail was set, and the *Cinque Ports* made off out of the bay and into the Pacific. He watched with straining eyes until her sails dipped down behind the horizon, and the whole vast blue of ocean was left stretching empty and lone before him.

How long he stood there, almost in a stupor[10] staring off to sea, he never knew, but suddenly he became aware that the stillness about him was so intense, it seemed of a truth to shriek in his ears. Thus brought back to himself, he looked about and observed that the sun was low in the sky. In a short time darkness would swoop down upon his solitude. Now he had no knowledge whether or no savage beasts abounded on the island, and he judged it to be most necessary that he find a shelter ere nightfall.

Accordingly, though with weak and trembling knees, he searched along the shore. In a little ravine at no great distance back from the beach, he came upon a cave that offered a most excellent retreat and lay not far from a stream of fresh water.

Hither he dragged his belongings from the place on the sand where they had been dumped, and being now at liberty and of a mind to take stock of the same, he found he had with him a sea chest containing his bedding and a few extra articles of clothing, a firelock,[11] a pound of gunpowder, a large quantity of bullets, a hatchet, a knife, a kettle, a Bible, several books that concerned navigation, and his mathematical instruments. In provisions for the sustenance[12] of life, he had but the quantity of two meals. It being then nearly dark, he was obliged to appease[13] his hunger by consuming a share from his slender store. He then closed the entrance to his cave by means of his sea chest and laid himself down to sleep with his firelock close by his side. Several times during the night he fancied he heard growling and roaring as of wild beasts; but the darkness passed without incident, and the sun rose with remarkable splendor.

---

[10]stupor—daze
[11]firelock—an old style of gun
[12]sustenance—nourishment; food that supports life or health
[13]appease—to make calm; to satisfy

It was early October, being spring in that latitude, and within the verdant[14] little gorge[15] where the cave was situated, all was bud and bloom and twitter of birds and gladsome play of sunlight and shadows. Selkirk, notwithstanding, had eyes for none of the beauties about him. He thought only of the misfortune, swift and terrible, that was come upon him. For days he sat moping and brooding by the seashore, straining his eyes to catch sight of a sail. Not until the darkness of night made it impossible longer to watch, did he close his eyes, and then he slept but poorly. As to eating, he never ate anything at all until the extreme of hunger constrained him, and even then he ate only of the crayfish and turtle to be found on the shore, for he felt spellbound to the beach. Fortunately he had with him a kettle, and by patient trial he learned to get fire by rubbing two sticks together on his knees, after the Indian fashion. Sometimes he broiled the shellfish and sometimes he boiled them, but he found nothing that he ate to his taste for want of salt to season it.

The whole island was in truth rich in natural beauties, in hills and valleys, delightful springs and leaping mountain streams, but Selkirk saw no beauty in it anywhere. To him its loneliness, its deadly stillness, made it all as frightful as some distorted vision of a dream. He only left the shore to climb up to a certain high point by the side of El Yunque, whence a gap in the trap-rock offered a still wider view of the sea. He made no count of days, he took no care of himself, of his clothing, or the cave in which he lived. All his soul was absorbed in that one thought, to watch for a sail, and he wore a beaten track from the shore to his lookout, from his lookout to the shore.

---

[14]verdant—green because of plant growth
[15]gorge—a deep, narrow valley with high, rocky sides

Along in November, as he slept an uneasy sleep within his cave, he was suddenly awakened by the increase of that growling and roaring as of wild beasts which had disturbed his first night on the island. It sounded somewhat between the howling of wolves and the thunderous roar of larger beasts and was of a nearness to make him hold all night close by his firelock. He never closed his eyes again for uncertainty, but when the sun was risen and he stepped cautiously out of his cave towards the shore, there before him on the beach he saw myriads[16] of seals that had come up out of the sea during the night. Some were in the water, but more were on the land; and these were moving their heads about, raising themselves on their flippers, roaring and bellowing. It being Selkirk's custom at once to go to his lookout on the beach, he approached the seals with some uncertainty as to their temper in letting him pass through. He held his firelock ready to beat them off with the butt in case they made at him, but he found them so surly and determined not to give way, that he was forced to beat a retreat before them. It appeared this was the spot where it was their custom to come each year and raise their young, and though seals be usually peaceable creatures, as there came to be many young among them, the old ones grew still more surly. They would rise up on their flippers in their desire to protect the whelps[17] and make at a man fiercely like an angry dog, if he offered to go among them. Moreover, day and night, they kept up a continuous noise of a hideous sort. So Selkirk was obliged to avoid the beach and largely to keep his lookout from the high place on the side of El Yunque, and in his present state of mind the dreadful howlings and voices of these monsters of the deep seemed almost too terrible to be borne. Many a time from sheer impatience and impotent inward rage against the helplessness of his wretched lot he shook his fists and cried aloud; and as no sail appeared day after day, he even meditated casting himself into the sea. "Could the thought of man," he often demanded of himself, "devise a more utterly miserable lot than life alone on a desert isle?"

And then at last one day as he was going through his sea chest in search of some trifle[18] or other, his hand fell upon the Bible, and he drew it forth with a strange tugging at his heartstrings. It was nothing that he himself cherished or would have thought of putting there. It must have been his mother who had slipped it in among the linens her hands had packed with tender care,

---

[16]myriads—extremely large numbers
[17]whelps—young animals
[18]trifle—something of little value

and as he drew it forth on this particular day in the midst of that lonely island, it took his thoughts with painful vividness back home. There rose before him in a flash the rolling downs[19] of Fifeshire, the great gray cliffs along the shore, and nestling beneath them, the little town of Largo. At the west end of the village there was his home, his father's cozy, homey dwelling, surrounded by its garden, and there by the window sat his mother knitting, looking off to sea and longing for news of him. Unconsciously his hand caressed the Bible; he climbed the height to his lookout, sat down with the book on his lap, and buried his face in his hands. He could see it all so clearly.

And now there rose before him, all overgrown with ivy, so peaceful and serene, the kirk itself. He could

---

[19]downs—grassy meadows

see the light that streamed in through its stained-glass windows, the congregation there in Sabbath day attire with fresh and happy faces, and over all a Sabbath air of quiet joy and calm. He could see his mother by his side, her eyes aglow with pride in him—so much she had expected from this, her stalwart son. And then he minded how during the very services in the kirk, his hot temper had led him to start a-brawling. His mother's eyes grew dark with shame, men thrust him out by force, and on the books of the kirk he could see the record written as with points of fire: "Alexander Selkirk having been for his indecent behavior summoned for trial before the kirk sessions on this 27th day August, 1695, did not appear, being gone away to the seas."

Yes, that was what he had done— run away from his punishment to the seas; and, worse still, not three years agone, when he was a man grown and home once more, he had been summoned again before the kirk sessions and publicly rebuked before the whole congregation for quarreling with his brothers and raising a tumult in his father's home. Suddenly his shoulders shook with sobs, and all his soul revolted against that unruly temper that had caused him so much trouble all his life. Had it not been for that same temper, he would not have been here alone and miserable on a desert island. He wept as he had not done since he was a lad at his mother's knee. The tears he shed left him greatly purified and refreshed, even as the earth after a thunderstorm. Slowly he opened the book on his knees and read the following:

"They wandered in the wilderness in a solitary way; they found no city to dwell in.

"Hungry and thirsty, their soul fainted in them.

"Then they cried unto the Lord in their trouble, and he delivered them out of their distresses.

"The wilderness and the solitary place shall be glad for them; and the desert shall rejoice, and blossom as the rose.

"Say to them that are of a fearful heart, Be strong, fear not: behold, your God will come . . . and save you."

Suddenly those words applied to him and to his need. Misery had melted the pride of a stubborn heart, and his thoughts drew near to the Creator of the universe. He read on and on, and with every word he read, his loneliness diminished; hope took the place of despair, and more and more his spirit rose within him. At length, with new vigor and purpose, he closed the book and strode down from the height to his cave.

Solitary Peace

Now for him everything was changed. He realized for the first time that life on Juan Fernandez would be what he made it. If he lived miserably, doing nothing to better his condition and pinning all his hope of happiness on the chance of a stray sail making its way toward the island at some hazy time in the future, he might waste away a lifetime in despair.

He set to work at once. First of all he saw that he had let his cave grow filthy. He spent some time in cleaning it out and washing of clothes and bedding. As he worked he was able sometimes to whistle. Moreover, it was a remarkable fact that the howling of the seals no longer annoyed him; he could even hear their voice with pleasure as furnishing a certain sense of companionship. The change within his own spirits made him approach them in so different a manner, with such confidence and assurance that now, when occasion demanded, he could safely make his way through them. It is true that loneliness and despair returned at times to tempt him, but he had henceforth always wherewithal to resist them through reading of the Scriptures and thinking on the words therein set down.

Having put things in such order about his cave as they had not been in since his arrival on the island, he began next to consider the question of food. As he had been unwilling to leave the beach and living on that food the most easily procurable[20] there, he had been eating almost nothing but turtle, until he could scarce brook[21] the thought of turtle again. Now he arranged at stated intervals, morning and evening, to go to his lookout on the rocks, but the rest of the time he put the matter of sails out of his mind and went about his business of providing for his natural wants. Accordingly, he traveled inland, and on the heights back from the shore found a plenty of goats. Juan Fernandez, the Spanish sailor who had first discovered the island a century or more ago and given it his name, had resided there for some time, stocking the place with goats. The wild creatures of this time were descendants of those domestic beasts Juan Fernandez left behind at the time of his final abandonment of the island. By means of his gun, Selkirk was thus able to provide himself with goat's flesh, and he perceived that the fruit of the pimento, which is the same as the Jamaica pepper and has a most delicious smell, would season his meat instead of salt. He therefore soon learned to

[20]procurable—able to be obtained or acquired
[21]brook—bear; tolerate

prepare victuals[22] he could truly relish. In particular he was able to make a most excellent broth. Being still, however, greatly in want of fresh vegetables, he decided to set out and explore the island in search of the same.

He found Juan Fernandez to be about thirteen miles in length by four in width, rocky and mountainous everywhere, the mountains being covered with green to the skyline, except where face of rock formed a beautiful contrast to the luxuriant pale vegetation. The steep paths up the hills were bordered by flowering shrubs and herbs. In several brooks at no great distance from his cave he found watercress of an excellent flavor, and to his delight, he discovered growing among the trees of the island, the cabbage palm which yields most edible leaf buds quite after the manner of the common cabbage.

In several places he came upon the ruins of huts or shelters that had probably been erected in times past by the few sailors preceding him who had spent periods of greater or less length on the island, though never before like him alone, being always in companies of three or four. He searched well in these places, but found nothing of any value left

[22]victuals (vĭt´lz)—food

behind, save that from one he was able to procure a few nails. In the rank growth near these ruins, however, radishes, parsnips, and turnips were growing. These appeared at present to be wild, but were undoubtedly offspring of seeds originally sown by someone of the earlier inhabitants of the island. Thus provided with a welcome addition to his food supply, Selkirk returned to his cave, a spot now quiet and serene enough since the seals had long since departed.

It was now well along in February, being the close of summer. Selkirk had long since carved on a tree the date of his arrival on the island, and by computing the number of days during which he had kept not track of the passage of time, he had from then on carried on an accurate system of markings by which he was always able to ascertain[23] the date. With autumn coming on and winter in view, he began to think of building himself a hut. Even in that climate where trees were green the year around, he knew that frost was common at night in winter, that snow would sometimes be found on the ground, and there would be much rain; therefore, he felt the need of more shelter than his cave. He felt more than ever that he was like to stay years or perhaps forever in that place.

After thinking the matter over carefully, he came to this conclusion—he must build his hut well back from the shore in a most sheltered and inaccessible spot, for by this time his powder was gone and he had no means of defense. He was now well satisfied that no savage beasts dwelt on the island, but he had this to take into consideration—if a boat ever did land, it was likely to hold men from whom he must flee. He knew well enough the character of the rough adventurers who sailed those seas— buccaneers, pirates, outlaws. Moreover at this time, with France and Spain being both at war with England, to fall into the hands of a Frenchman or Spaniard would have been to be captured by a foe. At length he made up his mind that if a French vessel put in he would surrender, trusting the nature of the French to deal honorably by him even though he were an enemy. But if the vessel were Spanish, he would flee and hide himself and never give up, for he knew that Spain never let a single Englishman return to Europe who had any knowledge of the South Seas. If he were to fall into the hands of Spanish sailors, they would either kill him or make him a slave to work in their rich South American mines. This much was certain then—he must build his hut where it would be a safe

---

[23]ascertain—to find out

retreat in case of need. Therefore, he climbed the rocks by an intricate path, and finding hidden high up among them a beautiful little glade on the edge of a spacious wood, a spot most difficult to come at, and so concealed as to be well nigh undiscoverable, he selected that spot as the site for his hut.

By the exercise of much toil and patience, he then cut down with the small axe at his disposal a sufficient number of pimento trees for his purpose. These he was obliged to join most accurately and carefully together by means of notches, having a great scarcity of nails. On the plains and small hills of the island there abounded a species of grass which grew to the height of seven or eight feet. This he cut most laboriously with his knife, and, on being dried, it proved to produce straw resembling that of oats. With this he thatched his hut. He then constructed a framework for a bed, covered it with straw, and spread thereon his bed clothes, a most welcome change after months of lying on the hard ground. Being still uncertain whether or no his hut was weatherproof, he hung the walls on the inside with well-tanned skins of goats.

He had now for some time, since he had used the last of his powder, been presented with a new problem in the matter of procuring his goats. Being determined, however, to be overcome of no adverse circumstance, he one day made after a goat on foot. The creature was too fleet for him, but when a young kid crossed his path, he found himself able to overtake that and seize it with his bare hands. As he daily exercised to increase his speed, he was soon able to overtake the grown goats as well. He made after them first as they slackened speed to climb an ascent, but with gradual practice and owing to the moderate and temperate life he led, which kept him in fine bodily trim, he was at last able to run down even the fleetest goats at full speed on level ground.

With the poor tools at his command, it took him many weeks to build his hut which he made of a spacious size. But with this hut being complete, he found his energy by no means flagging, and ere the rainy season began, he built at no great distance from it a second and smaller hut wherein he might cook his victuals.

Thus when winter came he was well prepared to meet it. The weather was never tempestuous,[24] but there was some frost and snow, a little hail, and great quantities of rain. In the larger hut he slept and passed the long periods of downpour. It had openings for windows which rendered it exceedingly light and pleasant, and over these openings in case of need to keep out the rain or cold, could be dropped the goatskin coverings. Here within, he was cozy and snug enough, and he led a most orderly and comfortable life, instituting there the simple but beautiful form of family worship to which he had been accustomed in his father's home. Soon after he left his bed and before he began the duties of the day, he sang a psalm, then read a portion of the Scriptures, finishing with devout prayer. Moreover he always repeated his devotions aloud in order to hear the sound of a human voice and retain his ability to speak

---

[24]tempestuous—stormy

the English tongue. The remainder of his time he occupied himself with making various articles of furniture, with carving dishes and utensils out of wood, and in studying his books on navigation.

The winter offered but one incident of any importance and that was the coming up onto the beach early in July of great quantities of sea lions. These strange creatures differ little in shape of body from seals, but they are larger (being sometimes twenty feet long and of two tons weight). They have another sort of skin, their fur being shorter and coarser than that of the seal, and their heads are much larger in proportion, with very large mouths, monstrous big eyes, and exceedingly heavy whiskers, the hair of which is stiff enough to make tooth pickers. These creatures stayed from July to September and were never observed during that time to go into the water but lay covering the shore above a musket shot from the waterside. But by this time Selkirk was in such good spirits that he was quite able to make his way safely through them whenever he needed to approach the shore.

With the return of spring, he found himself in a very different state of mind from what he had been the year before. When the rains ceased and it began to bud and twitter without, his heart leaped up and was glad within him. In the woods nearby the flowers appeared, and there was a sort of blackbird with a red vest that came most tamely about his dwelling. Moreover, as the season advanced, there was scarcely a plant of myrtle or of a shrub with long dark bells like the myrtle, which was not inhabited by a pair of varicolored hummingbirds, no bigger than bumblebees, and these little creatures whirring and buzzing over the flowers filled Selkirk with delight.

The fall before, he had carefully collected seeds of the vegetables that grew in different parts of the island, and this spring he cultivated a goodly patch of ground near his hut, having no implement[25] with which to till the ground save his knife and ax. Here he planted a garden, which he kept free of weeds and in most excellent and orderly condition.

His one trouble now was that he was greatly pestered with rats, his hut being overrun with the vermin and they so bold as to gnaw his clothes and even his feet when sleeping. On considering how to rid himself of this pest, he determined to catch and tame some of the wild cats that inhabited the island. These creatures, though of a color like the real wildcat, were not in truth that creature, as might be told from their smaller size and from their

[25]implement—a tool or piece of equipment

tails which were thin and tapered at the end, while the wildcat's tail is bushy and of uniform size throughout. They, like the rats, were descendants of domestic creatures that had come ashore from some boat or other that had put in to shore in times past to gather wood and water at the island. Nevertheless, though they were offspring of the tamest of beasts, they were as fierce and wild as wildcats and of an agility that made them well-nigh impossible to catch, so quickly could they slip out of one's very grasp and up into the trees. They formed their nests in rocky crevices or hollow trees and, when disturbed there, would rise up and give fight, snarling and spitting fiercely, every hair on their bodies bristling with rage. Selkirk, however, was able to procure some kittens which through patient care and feeding he tamed, and these being grown, speedily delivered him from the rats and kept his hut clean of the pests ever after.

Having succeeded well in taming the cats, he began also to tame kids that he might have food within easy reach in case of need. In this wise his hut was soon surrounded with tame creatures.

Pursuing goats up the mountain-sides was by no means without danger, for the soil at any great height was very light and shallow, the vegetation being mostly a scrubby undergrowth, and if a man seized hold of this to help himself up the slope, the whole was like to give way, come up by the roots, and precipitate[26] him down the steep. Once Selkirk so eagerly pursued a goat that he caught hold of it on the brink of a precipice[27] of which he was not aware, the bushes having hid it from him. So he fell over from a great height with the goat under him and lay at the bottom of the cliffs for a matter of twenty-four hours before he came to his senses—the amount of which time he calculated by the change in the moon since last he observed it. Having then crawled a mile back to his cottage, he there remained some ten days ere he was able to stir out again.

As time passed he began to be greatly troubled that, with so much using, his knife was wore clean to the haft.[28] He mourned beyond measure the loss of so valuable and necessary an implement. One day, however, as he wandered on the beach, keeping a sharp lookout as he always did for aught that might be of use, what should he spy, half buried in the sand, but some iron hoops. Doubtless they had been cast away by some ship as altogether unworthy, but to him they were a treasure then more priceless than a shipload of Spanish gold. Taking them back to his hut, he there broke off a piece, beat it thin, and ground the edge upon stones. Thus by the exercise of a little ingenuity, he was able to provide himself with a knife.

The knife, as may well be believed, was not the only one of his belongings that wore out. In due course of time his clothes did likewise. He then made himself a coat, cap, and breeches of goatskin with the hair outside. These he stitched together with little thongs of leather which he cut from the skins and attached to a nail. Having plenty of linen cloth by him, thanks to the care of his mother, he sewed himself shirts, when his wore out, using the nail again for a needle and using for thread the worsted that he unraveled from an old pair of stockings. As his bedding gave way, he replaced that also by goatskins. Only with the wearing through of his shoes did he find here an article that he could not replace. Nevertheless, as he was forced to shift without them, he found his feet grow so hard that he could run anywhere, even over the sharp jagged rocks, without the slightest annoyance. Thus even the loss of his shoes remained no great inconvenience.

---

[26]precipitate—to throw down from a high place
[27]precipice—a steep cliff
[28]haft—handle

Priceless Treasure

One day as he stood on his lookout scanning the sea for a sail (it must have been about in the second year of his solitude) he did indeed, to the joy of his soul, see a sail bearing straight for the island. Leaving all else, he stayed at the lookout, never taking his eyes off the ship, his heart beating high with hope. But as it drew well within the range of vision, he saw to his dismay that it was a high and clumsy vessel, its stem and stern built up like castles—Spanish without a doubt. Now as he had fully made up his mind rather to stay forever on the island than fall into the hands of the Spaniards, he watched until he made sure they were going to land, and then retired at once to his inaccessible retreat, where he stayed quietly, never once moving out of it so long as they remained on the island. From among the rocks he kept a sharp lookout over their encampment below, and he found the sight of humankind and the sound of their voices so agreeable even though he knew them to be enemies of a fierce and relentless kind, that he was often almost compelled[29] to go down and join them. More than once some of the men strayed up the rocks straight in the direction of his hut, but fortunately he had built it so far beyond the distance of any easy climb that they never penetrated so far. At last, having taken aboard wood and water, they made off, and Selkirk found himself once more the solitary master of the isle.

Curiously enough, it was not many months later, that he again espied a ship coming toward the island. This time, however, she was not of so distinct a type that he could at once decide whether she was Spanish or French. Desiring a closer examination, he ran eagerly down toward the beach, and was proceeding along through the underbrush with insufficient caution, when he suddenly came straight upon several of the crew before he even so much as knew they had landed. On the instant he perceived they were Spanish and made off. The others were struck dumb with astonishment at coming suddenly on so wild appearing a man on what they had believed to be an uninhabited island. However, they recovered themselves at once, fired shots after him, and followed hot on his heels. They being close upon him, he suddenly shinnied up a tree and hid himself in its branches. The Spaniards pursued him to the very foot of the tree and there losing track of him lingered long on the

---

[29]compelled—forced

354

spot just beneath him. They even looked up frequently into the branches and Selkirk's heart went pounding, for had they perceived him, he could scarcely have gotten out of range of their firelocks; but so dense were the leaves that they did not discover him, and at length they retired once more to their camp.

Henceforth, after his disappointment in this second ship, Selkirk seemed even less than ever to set his heart on leaving the island. And indeed after this, no other ship again came near.

He dwelt now in a state of great cheerfulness and even joy, not only reconciled[30] to his lot but also taking much pleasure in it. For the greater part of the year the sky was cheerful and serene, the air temperate, and his little hut was on the edge of a spacious wood abloom with flowers. He kept it always clean and well-ordered and had even come to ornament it with the fragrant green boughs of trees so that it formed a delicious bower around which played soft and balmy breezes. It grew to seem to him much like home, and he came back to it always after an absence with that pleasant warming of the inner man always experienced by one coming home. Moreover, his cats and tame kids became exceedingly dear to his heart. Though he had at first thought of taming them only to meet his own physical needs, he soon found himself having grown mightily fond of the little creatures, and as they grew to love him in return, they in some measure satisfied that natural craving for companionship and affection which dwells ever deep in the heart of man. The kids would come leaping to meet him,

---

[30]reconciled—having come to accept

licking his hands almost like dogs; and the cats would rub against his legs and vie with one another to curl up, purring in his lap. He would amuse himself often by teaching his pets to dance and do tricks, singing rousing old songs, and himself dancing with them to the music of his own voice. It was a strange and pretty sight, that!—the great man in his rough and shaggy garments, his face softened with joy of the little creatures, dancing and springing about in their midst, as though they were friends all speaking one language, the language of love that is foreign to none of God's creatures.

Selkirk had his garden, too, and indeed by application of his wits conquered all the inconveniences of his solitude. For food he had all he could wish for of variety and profusion right at hand—goat's flesh and milk, turtle, crayfish, fish, turnips, parsnips, radishes, cabbage, watercress, and a variety of small but delicious black plum, the only article of his diet now not easily procurable, for they grew in places hard to come at high up in the mountains, but were sufficiently delicious to repay the effort of gathering them. He perceived, too, that taste is much a matter of habit, for he had grown to relish his food seasoned with pimento quite as well as when he had it seasoned with salt.

The wood of the pimento he used entirely for firewood and as it burned, it gave off a most delicious fragrance and served him both for warmth and candle, throwing up a splendid blaze that lit all the darkness about. He was by this time intimately familiar with all the little by-paths of his mountain kingdom and could bound from crag to crag and slip down precipices with the utmost confidence.

So as he surveyed all the beauty and comfort about him and recalled the misery of his earlier state on the island, it seemed to him that his own change of heart had indeed made the promise come true—"The wilderness and the solitary place shall be glad for them and the desert shall rejoice and blossom as the rose."

He no longer missed the society of men. The strife and struggle of humankind seemed far away; God seemed very near. He read, "Behold the hour cometh, yea is now come that ye . . . shall leave me alone, and yet I am not alone because the Father is with me." And as he stood beneath the calm and smiling sky, with the beauty of all outdoors about and the sea stretching endlessly before him, he felt such a sense of nearness to the Spirit, as he had never known in all his life before, and his thoughts were full of reverence and simple childlike peace.

learn to gear this horse, the palace will be overrun by the enemy."

So they got the ropes from ten tents and tied the saddle to the giant horse. Then the Chattee-maker got a ladder and climbed up into the saddle. His wife, who worried about his falling off, tied him round and round with ten more sturdy ropes. She wrapped so many ropes around him that he and the horse looked to be one thing—one large animal with a ropey middle.

The great horse lost all patience now and bolted away at lightning speed. The Chattee-maker could only grab into the flying mane and hope the horse would go the right way.

After miles and miles of a thundering pace, under the afternoon sun and then the moon and then the early sun again, the Chattee-maker opened his eyes and tried to see where he was going. The land had changed. Instead of the lovely green of his village and the palace grounds, there was now a sandy place with banyan trees and spikey little plants whose leaves looked sharp as razors. And just ahead to his great wonder and dread was the enemy camp.

Inside the camp, the enemy Rajah was planning his attack. He was so sure of winning—as he had heard that the head of the opposing Army was only a Chattee-maker— that he had written up terms of surrender. In fact, he was so sure of winning—as he knew that the Army of his enemy was on holiday—he had even signed his name to the terms. All that was needed now would be to make the defeated Rajah sign his name.

Hard upon the camp came the Chattee-maker, whose resolve and courage were weakening a bit as he saw the huge array of tents and all the battle horses and elephants harnessed for war.

As he passed a big banyan tree, he reached out and grabbed it. But instead of that stopping his headstrong charger, the sandy soil let the roots slip loose and the tree came up like a plant. He could hardly see where he was going through the bushy branches.

Now he rode full out to battle with a great tree in his arms. The lookout for the enemy Rajah suddenly saw the Chattee-maker hurtling toward the camp. He rose up in alarm and ran to the Rajah's tent.

"Your Majesty! We have underestimated the enemy! Look!"

All the soldiers and the Rajah looked, and behold, a man bigger than a tree was galloping toward them without the least sign of fear or of slowing down.

The Rajah, a man who had seen many battles in his day, had never seen anything like this.

"No wonder they can leave only one man at a time to guard the king-

dom! If all the soldiers are as big as this, we are outnumbered if only ten come upon us. Run!"

And the Rajah and all his men fled, not even stopping to get on their horses or take any of their weapons.

When the Chattee-maker's horse thundered into the camp, he smelled the oats left behind by the fleeing horsemen and stopped running just as suddenly as he had begun. The Chattee-maker, once he recovered from the bone-jarring ride, worked out of his ropes and got down.

He walked on wobbly legs through the camp, wondering why the enemy had fled from him. After a while, he decided not to question this happy turn of events and went about gathering up weapons and treasure of every kind. He loaded up the elephants and the horses with all that they could carry. Then he tied the horses and the elephants together in a long parade, putting his great horse at the front.

As he left the camp that he had stripped of everything, he noticed a paper fluttering under the edge of a tent. He stopped to pick it up. It looked like the writing and the paper that his Rajah had used to make him Head of the Army only a few days before. Since the Chattee-maker could not read, he put the paper in his tunic, to ask someone who could read what it said.

For many days, he walked back, leading the long line of riches-laden animals. When he got near the palace, a lookout spotted him and alerted the city. Thousands of people ran out to meet him, including his Rajah. But the first to reach him was his wife, who was crying for joy to see him alive.

"Look," he said, "we're really and truly rich now!"

"And so we are," said his wife, for though she was happier that he was alive than that he was rich, she was not about to wish them poor again.

The Rajah ran up to greet him. "How wise it was to make such a hero the Head of the Army. No general was ever braver! You took the enemy single-handedly."

The Chattee-maker handed the Rajah the rope that held the great charger and thus all the war horses and elephants loaded with treasure he could do was shout threats at his enemy.

Uri was running from one side of the raft to the other, furious with excitement. A large wave sheeted across the reef. At that second the dog's shift in weight tipped the raft at a perilous[10] angle. With a helpless yelp, Uri slid off into the water. Mafatu sprang to catch him, but he was too late.

Instantly the hammerhead whipped about. The wave slewed the raft away. Uri, swimming frantically, tried to regain it. There was desperation in the brown eyes—the puzzled eyes so faithful and true. Mafatu strained forward. His dog. His companion. . . . The hammerhead was moving in slowly. A mighty rage stormed through the boy. He gripped his knife. Then he was over the side in a clean-curving dive.

Mafatu came up under his enemy. The shark spun about. Its rough hide scraped the flesh from the boy's shoulder. In that instant Mafatu stabbed. Deep, deep into the white belly. There was a terrific impact. Water lashed to foam. Stunned, gasping, the boy fought for life and air.

It seemed that he would never reach the surface. *Aué,* his lungs would burst! . . . At last his head broke water. Putting his face to the surface, he saw the great shark turn over, fathoms[11] deep. Blood flowed from the wound in its belly. Instantly gray shapes rushed in—other sharks, tearing the wounded hammerhead to pieces.

Uri—where was he? Mafatu saw his dog then. Uri was trying to pull himself up on the raft. Mafatu seized him by the scruff and dragged him up to safety. Then he caught his dog to him and hugged him close, talking to him foolishly. Uri yelped for joy and licked his master's cheek.

It wasn't until Mafatu reached shore that he realized what he had done. He had killed the *ma'o* with his own hand, with naught but a

bone knife. He could never have done it for himself. Fear would have robbed his arm of all strength. He had done it for Uri, his dog. And he felt suddenly humble with gratitude.

---

[10]perilous—dangerous
[11]fathom—a measurement of depth equal to about six feet

Sir Alexander Fleming:
Master of His Craft

Karen Wilt
illustrated by Jim Hargis

*"Before you can notice any strange happening, you have got to
be a good workman; you have got to be a master of your craft."*
—*Sir Alexander Fleming*

"Now look at this; this is very interesting," Dr. Fleming said.

His friend unbuckled his dripping mackintosh[1] and replaced it with a white lab coat. Peering into the microscope, he caught sight of a bluish, brushy mold. "Yes, very interesting, but not staphylococci.[2] The research council needs that article with your results in it, and now another culture[3] is ruined."

Dr. Fleming picked up the glass petri dish[4] which had held the research of long days and late nights. The flat round container fit perfectly in the palm of his hand. The staphylococci colony was contaminated[5] with the mold—and useless for research work. But under the microscope he could see the new mold attacking the bacteria—a bacteria that in the bloodstream or tissues of the strongest human could break down every natural defense and lead to death.

"This mold might be important," Dr. Fleming said. He took his platinum loop out and sterilized it. With the steady hands of an expert, he caught two or three mold spores—invisible to the naked eye—and dropped them into a test tube containing a nutritive broth on which molds grew well. Then he striped more of them across a slide and put it aside to grow.

[1]mackintosh—raincoat
[2]staphylococci (stăf´ ə lō kŏk´ sī)—a bacteria that causes boils or other severe infections
[3]culture—a growth of bacteria
[4]petri (pē´ trē) dish—a small flat covered dish used to grow microorganisms
[5]contaminated—made impure; polluted

Another scientist in the lab set his test tube on a rack and sighed. "The weather's so damp this summer, it's no wonder mold is ruining our work. You ought to be more careful to keep the window closed. Spores can fly right in from Praed Street. Every time we uncover a culture dish, something tiresome is sure to happen. Things fall out of the air." The other bacteriologist scrubbed at his bench with a disinfectant.[6]

"My rule in life is . . . ," Dr. Fleming began.

"I know, I know," the other said with a laugh. "Get everything possible out of your mistakes. I don't think you could have prevented that one."

Fog enveloped[7] the laboratory in a cold, soggy mist the next several weeks during the summer of 1928, shrouding[8] Dr. Fleming's work in mystery. The other colonies of staphylococci had no contamination. He completed his research in a flurry and sent off the article. Then, at last, he brought the strange new mold back to the microscope.

First he examined the slides. They had furry bits of mold clinging to them. Dr. Fleming painted a different bacteria in a circle around each one and set them aside to grow again. Then he gathered the flasks of nutritive broth. It had captured his attention several times during his staphylococci work. First the surface had grown into a thick, goopy white mass; then it had changed to a dull green moldy shade. Finally it had blackened, and the clear broth beneath it was transformed into a bright yellow color.

Dr. Fleming poured the unusual fluid from the flasks into other laboratory dishes. He streaked bacteria across them, just as he had done to the slides.

For several days he observed the mold. The bright yellow fluid and the spores on the slides had the same effect. They completely killed the bacteria.

"It looks as though we have got a mold that can do something useful," Dr. Fleming said to his assistant. "Bring me some more bacteria—the kind that causes infectious diseases."

Before long, slides and flasks littered the shelves and benches. Dr. Fleming stared at them under the microscope until his eyes burned. The mold and the bright yellow liquid fought battle after battle with the bacteria and almost always won. The germs causing strep throat, diphtheria, and staph infections would not grow near the mold culture and died if surrounded by it. Typhoid fever and influenza, however, didn't seem to be affected.

---

[6]disinfectant—a chemical used to destroy germs
[7]enveloped—enclosed completely
[8]shrouding—enfolding, as in a burial cloth

Dr. Fleming still could not be satisfied. He diluted the fluid and tried again. Each slide contained a weaker dose. One twentieth the original strength, one hundredth, a five hundredth—the mold broth hardly appeared yellow as weak as it was. Not daring to breathe, Dr. Fleming slipped each slide under the microscope. The mold continued working! The bacteria died.

Pulling out his old medical school books, Dr. Fleming hunted for the name of this amazing fungus. Thousands of molds lived in the air, earth, and sea. Finally, with the help of a botanist friend, he narrowed it down to the Penicillium family. He would call the mold fluid "penicillin."

Now the difficult experiments lay before him. First he gave a small dose to a rabbit. Hours passed, and the rabbit placidly[9] chewed the vegetables scattered in its cage. Dr. Fleming devised more experiments using mice. The penicillin produced no harmful effects on mice. Could it work on people?

One of the laboratory doctors caught a sinus infection. "Use me to experiment with that mold of yours," he said to Dr. Fleming.

[9]placidly—calmly or peacefully

"It's not in a pure form. Other substances in it might harm you or prevent it from working correctly," Dr. Fleming said.

"Well, if there are, it'll be another blunder to learn from. Someone has to be the first one."

Dr. Fleming agreed and cultured the infection. Two bacteria were present, one that penicillin could cure and one that it couldn't. Dr. Fleming washed out the sinus with the penicillin broth. The next test showed that the penicillin had killed one bacteria and not the other as Dr. Fleming had predicted.

But all the scientists knew that the penicillin fluid, grown directly from the mold, couldn't be administered to people. It hadn't been sterilized or converted[10] into a form that could be injected into the blood stream or capsulized.[11] Dr. Fleming tried to purify the penicillin fluid. As the liquid that held the penicillin evaporated, the mold grew weaker. Finally it disappeared completely. Dr. Fleming started over, and the penicillin vanished again—right in front of his eyes. To make a medicine, he had to have a powder or crystal base, not thin air! He passed the problem on to some chemists. They worked for several months, but the penicillin kept disappearing. Dr. Fleming sent samples of the penicillin mold and the fluid to scientists in other European countries and in America. No one could capture the penicillin to purify it and make it into a medicine.

"Give up," fellow scientists said.

Dr. Fleming sat down and wrote an article about his discovery. He gave lectures. Doctors and scientists listened politely, then returned to their own experiments and research. He wrote letters to friends and asked them to try to purify penicillin, but no one had time for such a challenging project.

---

[10]converted—changed something into something else
[11]capsulized—put into capsule form; encased

Meanwhile, trouble loomed ahead. Germany had amassed a huge army and had started to conquer Europe. England prepared for war. On September 3, 1939, eleven years after the Penicillium spore had contaminated Dr. Fleming's culture, England declared war on Germany.

Now the young scientists and doctors hurried to the battlefronts, and Dr. Fleming and the older workers tried to keep the lab in operation with a handful of people.

In a nearby laboratory, a young German Jew who had escaped Hitler's death camps read Dr. Fleming's papers. The work intrigued him. He asked for a grant of money to research further. In a few months Dr. Chain's laboratory shelves glistened with test tubes filled with a bright yellow fluid. Before long he discovered that the penicillin didn't just disappear when the fluid evaporated; it evaporated too! So he created a freeze-dry process that captured the penicillin before it could disappear into a vapor.

A year passed. The Germans had reached Dunkirk in France. They could invade England at any moment. Dr. Chain showed his findings to another scientist. A team of scientists soon bustled around the lab. At all costs the Germans must not destroy the mold. If England fell, one of them must escape and continue the research. All of them brought their coats to the lab. Stitch by stitch they took out the linings and dropped them into a vat filled with the liquid. Slowly the linings dried, and the men sewed them back into the coats. One of them would get away, and the spores from their coat linings would grow a new mold if England fell.

Meanwhile, Dr. Fleming read about their work. He had never given up hope that penicillin would one day fight the diseases of the world; so he hurried to the laboratory. Dr. Chain opened the door to his timid knock.

"You have made something of my substance," Dr. Fleming said.

"Are you Dr. Fleming?" Dr. Chain asked. "I thought you died in the bombings of London."

"I wish you had been with me in 1928 when I first discovered the stuff. So many years wasted." Dr. Fleming's eyes drank in the rows of petri dishes and flasks. His heart beat faster. "At last," he murmured, "at last."

Again experiments filled the hours—Dr. Fleming growing penicillin mold in his lab and Dr. Chain testing it in his. The lab animals showed no adverse[12] effects.

In February of 1941, a small bottle of pure penicillin rested on a refrigerator shelf. It represented hours of labor with microscopes and

---

[12]adverse—harmful or unfavorable

mold fluids. But all of the work was worth it, for now they had a large enough dose of pure penicillin to test on human illness. They needed only a volunteer.

Not long after that, the ringing of the telephone disrupted their quiet research work.

"Dr. Chain," the voice on the receiver boomed. "We have a desperate case of septicemia here at the hospital. We have done everything possible. Your work with this mold that kills bacteria—is there a chance?"

"It has never been used on humans." Dr. Chain rubbed the telephone receiver with his thumb. "Are you sure nothing else can be done?"

"We're at wits' end. The patient is a bobby.[13] He scratched the corner of his mouth. After it became infected, it spread to blood poisoning. Now it's moved into his lungs. With the war, we can't afford to lose any of the bobbies left behind."

"I'm just not sure. . . ." Dr. Chain said.

"Sir, he'll die without treatment."

"All right. I'll be there within the hour." Dr. Chain hung the receiver on the hook in slow motion. He

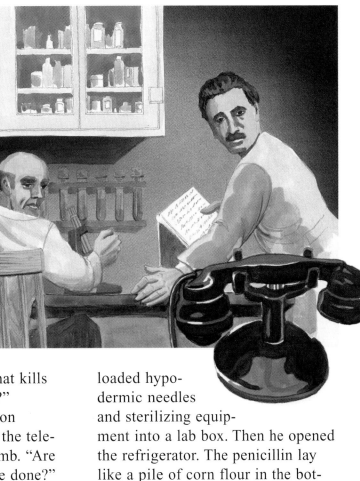

loaded hypodermic needles and sterilizing equipment into a lab box. Then he opened the refrigerator. The penicillin lay like a pile of corn flour in the bottom of the clear glass bottle. Each bright yellow crystal might prove to be worth its weight in gold. If it could cure. . . . Dr. Chain would see. The time had come.

The first injection was a strong one. The pale policeman had sunk so low that he didn't even feel the prick of the needle. Every three hours, all day, another injection was given. Dr. Chain paced the floor and watched every eyelash twitch, every slow

[13]bobby—the British nickname for policeman

labored breath, hoping that the signs of improvement were real, and not just part of his imagination. As he stumbled home in the darkened, bombed-out streets, he weighed the evidence. The policeman did not appear nearly so pale. He seemed to be breathing more easily. Tomorrow would tell. Dr. Chain fell into a restless sleep, his mind churning.

With the first hint of approaching dawn, Dr. Chain struggled through the thick London fog back to the hospital. The nurses greeted him with smiles. The policeman's temperature had fallen. He had awoken hungry!

One of the scientists from the team at Dr. Chain's laboratory pulled him aside.

"Dr. Chain, we have enough penicillin for two or three more injections. We can't get more until the cultures grow."

"Perhaps it will be enough for the man's own body defenses to fight off the rest," Dr. Chain said.

But when the injections were stopped, the policeman relapsed.[14] For a few days he struggled against the bacteria invading his body. On March 15, sad news reached the lab. The bobby had died. Penicillin had not proved itself yet.

The scientists turned back to their work. They needed more of the powder. Enough to last.

Two more cases of the illness turned up. This time, with the increased supply of penicillin, both people were cured.

Now the need to produce penicillin skyrocketed. But with the war raging, all the factories manufactured guns, airplanes, and bombs. The wounded didn't need those things as much as the curing power of penicillin. Working around the clock, the scientists begged for help. Calls came every hour for the new miracle drug. Dr. Chain asked the head of the laboratory to take a sample to America. After seeing penicillin rescue people from the brink of death, several corporations promised to produce it.

Thousands that might have died, lived. Thanks poured down on Dr. Fleming. He continued to work in his laboratory, trying to avoid talking to newspaper and radio reporters.

In June of 1944, the king of England invited Dr. Fleming to Buckingham Palace. With the chance that German bombers might disturb the ceremony, the servants prepared a special room in the palace basement. There the king knighted Dr. Fleming as Sir Alexander Fleming in honor of his discovery of a little mold spore that fell by accident into a dish.

[14]relapsed—fell back into a previous condition

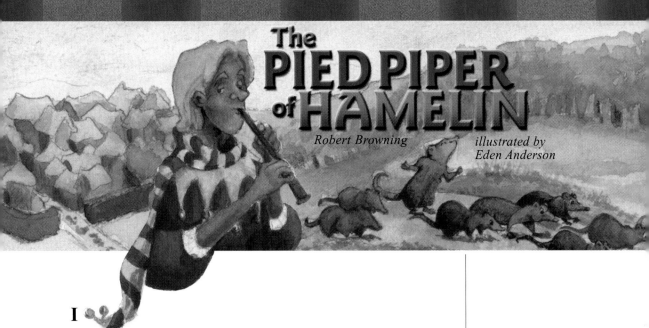

The PIED PIPER of HAMELIN

Robert Browning

illustrated by
Eden Anderson

I

Hamelin Town's in Brunswick,
By famous Hanover city;
The river Weser, deep and wide,
Washes its wall on the southern side;
A pleasanter spot you never spied;
But, when begins my ditty,[1]
Almost five hundred years ago,
To see the townsfolk suffer so
From vermin,[2] was a pity.

[1]ditty—a song

[2]vermin—unpleasant insects
   or small animals

II

Rats!
They fought the dogs and killed the cats,
And bit the babies in the cradles,
And ate the cheeses out of the vats,
And licked the soup from the cook's own ladles,
Split open the kegs of salted sprats,[3]
Made nests inside men's Sunday hats,
And even spoiled the women's chats
By drowning their speaking
With shrieking and squeaking
In fifty different sharps and flats.

[3]sprats—small fish

III

At last the people in a body
To the Town Hall came flocking:
" 'Tis clear," cried they, "our Mayor's a noddy;[4]
And as for our Corporation—shocking

5ermine—the white fur of
the ermine (a kind of
weasel)

To think we buy gowns lined with ermine[5]
For dolts that can't or won't determine
What's best to rid us of our vermin!

6obese—very fat

You hope, because you're old and obese,[6]
To find in the furry civic robe ease?
Rouse up, sirs! Give your brains a racking,
To find the remedy we're lacking,
Or, sure as fate, we'll send you packing!"
At this the Mayor and Corporation

7consternation—shock;
bewilderment

Quaked with a mighty consternation.[7]

IV

An hour they sat in council,
At length the Mayor broke silence:

8guilder—a unit of
currency; money

"For a guilder[8] I'd my ermine gown sell,
I wish I were a mile hence!
It's easy to bid one rack one's brain—
I'm sure my poor head aches again,
I've scratched it so, and all in vain.
Oh for a trap, a trap, a trap!"
Just as he said this what should hap
At the chamber door but a gentle tap?
"Bless us," cried the Mayor, "what's that?"
(With the Corporation as he sat,
Looking little though wondrous fat;
Nor brighter was his eye, nor moister

Than a too-long-opened oyster,
Save when at noon his paunch[9] grew mutinous[10]
For a plate of turtle green and glutinous[11])
"Only a scraping of shoes on the mat?
Anything like the sound of a rat
Makes my heart go pit-a-pat!"

[9]paunch—stomach

[10]mutinous—rebellious

[11]glutinous—sticky

V

"Come in!"—the Mayor cried, looking bigger:
And in did come the strangest figure!
His queer long coat from heel to head
Was half of yellow and half of red;
And he himself was tall and thin,
With sharp blue eyes, each like a pin,
And light loose hair, yet swarthy[12] skin,
No tuft on cheek nor beard on chin,
But lips where smiles went out and in;

[12]swarthy—dark-colored

There was no guessing his kith and kin:[13]
And nobody could enough admire
The tall man and his quaint attire.
Quoth one: "It's as my great-grandsire,
Starting up at the Trump of Doom's tone,
Had walked this way from his painted tombstone!"

[13]kith and kin—friends and
family

VI

He advanced to the council-table:
And, "Please your honors," said he, "I'm able,

By means of a secret charm, to draw
All creatures living beneath the sun,
That creep or swim or fly or run,
After me so as you never saw!
And I chiefly use my charm
On creatures that do people harm,
The mole and toad and newt and viper;
And people call me the Pied Piper."
(And here they noticed round his neck
A scarf of red and yellow stripe,
To match with his coat of the self-same check;
And at the scarf's end hung a pipe;
And his fingers, they noticed, were ever straying
As if impatient to be playing
Upon his pipe, as low it dangled
Over his vesture[14] so old-fangled.)
"Yet," said he, "poor piper as I am,
In Tartary[15] I freed the Cham,
Last June, from his huge swarms of gnats;
I eased in Asia the Nizam[16]
Of a monstrous brood of vampire bats:
And as for what your brain bewilders,
If I can rid your town of rats,
Will you give me a thousand guilders?"
"One? fifty thousand!"—was the exclamation
Of the astonished Mayor and Corporation.

[14]vesture—clothing

[15]Tartary—area of Europe and West Asia

[16]Nizam—former title of a ruler in India

VII

Into the street the Piper stepped,
Smiling first a little smile,
Then, like a musical adept,[17]
To blow the pipe his lip he wrinkled,
And green and blue his sharp eyes twinkled,
Like a candle-flame where salt is sprinkled;
And ere three shrill notes the pipe uttered;
You heard as if an army muttered;
And the murmuring grew to a grumbling;
And the grumbling grew to a mighty rumbling;
And out of the houses the rats came tumbling,
Great rats, small rats, lean rats, brawny rats,
Brown rats, black rats, gray rats, tawny rats,
Grave old plodders, gay young friskers,
Fathers, mothers, uncles, cousins,
Cocking tails and pricking whiskers;
Families by tens and dozens,
Brothers, sisters, husbands, wives—
Followed the Piper for their lives.
From street to street he piped advancing,
And step for step they followed dancing,
Until they came to the river Weser,
Wherein all plunged and perished!
—Save one who, stout as Julius Caesar,
Swam across and lived to carry
(As he the manuscript he cherished)
To Rat-land home his commentary:[18]
Which was, "At the first shrill notes of the pipe,
I heard a sound as of scraping tripe,[19]
And putting apples, wondrous ripe,
Into a cider-press's gripe:[20]
And a moving away of pickle-tub-boards,

[17]adept—expert;
professional

[18]commentary—explanation

[19]tripe—the lining of a
cow's stomach, used for
food
[20]gripe—handle; grip

And a leaving ajar of conserve-cupboards,
And a drawing the corks of train-oil-flasks,[21]
And a breaking the hoops of butter casks:
And it seemed as if a voice
(Sweeter far than by harp or by psaltery[22]
Is breathed) called out, 'O rats, rejoice!
The world is grown to one vast drysaltery![23]
So munch on, crunch on, take your nuncheon,[24]
Breakfast, supper, dinner, luncheon!'
And just as a bulky sugar-puncheon,[25]
All ready staved,[26] like a great sun shone
Glorious scarce an inch before me,
Just as methought it said, 'Come, bore me!'
—I found the Weser rolling o'er me."

VIII

You should have heard the Hamelin people
Ringing the bells till they rocked the steeple.
"Go," cried the Mayor, "and get long poles,
Poke out the nests and block up the holes!
Consult with carpenters and builders,
And leave in our town not even a trace
Of the rats!"—when suddenly, up the face
Of the Piper perked in the market-place,
With a "First, if you please, my thousand guilders!"

[21]train-oil-flasks—containers of oil taken from whale blubber

[22]psaltery—ancient stringed musical instrument

[23]drysaltery—seller of salted or dried meats, pickles, etc.

[24]nuncheon—a snack

[25]puncheon—a cask or container

[26]staved—broken

IX

A thousand guilders! The Mayor looked blue;
So did the Corporation too.
To pay this sum to a wandering fellow
With a gypsy coat of red and yellow!
"Beside," quoth the Mayor with a knowing wink,
"Our business was done at the river's brink;
We saw with our eyes the vermin sink
And what's dead can't come to life, I think.
So, friend, we're not the folks to shrink
From the duty of giving you something for drink,
And a matter of money to put in your poke;[27]
But as for the guilders, what we spoke
Of them, as you very well know, was in joke.
Beside, our losses have made us thrifty;
A thousand guilders! Come, take fifty!"

[27]poke—sack

X

The Piper's face fell and he cried
"No trifling![28] I can't wait, beside!
I've promised to visit by dinnertime
Baghdad, and accept the prime
Of the Head-Cook's pottage, all he's rich in,
For having left, in the Caliph's kitchen,
Of a nest of scorpions no survivor:
With him I proved no bargain-driver,
With you, don't think I'll bate[29] a stiver![30]
And folks who put me in a passion
May find me pipe after another fashion."

[28]trifling—playing with something carelessly

[29]bate—to take away; subtract

[30]stiver—something of little value

XI

"How?" cried the Mayor, "d'ye think I brook[31]
Being worse treated than a Cook?
Insulted by a lazy ribald[32]
With idle pipe and vesture piebald?[33]
You threaten us, fellow? Do your worst,
Blow your pipe there 'til you burst!"

XII

Once more he stepped into the street
And to his lips again
Laid his long pipe of smooth straight cane;
And ere he blew three notes (such sweet
Soft notes as yet musician's cunning
Never gave the enraptured[34] air)
There was a rustling that seemed like a bustling
Of merry crowds justling at pitching and hustling,
Small feet were pattering, wooden shoes clattering,
Little hands clapping and little tongues chattering,
And, like fowls in a farm-yard when barley is scattering,
Out came the children running.
All the little boys and girls,
With rosy cheeks and flaxen[35] curls,
And sparkling eyes and teeth like pearls,
Tripping and skipping, ran merrily after
The wonderful music with shouting and laughter.

XIII

The Mayor was dumb, and the Council stood
As if they were changed into blocks of wood,
Unable to move a step, or cry
To the children merrily skipping by,
—Could only follow with the eye
That joyous crowd at the Piper's back.
But how the Mayor was on the rack,
And the wretched Council's bosoms beat,
As the Piper turned from the High Street
To where the Weser rolled its waters
Right in the way of their sons and daughters!
However he turned from South to West,
And to Koppelberg Hill his steps addressed,
And after him the children pressed;
Great was the joy in every breast.
"He never can cross that mighty top!
He's forced to let the piping drop,
And we shall see our children stop!"
When, lo, as they reached the mountainside,
A wondrous portal[36] opened wide,
As if a cavern was suddenly hollowed;
And the Piper advanced and the children followed,
And when all were in to the very last,
The door in the mountainside shut fast.
Did I say, all? No! one was lame,
And could not dance the whole of the way;
And in after years, if you would blame
His sadness, he was used to say,—
"It's dull in our town since my playmates left!
I can't forget that I'm bereft
Of all the pleasant sights they see,
Which the Piper also promised me.

[36]portal—a doorway or
entrance

For he led us, he said, to a joyous land,
Joining the town and just at hand,
Where waters gushed and fruit-trees grew,
And flowers put forth a fairer hue,[37]
And everything was strange and new;
The sparrows were brighter than peacocks here,
And their dogs outran our fallow deer,
And honey-bees had lost their stings,
And horses were born with eagle's wings;
And just as I became assured
My lame foot would be speedily cured,
The music stopped and I stood still,
And found myself outside the hill,
Left alone against my will,
To go now limping as before,
And never hear of that country more!"

XIV

Alas, alas for Hamelin!
There came into many a burgher's pate[38]
A text which says that heaven's gate
Opes[39] to the rich at as easy rate
As the needle's eye takes the camel in!
The Mayor sent East, West, North, and South,
To offer the Piper, by word of mouth,
Wherever it was men's lot to find him,
Silver and gold to his heart's content,
If he'd only return the way he went,
And bring the children behind him.

But when they saw 'twas a lost endeavor,
And Piper and dancers were gone forever,
They made a decree that lawyers never
Should think their records dated duly

[37]hue—a color; shade

[38]burgher's pate—villager's mind

[39]opes—opens

into the house, into the room that had been his father's. Only when the door had closed and the footsteps receded down the hallway did he allow the tears to fall.

The next morning, Alonzo left for his job on a road-repair crew, telling Philip to make himself at home. Relieved, Philip had his devotions alone. Then, curious about the house where his father had lived so many years, he wandered about, exploring the cool, whitewashed rooms. Following a flight of hand-hewn steps, he found himself on the roof.

Fascinated, Philip looked down at the village. From his vantage point,[4] he could see over the roofs of the other houses. Down below, two women shook rugs as they chattered to each other; another carried baskets of corn into a *piki*[5] oven, and a neighbor worked on a battered jeep. Beyond the village, rocky crags thrust like jagged teeth against an incredibly blue sky.

When he lowered his gaze again, he saw three boys about his age climbing up toward the house. Philip studied them carefully. They too wore jeans, shirts, and sneakers, but any resemblance to Philip ended there. Their clothing was worn and somewhat stained with the ever-present red dust. Bright strips of cloth wound around their foreheads hardly constrained their tousled black hair. When Philip leaned forward to watch their progress, one of the boys looked up. He motioned to the others. Philip couldn't understand the bold burst of comments, but he stepped back out of sight, his face burning.

When he turned to go, he saw the eagle. It lay limply on the brick of the roof, its talons secured to a post. Philip approached it cautiously. The eagle's eyes, dull and listless, followed his approach without interest. Philip reached out a hand to touch its head.

"Back off!"

Startled, Philip obeyed automatically. Then, half-frightened, half-defensive, he turned to face his grandfather who had returned home.

Alonzo stepped onto the roof. "The eagle is wild. We brought him down from his nest only two days ago."

"This is the eagle Paulo told me about?"

"Yes. He will remain with us through late summer, a welcome member of our household. Then, when the kachinas[6] return to the mountain ridges, the eagle will be sacrificed."

---

[4]vantage point—place that provides a good view
[5]piki—thin bread made from corn
[6]kachinas—Hopi term for imaginary spirits, believed to bring rain

"But there is no need for sacrifice anymore," Philip began. "When Christ died—"

With a sharp sound Alonzo cut him off. "Each year the eagle spirit pleads with its ancestors for rain. Without its intervention the crops would perish."

He inspected the eagle carefully. "Perhaps we chose the wrong eagle. This one fights too much. He has become weak from lack of food and water. If he dies," Alonzo said, looking troubled, "we will have a bad year."

The eagle heard the man's voice. Focusing with an effort and shaking its wings, it made a weak attempt to attack Alonzo.

"Maybe it remembers that you took it from its nest," Philip suggested.

Alonzo raised bushy eyebrows, giving the boy an appraising look.

"That never happened before," he said slowly, "but perhaps you are right. Come closer. I don't think he has the strength to hurt you, anyway."

Philip stepped forward and took Alonzo's place. The eagle made no movement toward him. Alonzo didn't stop Philip as he lifted the bowl of water to the eagle. At first it resisted; then it took a few drops.

"Enough," Alonzo said quietly. "Put it down. He will drink now."

Gently Philip placed the bowl on the bricks in front of the bird and stepped back. After a moment the eagle drank.

"You were right, Philip," Alonzo said, placing a hand on the boy's shoulder. "So—it becomes your job to care for the eagle, as it was mine and my father's before me. Fresh meat will be brought daily. He will be fed only the best."

The next morning Philip discovered who brought the fresh meat. When he entered the kitchen for breakfast, one of the three boys he had seen the day before waited beside the door. From his hand dangled a freshly killed rabbit. As the boy waited for Alonzo to pay for the rabbit, he slowly swung it in a circle, eyes fixed on Philip.

Without changing his steady gaze, he spoke to Alonzo with quick, strange words. Alonzo glanced at Philip and replied in the same language, more amused than annoyed. Philip flushed. The boy gave him a mocking salute and slipped out the door.

"Who was that?" Philip asked.

"Dennis Qumevedo," Alonzo answered. "A grandson of a friend. A good Hopi."

Philip accepted the rebuke without answering. There was no answer he could give. Instead, he changed the subject.

"How do I feed the eagle?"

"Come, I will show you."

Philip followed his grandfather up the stairs to the roof and then carefully followed his instructions. After the eagle had eaten, Philip asked, "What's his name?"

"At the ceremony he was given the name 'He Who Sails on the Wind.'"

Philip struggled with the Hopi syllables for the eagle's name until Alonzo nodded. "That's close enough," he said as he went back to the stairs.

Philip tried once more alone, then gave up. "I think I'll call you Sailor. What do you think, bird?"

The eagle chirped deep in his throat and stretched his beak toward Philip. Philip laughed at the display of attention. "The hand that feeds, huh, Sailor?"

As the days passed, Philip sought out Sailor's rooftop sanctuary[7] more and more frequently. Though the bird launched himself at Alonzo on sight, he seemed to enjoy Philip's presence. And Philip enjoyed the unconditional affection the eagle displayed. It was nice at last—for the first time since the death of his parents—to feel loved and needed.

Often he took his father's Bible to the rooftop with him and had his devotions by the light of the early-morning sun. Following the penciled notations in the margins gave him comfort, a feeling that something of his life remained the same, unchanged. He knew his grandfather was aware of the devotions, but his grandfather made no reference to the daily Bible reading nor to their first conversation about prayer. Philip sensed that Alonzo gave him grudging respect for continuing to do what he thought was right.

---

[7]sanctuary—an area where wild animals and birds are protected

As June came, religious ceremonies in the villages became more frequent. Each time a ceremony was held in the Eagle Clan, Alonzo insisted that Philip accompany him. Philip did learn to appreciate the thin *piki* bread made from blue corn, the juicy ears of roasted sweet corn, and the other delicacies so freely given in the houses of the Eagle Clan. But to accept that the kachina spirits lived on the mountaintops, to accept that snakes and eagles had anything to do with rain—Philip knew better. He found it impossible to remain silent, even to avoid angering his grandfather.

Each night Philip prayed that, when given the opportunity, he would say only what was right and that he would say it in the right spirit. It wasn't easy, especially when Dennis and his friends taunted him openly. Frequently Philip lost his good intentions and spoke sharply, then wished he had held his tongue. Common sense told him he gained nothing and only brought on more confrontations.[8]

One such event took place in Paulo's crossroads store. Dennis and his friends were already there when Philip and Alonzo drove up.

The three boys lounged around the drink box. They greeted Alonzo respectfully, and then turned their attention to Philip.

"Wait here with the boys," Alonzo told Philip. "I won't be long."

Philip sighed. He knew Alonzo wanted him to get along with the Hopi boys. He took a deep breath and said, "Hello."

The boys looked at each other and grinned.

When the screen door closed behind Alonzo, Dennis put his drink bottle down and stepped forward. He stopped about six inches from Philip. He did nothing, said nothing. He just stood there, his eyes boring into Philip's. Philip had to force himself not to step back.

The others moved in closer. Not a word was said, not a gesture made toward him, but the tension between the four boys increased. Trying desperately to ignore the impassive[9] faces, Philip broke the silence with the first thing that came to mind. "How do you trap the rabbits?"

There was no answer, no movement, no lessening of the boys' strange concentration. Philip found himself racing mentally through Bible verses to maintain the courage to stand against the silent attack.

A voice behind him shattered the tension. "What's going on, boys?"

The three boys stepped back as a tall man, dressed neatly in work clothes, stepped up on the porch. His keen gaze missed nothing. He

[8]confrontations—face-to-face conflicts; arguments
[9]impassive—expressing no emotion

stopped beside Philip and, hands resting easily on his hips, waited for a reply.

Dennis glanced at Philip, then said, "Nothing, Mr. Timmons. We were just leaving."

Philip relaxed, his muscles trembling.

Mr. Timmons remained beside him, watching as the boys edged away.

"How about coming to the mission Saturday, boys?" he asked cheerfully. "We're having a workday, then refreshments. Be glad to have you."

"No, thanks. There's a snake dance Saturday." Dennis jumped off the porch and, followed by the other two, swung easily into the back of his father's pickup.

Mr. Timmons turned to Philip. "Seemed sort of tense there for a moment. I'm Dave Timmons. I run the mission here."

"Mission?"

Mr. Timmons looked surprised. "Sure. The flat, rectangular building on the other side of the village. You haven't seen it?"

"I didn't even know it existed," Philip replied. "I feel like I've been everywhere else, though." He held out his hand. "I'm Philip Talihema. My grandfather is—"

"Alonzo. I think I understand. I heard your parents were Christians and that there had been some trouble about it."

"You can say that again." Philip sighed. "Grandfather is determined to make me a good Hopi, even if Dad wasn't."

"And?"

"Impossible. I'm a Christian."

"Then the last few weeks must have been hard on you. Why don't you come down to the mission and talk about it?"

"That'll be great!"

"See you then. Come any time." Mr. Timmons gave his shoulder a sympathetic squeeze.

As Dave Timmons entered the store, Alonzo came out. He responded to the missionary's greeting with a cold nod.

"What'd *he* want?" he asked Philip.

"He invited me to the mission," Philip replied warily.

"In the truck," Alonzo snapped. When Philip obeyed, his grandfather fixed him with a stern look. "You are not to go to the mission, not now, not ever. And stay away from Dave Timmons!"

"Yes, sir." Philip leaned back against the seat and closed his eyes to fight the despair that swept over him.

Son of My Son

In the succeeding weeks, Philip concentrated on learning as much as he could about golden eagles. He discovered that they prefer a varied diet. Since the care of the eagle had proven to be a safe subject in the past, he asked Alonzo to teach him how to trap other small animals for feed.

The next weekend, Philip and his grandfather left food and water for Sailor and packed the pickup. Before sunup they were bumping down the narrow streets, on their way to the canyons for a combination camping and trapping expedition.

Sunrise in the canyons caught Philip by surprise. He hadn't expected the range of light and shadow that brought the normally dull-red rock cliffs alive with color. Alonzo stopped the pickup near the rim of a canyon so Philip could watch as the sun appeared over the opposite edge.

The early morning breeze ruffled his hair and whispered in the needles of the scrawny piñon trees behind him. He wanted to say how beautiful it was, but he could think of no words to describe what he felt. Music, maybe, but not words.

Philip found it impossible to stand there and not think of God. For the first time he felt Hopi, sensing the reverence of ages for this place. He glanced at Alonzo's quiet face and, with sudden understanding, realized how nature could play such an important part in the religious tradition of the Hopis.

When the sky lightened, they left the rim and packed their equipment down a rough trail to the canyon floor. As they set up camp near a water hole, Alonzo pointed out the most likely places to set traps.

Later, he showed Philip how to construct tiny noose traps and how to set out triggered boxes for larger animals. After baiting the traps, they retired to camp to eat lunch and to relax in the shade. Philip lay under an overhanging rock and watched the play of light on the canyon wall.

"The rocks look different from the way they did this morning," he observed.

"You have a good eye," Alonzo said, approvingly. "It's easy to get lost in the canyons if you don't pick out landmarks, then allow for the changes made by the shadows. The canyons and ravines can become deathtraps if a person doesn't know what he's doing."

"When will we check *our* traps?"

"In the morning," Alonzo replied, a little sleepily. "The smaller animals have the sense to stay out of the sun. They'll come out at dusk."

The birds were the first to appear. As shadows painted the canyon

in deep purples, quail and doves fluttered over Philip's head.

"They'll take water, then roost for the night," Alonzo said quietly. "Look."

Turning his head fractionally, Philip glimpsed a red fox merging[10] back into the rocks beside the water. As he lay silently watching, a mule deer moved warily into the open. Before dark obscured his vision, he had seen a coyote and its mate, a family of badgers, and a lone skunk seek water from the hole. At full dark, Alonzo rose from his side and started a campfire. Philip, surprised at the chill in the night air, sought its warmth.

In the morning the traps yielded a good selection of small animals for the eagle. The bagged animals, added to the traps and packs, made awkward bundles to lug back up the steep trail to the truck. Halfway there, Philip slipped on loose rock and fell. Crumbling earth and cascading rock almost shot him over the edge.

"Danny!"

[10]merging—blending together gradually

equipment and traps in the back with the bag of animals.

"These won't last long," Philip said as Alonzo started the truck. "Sailor sure eats a lot."

"He's a healthy, growing eagle, thanks to you," Alonzo replied. "What we have will last about a week. Then, if you want, we can come again."

"Sure!" Philip responded enthusiastically.

"Saves me money, anyway." Alonzo grimaced. "That Dennis raised his price on fresh rabbit again. At his prices, we might as well eat the rabbit ourselves."

"We didn't get any rabbit," Philip said. "How does Dennis get his?"

"Depends on whether his customers want a hole through it or not. We'll go rabbit hunting next weekend."

The first of the week, Alonzo met frequently with the other men in the *kiva*,[11] praying and planning the coming ceremonies. Left on his own, Philip took his books to the rooftop. In the bookcase in his father's room he had found a book on training eagles.

After feeding Sailor, Philip inspected the bird's perch. Sailor leaned forward, chirping and preening. Philip rubbed the bird's head gently as he fingered the bonds that held the

Philip, hanging on to a thick root, heard his father's name. He looked up into his grandfather's strained face.

Alonzo pulled him to safety, then spoke gruffly. "Watch out along the edge."

Philip nodded without commenting on the use of his father's name. He followed his grandfather, this time watching his feet instead of the view. They dumped the camping

[11]kiva—Hopi term for an underground room where men of the tribe hold meetings and ceremonies

eagle to the perch. "I wonder if I could train you to the fist," he whispered, holding out his hand. Sailor flexed his talons[12] and shifted back and forth on the perch, eyeing the hand. "I bet I could!"

A shout from below took him to the stairs. Down in the kitchen, Dennis stood holding a rabbit. When he saw Philip, he frowned. "Where's your grandfather?"

"He's at the *kiva*," Philip responded, trying to keep his voice pleasant. "He told me to tell you we wouldn't be needing any more rabbits for a while."

Dennis's black eyebrows met. "The eagle die?"

Philip shook his head. "No, we're trapping our own, now."

Black eyes sparked with anger. "*I* supply the rabbits!"

"You can talk to Grandfather if you like," Philip said more calmly than he felt.

Dennis swung away. "Forget it," he said unpleasantly. "Wouldn't have been much longer anyway. Soon the kachinas will return to the ridges— and so will your eagle!"

Philip stared at his retreating figure in shock. He had almost forgotten the eagle's purpose. Quickly he calculated on his fingers. Three more weeks until the end of July. Only three more weeks!

The bird pulled away as Philip approached, watching him uneasily

and making sharp, questioning screeches. Philip forced himself to slow down and move calmly. Still, some of his turmoil communicated to the bird, and he remained flustered, watching Philip warily.

Philip returned to his books to wait. He read with surprise that eagles have to learn how to fly. Silently he inspected the tethered[13] bird. Without stopping to consider the consequences, he reached over and loosened the cords.

Sailor remained on the perch.

"Shoo! Shoo!" Philip waved his arms. "Don't you know how to fly at all? Look!"

Wildly, he ran around the rooftop, flapping his wings up and down. Head tilted to one side, Sailor regarded him with a glint in the visible eye.

Philip laughed and sat down, exhausted.

"I bet you think I've gone bananas," he told the bird soberly. "And I have. If I let you loose, I might as well pack my bags. Where'll I go? What'll happen to me? And where will you go?"

Sailor lifted his wide wings and propelled himself across the roof to land beside Philip. "So you can fly," Philip murmured. He watched the bird hop about the rooftop, lifting its

---

12talons—claws
13tethered—tied up

wings experimentally. It made several practice liftoffs, always coming back to Philip. When it stopped near the perch and turned its head, Philip got up.

"No, I'll not tie you up again. You shouldn't end up as feathers on a prayer bush. You should ride the wind, just as your name says." He waved his arms again, shouting, "Fly, fly while you can!"

The eagle turned as if to listen to the wind. Then, spreading its wings, it launched into the blue sky.

Philip shaded his eyes and watched the bird spiral upward until it was only a speck against the sky. When it disappeared beyond the crags, Philip removed the perch and any evidence of feeding, hoping the bird would not return out of habit.

He descended the stairs wearily. He was in his room packing his old suitcase when Alonzo entered. His grandfather's startled gaze took in the scattered clothing and open suitcase.

"What's going on?"

Philip faced his grandfather resolutely.[14] "I let the eagle go."

Alonzo's face grayed. He rushed out of the room and up the stairs. For a long time there was silence in the house. Philip sat on the bed and waited. At last he heard slow footsteps on the stairs.

Alonzo stood in the doorway, looking tired.

"Why? Why did you do such a thing?"

"I didn't want to see his feathers on the bush," Philip said, looking down at his own clenched hands. "I'm sorry."

"What's done is done. Put your clothes away." Alonzo turned and left Philip alone in the room.

---

[14]resolutely—firmly; determinedly

408

The next few weeks went by with paralyzing slowness for Philip. He had expected anger and rejection from his grandfather. Instead, his attitude was that of defeat. Philip found it harder to endure than any punishment he could imagine. When Alonzo's attitude toward him began to soften and the days became more normal, Philip accepted the change gratefully and without question.

On the night of the owl ceremony, Philip discovered the extent of his grandfather's disgrace. He and Alonzo arrived at the ceremony late. The kachinas[15] already danced in the cleared space, shaking whips at the "clowns" that represented Hopis who had deserted the ways of their people. Alonzo walked stiffly beside Philip. The crowd parted before them, murmuring disapprovingly. When they stopped near the front, people moved away a little, leaving them in a slightly cleared space. Philip had never felt so exposed. One glance at his grandfather's face told him he felt the same.

The rhythmic rattling of the turtle shells and bells attached to the kachina's knees pulled Philip's attention back to the ceremony. The owl kachina had appeared to warn the wayward Hopis of their punishment.

Masked and brightly costumed, the faceless owl circled the clearing, cracking a whip. When it reached Philip and his grandfather, it stopped. The crowd murmured in surprise as the owl turned away from the clown it was supposed to "chastise" and moved toward Philip. The owl shouted menacingly[16] in Hopi and shook the whip threateningly at Philip. When Philip tried to back away, a sharp push from behind thrust him into the clearing. He half turned and saw Dennis disappearing back into the crowd.

The whip cracked. Stunned, Philip whirled to face the owl. The kachina raised the whip again, high over its head.

"Stop!"

Alonzo shouldered past the onlookers and stood beside Philip. His eyes bored into the masked eyes of the owl. "This is my grandson, the son of my son."

The owl hesitated. Then it stepped back, acknowledging both the spoken and unspoken message.

Alonzo put his hand on Philip's back. "Come."

They returned to the house in silence. When Philip started to his room, Alonzo stopped him. "Let's talk," he said, motioning for Philip to follow him into the kitchen.

He poured two glasses of milk and sat down at the table. "I apologize for what happened out there. The owl kachina is a friend of

---

[15]kachinas—a masked dancer in costume representing an imaginary spirit
[16]menacingly—threateningly

mine—Dennis's grandfather. What they tried to do is wrong. No one is supposed to be punished at the ceremonies."

"What I did was worse than I thought." Philip sat down. "I've made a mess of things, haven't I?"

"Neither one of us has done too well," Alonzo said wearily. "I guess I tried to remake my son, Danny, the way he was before I drove him away. I won't make that mistake again. And you, you've just been trying to fit in. You don't have to follow the religious practices of the Hopis to be part of the tribe, Philip. There are many who don't."

At Philip's surprised look, Alonzo dropped his gaze to his glass. "If you had looked, you'd have noticed that not everyone was at the ceremony. I tried to keep you away from the others because I thought your faith would weaken if not encouraged. Instead, it seems to have grown stronger. Perhaps it is time you visited the mission."

He drained his glass and stood up.

"Now?" Philip asked incredulously.[17]

"Why not? I hear there's a party." Alonzo managed a smile. "Probably to keep the Christians away from the owl ceremony."

"But what about Sailor?"

"He's free, isn't he?" Alonzo said gruffly. "Maybe he'll come back; maybe he won't. There was an eagle when I was eight—well, that's another story. If anything else is said about the eagle, I'll take care of it. Now, wipe your mustache off, and let's go. You're late as it is."

Philip hastened to obey. At the door of the house, as they headed for the truck, his grandfather put on his old felt hat and looked down at the boy. He held out his hand and said, "Welcome home, Philip Talihema."

---

[17]incredulously—shocked and disbelievingly

Almanacs

Rachel Larson

The History of Almanacs

Ever since their introduction, almanacs have served as ready reference sources. They contain a great deal of practical information about the current year of publication as well as past events. You can find information about such topics as world governments, historical events, people, transportation, education, communication, and sports. Best of all, the information is organized, summarized, and recorded as tables and charts in easy-to-use formats. Almanacs are readily found in libraries. Because of their size, relatively low cost, and easy accessibility, almanacs have become a popular reference source.

Geoffrey Chaucer first used the English word "almanac" in 1391. In the fifteenth century, almanacs were prepared for specific periods of time. These ten-year lists combined weather and celestial predictions with a calendar of special church holidays. Samuel Danforth printed the first extant (still existing) American almanac in 1648 (MDCXLVIII). Two of the most popular almanacs in colonial

An excerpt from Poor Richard's Almanac

America were compiled by Nathaniel Ames of Dedham, Massachusetts, and by Benjamin Franklin in Philadelphia. Franklin's work, *Poor Richard's Almanac,* gained lasting fame for its witty sayings about human nature. "Early to bed, and early to rise, makes a man healthy, wealthy, and wise" is one example of the sayings he included as space fillers. *The Farmer's Almanac* has been published since 1792 and retains the longest record for annual almanac printings.

Families that purchased almanacs from print shops got the same filler pages but bound them with different materials based on how much money they had or wanted to spend on a binding. Since most families bought almanacs each year, paper or cloth covers were widely used. In addition, since almanacs were printed on only one side of the page, and since paper (which was made from cotton rags) was somewhat scarce and expensive, the backs of the pages were inscribed by a quill pen with a family's own information and writings. Records of births of children, deaths of local people, spring arrivals of livestock, diaries, and comments on the weather are found inscribed on these pages.

General Information in Almanacs

Today's almanacs serve some of the same purposes as their predecessors,[1] but they have increased in size and have added features. As a result, they are useful sources of information. Portions of almanacs can also be found through electronic access, but these must be evaluated by your teacher or your parent.

Almanacs often list "headline" or big news stories in the chronological order they occurred in that year.

[1]predecessors—things that came before or had a function before another

The sleeping fox catches no poultry.

Haste makes waste.

A penny saved is a penny earned.

Little strokes fell great oaks.

Lost time is never found again.

–*Benjamin Franklin*

Remember, however, that such accounts are concise.[2] But you could easily find the date of the event and later find an in-depth account in a newspaper or periodical for that date in the library.

Almanacs are useful for making comparisons. You can also use them to evaluate trends in natural events, such as average rainfall or population growth.

If you searched for answers to the following questions, you could find the information in a current almanac. The authors gather their facts from census materials, historical data, and other published material. Then they summarize the information with charts and tables.

- Which country has the fewest miles of railroad?

- Which seven countries have one car for every two people?

- Which countries have the fewest cars or the most people per car?

- Which two countries other than the United States have the most airline passenger miles flown?

[2]concise—brief and clear

Common Transportation Statistics					
Country	Railroad Miles	Cars	Persons Per Car	Airplane Passenger Miles	Airports
Australia	22,385	8,700,000	2	47,200,000,000	400
Bangladesh	1,681	134,073	948	2,000,000,000	8
Brazil	18,578	14,000,000	12	26,300,000,000	139
Canada	44,182	13,300,000	2	38,400,000,000	301
China	45,319	4,700,000	265	45,300,000,000	113
Egypt	2,989	1,280,000	53	5,600,000,000	11
France	19,874	25,500,000	2	52,600,000,000	61
Germany	54,994	41,330,000	2	53,600,000,000	40
India	38,935	4,250,000	235	15,000,000,000	66
Italy	9,944	31,000,000	2	23,600,000,000	34
Japan	12,511	46,640,000	3	93,900,000,000	73
Mexico	16,543	8,200,000	12	14,700,000,000	83
Russia	94,400	13,710,000	11	30,600,000,000	75
United Kingdom	23,518	25,590,000	2	98,100,000,000	57
United States	137,900	129,730,000	2	599,400,000,000	834

Although almanacs provide a source of "trivia," you can also evaluate this concise information for trends and other patterns. Reading the tables and charts in an almanac provides information for answering questions such as the following:

- Which countries have more newspapers per 1,000 people than the United States?

- Does India have more radios or televisions per 1,000 people?

- In which six countries do more than half of the people have phones?

- Which country has the most televisions per 1,000 people?

Now look at the Common Communication Statistics table shown below. From this information you can see the current trends of communication differences in various countries. It appears that radios and phones are more numerous for communication, and most countries have more radios than televisions.

Use the table of contents to get a general idea of the subjects covered. Then take time to look at the index. Finally, browse through the volume and look for topics of special interest to you. As you become more familiar with this useful resource tool, you may decide that it would be a handy item to have along with a good dictionary in your home library.

Common Communication Statistics*				
Country	Newspapers	Phones	Radios	Televisions
Australia	258	513	1,148	641
Bangladesh	0.4	2.5	65	5
Brazil	47	116	348	193
Canada	215	621	919	647
China	23	68	177	189
Egypt	43	59	312	110
France	235	576	860	579
Germany	375	566	1,836	551
India	21	17	117	21
Italy	126	458	790	436
Japan	578	479	799	619
Mexico	115	99	227	192
Russia	267	184	341	379
United Kingdom	383	539	1,194	612
United States	238	633	2,122	776

* All figures per 1,000 population

DISTANT REALMS 5

Blotto

adapted from original version
illustrated by Timothy N. Davis

by H. Mortimer Batten

Of all the wild animal pets I have ever known, Jim Standing's bear cub Blotto was the most amusing. I met Jim when I was forest-ranging in British Columbia, and he was inspector of a long stretch of railway line.

Jim's cabin stood alongside the railway line. You could hardly call Jim's place a railway station, since day after day the great transcontinental trains thundered right past his cabin. Only one train stopped there each week—if you could call it a train. It had a single coach and an engine which puffed over the mountains for the sole purpose of bringing mail, papers, and food to the men working on the line. When it arrived, Jim would pull a long lever, and the engineer would reverse the little engine onto Jim's private siding.[1] Jim would be supplied with all he needed from the coach, and after the midday regular had gone roaring past, he would pull the lever again, and the little engine would go snorting off to the cabin of the next man.

---

[1]siding—a short length of railroad track that goes off the main track

Jim had no signals to mind, but he always carried a red flag under his arm when he made the daily rounds of the tracks. He might find something wrong with one of the bridges that spanned the roaring rivers, or possibly in the dry heat the railway ties might be smoldering. Every day he tapped out messages on the telegraph in his cabin, relaying the times at which trains passed and the number of coaches they pulled—to make sure none had dropped off during the steep ascent of the mountains. Thus, Jim had plenty to do and was satisfied with his lot.

Among Jim's visitors early one summer was an Indian carrying a black bear cub. When Jim asked him how he had caught the little creature, the Indian explained that he had crept up on its mother while she was drinking and had suddenly shouted a ringing "Whoop!" The mother bear had fallen headfirst into the river and had swum across, and the cub, having lost sight of her, had run to the Indian by mistake. Jim was touched by the animal's amusing ways and offered to keep the bear cub.

Why Jim called him Blotto, I do not know. Perhaps it was because he was as much like a blot of ink as anything else when he first arrived. He was fed on evaporated milk, sugar, bread, and scraps of bacon fat, and he grew fast. He was always thirsty. He would drink milk and water till he was blown up like a balloon and could do nothing but lie flat on the ground, whimpering because he could drink no more.

As he became more active, no puppy could have been more amusing. At first when the trains came thundering by, Blotto did not like them. The cub would run into the cabin and hide his head under the worn wolfskin mat beside Jim's bed. But Blotto soon got used to the trains and would sit up at the cabin door to watch them pass.

Day after day Blotto got into mischief and was spanked, but he was a wise bear, for there were certain things he never did twice. Only once did he eat the soap, crying and foaming all the time he munched it.

Only once did he amuse himself by batting the pepper pot around, pretending it was a ball; and only once did he hit the teakettle because it hissed steam at him.

When Blotto's spirits became too high, Jim had only to offer the cub soap or show him the pepper pot or point to the kettle, and Blotto would suddenly remember an important appointment outside.

Realizing that someday Blotto might have to look after himself, Jim set to work to teach him the lessons he would have learned from his mother. He showed Blotto how to hunt ants and slugs by turning over stones and dead logs, and how to hunt beetles by tearing up moss. Jim hissed a warning at Blotto when the cub tried to catch a little red snake but urged him to go as hard as he could after the fat black ones. Then one morning Jim found a bees' nest full of honey in a hollow tree and called, "Hi, Blotto! Honey! Come quick! Hurry!"

It did not take Blotto long to smell the honey, and it did not take Jim long to smash open the tree with his hammer, leaving Blotto to enjoy that feast.

After that, Blotto spent a good deal of his time hunting honey. When he found a nest he could not reach, he would yell for Jim. Then after dark they would go back to the honey tree armed with a lantern and an ax, for Jim liked honey too.

But of all his pastimes, Blotto loved one better than any other. Near the cabin a sun-dried tree trunk stood up from the earth. It was five feet long, tough, hard, and as thick as a man's wrist. Blotto would take the trunk between his forepaws and pump it backward and forward, grunting in time with his movements. Whenever Jim passed the trunk, he would point to it and shout, "Pump, Blotto! Pump!" And the louder Jim urged, the harder Blotto pumped, till often they finished up with Jim pumping wildly in the air in time with Blotto's pumping. Then the cub would lose his grip on the trunk and go somersaulting backward in a cloud of dust, while the trunk sprang back, trembling.

Blotto was a born mimic, and Jim would often find the cub clumsily imitating something his master had done. For example, each morning while the bacon was sizzling, Jim would wash in a bucket by the cabin door. Looking around, he would see Blotto going through the motions of washing his face and neck, patting himself just as Jim did. One day Jim discovered how Blotto got the strange idea of pumping the tree trunk.

On this particular day Jim was expecting the relief train, so he went to the shunt[2] line early to check the points. Gripping the long lever that worked the points,[3] Jim threw it backward and forward a time or two to make sure it was working properly. The cub watched him, and as Jim walked away, he turned to see Blotto pumping away at the point lever just as he had done!

This was terribly dangerous! If Blotto pumped the point lever on his own, he might leave the points in the wrong position and shunt one of the trains onto the siding, which was only a hundred yards long, and cause a terrible accident.

Jim dashed up, shouting angrily, and as Blotto darted aside, Jim took a kick at his hindquarters to teach him a lesson. But Blotto dodged the kick, and all that happened was that one of Jim's shoes went soaring into the air and fell close to Blotto. The cub dutifully picked up the shoe and ran for home, and Jim had to expose one foot to the cinders all the way back to the cabin.

Jim was determined to teach Blotto a lesson about those points. Taking him back to the shunt line, Jim sprinkled the lever with pepper. Holding the cub by his neck over the point lever, Jim said, "Now don't you do that again!"

As soon as Blotto was free, he ran home sneezing. When Jim reached the cabin, there was Blotto

---

[2]shunt—the directional track used for changing course
[3]points—movable parts of a railroad switch

pumping the branch and sneezing every time he pumped.

Soon after the pumping episode, two forest rangers came to visit Jim. They were met at the door of the cabin by Blotto. He stared at them curiously and then turned two somersaults and ran into the cabin. The rangers found him with his head hidden under the wolfskin, yelling at the top of his voice. However, one of the rangers had a bag of raisins, so it did not take him long to make friends with Blotto.

Soon Jim turned up, and that evening the three men laughed at Blotto's antics. But at suppertime one of the rangers suddenly looked grave. "Look here, Jim," he said. "What do you intend to do with that bear? The railway people won't let you keep him after he grows up, and already he's big enough to be dangerous."

Jim laughed heartily. "Dangerous!" he scoffed. "Did you ever hear of a dangerous black bear? They're the softest, silliest old things in all the woods. Blotto will just stay with me."

The ranger shook his head. "That may be true as far as it goes," he answered. "Bears are good-natured and well-meaning, but they do not know their own strength. One day you will pat Blotto affectionately, and in return he'll give you a pat that will send you to the hospital."

Again Jim laughed. "Blotto will never hurt me," he replied. "He loves me too much."

But the ranger was serious. "Well, that may be your point of view, but I shall have to report him all the same. The railway company will forbid your keeping him. What will become of Blotto then?"

Jim did not really know. It was a point which, in the back of his mind, had puzzled him for a long time. That was why he had taught Blotto to hunt for himself. Jim hoped that eventually Blotto would wander back into the woods and join the free, wild creatures. Jim was disturbed until the other ranger spoke up.

"Look here, Jim," he said. "You just carry on with your bear cub, but do everything you can to make Blotto wander off into the woods. We'll not report him yet. I think he'll go off on his own when autumn comes. Henry and I will be on our way now, before the light goes. It was a swell supper, Jim. Good-bye, and we wish you well!"

As the rangers left on their long journey through the wilderness, they looked back and saw Blotto on his hind legs next to Jim at the cabin door.

After that, Jim watched the growth of his bear cub rather sadly, knowing that before long Blotto would be too big and powerful for a household pet. He realized this fully one evening when the bear cub carried a huge boulder into the cabin in order to eat three ants that were clinging to it. He evidently expected Jim to eat at least one of the ants, for he slunk away with a pained expression when Jim told him to carry out the rock. It was all Jim could do to lift the stone.

Another evening a pack rat appeared in the cupboard, and Jim and Blotto set to work to hunt it out. Suddenly the rat ran across the floor. Blotto aimed a blow at it that would have knocked a cow off its feet. He missed the rat, but he knocked Jim's legs out from under him and sent him sprawling. Yet Blotto was so well-meaning and good-natured that except for his size and strength he was a most desirable companion.

One day Jim decided that the points of the shunt line needed oiling, so he went out with his oil can and spanner,[4] leaving Blotto to hunt bees. Arriving at the points, he found them clogged with rust.

There was one big nut Jim could not move, and as he pulled with all his weight on the long-handled spanner, the bolt suddenly broke. Jim fell over backward, caught his heels on the rail, and went somersaulting down the embankment toward the river—an avalanche[5] of stones bounding after him.

Jim landed on a ledge. But when he tried to get on his feet, he found he couldn't. His right hip seemed to be out of place, and his leg was useless to him. He knew that he had really injured himself.

What a situation, thought Jim. But he decided it might have been much worse. When the men down the line got no message from his telegraph, they would know that something was wrong and would hurry to rescue him. Then suddenly Jim realized with horror that the next train was due to arrive within an hour. Jim looked at his watch—no, it was due within thirty minutes! He must have been unconscious!

Then a terrible question flashed into his mind. How had he left the points? With a mighty effort he was able to raise himself so that he could see the end of the long lever. It was pointed in the wrong direction! When the train came along, it would be thrown into the siding to crash over the buffers,[6] then down into the river!

---

[4]spanner—wrench
[5]avalanche—a large mass of rocks sliding down a hill
[6]buffers—things that separate and protect

Jim tried to struggle up, but he was quite helpless. Within minutes a railway accident was bound to occur unless a miracle of some kind happened.

Just then Jim heard a high-pitched "Kia-wa-wa!" which simply meant that Blotto had discovered a bees' nest and had been stung on the snout.

A wild idea flashed into Jim's mind. "Blotto!" he yelled. "Hi! Come here, Blotto!"

Jim shouted until his lungs hurt. It seemed an eternity before the bear came. His wooly head appeared over the edge of the embankment, and he looked down at Jim inquiringly.

"Pump, Blotto! Pump!" shouted Jim.

Blotto's eyes gleamed. He looked around and saw the long lever. It was tempting, and Blotto liked to play that game. Taking the lever in his paws, the bear began to jerk it violently backward and forward, while the points engaged and disengaged with a clicking sound. At length he looked down at Jim as much as to say, "That enough?" Jim could hear the far-off thunder of the train, and he saw that the lever was still in the wrong position.

"Pump, Blotto! Pump!" he shrieked. The train was coming. Nearer and nearer it came. "Blotto, pump! Pump!" Jim yelled.

Blotto grunted, then put one paw over his nose, as if he still remembered the pepper. But with the other paw he gave the lever a good yank, and over went the points to the "safe" position.

"Ants, Blotto!" Jim howled. "Ants—honey—slugs—soap—come here quick!" And Blotto, all curiosity, forgot about the lever and ambled[7] down the slope toward Jim, as the train sped safely on its way overhead.

Somehow, by painfully dragging himself along on his left side, Jim made it to the cabin where he reported his accident by telegraph.

The next train stopped to take Jim to the hospital. Blotto looked on helplessly, but when the train steamed out, the bear fell in behind the train and followed it. If Jim was going, so was he!

[7]ambled—walked unhurriedly; strolled

An hour later an outpost railway man saw the bear cub ambling down the tracks past his cabin, still in pursuit of the train, now fifty miles ahead. Later in the day the men at Cracardo Sawmills saw Blotto still chasing the train, which was now speeding down the opposite slope of the Rockies. They saw him go to the stream and drink gallons of water, after which he went on more slowly, looking like a fur-clad barrel, a cloud of flies about his head. That was the last ever heard of him.

Somewhere along that stretch of tracks through the wilderness the black bear's interest probably turned from Jim to the matter of food. He must have wandered off the right of way.

Blotto returned to the wild with honor to his name. And in a freight-yard job far from his lonely cabin, Jim often thought of the black bear with many chuckles and a warm spot in his heart.

The Medieval Knight

Amy Miller
illustrated by Kathy Pflug

When we hear of knights, we typically think of courageous men such as King Arthur who have been portrayed in the famous legend about the Knights of the Round Table. We remember the tales of brave knights defending beautiful ladies and performing daring deeds. Although there were times of heroic deeds, a knight endured much training to earn his title.

The page served in the household where he learned respect for authority and courtly manners. He also learned to fight with swords and played strategy games to improve his mind.

Becoming a Knight

As the role of the medieval[1] knight developed, it became common for landowners to send their sons at a young age to the home of a nobleman to be trained as a knight. Often leaving home at eight years of age, a boy served in household duties as a *page*. As a result of serving his master and the ladies of the house, the boy learned at an early age about courtly manners.

At about fourteen years of age, the *page* was then apprenticed to a knight. During the teenage years, the boy learned to fight and was called a *squire*. The squires spent almost all of their time in rigorous physical training. All day long they exercised, wrestled one another, learned acrobatics, and built their strength. In times of war or battle, the squire served the knight to which he was

---

[1]medieval—applying to anything in the Middle Ages (A.D. 500-1500)

apprenticed, carrying the knight's armor and aiding him in battle. If the knight was unhorsed, the squire helped the knight to his feet (since the armor was very hard to move around in), helped him remount his horse, and provided him with new weapons.

In the late teen years, the *squire* might become a *bachelor* who served as a leader of the squires. Often, a nobleman would have a dormitory full of young squires training to become knights, with only one or two seasoned knights to train them. Thus, the bachelors were given overseer duties.

Finally, at about age twenty or twenty-one, a successful squire was eligible to be knighted. However, the knight had first to prove himself in battle or in *joust* before he could become a knight. Not all squires would become knights just because they were a certain age.

The ceremony that took place could be either very lengthy or very short, depending on the situation. Another knight, a prince, or even the king himself knighted a man on the battlefield when one had proved himself worthy of becoming a knight. During times of peace, the ceremony of knighthood might have included ritual bathing, all-night prayer ceremonies, or even a specific haircut style. Often a great feast of celebration accompanied the ceremony. To be knighted by the king was a great honor not bestowed on many knights.

The squire was servant to his lord or to the knight he was apprenticed to. He wrestled, jousted with a dummy target, and strengthened his body for the day of battle.

Some men were knighted on the battlefield, others in formal ceremony. The knight received his weapons and armor from the nobleman whom he served.

Practicing for Battle

After leaving the structure of the dormitory life, knights still needed to practice their skills in order to keep in good shape for the day of battle. This practice came in the form of tournaments. Originally, the tournaments took the form of mock battles. The knights would form two teams and meet on the battlefield—without rules or regulations. They did not even blunt the ends of their sharp weapons. As a result, many valuable knights were killed in practice. Eventually, rules were made to keep the tournaments safe.

Another form of the tournament involved knights practicing one-on-one in a *joust*. Special lances with blunt or rounded tips protected the knights from killing one another in practice, but many were still wounded. The object of this tournament was to either break your lance when striking the opponent, or to knock him off his horse—or "unhorse" him—with one blow. In some tournaments, the contest continued on foot with swords or other smaller weapons after one knight had been unhorsed.

The Tradition of Titles

Upon becoming a knight, the young man was given the title "Sir." This is different from our use of the word today in that it became a part of his name so that people knew what position he held. It was a title like "Doctor." It came with a position that was earned. In this way, the knight was different from the nobility. Noblemen had titles, such as "prince" or "earl," that were usually given to them at birth.

The titles and levels of nobility have changed over the years in England, but in the Middle Ages, the earl was of the highest rank just below the prince. Earls owned more land than anyone except the king and his immediate family. Owning land also gave them great power.

²estate—property in land and buildings

While the king was always called "His Majesty," the earl was commonly addressed in two different ways. As with other noblemen, the earl's title was joined to the name of his estate.² If his estate was named Kenilworth, he might be called "The Earl of Kenilworth." If his family name was Fairfax, he might be called "Lord Fairfax." Both names could be used to refer to the same person.

Today there are still knights, kings, and earls. Kings and earls are born into their position with these titles. In times past the honor given to a knight was for military recognition. Now, a knight earns his title through great accomplishments in many areas that bring honor to his country.

Armor of the medieval knight

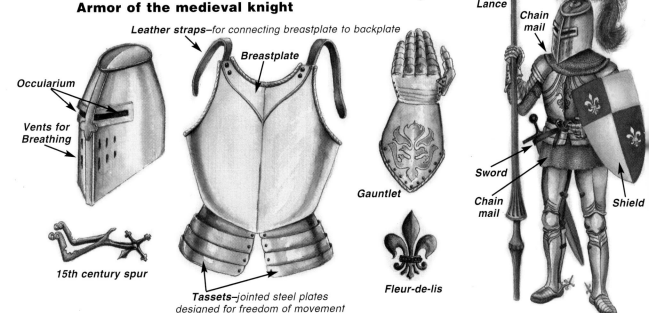

Occularium

Vents for Breathing

Leather straps–for connecting breastplate to backplate

Breastplate

Gauntlet

Fleur-de-lis

15th century spur

Tassets–jointed steel plates designed for freedom of movement

Lance

Chain mail

Sword

Chain mail

Shield

CHAMPION IN TRUTH

from Men of Iron *by Howard Pyle,*
adapted by Amy Miller
illustrated by Johanna Ehnis

Myles Falworth, the son of a wrongfully outlawed nobleman, has been sent to a powerful kinsman[1] to learn the arts of knighthood. While under the silent watch of the earl of Mackworth, Sir James Lee, a seasoned one-eyed knight, undertakes the task of bringing Myles from boyhood to the strength of manhood required of a true knight. Myles does not fully understand the reason that his blind father has been forced into hiding for the past twelve years, but he has recently come to understand that the great earl of Mackworth in his silence has always been on his side. Myles, being modest, though fearless, does not recognize the strength of his skill and ability that has been acknowledged by Sir James and the earl. Myles is destined to rise above his fellow squires and be used greatly to right the wrongs of an evil enemy.

Hero of the Hour

That same afternoon the squires' quarters were thrown into such an uproar of excitement as had, perhaps, never before stirred them. About one o'clock in the afternoon, the earl himself and Lord George came walking slowly across the Armory Court wrapped in deep conversation and entered Sir James Lee's office.

All the usual hubbub of noise that surrounded the neighborhood of the dormitory and the armory was stilled at their coming, and when the two noblemen had entered Sir

---

[1]kinsman—relative

428

James's office, the lads and young men gathered in knots, discussing with awe-filled interest what that visit might signify.

After some time Sir James Lee came to the door at the head of the long flight of stone steps and, whistling, beckoned one of the smaller pages to him. He gave a short order that sent the little fellow flying on some mission. In the course of a few minutes he returned, hurrying across the stony court with Myles Falworth, who presently entered Sir James's office. It was at this sight that the intense half-suppressed excitement reached its height of fever heat. What did it all mean? The air was filled with a thousand vague,[2] wild rumors—but the very wildest imaginations fell short of the real truth.

Myles entered, pale-faced, to find the earl, Lord Mackworth, sitting at the table in the seat that Sir James Lee usually occupied. Lord George, the earl's brother, half-sat, half-leaned in the window place. Sir James, the hardy one-eyed knight, stood with his back to the empty

[2]vague—not clear

fireplace, his hands clasped behind him. All three were very serious.

With great purpose, the earl of Mackworth explained to Myles that as he knew, the king was making a most opportune[3] visit to his household. The earl planned to take advantage of the occasion to have young Myles Falworth knighted with full honors. In order to prove his worth as a knight, he must face a renowned champion in a jousting match. The Comte[4] de Vermoise, visiting from France, was travelling with the king. In the company of the Comte was his greatest knight.

"Hast thou ever heard of the Sieur de la Montaigne?" asked the earl.

The stunned Myles indicated that he had with much astonishment and trembling as he realized this was his intended opponent.

Sensing Myles's unaccustomed fear, the earl questioned, "Speak from thy heart, Myles; why art thou afraid?"

"Because," said Myles, "I am so young, sir. I am but a raw boy. How should I dare be so hardy as to venture[5] to set lance against such a one as the Sieur de la Montaigne? What would I be but a laughing-stock for all the world who would see me so foolish as to venture against one of such ability and skill?"

Lord George, who had openly shown favor towards Myles, spoke in his behalf, "Nay, Myles, thou thinkest not well enough of thine own skill and ability. Thinkest thou we would undertake to set thee against him, if we did not think that thou couldest hold thine own fairly well?"

Warmed by the approval of his esteemed friend, Myles responded to the honor of such a challenge, "If thou bid me do so, I will fight him."

"There spake my brave lad!" cried Lord George heartily.

"I give thee joy, Myles," said the earl, extending his hand, which Myles took and kissed. "And I give thee double joy. I have talked with the King concerning thee this morning, and he hath consented to knight thee—yea, to knight thee with all honors of the Bath—provided thou wilt match thee against the Sieur de la Montaigne for the honor of England and Mackworth."

The conversation concluded, the earl gave Myles into the hands of Lord George to prepare him with garments and all readiness for the upcoming ceremonies. Lord George told Myles of the appointed time to meet in his apartment to be outfitted and dismissed him.

Then Myles went out stupefied, dazed, bewildered. His first thought,

---

[3]opportune—taking place at a good time
[4]Comte—high-ranking noble in the French court
[5]venture—to dare to

as always, was to tell his long-time loyal friend, Francis Gascoyne, of this great event. Not seeing him, he said not a word in answer to the eager questions poured upon him by his fellow squires but walked straight away. He hardly knew where he went, but by and by he found himself in a grassy angle below the end of the south stable, a spot overlooking the outer wall and the river beyond. He looked around. No one was near, so he flung himself at length, burying his face in his arms. How long he lay there he did not know, but suddenly someone touched him upon the shoulder, and he sprang up quickly. It was Gascoyne.

"What is to do, Myles?" said his friend anxiously. "What is all this talk I hear concerning thee up yonder at the armory?"

"Oh, Gascoyne!" cried Myles, with a husky choking voice. "I am to be knighted—by the king—by the king himself, and I—I am to fight the Sieur de la Montaigne."

They stood for a while quite silent, and when at last the stillness was broken, it was Gascoyne who spoke, in a choking voice.

"Thou art going to be great, Myles," said he. "I always knew that it must be so with thee, and now the time hath come. Yea, thou wilt be great and live at court amongst noble folk, and kings perhaps. Presently thou wilt not be with me anymore and wilt forget me by and by."

"Nay, Gascoyne, never will I forget thee!" answered Myles. "I will always love thee better than anyone in the world, saving only my father and my mother."

Gascoyne shook his head and looked away, swallowing at the dry lump in his throat. Suddenly he turned to Myles. "Wilt thou grant me a boon?"[6]

"Yea," answered Myles. "What is it?"

"That thou wilt choose me for thy squire."

"Nay," said Myles, "how canst thou think to serve me as squire? Thou wilt be a knight thyself someday, Gascoyne, and why dost thou wish now to be my squire?"

"Because," said Gascoyne, with a short laugh, "I would rather be in thy company as a squire than in mine own as a knight, even if I might be a banneret."

Myles flung his arm around his friend's neck. "Thou shalt have thy will," said he, "but whether knight or squire, thou art mine own true friend."

Then they went slowly back together to the castle world again.

---

[6]boon—benefit; blessing

At two o'clock Myles went to Lord George's apartments. There his friend and patron[7] dressed him out in a costume better fitted for the ceremony of presentation. Myles had never worn such splendid clothes in his life, and he could not help feeling that they became him well.

"Sir," said he, as he looked down at himself, "sure it is not lawful for me to wear such clothes as these."

In those days there was a law, known as a sumptuary law, which regulated by decree the clothes that each class of people were privileged to wear. It was, as Myles said, against the law for him to wear such garments as those in which he was clad—either velvet, crimson stuff, fur, or silver or gold embroidery—nevertheless such a solemn ceremony as presentation to the king excused the temporary overstepping of the law, and so Lord George told him. As he laid his hand upon the lad's shoulder and held him off at arm's length, he added, "And I pledge thee my word, Myles, that thou art as sturdy and handsome a lad as ever mine eyes beheld."

"Thou art very kind to me, sir," said Myles.

Lord George laughed and then, giving him a shake, let go his shoulder.

[7]patron—a person who helps or supports another by giving him money or things

It was about three o'clock when little Edmond de Montefort, Lord Mackworth's favorite page, came with word that the King was then walking in the earl's private garden.

"Come, Myles," said Lord George, and then Myles arose from the seat where he had been sitting, his heart throbbing wildly.

At the wicket[8] gate of the garden, two gentlemen-at-arms stood guard in half armor. They saluted Lord George and permitted him to pass with his charge. As he laid his hand upon the latch of the wicket, he paused for a moment and turned.

"Myles," said he, in a low voice, "thou art a thoughtful and cautious lad. For thy father's sake be thoughtful and cautious now. Do not speak his name or betray that thou art his son." Then he opened the wicket gate and entered.

Following the lead of Lord George, Myles was brought before the king.

"Thou art a right champion in truth," he said, looking Myles over with smiling eyes. "Such was Sir Galahad when he came to Arthur's court. And so they tell me, thou hast the stomach to brook[9] the Sieur de la Montaigne, that tough old boar of Dauphiny. Hast thou in truth the courage to face him? Knowest thou what a great thing it is that thou hast set upon thyself—to do battle, even in sport, with him?"

"Yea, Your Majesty," answered Myles; "well I know it is a task perhaps beyond me. But gladly would I take upon me even a greater undertaking, and one more dangerous, to do Your Majesty's pleasure!"

The king looked pleased. "Now that was right well said, young man," said he, "and I like it better that it came from such young and honest lips." The king turned and introduced Myles to the Sieur de la Montaigne. Each measured his opponent hastily. The contrast between the two was very great—the one a young novice, the other a seasoned warrior.

The meeting over, Myles withdrew under the charge of Lord George. Myles paused to talk with the gentlemen attendants, finding himself, with a certain triumphant exultation,[10] the peer of any and the hero of the hour.

That night was the last that Myles and Gascoyne spent lodging in the dormitory in their squirehood service. The next day they were assigned apartments in Lord George's part of the house and thither they transported themselves and their belongings, amid the awestruck wonder and admiration of their fellow squires.

---

[8]wicket—small gate built in or near a larger gate
[9]brook—to put up with
[10]exultation—joy; delight

In Myles Falworth's day, one of the greatest ceremonies of courtly life was that of the bestowal of knighthood by the king, with the honors of the Bath. By far the greater number of knights were at that time created by other knights, or by nobles, or by officers of the crown. To be knighted by the king in person distinguished the recipient for life. It was this signal honor that the earl, for his own purposes, wished Myles to enjoy, and for this end he had laid not a few plans.

The accolade was the term used for the creation of a knight upon the field of battle. It was a reward of bravery or of commendable service and was generally presented in a more or less offhand way; but the ceremony of the Bath was an occasion of the greatest courtly moment, and it was thus that Myles Falworth was to be

knighted in addition to the honor of a royal belting.

After following all of the ceremonious details in clothing, grooming, and a night spent in prayer in the dark and mysterious castle chapel, the time came for Myles to appear before the king and all witnesses gathered in the Great Hall. Myles knew that he was very pale; he felt rather than saw the restless crowd of faces upon either side, for his eyes were fixed directly

before him, upon the platform whereon sat the king. The earl of Mackworth stood at the king's right hand, the Comte de Vermoise upon the left, and the others ranged around and behind the throne. It was with the same tense feeling of dreamy unreality that Myles walked slowly up the length of the hall, measuring his steps by those of Gascoyne. Suddenly he felt Lord George touch him lightly upon the arm, and almost instinctively he stopped short—he was standing just before the covered steps of the throne.

He saw Gascoyne mount to the third step, stop short, kneel, and offer the sword and the spurs he carried. The king took the weapon and laid it across his knees. Then the squire bowed low and, walking backward, withdrew to one side, leaving Myles facing the throne. The king unlocked the spur chains from the sword hilt, and then, holding the gilt[11] spurs in his hand for a moment, he looked Myles straight in the eyes and smiled. Then he turned and gave one of the spurs to the earl of Mackworth.

The earl took it with a low bow, turned, and came slowly down the steps to where Myles stood. Kneeling upon one knee, and placing Myles's foot upon the other, Lord Mackworth set the spur in its place and latched the chain over the instep. He drew the sign of the cross upon Myles's bended knee, set the foot back upon the ground, rose with slow dignity, and bowing to the king, drew a little to one side.

As soon as the earl had fulfilled his duty, the king gave the second spur to the Comte de Vermoise, who set it on Myles's other foot with the same ceremony that the earl had observed, withdrawing as he had done to one side.

An instant pause of motionless silence followed, and then the king slowly arose and began deliberately to unwind the belt from around the scabbard of the sword he held. As soon as he stood, the earl and the count advanced and, taking Myles by either hand, led him forward and up the steps to the platform above. As they drew a little to one side, the king stooped and buckled the sword belt around Myles's waist; then rising again, he lifted his hand and struck him upon the shoulder, crying in a loud voice, "Be thou a good knight!"

Instantly a loud sound of applause filled the whole hall, in the midst of which the king laid both hands upon Myles's shoulders and kissed him upon the right cheek. So the ceremony ended. Myles was no longer Myles Falworth, but Sir Myles Falworth, Knight by Order of the Bath and by the grace of the king!

---

[11]gilt—covered in gold or gold in color

Young Heart of Iron

And now, at last, had come the day of days for Myles Falworth. This was the day when he was to put to the test all that he had learned in the three years of his training, the day that was to disclose[12] what promise of future greatness there was in his strong young body. And it was a noble day, one of those in late September when the air seems sweeter and fresher than at other times and the sun bright and as yellow as gold.

At either end of the lists[13] stood the pavilions[14] of the knights. That of Myles was at the southern extremity and was hung, by the earl's desire, with cloth of the Beaumont colors, black and yellow, and displaying the crest of the house of Beaumont. Myles, partly armed, stood at the doorway of the pavilion, watching the folk gathering at the temporary wooden stands.

The ladies of the house were already seated, and the ushers were bustling hither and thither, assigning the others their places. A considerable crowd of common folk from the town had already gathered at the barriers opposite;

and as he looked at the restless and growing multitude, Myles felt his heart beat quickly and his flesh grow cold with a nervous anxiety.

Suddenly there came a loud blast of trumpets. A great gate at the farther boundary of the lists was thrown open, and the king appeared, riding upon a white horse, preceded by the king-at-arms and the heralds, attended by the earl and the Comte de Vermoise, and followed by a crowd of attendants. Just then Gascoyne, who was lacing some of the armor plates with new thongs, called Myles, and he turned and entered the pavilion.

As the squires were adjusting these last pieces, strapping them in place and tying the thongs, Lord George and Sir James Lee entered the pavilion. Lord George took the young man by the hand and with a pleasant smile wished him success in the coming encounter.[15]

Sir James seemed anxious and disturbed. He said nothing, and coming forward, examined the armor piece by piece, carefully and critically, testing the various

---

[12]disclose—to make known
[13]lists—stadium for jousting
[14]pavilions—fancy or elaborate tents
[15]encounter—a brief meeting

436

straps and leather points and thongs to make sure of their strength.

"Sir," said Gascoyne, who stood by watching him anxiously, "I do trust that I have done all properly and well."

"I see nothing amiss, sirrah,"[16] said the old knight, half grudgingly. "So far as I may know, he is ready to mount."

Myles mounted and rode out to meet his opponent to hear the challenge read. The marshal bade the speaker read the challenge of the Sieur de la Montaigne, which, unrolling the parchment, he began to do in a loud, clear voice so that all might hear. As soon as the speaker had ended, the marshal bade him call the defendant of the other side.

After repeating his challenge, Myles drew back to where Gascoyne awaited him. Mounting upon a stool, Gascoyne covered his friend's head with the great jousting helmet, fastening the leathern points that held it to the iron collar.

As he was tying the last thong, a messenger came from the herald, saying that the challenger was ready, and then Myles knew the time had come. Reaching down and giving Sir James a grip of the hand, he drew on his armored gloves, took the jousting lance that Gascoyne handed him, and turned his horse's head toward his end of the lists.

As Myles took his place at the south end of the lists, he found the Sieur de la Montaigne already at his station. Myles peered through the peephole in the face of the huge helmet; a crosswise slit known as the occularium. Through it, he could see, like a strange narrow picture, the farther end of the lists, where the spectators upon either side were moving and shifting. In the center of all, his opponent sat with spear point directed upward, erect. The Sieur de la Montaigne was as motionless as a statue of iron, the sunlight gleaming and flashing upon his polished plates of steel, and the ornamental harness of his horse swaying and fluttering in the rushing of the fresh breeze.

Upon that motionless figure Myles's sight gradually centered, with every sense keenly in tune. He knew that in the next moment the signal would be given that was to bring him either glory or shame from that iron statue. He ground his teeth together with stern resolve to do his best in the coming encounter and murmured a brief prayer in the hollow darkness of his huge helmet. Then with a shake he settled himself more firmly in his saddle, slowly raised his spear point until the shaft reached the exact angle, and there allowed it to rest

---

[16]sirrah—term used to address a person of lower status

motionless. There was a moment of dead, tense, breathless pause; then he felt rather than saw the marshal raise his baton. He gathered himself together, and the next moment a bugle sounded loud and clear. In one blinding rush he drove his spurs into the sides of his horse and in answer felt the noble steed spring forward with a bound.

Through all the clashing of his armor reverberating[17] in the hollow depths of his helmet, he saw the mail-clad figure from the other end of the lists rushing towards him, looming larger and larger as they came together. He gripped his saddle with his knees, clutched the stirrups with the soles of his feet, and bent his body still more forward. In the instant of meeting, with almost the blindness of instinct, he dropped the point of his spear against the single red fleur-de-lis[18] in the middle of the oncoming shield.

There was a thunderous crash that seemed to rack every joint. He heard the crackle of splintered wood. He felt the momentary trembling recoil of the horse beneath him, and in the next instant he had passed by. As he reined in the rushing horse at the far end of the course, he heard faintly in the dim hollow recess[19] of the helmet the loud shouts and the clapping of those who looked on. He found himself gripping the end of a broken spear with nervous intensity, his mouth clammy with excitement, and his heart thumping in his throat.

[17]reverberating—echoing
[18]fleur-de-lis (flûr′ də-lēz)—the symbol of the French king
[19]recess—a small hollow place or indentation

attendant followed behind, bearing his shield and helmet.

Gascoyne had picked up Myles's fallen helmet as the Sieur de la Montaigne moved away, and Lord George and Sir James Lee came walking across the lists to where Myles still sat. Then, the one taking his horse by the bridle rein, and the other walking beside the saddle, they led him before the raised platform where the king sat.

Even the Comte de Vermoise, mortified and amazed as he must have been at the overthrow of his best knight, joined in the praise and congratulation that poured upon the young conqueror.

Returning to the pavilion, Gascoyne had just removed Myles's breastplate and gorget, when Sir James Lee burst in. All his grim coldness was gone, and he flung his arms around the young man's neck, hugging him heartily and kissing him on either cheek.

"Mine own dear boy," he said, holding him off at arm's length and winking his one keen eye rapidly, as though to wink away a dampness of which he was ashamed—"Mine own dear boy, I do tell thee truly this is as sweet to me as though thou wert mine own son; sweeter to me than when I first broke mine own lance in triumph and felt myself to be a right knight."

"Sir," answered Myles, "what thou sayest doth rejoice my heart. But it is only just to say that both his breast piece and overgirth were burst in the stitches before he ran his course, for so I saw with mine own eyes."

"Burst in the stitches!" snorted Sir James. "Thinkest thou he did not know in what condition was his horse's gearing? I tell thee he went down because thou didst strike fair and true, and he did not so strike thee. Had he been Guy of Warwick, he had gone down all the same under such a stroke and in such a case."

Now that Myles has proven himself to be an able and noble knight, the real test lies ahead. Under the direction of his friend, the earl of Mackworth, Myles spends six months in France with the Prince of Wales. There he gains experience in battle and returns mature and confident, yet still noble in character. The battle between his father's and the earl's enemy awaits him. Myles has the chance to see justice brought to his friends and family after many long years of silent injustice being borne by his loved ones. Myles demonstrates true knightliness by championing his father in the case which could easily take his life.

Oliver Twist

from the novel by Charles Dickens   *illustrated by Jim Hargis*

Charles Dickens wrote his novels column by column for the news-papers. He told a little more each day, spinning the book out as long as possible. After several months, the chapters were collected and put into book form. Dickens used his stories to reflect social and politi-cal problems of his time. You will notice in this story the number of children being taught to pick pockets and rob from stores. The most famous of these young criminals is the Artful Dodger, chief of child pickpockets. The Dodger is the prize student of a man called Fagin. You will also meet Mr. Fang, the picture of a bullying petty[1] magis-trate[2] who has nobody over him to make sure he rules his courtroom fairly. This part of Oliver Twist comes after the Dodger has delivered Oliver to Fagin to be cared for and taught burglary. Mistakenly, Oliver thinks Fagin is a kindly man who takes in orphans.

[1]petty—of low rank
[2]magistrate—a judge with limited authority

Curious Games

It was late next morning when Oliver awoke from a sound, long sleep. There was no other person in the room but the old man, who was boiling some coffee in a saucepan for breakfast, and whistling softly to himself as he stirred it round and round with an iron spoon. He would stop every now and then to listen when there was the least noise below: and when he had satisfied himself, he would go on, whistling and stirring again, as before.

Although Oliver had roused himself from sleep, he was not thoroughly awake. He saw the old man with his half-closed eyes, heard his low whistling, and recognized the sound of the spoon grating against the saucepan's sides; and yet his selfsame senses were mentally engaged at the same time in busy action with dreams of everybody he had ever known.

When the coffee was done, the old man drew the saucepan to the hob. He turned round and looked at Oliver, who was to all appearance asleep.

After satisfying himself upon this head,[3] the old man stepped gently to the door which he fastened. He then drew forth, from some trap in the floor, a small box, which he placed carefully on the table. His eyes glistened as he raised the lid and looked in. Dragging an old chair to the table, he sat down and took from it a magnificent gold watch, sparkling with jewels.

"Aha!" said the old man, with a hideous grin. "Clever dogs! Clever dogs! Staunch[4] to the last! Never told the old judge where they were. Never peached[5] upon old Fagin! And why should they? It wouldn't have loosened the knot of the noose a minute longer. No, no, no! Fine fellows! Fine fellows!"

The old man once more deposited the watch in its place of safety. At least half a dozen more were severally[6] drawn forth from the same box and surveyed with equal pleasure; besides rings, brooches, bracelets, and other articles of jewelry, of magnificent materials, and costly workmanship.

Having replaced these trinkets, and leaning back in his chair, he muttered:

"What a fine thing capital punishment[7] is! Dead men never repent; dead men never bring awkward stories to light. Ah, it's a fine thing for the trade! Five of 'em strung up in a row, and none left to share booty,[8] or turn white-livered!"

---

[3]head—critical point
[4]staunch—loyal
[5]peached—tattled
[6]severally—one at a time
[7]capital punishment—penalty of death
[8]booty—stolen possessions

As the old man uttered these words, his bright dark eyes, which had been staring vacantly before him, fell on Oliver's face; the boy's eyes were now fixed on his in silent curiosity. It was enough to show the old man that he had been observed. He closed the lid of the box with a loud crash; and, laying his hand on a bread knife which was on the table, started furiously up. He trembled very much though; for even in his terror, Oliver could see that the knife quivered in the air.

"What's that?" said the old man. "What do you watch me for? Why are you awake? What have you seen? Speak out, boy! Quick—quick! For your life!"

"I wasn't able to sleep any longer, sir," replied Oliver, meekly. "I am very sorry if I have disturbed you, sir."

"You were not awake an hour ago?" said the old man, scowling fiercely on the boy.

"No! No, indeed!" replied Oliver.

"Are you sure?" cried the old man with a still fiercer look than before and a threatening attitude.

"Upon my word I was not, sir," replied Oliver, earnestly. "I was not, indeed, sir."

"Tush, tush, my dear!" said the old man, abruptly resuming his old manner, and playing with the knife a little, before he laid it down; as if he had caught it up, in mere sport. "Of course I know that, my dear. I only tried to frighten you. You're a brave boy. Ha! ha! You're a brave boy, Oliver." The old man rubbed his hands with a chuckle, but glanced uneasily at the box, notwithstanding.

"Did you see any of these pretty things, my dear?" said the old man, laying his hand upon it after a short pause.

"Yes, sir," replied Oliver.

"Ah!" said the old man, turning rather pale. "They—they're mine, Oliver; my little property. All I have to live upon, in my old age. The folks call me a miser,[9] my dear. Only a miser; that's all."

Oliver thought the old gentleman must be a decided miser to live in such a dirty place, with so many watches; but, thinking that perhaps his fondness for the Dodger and the other boys cost him a good deal of money, he only cast a deferential[10] look at the old man, and asked if he might get up.

"Certainly, my dear, certainly," replied the old gentleman. "There's a pitcher of water in the corner by the door. Bring it here, and I'll give you a basin to wash in, my dear."

Oliver got up, walked across the room, and stooped for an instant to raise the pitcher. When he turned his head, the box was gone.

---

[9]miser—a stingy person who lives like a poor person to save money
[10]deferential—respectful

446

He had scarcely washed himself and made everything tidy by emptying the basin out of the window, when the Dodger returned, accompanied by a very sprightly young friend, whom Oliver had seen on the previous night, and who was now introduced to him as Charley Bates. The four sat down to breakfast on the coffee and some hot rolls and ham which the Dodger had brought home in the crown of his hat.

"Well," said the old man, glancing slyly at Oliver, and addressing himself to the Dodger, "I hope you've been at work this morning, my dears?"

"Hard," replied the Dodger.

"As nails," added Charley Bates.

"Good boys, good boys!" said the old man. "What have *you* got, Dodger?"

"A couple of pocket books," replied that young gentleman.

"Lined?" inquired the old man, with eagerness.

"Pretty well," replied the Dodger, producing two pocketbooks, one green, and the other red.

"Not so heavy as they might be," said the old man, after looking at the insides carefully; "but very neat and nicely made. Ingenious workman, ain't he, Oliver?"

"Very, indeed, sir," said Oliver. At which Mr. Charles Bates laughed, very much to the amazement of Oliver, who saw nothing to laugh at.

"And what have you got, my dear?" said Fagin to Charley Bates.

"Wipes," replied Master Bates, at the same time producing four pocket handkerchiefs.

"Well," said the old man, inspecting them closely; "they are very good ones, very. You haven't marked them well, though, Charley; so the marks shall be picked out with a needle, and we'll teach Oliver how to do it. Shall us, Oliver, eh? Ha! ha! ha!"

"If you please, sir," said Oliver.

"You'd like to be able to make pocket handkerchiefs as easy as Charley Bates, wouldn't you, my dear," said the old man.

"Very much indeed, if you'll teach me, sir," replied Oliver.

Charley Bates saw something so ludicrous[11] in this reply, that he burst into another laugh.

"He is so jolly green!"[12] said Charley when he recovered, as an apology to the company for his impolite behavior.

The Dodger said nothing, but he smoothed Oliver's hair over his eyes, and said he'd know better, by and by; upon which the old gentleman changed the subject by asking whether there had been much of a crowd at the execution[13] that morning. This made him wonder more and more; for it was plain from the

---

[11]ludicrous—absurd or ridiculous
[12]green—inexperienced
[13]execution—event of putting to death

replies of the two boys that they had both been there; and Oliver naturally wondered how they could possibly have found time to be so very busy.

When the breakfast was cleared away, the merry old gentleman and the two boys played at a very curious and uncommon game, which was performed in this way. The merry old gentleman, placing a snuffbox in one pocket of his trousers, a note-case in the other, and a watch in his waistcoat pocket, with a guard-chain round his neck, and sticking a mock diamond pin in his shirt, buttoned his coat tight round him, and putting his spectacle-case and handkerchief in his pockets, trotted up and down the room with a stick, in imitation of the manner in which old gentlemen walk about the streets any hour in the day.

Sometimes he stopped at the fireplace, and sometimes at the door, making believe that he was staring with all his might into shop-win-

dows. At such times, he would look constantly round him, for fear of thieves, and would keep slapping all his pockets in turn, to see that he hadn't lost anything, in such a very funny and natural manner, that Oliver laughed till the tears ran down his face.

All this time, the two boys followed him closely about: getting out of his sight, so nimbly, every time he turned round, that it was impossible to follow their motions. At last, the Dodger trod upon his toes, or ran upon his boot accidentally, while Charley Bates stumbled up against him behind; and in that one moment they took from him, with the most extraordinary rapidity, snuffbox, note-case, watch-guard, chain, shirt-pin, pocket handkerchief, even the spectacle case. If the old gentleman felt a hand in any one of his pockets, he cried out where it was; and then the game began all over again.

At length, Charley Bates expressed his opinion that it was time to pad the hoof. This, it occurred to Oliver, must be French for going out; for, directly afterwards, the Dodger and Charley went away together, having been kindly furnished by the amiable[14] old man with money to spend.

"There, my dear," said Fagin. "That's a pleasant life, isn't it? They have gone out for the day."

"Have they done work, sir?" inquired Oliver.

"Yes," said the old man; "that is, unless they should unexpectedly come across any, when they are out; and they won't neglect it if they do, my dear, depend upon it. Make 'em your models, my dear. Make 'em your models," tapping the fire-shovel on the hearth to add force to his words; "do everything they bid you, and take their advice in all matters— especially the Dodger's, my dear. He'll be a great man himself, and will make you one too, if you take pattern by him—is my handkerchief hanging out of my pocket, my dear?" said the old man, stopping short.

"Yes, sir," said Oliver.

"See if you can take it out, without my feeling it, as you saw them do, when we were at play this morning."

Oliver held up the bottom of the pocket with one hand, as he had seen the Dodger hold it, and drew the handkerchief lightly out of it with the other.

"Is it gone?" cried the old man.

"Here it is, sir," said Oliver, showing it in his hand.

"You're a clever boy, my dear," said the playful old gentleman, patting Oliver on the head approvingly. "I never saw a sharper lad. Here's a shilling for you. If you go on in this way, you'll be the greatest man of the time. And now come here, and I'll show you how to take the marks out of the handkerchiefs."

Oliver wondered what picking the old gentleman's pocket in play had to do with his chances of being a great man. But, thinking that the old man, being so much his senior, must know best, he followed him quietly to the table, and was soon deeply involved in his new study.

For many days Oliver remained in the old man's room, picking the marks out of the pocket-handkerchiefs (of which a great number were brought home) and sometimes taking part in the game already described which the two boys and the old man played, regularly, every morning. At length, he began to want fresh air, and took many occasions of earnestly begging the old gentleman to allow him to go out to work with his two companions.

---

[14]amiable—friendly and good-natured

At length, one morning, Oliver obtained the permission he had so eagerly sought. There had been no handkerchiefs to work upon for two or three days, and the dinners had been rather meagre.[15] Perhaps these were reasons for the old gentleman's giving his assent;[16] but, whether they were or no, he told Oliver he might go, and placed him under the joint guardianship of Charley Bates and his friend the Dodger.

The three boys sallied out; the Dodger with his coat-sleeves tucked up, and his hat cocked, as usual; Charley Bates sauntering along with his hands in his pockets; and Oliver between them, wondering where they were going, and what branch of manufacture he would be instructed in, first.

The pace at which they went was such a very lazy saunter that Oliver soon began to think his companions were going to deceive the old gentleman by not going to work at all. The Dodger had a vicious habit, too, of pulling the caps from the heads of small boys and tossing them down, while Charley Bates pilfered[17] apples and onions from the open stalls on the street and thrust them into pockets which were surprisingly big. Oliver was on the point of declaring his intention of seeking his way back, when his thoughts were suddenly directed into another channel, by a very mysterious change of behavior on the part of the Dodger.

They were just emerging from a narrow court not far from the open square when the Dodger made a sudden stop; laying his fingers on his lip, he drew his companions back again, with the greatest caution.

"What's the matter?" demanded Oliver.

"Hush!" replied the Dodger. "Do you see that old cove[18] at the book-stall?"

"The old gentleman over the way?" said Oliver. "Yes, I see him."

"He'll do," said the Dodger.

"A prime plant," observed Master Charley Bates.

Oliver looked from one to the other, with the greatest surprise; but he was not permitted to make any inquiries. The two boys walked stealthily[19] across the road and slunk close behind the old gentleman. Oliver walked a few paces after them and stood looking on in silent amazement.

The old gentleman was a very respectable-looking person, with a powdered head and gold spectacles. He was dressed in a green coat with a black velvet collar, wore white trousers, and carried a cane under his arm. He had taken up a book from the stall, and there he stood, reading away, as hard as if he were

---

[15]meagre—lacking in quantity; poor
[16]assent—consent; agreement
[17]pilfered—stole
[18]cove—(British) man
[19]stealthily—moving cautiously or sneakily

in his chair, in his own study. It is very possible that he fancied himself there, indeed; for it was plain that he saw not the bookstall, nor the street, nor the boys, nor anything but the book itself, which he was reading straight through, slowly turning over each page with the greatest interest and eagerness.

What was Oliver's horror and alarm as he stood a few paces off, looking on with his eyelids as wide open as they would possibly go, to see the Dodger plunge his hand into the old gentleman's pocket, and draw from thence a handkerchief! To see him hand the same to Charley Bates; and finally to behold them, both, running away round the corner at full speed!

In an instant the whole mystery of the handkerchiefs, and the watches, and the jewels, and the old man, rushed upon the boy's mind. He stood, for a moment, with the blood tingling through all his veins from terror; then, confused and frightened, he took to his heels; and, not knowing what he did, made off as fast as he could lay his feet to the ground.

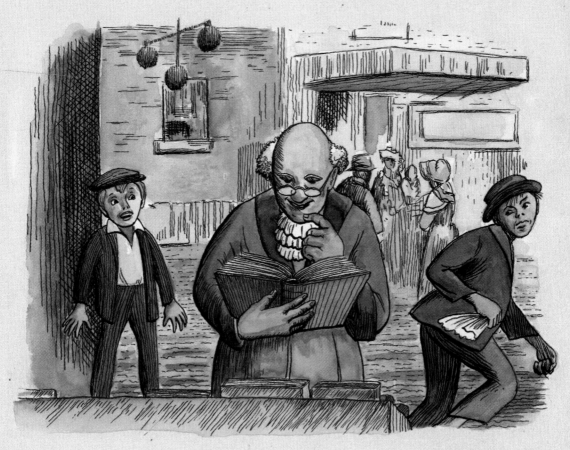

Young Pickpocket

This was all done in a minute's space. In the very instant when Oliver began to run, the old gentleman, putting his hand to his pocket, and missing his handkerchief, turned sharp round. Seeing the boy scudding away at such a rapid pace, he very naturally concluded him to be the culprit; and, shouting "Stop thief!" with all his might, made off after him, book in hand.

But the old gentleman was not the only person who raised the hue-and-cry. The Dodger and Charley Bates had merely hidden in the very first doorway round the corner. They no sooner heard the cry and saw Oliver running than they issued forth, shouting "Stop thief!" and joined in the pursuit like good citizens.

Oliver went like the wind, with the old gentleman and the two boys roaring and shouting behind him.

"Stop thief! Stop thief!"

There is a magic in the sound. The tradesman leaves his counter, and the car-man his wagon; the butcher throws down his tray; the baker his basket; the milkman his pail; the errand boy his parcels; the schoolboy his marbles; the paviour[20] his pickaxe; the child his battle-dore.[21] Away they run, pell-mell, helter-skelter, slap-dash: tearing, yelling, screaming, knocking down the passengers as they turn the corners, rousing up the dogs, and astonishing the fowls; and streets, squares, and courts re-echo with the sound.

"Stop thief! Stop thief!" The cry is taken up by a hundred voices, and the crowd grows at every turning. Away they fly, splashing through the mud, and rattling along the pavements: up go the windows, out run the people, onward bear the mob, and, joining the rushing throng, swell the shout, and lend fresh vigor to the cry, "Stop thief! Stop thief!"

There is a passion for *hunting something* deeply implanted in the human heart. One wretched[22] breathless child, panting with exhaustion, terror in his looks, agony in his eyes, large drops of perspiration streaming down his face, strains every nerve to make head upon his pursuers. And as they follow on his track and gain upon him every instant, they hail his decreasing strength with still louder shout, and

---

[20]paviour—man who paves streets
[21]battledore—a flat wooden paddle used in an early
form of badminton
[22]wretched—very unhappy or unfortunate

because he had seen him running away. He expressed his hope that the magistrate would deal as leniently[34] with him as justice would allow.

"He has been hurt already," said the old gentleman in conclusion. "And I fear," he added, with great energy, looking towards the bar, "I really fear that he is ill."

"Oh! Yes, I dare say!" said Mr. Fang, with a sneer at Oliver. "Come, none of your tricks here, you young vagabond; they won't do. What's your name?"

Oliver tried to reply, but his tongue failed him. He was deadly pale, and the whole place seemed turning round and round.

"What's your name, you hardened scoundrel?" demanded Mr. Fang. "Officer, what's his name?"

This was addressed to a bluff old fellow, in a striped waistcoat, who was standing by the bar. He bent over Oliver and repeated the inquiry; but finding him really incapable of understanding the question, and knowing that his not replying would only infuriate the magistrate the more and add to the severity[35] of his sentence; he hazarded[36] a guess.

"He says his name's Tom White, your worship," said the kindhearted thief-taker.

"Oh, he won't speak out, won't he?" said Fang. "Very well, very well. Where does he live?"

"Where he can, your worship," replied the officer, again pretending to receive Oliver's answer.

"Has he any parents?" inquired Mr. Fang.

"He says they died in his infancy, your worship," replied the officer, hazarding the usual reply.

At this point of the inquiry, Oliver raised his head and, looking round with imploring eyes, murmured a feeble prayer for a drink of water.

"Stuff and nonsense!" said Mr. Fang. "Don't try to make a fool of me."

"I think he really is ill, your worship," remonstrated the officer.

"I know better," said Mr. Fang.

"Take care of him, officer," said the old gentleman, raising his hands instinctively. "He'll fall down."

"Stand away, officer," cried Fang. "Let him, if he likes."

Oliver availed himself of the kind permission and fell to the floor in a faint. The men in the office looked at each other, but no one dared to stir.

"I knew he was shamming,"[37] said Fang, as if this were proof of the fact. "Let him lie there; he'll soon be tired of that."

---

[34]leniently—not strictly or severely
[35]severity—strictness and harshness
[36]hazarded—attempted
[37]shamming—faking

into the office, and advanced towards the bench.

"Stop! Stop! Don't take him away! Stop a moment!" cried the newcomer, breathless with haste.

"What is this? Who is this? Turn this man out. Clear the office!" cried Mr. Fang.

"I *will* speak," cried the man; "I will not be turned out. I saw it all. I keep the bookstall. I demand to be sworn. I will not be put down. Mr. Fang, you must not refuse, sir."

The man was right. His manner was determined, and the matter was growing rather too serious to be hushed up.

"Swear the man," growled Mr. Fang, with a very ill grace. "Now, man, what have you got to say?"

"This," said the man. "I saw three boys, two others and the prisoner here, loitering[39] on the opposite side of the way, when this gentleman was reading. The robbery was committed by another boy. I saw it done, and I saw that this boy was perfectly amazed by it." Having by this time recovered a little breath, the worthy bookstall keeper proceeded to relate,

"How do you propose to deal with the case, sir?" inquired the clerk in a low voice.

"Summarily,"[38] replied Mr. Fang. "He stands committed for three months—hard labour of course. Clear the office."

The door was opened for this purpose, and a couple of men were preparing to carry the insensible boy to his cell; when an elderly man of decent but poor appearance, clad in an old suit of black, rushed hastily

---

[38]summarily—quickly and without care for detail
[39]loitering—standing about in an idle manner

in a more coherent[40] manner, the exact circumstances of the robbery.

"Why didn't you come here before?" said Fang, after a pause.

"I hadn't a soul to mind the shop," replied the man. "Everybody who could have helped me had joined in the pursuit. I could get nobody 'til five minutes ago, and I've run here all the way."

"The prosecutor[41] was reading, was he?" inquired Fang, after another pause.

"Yes," replied the man. "The very book he has in his hand."

"Oh, that book, eh?" said Fang. "Is it paid for?"

"No, it is not," replied the man, with a smile.

"Dear me, I forgot all about it!" exclaimed the absent old gentleman, innocently.

"A nice person to prefer a charge against a poor boy!" said Fang, with a comical effort to look humane.[42] "I consider, sir, that you have obtained possession of that book, under very suspicious circumstances, and you may think yourself very fortunate that the owner of the property declines to prosecute. Let this be a lesson to you, my man, or the law will overtake you yet. The boy is discharged. Clear the office."

"Why you—" cried the old gentleman, bursting out with the rage he had kept down so long, "Why you! I'll—"

"Clear the office!" said the magistrate. "Officers, do you hear? Clear the office!"

The mandate was obeyed; and the indignant Mr. Brownlow was conveyed out, with the book in one hand, and the bamboo cane in the other, in a perfect frenzy of rage and defiance. He reached the yard, and his passion vanished in a moment. Little Oliver Twist lay on his back on the pavement, with his shirt unbuttoned, and his temples bathed with water; his face a deadly white; and a cold tremble convulsing his whole frame.

"Poor boy, poor boy!" said Mr. Brownlow, bending over him. "Call a coach, somebody, pray. Directly!"

A coach was obtained, and Oliver having been carefully laid on the seat, the old gentleman got in and sat himself on the other.

"May I accompany you?" said the bookstall keeper, looking in.

"Bless me, yes, my dear sir," said Mr. Brownlow quickly. "I forgot you. Dear, dear! I have this unhappy book still! Jump in. Poor fellow! There's no time to lose."

The bookstall keeper got into the coach, and away they drove.

---

[40]coherent—understandable
[41]prosecutor—one who formally accuses another of a crime in court
[42]humane—not cruel; kind

THE OPEN ROAD

adapted from The Wind in the Willows, *by Kenneth Grahame*
illustrated by Linda Slattery

Kenneth Grahame began telling his son The Wind in the Willows *as a series of bedtime stories. When it came time for the boy to go away for vacation, he wouldn't go for fear of missing any adventures his father had to tell. Grahame promised to send his son letters that would continue the story. From these letters, he later wrote his famous novel, and it has been a favorite with children in England and America.*

The characters, though animals, conduct themselves with very British manners and taste. Mole is the curious, friendly, and innocent visitor who is staying with his friend the Water Rat, an amiable, well-off, and poetic citizen of the upper middle class. The Water Rat possesses both charm and good sense, in contrast to Toad of Toad Hall, who is silly, conceited, and sometimes pompous.[1] The three are full of good intentions and try to help each other out of various scrapes, but Toad, for all his family background and upbringing, manages to keep the riverbank lively for everybody.

[1]pompous—overly conscious of one's importance

The Life Adventurous

"Ratty," said Mole suddenly, one bright summer morning, "if you please, I want to ask you a favor."

The Rat was sitting on the river bank, singing a little song. He had just composed it himself, so he was very taken up with it and would not pay proper attention to Mole or anything else. Since early morning he had been swimming in the river in company with his friends the ducks. And when the ducks stood on their heads suddenly, as ducks will, he would dive down and tickle their necks just under where their chins would be if ducks had chins, 'til they were forced to come to the surface again in a hurry, spluttering and angry and shaking their feathers at him, for it is impossible to say quite all you feel when your head is under water. At last they implored him to go away and attend to his own affairs and leave them to mind theirs. So the Rat went away, and sat on the riverbank in the sun, and made up a song about them, which he called

"Ducks' Ditty"
All along the backwater,
Through the rushes tall,
Ducks are a-dabbling,
Up tails all!

Ducks' tails, drakes' tails,
Yellow feet a-quiver,
Yellow bills all out of sight
Busy in the river!

Slushy green undergrowth
Where the roach swim—
Here we keep our larder,[2]
Cool and full and dim.

Everyone for what he likes!
We like to be
Heads down, tails up,
Dabbling free!

High in the blue above
Swifts whirl and call—
We are down a-dabbling
Up tails all!

"I don't know that I think so *very* much of that little song, Rat," observed the Mole cautiously. He was no poet himself and didn't care who knew it, and he had a candid[3] nature.

"Nor don't the ducks neither," replied the Rat cheerfully. "They say, '*Why* can't fellows be allowed to do what they like *when* they like and *as* they like, instead of other fellows sitting on banks and watching them all the time and making remarks and poetry and things about them? What *nonsense* it all is!' That's what the ducks say."

[2]larder—a place to store food
[3]candid—open and honest; sincere

"So it is, so it is," said the Mole, with great heartiness.

"No, it isn't!" cried the Rat indignantly.

"Well then, it isn't, it isn't," replied the Mole soothingly. "But what I wanted to ask you was, won't you take me to call on Mr. Toad? I've heard so much about him, and I do so want to make his acquaintance."

"Why, certainly," said the good-natured Rat, jumping to his feet and dismissing poetry from his mind for the day. "Get the boat out, and we'll paddle up there at once. It's never the wrong time to call on Toad. Early or late he's always the same fellow. Always good-tempered, always glad to see you, always sorry when you go!"

"He must be a very nice animal," observed the Mole, as he got into the boat and took the sculls,[4] while the Rat settled himself comfortably in the stern.

"He is indeed the best of animals," replied Rat. "So simple, so good-natured, and so affectionate. Perhaps he's not very clear—we can't all be geniuses; and it may be that he is both boastful and conceited. But he has got some great qualities, has Toady."

Rounding a bend in the river, they came in sight of a handsome, dignified old house of mellowed[5] red brick, with well-kept lawns reaching down to the water's edge.

"There's Toad Hall," said the Rat, "and that creek on the left, where the notice-board says, 'Private. No landing allowed,' leads to his boathouse, where we'll leave the boat. The stables are over there to the right. That's the banqueting hall you're looking at now—very old, that is. Toad is rather rich, you know, and this is really one of the nicest houses in these parts, though we never admit as much to Toad."

They glided up the creek, and the Mole shifted his sculls as they passed into the shadow of a large boathouse. Here they saw many handsome boats, slung from the crossbeams or hauled up on a slip,[6] but none in the water; and the place had an unused and a deserted air.

The Rat looked around him. "I understand," said he. "Boating is played out. He's tired of it and done with it. I wonder what new fad he has taken up now? Come along and let's look him up. We shall hear all about it quite soon enough."

---

[4]sculls—oars
[5]mellowed—seasoned with age
[6]slip—a place to park a ship or boat

They disembarked and strolled across the flower-decked lawns in search of Toad, whom they presently happened upon resting in a wicker garden-chair, with a preoccupied[7] expression of face, and a large map spread out on his knees.

"Hooray!" he cried, jumping up on seeing them. "This is splendid!" He shook the paws of both of them warmly, never waiting for an introduction to the Mole. "How *kind* of you!" he went on, dancing round them. "I was just going to send a boat down the river for you, Ratty, with strict orders that you were to be fetched up here at once, whatever you were doing. I want you badly—both of you. Now what will you take? Come inside and have something! You don't know how timely it is, your turning up just now!"

"Let's sit quiet a bit, Toady!" said the Rat, throwing himself into an easy chair, while the Mole took another chair by the side of him and made some civil remark about Toad's "delightful residence."

"Finest house on the whole river," cried Toad boisterously. "Or anywhere else, for that matter," he could not help adding.

Here the Rat nudged the Mole. Unfortunately the Toad saw him do it, and turned very red. There was a moment's painful silence. Then Toad burst out laughing. "All right, Ratty," he said. "It's only my way, you know.

And it's not such a very bad house, is it? You know you rather like it yourself. Now, look here. Let's be sensible. You are the very animals I wanted. You've got to help me. It's most important!"

"It's about your rowing, I suppose," said the Rat, with an innocent air. "You're getting on fairly well, though you splash a good bit still. With a great deal of patience, and any quantity of coaching, you may—"

"O, pooh! Boating!" interrupted the Toad, in great disgust. "Silly boyish amusement. I've given that up *long* ago. Sheer waste of time, that's what it is. It makes me downright sorry to see you fellows, who ought to know better, spending all your energies in that aimless manner. No, I've discovered the real thing, the only genuine occupation for a lifetime. I propose to devote the remainder of mine to it and can only regret the wasted years that lie behind me, squandered[8] in trivialities.[9] Come with me, dear Ratty, and your amiable friend also, if he will be so very good, just as far as the stable-yard, and you shall see what you shall see!"

He led the way to the stable-yard accordingly, the Rat following with a most mistrustful expression; and there, drawn out of the coach house

---

[7]preoccupied—distracted; lost in thought
[8]squandered—wasted
[9]trivialities—worthlessness; things of little importance

into the open, they saw a gipsy[10] caravan,[11] shining with newness, painted a canary-yellow picked out with green and red wheels.

"There you are!" cried the Toad, straddling and expanding himself. "There's real life for you, embodied in that little cart. The open road, the dusty highway, the heath, the common, the hedgerows, the rolling downs! Villages, towns, cities! Here today, up and off to somewhere else tomorrow! Travel, change, interest, excitement! The whole world before you, and a horizon that's always changing! And mind, this is the very finest cart of its sort that was ever built, without any exception. Come inside and look at the arrangements. Planned 'em all myself, I did!"

The Mole was tremendously interested and excited and followed him eagerly up the steps and into the interior of the caravan. The Rat only snorted and thrust his hands deep into his pockets, remaining where he was. It was indeed very compact and comfortable. Little sleeping-bunks—a little table that folded up against

---

[10]gipsy or gypsy—one who moves from place to place
[11]caravan—a large covered vehicle

the wall—a cooking-stove, lockers, bookshelves, a birdcage with a bird in it; and pots, pans, jugs, and kettles of every size and variety.

"All complete!" said the Toad triumphantly, pulling open a locker. "You see—biscuits, potted lobster, sardines—everything you can possibly want. Soda water here, letter paper there—you'll find," he continued, as they descended the steps again, "you'll find that nothing whatever has been forgotten, when we make our start this afternoon."

"I beg your pardon," said the Rat slowly, as he chewed a straw, "but did I overhear you say something about 'we' and 'start' and 'this afternoon'?"

"Now, you dear good old Ratty," said Toad imploringly, "don't begin talking in that stiff and sniffy sort of way because you know you've *got* to come. I can't possibly manage without you, so please consider it settled, and don't argue—it's the one thing I can't stand. You surely don't mean to stick to your dull fusty[12] old river all your life, and just live in a hole in a bank, and *boat*? I want to show you the world! I'm going to make an *animal* of you, my boy!"

"I don't care," said the Rat doggedly.[13] "I'm not coming, and

that's flat. And I *am* going to stick to my old river, *and* live in a hole, *and* boat, as I've always done. And what's more, Mole's going to stick to me and do as I do, aren't you, Mole?"

"Of course I am," said the Mole loyally. "I'll always stick to you, Rat, and what you say is to be—has got to be. All the same, it sounds as if it might have been—well, rather fun, you know!" he added wistfully. Poor Mole! The Life Adventurous was so new a thing to him, and so thrilling; and this fresh aspect of it was so tempting; and he had fallen in love at first sight with the canary-colored cart and all its little fitments.[14]

The Rat saw what was passing in his mind, and wavered.[15] He hated disappointing people, and he was fond of the Mole, and would do almost anything to oblige him. Toad was watching both of them closely.

"Come along in and have some lunch," he said diplomatically,[16] "and we'll talk it over. We needn't decide anything in a hurry. Of course, I don't really care. I only want to give pleasure to you fellows. 'Live for others!' That's my motto in life."

---

[12]fusty—damp and decaying
[13]doggedly—persistently
[14]fitments—furnishings
[15]wavered—became uncertain
[16]diplomatically—tactfully; careful of others' feelings

Changing Horizon

During luncheon—which was excellent, of course, as everything at Toad Hall always was—the Toad simply let himself go. Disregarding the Rat, he proceeded to play upon the inexperienced Mole as on a harp. Naturally a voluble[17] animal, and always mastered by his imagination, he painted the prospects of the trip and the joys of the open life and the roadside in such glowing colors that the Mole could hardly sit in his chair for excitement. Somehow, it soon seemed taken for granted by all three of them that the trip was a settled thing; and the Rat, though still un-convinced in his mind, allowed his good nature to override his personal objections. He could not bear to disappoint his two friends, who were already deep in schemes and antici-pations, planning out each day's separate occupation for several weeks ahead.

When they were quite ready, the now triumphant Toad led his com-panions to the paddock[18] and set them to capture the old grey horse, who, without having been consulted,[19] and to his own extreme annoyance, had been enlisted by Toad for the dustiest job in this dusty expedition. He frankly pre-ferred the paddock, and took a deal of catching. Meantime Toad packed the lockers still tighter with neces-saries, and hung nosebags, nets of onions, bundles of hay, and baskets from the bottom of the cart. At last the horse was caught and harnessed, and they set off, all talking at once, each animal either trudging by the side of the cart or sitting on the shaft, as the humor took him. It was a golden afternoon. The smell of the dust they kicked up was rich and satisfying; out of thick orchards on either side of the road, birds called and whistled to them cheerily; good-natured wayfarers, passing them, gave them "Good day," or stopped to say nice things about their beautiful cart; and rabbits, sitting at their front doors in the hedgerows, held up their forepaws and said, "O my! O my! O my!"

Late in the evening, tired and happy and miles from home, they drew up on a remote common far from habitations, turned the horse loose to graze, and ate their simple supper sitting on the grass by the side of the cart. Toad talked big about all he was going to do in the days to come, while stars grew fuller and larger all around them, and a yellow moon, appearing suddenly and silently from nowhere in particu-lar, came to keep them company and

---

[17]voluble—able to express oneself well with words
[18]paddock—a fenced field
[19]consulted—asked for advice

listen to their talk. At last they turned in to their little bunks in the cart; and Toad, kicking out his legs, sleepily said, "Well, good night, you fellows! This is the real life for a gentleman! Talk about your old river!"

"I *don't* talk about my river," replied the patient Rat. "You *know* I don't, Toad. But I *think* about it," he added pathetically, in a lower tone: "I think about it—all the time!"

The Mole reached out from under his blanket, felt for the Rat's paw in the darkness, and gave it a squeeze. "I'll do whatever you like Ratty," he whispered. "Shall we run away tomorrow morning, quite early—*very* early—and go back to our dear old hole on the river?"

"No, no, we'll see it out," whispered back the Rat. "Thanks awfully, but I ought to stick by Toad 'til this trip is ended. It wouldn't be safe for him to be left to himself. It won't take very long. His fads never do. Good night!"

The end was indeed nearer than even the Rat suspected.

After so much open air and excitement the Toad slept very soundly, and no amount of shaking could rouse him out of bed next morning. So the Mole and Rat got up quietly and manfully, and while the Rat saw to the horse, and lit a fire, and cleaned last night's cups and platters, and got things ready for breakfast, the Mole trudged off to the nearest village, a long way off, for milk and eggs and various necessaries the Toad had, of course, forgotten to provide. The hard work had all been done, and the two animals were resting, thoroughly exhausted, by the time Toad appeared on the scene, fresh and cheerful, remarking what a pleasant, easy life it was they were all leading now, after the cares and worries and fatigues of housekeeping at home.

They had a pleasant ramble that day over grassy downs and along narrow by-lanes, and camped, as before, on a common, only this time the two guests took care that Toad should do his fair share of work. In consequence, when the time came for starting next morning, Toad was by no means so rapturous[20] about the simplicity of the primitive[21] life, and indeed attempted to resume his place in his bunk, whence he was hauled by force. Their way lay, as before, across country by narrow lanes, and it was not 'til the afternoon that they came out on the highroad, their first highroad; and there disaster, fleet and unforeseen, sprang out on them—disaster momentous indeed to their expedition, but simply overwhelming in its effect on the after-career of Toad.

They were strolling along the highroad easily, the Mole by the

[20]rapturous—delighted; overjoyed
[21]primitive—simple; crude

The Sparrow Hawk 475

WORTH MORE THAN SPARROWS

Eileen M. Berry

You're walking through the long, weedy grass of an abandoned field. As the grasses part beneath your feet, a sudden rustle of wings startles you. A little bird flies up, lands a short distance away, and begins to run through the grass like a mouse.

You keep walking at a steady pace, following the bird with your eyes. If the bird were not moving and rustling the grass, you probably would not notice it at all. Its brown and gray feathers blend in perfectly with the colors of the leaves and dry grasses around it. Perhaps you've heard it sing before without being able to see it. That little bird is a sparrow.

Most sparrows are not brightly colored. Their drab[1] feathers blend in

---
[1]drab—not bright; dull

so well with their surroundings that they are able to hide easily. And yet, Jesus tells us that not one sparrow ever escapes the notice of our Heavenly Father.

"Are not two sparrows sold for a farthing? [worth about a penny] and one of them shall not fall on the ground without your Father" (Matthew 10:29). How much do you know about these little creatures that are so special to God?

More than fifty species of sparrows live in North America. Seaside sparrows live near salt water. Field sparrows make their homes in overgrown fields and pastures. Black-throated sparrows build their nests in desert cacti.

One way to distinguish between types of sparrows is to observe their colors and markings. The white-crowned sparrow, thought by many

Sparrows usually sing from a perch that is in the open. Song sparrow (left), White-crowned sparrow (right).

to be the most beautiful variety, has a distinctive white stripe along its black forehead, and a white stripe above each eye. It has a pearly gray breast and vivid black, white, and brown streaks on its back and wings. Scientists have done experiments with this type of bird to learn more about *migration,* the movement of birds to a different climate when the seasons change. White-crowned sparrows are often found in areas with dense brush, and sometimes in the winter they make their homes in southern woods and gardens.

Another way to tell sparrows apart is by listening to their songs. Male sparrows do most of the singing, and they often like to perch on the tops of rocks or tall strands of grass while they sing. The song sparrow is thought to have the most musical song of all the sparrows. Some people say that the song sounds like this: "Maids, maids, maids, put on the kettle, ettle, ettle." This is its most common song, but some song sparrows can sing twenty different melodies and hundreds of variations on those tunes. Another type of sparrow, the white-throated sparrow, can be found in Canada during breeding season. Some people say that its song sounds like this: "Sweet, Sweet Canada, Canada, Canada."

Almost all kinds of sparrows have certain things in common. They are about five or six inches long and have cone-shaped bills. Almost all sparrows eat seeds or insects, except for the seaside sparrow, which eats crabs, snails, and other small sea creatures. Sparrows like to build their nests near the ground. The cup-shaped nests are usually made of grass and sometimes lined with hair. The mother sparrow lays four or five eggs, which hatch in about two weeks. Eggs may be blue, pale green, white, or speckled with brown.

The Heavenly Father cares for sparrows. He made each one with the special markings it needs to hide itself from enemies. He provides the food and nesting materials that each one needs. He gives each one a song to sing.

Jesus told his disciples that not one sparrow is forgotten by God. "Fear not therefore," He said. "Ye are of more value than many sparrows" (Luke 12:6, 7).

If God cares so much about sparrows, how much more does He care about you? If He sees each sparrow that falls, how much more does He see and sympathize when you fail, get hurt, or grow discouraged? He made you and knows exactly what you need. You are worth more to Him than *many* sparrows.

Nonprint Media

The word *library* usually brings to mind a picture of long rows of books, of people quietly searching for or reading books, and of a librarian surrounded with stacks of more books. In reality, modern libraries have many sources of information other than books.

Suppose you had been the author of either the article about knights or the article about sparrows that you just read. Although you would have based a lot of your writing on personal experience and ideas you already had established, you would broaden your base of information with research. You would probably have started your research in some of the usual places: an encyclopedia to give you an overview of information, books from the science or history sections of the library, or articles in magazines that

Visual and audio sources are valuable references in research.

specialize in nature information. But if you wanted to learn even more about knights or sparrows, you could have looked at several other sources.

Kinds of Nonprint Media

Pictures of knights or sparrows might be found in a picture file, on a poster, or on projection materials such as slides or filmstrips. All of those sources, of course, have pictures on other topics that would be helpful in research. You can find a wide variety of visuals such as a photograph of the highest mountain in the world or a slide of the magnified cross section of a dandelion stem. The next time you do research, be sure to keep in mind these visual sources in the library.

The sound of a sparrow song or a story about knights might be found on an audio recording.

A film, a sound filmstrip, or a video recording could give added information that is both visual and auditory. Libraries may also have computer access to additional information that is both auditory and visual.

Although research involving these sources takes more time, the investigation of various sources is especially valuable to a writer who is dealing with a topic with which he has had very little personal experience.

Another type of nonprint media is referred to by librarians as *realia.* Collections of real objects cover a wide range of items. Real bird's nests, rock collections, science models, stamps, or coins are examples of real objects kept by some libraries to provide information for library users.

Locating and Using Nonprint Media

In some libraries you may use the card catalog or computer to locate some of the nonprint media.

Recordings of music, for instance, are cross-referenced by musician, selection, and composer. Recordings of plays or stories can be located by author or title, and recordings of historical events can be found by subject. A search for recorded stories about knights or kings might take you to a recording about King Arthur's adventures or William Shakespeare's play of *King Henry IV.*

In some libraries you can even use the card catalog or computer to locate slides, filmstrips, films, or video recordings, and a specific area

480

SL52   Sparrows. Chicago, Educational
Slides, Inc. 12 2x2 in. slides. col.

Contents. Dl Tree sparrow. D2 White-
crowned sparrow. D3 Seaside sparrow. D4
Swan sparrow. D5 Black-chinned sparrow.
D8 Song sparrow. D9 Vesper sparrow. D10
Lincoln's sparrow. D11 White-throated spar-
row. D12 Lark sparrow

*The card catalog, computer, or reference librarian can
direct you to a variety of nonprint media in the library.*

in the library might be available for you to view the materials.

The picture or poster file, however, might have a specialized filing system that would require the assistance of a librarian.

Storage for realia also varies from one library to another. Some items might be in display cases much like a miniature museum, and other things are stored out of sight and brought out upon request. One library, for instance, keeps in suitcases some artifacts and costumes from every country. Students doing reports on countries can check out the collection to help them with their research and class presentations. Sometimes libraries specialize in realia that is important to the locality. A library along the coast might have a collection of model ships on display, while a library specializing in nature could have a collection of sparrow nests or even a display on sparrows.

So the next time you have research to do, don't stop at the encyclopedia section. Don't even stop after searching the card catalog or computer. Go to the reference librarian and find out what nonprint materials are available to help you learn even more about your topic.

Dream of Light

A true story by Sanela Tutaris with Eileen M. Berry
illustrated by Sanela Tutaris

John wrote of the Lord Jesus Christ, "That was the true Light, which lighteth every man that cometh into the world" (John 1:9). You may think that there is meaning and happiness in this life apart from God, but there is not. Everything is empty without Him. But with God, everything becomes clear and bright.

My name, Sanela, comes from the word that means dream. God made a story out of my life—perhaps so that you might read it and learn something about Him through it. Dare to trust Him because His Word is true and eternal. Dare to trust Him because He will give you life in abundance. Dare to trust Him for He is good, and He will reward you. Your joy will be full and unspeakable. Desire nothing except Him, and He will give you more than you could even dream.

Walking in Shadows

I lived in Bosnia for twelve years, growing up in a non-Christian family in the town of Bugojno.[1] Three different religious groups live in Bosnia—the Serbs, who are Serb Orthodox; the Croats, who are Catholic; and the Muslims. The three religions are combined in my family. My father's father is Muslim, and his mother is Catholic. When my mother left her Orthodox family to marry someone who was not Orthodox, her choice caused conflict within the family.

In 1992, fighting broke out in Bosnia. Each of these religious groups wanted control of the government. Families fought with one another, and sometimes family members even killed each other.

I will never forget that terrible night when my family and I were some of the last ones, if not the last, who stayed in a part of Bugojno where there was heavy street fighting. We heard the sound of shooting all around the house where we were staying. We were hiding on the ground floor, hoping that soldiers would not come inside. I was silent, scared, and very tired. Because the shooting continued all during the night, it was hard to sleep. However, I got used to it, and when it ceased I was surprised and even more scared than when there was noise because now there was a dead peace. It made me think about loved ones who were gone forever. What was left?

In the morning we left quietly. The whole place was lifeless. The traces of bullets were on every single house. Some of the houses were no longer there. Ugly burning walls replaced them. After the looting[2] and burning, all that was left of many of the stores were their signs. Dogs whined and howled in the street, making a weird, scary noise. I remember hearing the voice of a mother crying for her loved ones.

We went to another part of town where my grandparents and other relatives had come to live. It would be safer there with people around us. On our way we found a place where we could still buy bread. That was one of the last pieces of bread that my father would eat for many days.

We all lived in the basement of one building. For beds we used the

---

[1]Bugojno (boō goi´ nō)
[2]looting—stealing valuable things during time of war or chaos

tiny shelves attached to the walls. The other children and I slept on our sides because turning could easily make us fall off.

More than ever in my life I saw the love of my parents for us. Food was scarce, but each tiny bite of food that came our way went right to our mouths. During that terrible time, even a little cup of sugar was a miracle. My grandfather is diabetic, so the insulin and food shortage was especially hard for him. My grandmother lost so much weight that she could again wear the clothes she wore when she was young. But that was not the most important thing she lost. She lost her youngest son in the fighting. Everybody was losing. Even those who were causing this terrible situation were losing. Houses, health, lives, loved ones.

On May 29, 1992, when I was twelve, my mother, two sisters, and I left our town. For a long time, my mother had not wanted to leave. It was hard for us to believe that all that was happening around us was reality. Although we had already been living in war conditions for quite some time, my mom thought that this was just a temporary war and would soon cease. But after she saw tanks behind one of the buildings of our city, she finally decided that we had to escape. My father stayed in Bosnia to care for his parents throughout the war. He could not escape and did not want to.

Sanela's mother (left) and two sisters (right) fled war-torn Bosnia.

My mother, sisters, and I wanted refuge from the war, but we did not know exactly where we were going. We carried 100 DM, which is less than fifty American dollars, two bags, and a blanket. I did not want to leave my dad in all that noise, danger, and suffering. My father and I both cried when we parted, but tears did not help.

The four of us passed through thirteen blockades. Sometimes the soldiers at these blockades would be Serbs, sometimes Croats, and sometimes Muslims. They would stop us and ask if there was anyone with us who did not belong to their religious group. Seeing their guns made us afraid that this was the end for us. But we just kept quiet, and we got through each blockade without being harmed. Looking back now, I see that the Lord delivered us. He helped us to arrive safely in Croatia, a place where there was no war.

During our travels, we slept in all kinds of places: in a ship's dining room, in a bus station, and in a train that was standing empty. Once we found a refugee[3] camp in a swampy place, but the tents there were full of snakes. The other refugees told us that the snakes were not poisonous, but my mom did not want us to live there. We searched long for a different refugee camp, and we finally found one with much better living conditions. My mom got us into the camp by lying about her religion. She said that she

was a Croat-Catholic, though she was really a Serb-Orthodox. We left after ten weeks because she was afraid of being found out.

Through the help of some cousins in Slovenia, we crossed Slovenia and Hungary to get to Yugoslavia. Our cousins in Yugoslavia did not receive us because they already had enough of their own refugees. My mom started looking for another refugee camp. After a few days we came to a refugee center situated on a mountain, far away from any real civilization. I remember when we got there that I just cried. I could not eat the food they gave us. Many other refugees felt the same way, but we did not have a choice. We had to stay alive.

Many wicked things went on in refugee camps. The little refugee room where we lived was often very loud and noisy because of the fights in my family. That made me cry.

My grandmother on my mother's side had been moved into our camp. Once she told me, "God will give; you and your family will be together again." But I remembered something that my other grandmother back in Bosnia used to say: "Pink moments in life are so rare." I agreed with her.

I traveled to school on a bus with some other kids—seventy kilometers, or forty-three miles, both directions. After finishing primary school we moved to another refugee camp

[3]refugee—a person who flees from his own country to find protection or safety

to be a little closer to our high school. At first I boarded at the high school. But I had hard relationships with my roommates. Any love among us was only superficial;[4] each of us looked out for our own interests. We listened to terrible music and cheated in school.

After a while I decided to move back to the refugee camp. I had to travel to school by hitchhiking[5] because bus travel was rare and expensive. I envied my friends who went to school with me because they did not have to hitchhike to school or be called a refugee. I felt that I never had anything good happen to me. But I held to the hope that one day something beautiful would happen to me too.

During these years, my diary was my most faithful friend. I did not have people I could trust and hope in. But my diary was like a person who was always with me and always understood me. I often wished that it could speak to me. Now I know that what I really wanted was God.

I wrote often in my diary, trying to find some kind of solution to the problems in my life. But no solution was possible without God. I believed that there was some higher power because I saw things happening in my life outside of my will. But I could find no answers. Sometimes I would feel that my whole life was dark, filled with shadows. For me,

the world was lighted not by candles but by the lightning before the thunder. My whole purpose seemed to be fighting for survival, and I never knew what tomorrow would hold.

Sometimes I had bad dreams, and I had trouble concentrating on my schoolwork. I was afraid of people—especially my literature teacher, even though he was my idol[6] because he was so intelligent and worldly-wise. He picked on me in class because I was a refugee. I wanted so much to prove myself to him that I began reading everything I could find so that I would always know the answers in class.

I loved studying literature. Once I found a statement in a book that I recorded in my diary. "God give me strength to bear what I cannot change, give me courage to change what I can, and wisdom to distinguish these two." *If I succeed in doing this I will be happy,* I thought. But I could never succeed.

My literature teacher taught us that only by useful work can we give our life meaning and keep ourselves from oblivion[7] after we die. I did not want to be forgotten when I died. But this philosophy did not give me peace in my heart.

---

[4]superficial—on the surface; artificial
[5]hitchhiking—standing by the sides of roads and getting free rides from passing cars
[6]idol—a person who is admired or loved very much
[7]oblivion—nothingness

Coming to the Light

About this time, I met a group of Christians from England. They had traveled all the way from England to Yugoslavia to help refugees, giving us presents and telling us how good God is and how much He loves us. They told us that He spared not His own Son but delivered Him up for us all. Although some of the refugees turned to this Christ, many of them did not respond. But the Christians kept coming. I watched them and wished I could smile and have peace inside like my British friends.

One day these friends offered me a free trip to Paris, France. Going to Paris had been my lifelong dream. I longed to study art there and see the paintings in the Louvre.[8] I was eighteen years old now, and I wanted to leave my country; but I did not have money or papers to go. Miraculously, I got a visa[9] and went with my friends. We arrived in Paris at the end of January. They left me there and returned to England. Part of me wanted to go with them. I was a small, lost girl seeking light and a better life in a big city.

I was very lonely at first. I did not know French well, and I did not have anyone in Paris who loved me and cared for me. I got a job working as a nanny.[10] On my trips to the Louvre, I saw a lot of pictures of

Paris, France

Christ. I wondered why artists painted Him so often. Why had He died, if He was so good? I also wondered why the French people said *avant Jésus* and *après Jésus*— "before Jesus" and "after Jesus"— when referring to a date from history. We do not say that in my country. *Maybe Jesus was really here on earth,* I thought, *and maybe He was telling the truth.*

I had received a Gospel of John in my language from my Christian friends. When I started reading it,

---

[8]Louvre (loo´ vrə)—one of the largest art museums in the world, located in Paris, France
[9]visa—an authorized document giving permission to travel within a certain country or region
[10]nanny—one who cares for the children of one family

Dream of Light 487

Sanela finds the Bible to be true.

the first words were striking to me: "In the beginning was the Word, and the Word was with God, and the Word was God." I knew through reading a lot of literature that words are very important. Words can change lives. And those words did change my life.

On January 30, 1999, I signed on the back of that gospel that I had accepted Christ as my Savior. I realized that I was a sinner, that the Bible is true, that Christ was really here on this earth, and that He had died on the cross. Bad people had not killed Him, as I had once thought. He voluntarily gave His life for me; He died for my sins. I had found the Light that I had dreamed of for so long.

Afterwards, everything was changed. *I* was changed. I remember getting up in the morning and hardly

recognizing myself. My only thought was God. I wanted to have the whole Bible, but I could not find one in my language there in Paris. I went into a Bosnian library and asked about the Bible. People just looked at me strangely. The Yugoslavian library with its many books did not have it either. I cried to the Lord to give me His Word, and I could not understand why I could not find it. But God had better and higher ways for me.

I wanted to go somewhere to church with other believers. But I did not know where to go. I went to the nearest church. I did not like it very much. Everything seemed very religious, but it did not look to me like the people there had a personal relationship with Christ.

One day I found a tract under the door of my apartment building entrance. It had the name of a church on the back—an independent church pastored by a missionary from America. I decided to visit this church, but I wanted to be very careful. I was afraid that this missionary would teach me something that was not true. I did not have the Bible to find out the truth for myself. But I continued going to the church, and then one day the missionaries gave me a copy of the whole Bible in French. After that, I had more confidence in these missionaries. On the 20th of June 1999, Pastor Hansen of that same independent church baptized me.

Very slowly I started reading the French Bible, translating[11] almost every word and deeply meditating on those words. I read it all the time. Everything was so new to me, and God's Word so sweet. Reading the French Bible and later listening to the French New Testament on tapes helped me learn French quickly. God was accomplishing His higher purpose—not just for me to have His Word for myself but to enable me to give it to others. Now I could witness to French people. I was so excited to talk about Christ. As I rode the metro[12] all around Paris, I witnessed to people around me.

I still believed the Lord wanted me to study art, but I no longer wanted to go to the art schools in Paris. I told the missionaries about my desire to study, and they told me about the Christian schools in America. They showed me some bulletins from American schools. Out of all the schools, I liked Bob Jones University the most, but the prices were for me enormous. I pushed away my desires. "I am never going to be able to pay all this—even if I work all my life," I said. "My parents cannot help me; and by the time I earn all this money, I will be too old to go to college."

The missionaries reminded me that God has all the money in the world. "You will have to trust Him," they said. I began praying earnestly that the Lord would place me in the school where I would be taught the truth.

Two weeks later, a couple from America came to visit the missionaries. The husband was a graduate of Bob Jones, and he told me wonderful things about the school. This couple told me that they would try to help me. I did not take them seriously at first. Who would pay that kind of cost, not even for his own children but for somebody they had only known for a few hours? But they did help me. Once again, God miraculously provided a visa. I was at Bob Jones University that next school year in the fall of 1999, a week or two late, but happy to be there.

When I was first saved, I promised God that I would never leave Him nor forsake Him, no matter what my family said about it. I knew that they would be against my decision, and they were. Thankfully, my father accepted Christ about a year after I did. But the rest of my family was still unsaved. During my second year as an art major at Bob Jones, God did many miracles for me at Christmastime. He answered my own prayers and those of many friends and allowed me to travel home to Bosnia.

---

[11]translating—changing into another language
[12]metro—subway

I had many opportunities during my travels on the plane, bus, metro, and train to share the gospel. I even shared my new faith with a nun. When I came to Paris, I stayed with an unsaved family. One of my friends in this family had just lost her mother, and she was very open to the gospel.

When I took the twenty-four-hour bus ride to Yugoslavia, I prayed that the Lord would save everyone on the bus. For some reason, the driver of the bus asked me to serve the coffee to the passengers, and that gave me an opportunity to meet and witness to many of them.

At the border, customs officials did not even open my bags. I thanked the Lord that I had safely passed the border with almost two thousand tracts in my luggage.

Now I had to deal with my mother, who had explicitly[13] told me that I could come but without any Christian literature. When she discovered my very heavy bag, she asked me if it contained Christian literature. "Yes," I said. Rather than saying more, she just helped me carry it! My mom was more than kind to me, but she did not accept Christ. I look forward to seeing what the Lord will do in her heart.

My fourteen-year-old sister went to Greece the same day I came to Yugoslavia, so she was not there when I arrived. She left me a big message on the wall of our refugee room: I LOVE YOU A LOT. I thought, *You will see who loves.*

I took a very cheap train in Yugoslavia and went after her to Greece to tell her of God's love. I told her the gospel, and she cried as she understood Christ died for her sins. We prayed together, and she accepted Christ. She is a new person now.

The Lord gave me opportunities to witness to my grandparents, aunts and uncles, cousins, and friends. I was able to spend all night reading the New Testament to one of my aunts, and afterward she asked me for more Christian literature. Many seemed so hungry for the Word of God. I guess that is what happens after communism, war, and of course, the prayers of Christian people. Some of my friends and relatives are now saved, including an aunt and her two children. My cousin and one of my friends would like to come to Bob Jones someday to study.

Has God ever done so much in your life that you were speechless? Where would I be today if God had not saved me? *"Verily, verily, I say unto you, He that believeth on me, the works that I do shall he do also; and greater works than these shall he do; because I go unto my Father.*

---

[13]explicitly—clearly; specifically

And whatsoever ye shall ask in my name, that will I do, that the Father may be glorified in the Son. If ye shall ask any thing in my name, I will do it" (John 14:12-14).

How much God changed me. I hardly recognize myself when I look at my old diaries. I am praying that I will grow steadily in my Christian life and that I will become a fruitful servant of the Lord through Bible training. My only real desire is to know Him and study His Word in order to grow in His grace and love. Someday I would like to go back to my own country, or wherever God directs, to share this wonderful life and peace He has given me.

Sanela traveled many miles to share the gospel with her family. Pictured (top, left to right) are the following: Sanela's three friends, mother, and aunt; her father; sister; (bottom) Sanela with her mother and uncle.

Theme

Morgan Reed Persun

Theme and Plot

If someone asked you to tell him what "Yeoman Knight" is about in one sentence, what would you say? Perhaps you would say, "It's the story of a poor boy who wants to become a knight." That would be a good summary of the main part of the plot. But is that what the story is really about? The person might be asking you rather what the story *means*—what its *theme* is.

It is always easier to tell what a story is about than to tell what it means. Why is that? The first requires only that the reader remember a sequence[1] of events.

---

[1]sequence—order; arrangement

The second requires that he be able to figure out the message, or theme, that the sequence creates.

To describe the events (the plot) is not necessarily to tell the meaning (the theme.) But to understand what a story is really about, you have to study the events. All plots have three parts: beginnings, middles, and ends. And it is the endings—the resolutions—that help reveal[2] the themes of stories. In "Yeoman Knight" Geoffrey sets out to be a knight having only his wit, his courage, and his sense of duty. In the middle of the story he is tested in each of those three virtues twice. The ending of the story makes his quest[3] and his trials have meaning. Because his good action is eventually rewarded, the story's meaning is clear: do right no matter what, and in the end you will not be sorry.

You may be thinking—so why does an author write stories rather than just make a simple short statement (like the last sentence in the paragraph above)? Certainly that would be easier than composing[4] a whole story! But would the message be as memorable? Would you remember the stated theme of "Yeoman Knight" as well as you remember a story about Geoffrey and his loyalty to a duke who seemed for a while to have forgotten him?

Would you be as inclined[5] to be more loyal just from being *told* to be rather than by being *inspired* to be by a brave young man? Very likely not.

Stated and Unstated Themes

All right, you say, a story is more memorable than a statement. But why does the theme have to be figured out? Why can't it just be stated in the story somewhere? Sometimes, in fact, stories do have stated themes. Aesop's fables, for example, end with clearly defined meanings often headed "The Moral of the Story Is . . ." and followed by such axioms[6] as "Little friends may prove great friends" (the moral of the story about a lion and a mouse). It is as though the author has stepped forward and told you plainly, "Here is what I meant."

Other stories state their themes, but not in a prescribed[7] place and way as do Aesop's. In *Oliver Twist,* Dickens describes Oliver's reaction to seeing the Dodger pick a pocket: "He stood, for a moment, with the blood tingling through all his veins

---

[2]reveal—make known
[3]quest—mission; search for something of value
[4]composing—writing; creating
[5]inclined—having a preference
[6]axioms—sayings
[7]prescribed—set; prearranged

from terror; then, confused and frightened, he took to his heels." Although not directly stated, the theme comes through in Oliver's actions: stealing and deception are wrong. Even though done by a person who cares for him, theft is something Oliver cannot go along with. He flees, and in doing so, reinforces the theme of honesty at whatever cost.

But other writers do not state their themes at all. They understand that, for the most part, readers do not like to be told what to think. Readers want to come to their own conclusions about things. The challenge for such writers is to make memorable and engaging[8] stories with enough clues to get the point across without running the reader off. The message in "Yeoman Knight" is never stated outright by the author or any character. But, like folktales and fables, it has a universal theme about the virtues of courage and loyalty, which the author expects the reader to recognize.

Why is it important to know what a story means? Isn't it enough to say whether we like it or dislike it? The Bible commands Christians to be wise as serpents and harmless as doves. One way to know about the ways of the world without being tainted[9] by them is to read, and to read thoughtfully. To read about dishonesty and its results makes you wise about dishonesty without having been dishonest yourself. But it is crucial that you be able to tell whether the author implies that stealing is fine if you have a good reason for doing so or whether he is saying stealing, for whatever reason, will have consequences. The first is not a lesson you want to take in without thinking.

Just as you want to know that someone who is talking to you is telling you the truth, so you want to be able to judge the value of a story's theme. Then you will *really* know how to read.

---

[8]engaging—appealing
[9]tainted—polluted

The ROOM

Gloria Repp
illustrated by Preston Gravely

Candy swung at another cobweb with her broom. She frowned at the green paint flaking from the water-stained cement wall beside her. How could Dad feel called to pastor a church with a cramped little parsonage[1] like this? She coughed in the musty basement air. Dad had told them it was a small house, but until they'd moved in last week, she'd stubbornly hoped that somehow she could have her own room. Her own room, a quiet place she wouldn't have to share with her twin sisters.

"Absolutely not," her mother said from the top of the basement stairs.

"You can't possibly sleep down there, Candy. You'd catch pneumonia, it's so damp."

Candy sighed and started up the steps. Through the open doorway into her room, she caught sight of Leah's blonde head bent over *her* desk. "Leah!" she cried. "You'd better stay away from my rock collection." She wrinkled her nose at the crumpled papers and dolls on the floor. "Look at this mess! Can't you girls play without creating your own personal tornado?"

She turned to her mother. "See why I'd rather sleep in the basement? Mother, I'm almost twelve. Can't I have my own room?"

"I know, Candy," her mother said in a low voice. "We've all prayed about it." She put her hand on Candy's shoulder. "It could be worse, you know."

Candy jerked away angrily. "You just don't understand. I can never read or think without being interrupted, and they're always getting into my stuff . . ." She avoided her mother's eyes. "I'm going down by the river, okay?"

[1]parsonage—house provided for the pastor of a church

496

On her way through the living room she glanced at the pile of mail. There were a lot of letters with the yellow forwarding stickers that the post office used. She thought about taking Dad's over to his office at the church, but then she remembered he'd be in Columbus until Saturday night.

She was about to put the pile of mail back when she looked again at a thin blue envelope with a foreign stamp. It was for her! It must be from Te Van, her pen pal in Vietnam. The youth group in her former church had started writing some teenagers in Vietnam about a year before she left, and she had wondered how soon Te Van's latest letter would catch up with her.

Pocketing her letter, Candy stepped out onto the veranda.[2] There she paused, as she always did, to gaze in fascination at the misty blue-green hills of Kentucky that rolled into the distance just across the shimmering Ohio River. After a minute she trudged down the hill to her favorite shady spot and perched on a rock to watch the river slipping by. But today she couldn't enjoy it.

Restlessly she glanced back up the hill at the parsonage, remembering how Mrs. Lindquist kept insisting that it was such a wonderful old house. What had she called it—a historical monument dating from before the Civil War? "Well," Candy thought, "I wish it were bigger and a little less historical."

The letter from Vietnam crackled excitingly as she pulled it from her pocket. She skimmed through it, and suddenly Te Van's carefully drawn words seemed to leap out at her:

You have written that you are moving to a different house with your family. We moved also into a house with better walls, made of bamboo woven, with a tin roof. It is six children in my family and we are still crowded in the one room but it is bigger. My father tries to get his job back and then I can go again to the school. I like very much.

Candy felt her face grow red with embarrassment, even though nobody was there to see her shame. She felt that she had acted like a spoiled child, fussing about a room of her own. And yet—it was hard to live with Leah and Liz, no matter how happy Te Van was with a one-room house!

Candy shook her head. She was no Te Van, that was for sure! "Well," she told herself, "I can't make myself like it, but I guess I don't have to carry on like a six-year-old over it. I'll just have to live with sharing my room."

[2]veranda—porch or balcony with a roof

Now that she was quieter, Candy reached into her jacket for her pocket New Testament. One good thing about the new parsonage was that she could have her devotions right by the river. She had just finished reading when all at once she heard the twins tumbling down the hill.

"Candy, guess what!" Leah called. "David got to come home from school for the weekend."

"And the church brought over some paint," Liz added.

"Hurrah!" Candy cried. "David can help me paint tomorrow." Laughing together, they ran up the hill and into the house.

Early the next morning, Candy slipped out onto the veranda to find David already there, reading. He looked up with a grin.

"Hey, this is a fascinating old place, isn't it?" her brother said. "Too bad it's so small. I know how much you wanted a room of your own."

Candy answered quietly. "I guess we've got more room than some people do. I'll manage." Then she remembered. "Oh, there's a lady at church, Mrs. Lindquist. She's wanted to meet you ever since she found out you're majoring in history at college. She's crazy about Civil War stuff. And she's got a whole bunch of antiques in her house."

David's eyes lit up. "Let's go see her as soon as we've finished that painting, okay?"

It was while David was painting the hall ceiling that he noticed the loose panel of plasterboard. "Hey, Candy," he called from the ladder. "Get a hammer, would you? I might as well—" His words were lost as the panel clattered to the floor.

"Now, that's strange," he said. "Where's that hammer, Candy?"

"Right here." She climbed up the ladder behind him. "David, isn't that another ceiling under there?"

"Yes—seems to me like somebody was trying to cover something up." He pointed to a big square

patch. "Here's another panel coming off. Can you take it?"

"David," Candy cried. "That looks like a trap door. Push on it and see if it moves."

"Nope, won't budge."

"Push harder. Here, let me help you."

"It's probably been nailed shut for a hundred years, Candy. There's nothing up there anyway," said David.

"Maybe," she said slowly. "But I still don't understand . . ." She ran her fingers around the edge of the board. "Feel this, David. Some little cut-outs, maybe for—"

"Fingers!" David interrupted. "Pull!" Candy's heart lurched as the trap door bumped open onto the false ceiling.

"Let's get some more of these boards out of the way so the door can come down," David said. "Better find some flashlights too."

It wasn't long before Candy could scramble after David through the gaping hole and onto the attic floor.

"Hey, why's this floor so soft?" David said, shining his flashlight down to their feet. Under the dust, they could see squares of faded cloth.

"Quilts!" Candy exclaimed. "This floor is covered with quilts." She took a few more steps. In a cobwebby corner, she saw a dull gleam.

"Look, David, a candleholder, with a half-burned candle in it. She snatched it up. "It looks like old, tarnished silver."

"Probably pewter," he said from where he was examining a wall. "Look here, Cand." He shone his light on several window frames. "Someone did a good job of boarding over these windows. From the outside no one would ever guess there was an attic up here."

Candy stared thoughtfully across the dusty little attic with its secretive shadows. Why would anyone want to hide an attic? It was just a room. . . .

"David!" she cried. "David, this room! It can be my bedroom! The Lord has given me a room!"

"He sure has," David answered with a smile. He cocked his head. "Hey, it sounds like Mom's home with the twins. Wait till they see this. Let's take this candleholder down with us."

That night, Candy waited impatiently for David to get back. He had been gone for hours, and all he had said was "Got to check on something." Then he had taken off with the candleholder in a paper bag.

Finally David came in, slamming the door behind him, the way he did when he was excited. "Guess what I found out?" he said, grinning.

"Come on, tell us," Candy exclaimed.

"Well, Mrs. Lindquist was right about this house being built before the Civil War," he said. "I checked on the dates with her. We figured out that someone must have used the attic to hide runaway slaves that were on their way to freedom in Canada." Candy stared at him in amazement.

"No kidding," he said. "The slaves used to escape across the river from Kentucky into Ohio because Ohio was a free state. They called this an underground station—part of the underground railroad that helped slaves escape to freedom in the North. That's why it was all fixed so no one would ever suspect there was an attic up there."

"And the quilts on the floor," Candy exclaimed. "So the people wouldn't make any noise."

"This pewter candleholder is a real antique." David handed it to his mother and Candy for a closer look.

"I wonder who used it last?" Candy ran her fingers around the dented edge of the candleholder. "Can I keep this up in my room?"

"You might find some spiders up there, Candy," David teased. "Are you sure you won't feel creepy in your new bedroom?"

"I'm not worried." Candy's face glowed. "The Lord sure gave me my room. He can handle the spiders for me too!"

SECRETS in the WALLS

Eileen M. Berry

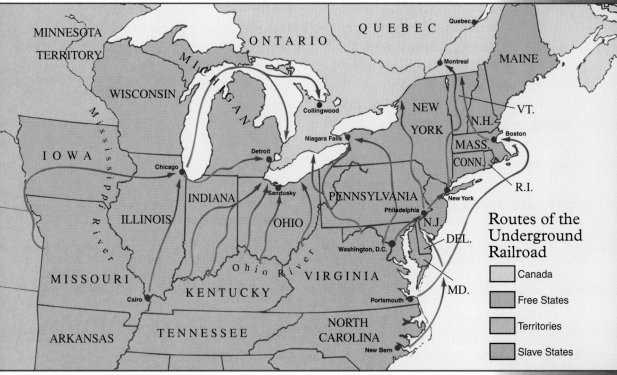

Routes of the Underground Railroad

- Canada
- Free States
- Territories
- Slave States

In the 1840s and 50s, many buildings in the northern United States had secret rooms. A shoe store had a little room tucked away behind a wall filled with shelves of shoeboxes. An inn had an underground tunnel connecting it to a log cabin. A house had a fake closet that was really an entrance to a passage leading far back within its walls. All of these buildings were part of a system called the Underground Railroad.

The Underground Railroad was a secret organization formed by people who wanted to help runaway slaves gain their freedom. In the decades before the American Civil War, thousands of slaves fled from their owners in the slave states of the South to safety in a northern free state or in Canada. All along the way, they followed a network[1] of specially mapped-out routes with safe places to stop for food and shelter. At these secret places, they would be hidden long enough for them to rest, regain strength, and sometimes receive new shoes or clothing before continuing their journey.

---

[1]network—a system or pattern

Traveling or working on the Underground Railroad was dangerous. The Fugitive[2] Slave Act of 1793 imposed[3] a fine of five hundred dollars on anyone who was caught harboring[4] an escaped slave. But then in 1850, a new Fugitive Slave Law was passed. This law raised the fine to one thousand dollars, and it also stated that people living in free states could be imprisoned for failing to return fugitive slaves to their owners.

The people who operated the Underground Railroad used the language of the railroad to avoid raising suspicion and being discovered. They referred to the places of safety as "stations" or "depots" and those who lived in them as "stationmasters." The people who made special trips south to encourage slaves to flee were called "pilots," and those who risked their lives to lead them on their journey were called "conductors." The fugitive slaves were often referred to as "passengers" or "cargo."

People helped slaves travel the Underground Railroad for various reasons. Many of the stationmasters were Quakers. They believed that all men were created equal, and they considered it their religious duty to help runaway slaves find a life of freedom in the North. One Quaker named Thomas Garrett calculated that he had assisted 2,322 slaves in the years between 1825 and 1863.

Some railroad workers were free blacks. Many had been born free in the North and had never known what it was like to labor for little or no pay, to be whipped by a harsh overseer, or to be separated from their families and sold to another plantation. Others had been born into slavery but had been granted freedom by their masters or had worked extra hard to buy their freedom.

William Still was a free black man whose parents had escaped from slavery before he was born. He spent his entire life serving the fugitive slaves who traveled the Underground Railroad. As clerk of the Pennsylvania Anti-Slavery Society and secretary of the Philadelphia Vigilance Committee,[5] he met thousands of runaway slaves who came through Philadelphia. He boarded[6] many fugitives in his home and helped them choose the safest escape routes to Canada, where the Fugitive Slave Law could not be enforced. He also kept careful records about each runaway slave that he met. He continued to keep them even after the Fugitive Slave Law of 1850, when many records were destroyed for fear

---

[2]fugitive—a person running away
[3]imposed—put on or assigned to a person something that is a burden
[4]harboring—giving shelter to; taking in

[5]Vigilance Committee—an unofficial group that watches out for crimes or other acts
[6]boarded—gave shelter or food, usually for pay

Born into a slave family on a plantation in Maryland, Harriet Tubman lived as a slave until she was twenty-nine years old. She often heard stories about the Underground Railroad while she was growing up, and one day she learned the location of the "station" nearest her. She fled in the middle of the night and traveled for many more nights on the ninety-mile route to freedom. When at last she reached the free state of Pennsylvania, she got a job as a cook in a hotel in Philadelphia.

But Tubman missed the family she had left behind in Maryland. She decided to travel back to try to rescue her sister and nieces and nephews. Though it was very dangerous for her to travel back into a slave state, Tubman believed it was worth the risk. She traveled to Baltimore, found her sister, and successfully guided her family members from station to station on the Underground Railroad, all the way to Philadelphia.

Harriet Tubman went on to become the most famous conductor on the Underground Railroad. Starting in 1852, she made two trips to Maryland every year until 1857 to bring her family members and other slaves out of bondage. She and William Still became close friends as she brought group after group of

of discovery. His records sometimes helped slaves locate family members from whom they had been separated. After the Civil War, William Still published these records in a book that gave us our most detailed information about the Underground Railroad.

Some workers on the Underground Railroad were escaped slaves who were not content to settle down in safety and freedom while so many others suffered on in slavery. One such woman was Harriet Tubman.

runaway slaves to be registered[7] in his office. Harriet Tubman was often called "the Moses of her people," for she helped to conduct more than three hundred slaves to freedom. She said of herself that she had "never run [her] train off the track, and . . . never lost a passenger." During the Civil War, she continued working for the North as a spy, scout, and nurse. Upon her death in 1913, she was buried in Auburn, New York, with full military honors.

On January 1, 1863, Abraham Lincoln's *Emancipation*[8] *Proclamation* freed the slaves in the Confederate States. Then in 1865, Congress passed the thirteenth amendment[9] to the Constitution and slavery ended. The Underground Railroad was no longer necessary. The secret rooms and passageways were sealed up, used for storage, or simply forgotten. But the thousands of slaves who had first tasted freedom at the end of that "railroad" would never forget the courageous people who had helped them on their way.

---

[7]registered—officially written on a list or record
[8]emancipation—freedom from slavery
[9]amendment—a change in a law

Amendment XIII: Slavery

Section 1. Neither slavery nor involuntary servitude, except as punishment for crimes whereof the party shall have been duly convicted, shall exist within the United States, or any place subject to their jurisdiction.

Section 2. Congress shall have power to enforce this article with appropriate legislation.

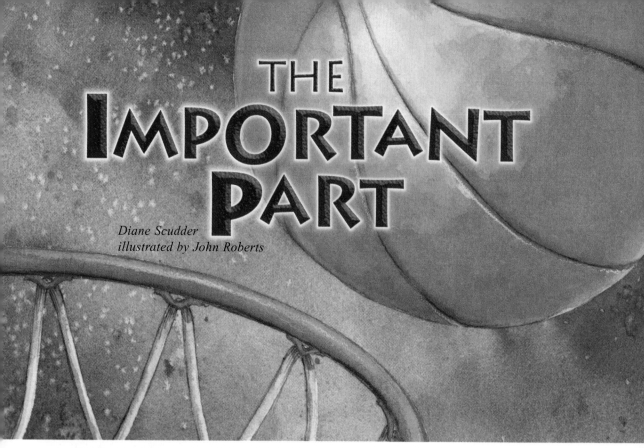

THE IMPORTANT PART

Diane Scudder
illustrated by John Roberts

A PART TO PLAY

"Come on! Play your positions!" Rodney yelled. "One minute 'til the bell rings. We can catch 'em—maybe beat 'em."

Joe glanced over at Rodney, the tallest player and captain of their basketball team. He had two players guarding him. "If only I could get the ball, I'd have a chance at the goal," Joe thought. Their team was behind by only one point.

Joe stepped under the basket. Now three of the other team members were crowding Rodney, since he was the best shot. But no one was guarding Joe.

"I'm free," Joe yelled from his position under the hoop. "Throw it here!"

Glen had the ball. He hesitated, looking quickly at Rodney and back at Joe. There were just too many guards around Rodney. Glen shot the ball over to Joe just as the bell rang.

Joe lined up his shot quickly and got the ball in the air before the bell stopped ringing. "This is it," he thought. "If I make it, we'll win the game." He watched as the ball arched through the air toward the hoop. Instead of swishing through the net, the ball hit the rim behind it and bounced back out.

"Come on, boys," Mrs. Taylor called from across the parking lot. "Time to come inside. Game's over."

The other team gave a big shout and ran for the door. Rodney's team followed more slowly. Joe kept his eyes on the ground.

"Why'd you throw it to Joe?" Rodney muttered to Glen. "You know he never hits anything."

Joe wasn't sure whether Rodney wanted him to overhear the comment or not. It didn't really matter. It was true. He sighed and pushed his hair back out of his eyes. His dad had always told him it didn't matter whether he won or lost as long as he did his best. Nobody else seemed to feel that way, though—especially Rodney.

Joe lifted his glasses and wiped the bridge of his nose. Whew, it was hot! If only all that running around had accomplished something—like getting him a basket. He seemed to hear his dad's voice in his mind. "If you keep practicing," he said, "you'll get better. Before long you'll be surprised at how well you play."

Joe's shoulders slumped as he walked toward the school building. It just wasn't working.

Joe got in line for a drink of water from the fountain before going back to his classroom.

"Please be quiet out there," Mrs. Taylor called.

Glen and Rodney stopped talking, but Joe watched their eyes sending messages back and forth. He was still trying to figure out what they were saying to each other when his turn at the drinking fountain came.

As Joe stepped forward and bent over the fountain, someone nudged him from behind. His teeth hit the metal spout of the fountain with a loud *thunk*. Tears of pain clouded his eyes as he jerked his head back.

Joe decided not to get a drink after all, and he walked past the rest of the line into the room as fast as he could. He felt his ears starting to turn red. His mouth hurt too, and he wanted to feel his lip and try to tell whether it was cut. Everyone in line must have heard the noise he'd made hitting the metal spout.

At the classroom door, Mrs. Taylor handed him a tissue from her pocket. "What happened to your lip, Joe?" she asked.

"I hit my mouth on the fountain." Joe didn't look up. The tissue was still pressed on his lip, so Mrs. Taylor couldn't hear him.

"What happened?" she asked again.

Joe took the tissue away from his lip. "I hit my mouth on the fountain," he said again in a louder voice. "It'll be all right."

Joe's mind wandered during the Heritage Studies lesson. He felt like his lip must be twice its normal size, and he supposed his ears were still pretty red. At least no one was looking at him. When Mrs. Taylor talked, everyone looked at her.

"What's wrong with me?" Joe wondered. "Why am I so clumsy?" Last night he had broken five dishes while he was clearing the table. He had meant to set a stack of plates on the table, but the bottom plate had hit the table's edge instead, and the unexpected bump had made him drop the whole stack. He still remembered the weary look on his mother's face as she bent to help him pick up the pieces of shattered plates.

Mrs. Taylor knocked gently on Joe's desk. "Joe, it's time to get busy," she told him. He was still looking at her, but everyone else in the class was busy with an assignment. "Read to the end of the chapter," Mrs. Taylor told him. "I want you to practice the note-taking skills and record what you learn about the Maya civilization of ancient America."

Joe started the assignment, determined to keep his mind on it and do a good job.

A few minutes later he heard his name. "Joe, come up to the desk," Mrs. Taylor called in that soft voice she used when everyone else was supposed to be working.

As he walked up the aisle toward her desk, Joe stumbled. He wasn't sure whether someone had tripped him on purpose or whether he'd caught his foot on something.

On Mrs. Taylor's desk, he saw a stack of papers clipped together. Some of the lines had been marked with yellow highlighter. Joe's eyes widened. They were scripts for the annual school play! The name *Mr. Harper* was written in the corner of the first set of pages.

"The other teachers and I would like you to take the part of Mr. Harper," Mrs. Taylor said. "It's the most important part in the play, and we know you can memorize the lines. It starts here." She pointed to the first line that was highlighted in yellow. "We won't start practices for two or three weeks yet, but we'd like you to start learning your lines."

Joe didn't take the pages when she held them out to him. "I don't think I can do it," he said.

"Oh, it's not all that long," she assured him, ruffling through the pages. "You don't have something to say on every page. I'm sure you won't have any trouble. You're always one of the first ones to recite the week's Scripture passage."

"I don't want to do it," Joe told her flatly.[1] He looked down at the floor. He wanted to say that he was sure he would trip as he walked onto the stage, that he knew he would do something to mess the whole play

[1]flatly—without emotion

up, but he didn't. He just kept staring at the floor.

Mrs. Taylor looked puzzled. "Joe, this is an opportunity to serve the Lord. We always have a big crowd for our plays, and some of the people who come aren't saved. This play has the gospel message in it very clearly."

She waited for Joe to say something. When he kept looking at the floor, she tried again. "We need you," she said. "Mr. Harper has to be played by an older boy, and you're probably the only one who can learn all the lines. Besides, I think you would do a wonderful job."

Mrs. Taylor looked pleadingly at Joe and waited, but Joe just kept looking at the floor. Finally she

sighed and said, "I don't know what to do. We were sure you would take the part." She paused, then said thoughtfully, "I don't intend to force you to do it if you don't want to. But you've always wanted to serve the Lord before. Will you pray about it, Joe?" she asked him. "If the Lord changes your mind, you can let me know before the end of the week."

Joe nodded politely and turned to walk back to his desk. "I'll be praying you'll make the right decision," Mrs. Taylor said.

Joe sighed as he sat down again. When Mrs. Taylor talked to him like that, he felt awful, but he didn't want to be in the play. He didn't want to hear the laughter of the audience as he messed up line after line.

HIS WORK, HIS WAY

Later, at home, Joe sat down at the dining-room table to finish his Heritage Studies notes.

His mother called to him from the kitchen. "Joe, please don't get too comfortable. We're having company, and I have to set the table."

Joe began removing his books from the table. "Who's coming?" he asked. He was glad his lip wasn't very swollen and the cut had been on the inside. He didn't want to have to tell anyone what had happened.

"Pastor Martin and his wife," his mother answered, smiling.

"Need any help?" Joe reached for the stack of dishes she was holding.

"Not tonight, Joe. You'd better try to finish that homework before dinner."

She said it very kindly, but Joe knew she didn't trust him with her best china.

Without a word, Joe went to his room, put his books on the desk, and lay down on his bed. "I hope Pastor Martin doesn't know about the part in the school play," he thought. "He might say something about it to mom at dinner, and I sure don't want her to know about it."

Joe knew his mother would tell him all the reasons he ought to be in the play. If he tried to convince her that he didn't want to do it, she would give him a disappointed look, and he knew he would end up taking the part just to keep her from being unhappy.

Yet Mrs. Taylor had not mentioned telling his parents about the part. She had left the decision up to him.

"I won't do it," Joe said out loud as he stared at the ceiling. He felt a cold, hard knot in the pit of his stomach. "I make mistakes at everything I do. It's bad enough to be a fool in front of my team and the whole class. I don't want to be one in front of the entire church."

Thinking about the church reminded Joe of the service three weeks ago when he had responded to the invitation. Pastor Martin had said that the Lord could use anyone who would let God take complete control of his life. Joe had raised his hand to say he was willing to serve the Lord anywhere, at home or abroad.

Pastor Martin had seen Joe's hand and prayed for him. "Bless these young ones who are giving their lives to Thee, Lord," he had said. Joe had been certain that God had a special, important work for him to do someday.

But now he wasn't so sure. He was quite certain God wouldn't want to use anyone like him. He was too clumsy. What if he never got over it? Joe didn't want people looking at him—and probably laughing— throughout his entire life. God used people like Pastor Martin. It was hard to imagine Pastor Martin ever tripping as he walked down an aisle or hitting his mouth on a water fountain.

"Maybe I'll learn to fix cars and get a job doing that," Joe thought. "I'll be underneath cars all the time, and no one will ever see me."

Joe remembered that Mrs. Taylor had told him to pray about being in the play. He closed his eyes. "God, please make sure my mother doesn't find out about the play. And please give me special direction if You want me in the play." But he was sure that God had already shown him what to do. God had shown him that he was too clumsy to do anything very important.

Joe got up and started working on his assignment again. He had just finished when he heard the doorbell ring. Pastor and Mrs. Martin had arrived. Joe hurried to the living room.

"Hi, Joe," Pastor Martin said. He shook Joe's hand just the way he would shake a grown-up's. "How are you?" he asked.

"I'm fine," Joe told him.

Mother invited everyone into the dining room.

Dad asked Pastor Martin to pray before the meal. Joe liked to listen to the pastor pray. He didn't pray long prayers, but he talked to God as if he really knew Him, as if he'd been talking to Him a lot for a long time.

As his mother began passing the food around, Pastor Martin asked Joe how he was doing in school. Joe said "fine" and was relieved when Pastor Martin didn't mention anything about the play.

Joe took a big helping of mashed potatoes. "Please pass the gravy," he said.

His mother smiled and passed him the gravy dish. Joe set the dish down beside him and dipped several big ladles of gravy onto his potatoes. He thought he was setting the ladle back into the half-empty gravy bowl, but something else must have happened. His mother whispered urgently, "Joe!"

When he looked, the ladle was on the tablecloth next to the bowl. There was gravy dripping down the side of the bowl and a big gravy smudge on the tablecloth.

Joe mumbled an apology and picked up the ladle. He tried to wipe the gravy up with his napkin, sure that his ears were turning red again.

Joe's mother patted his arm. "It will wash out," she said.

"Joe's really been having a hard time lately," Joe's dad said, passing the gravy on to Pastor Martin.

Pastor Martin laughed. "I remember when I went through that," he said. "For months my mother said I broke dishes faster than she could buy them. I had to use part of my allowance to pay for broken dishes."

Joe's dad gave him a playful wink across the table. "See, Son, you'll grow out of it," he said.

"Sure you will, Joe. I had an especially hard time because of my glasses. I wear contacts now." Pastor Martin picked up his water glass. "But I used to wear glasses that were thicker than the bottom of this glass. Most boys go through a clumsy stage when they begin growing rapidly, but mine was compounded[2] by my poor eyesight. Without anyone knowing it, my eyes began to change rapidly too. I was having a lot of trouble seeing. Things did improve some when I got my glasses changed."

"Maybe we should have Joe's eyes checked," his father said. "We never really thought about that. He has had those glasses for quite a while."

"That may not be the whole answer, but it might help." Pastor Martin smiled at Joe again. "I had a lot of problems when I was your age, Joe. I wonder how I ever lived through them. Not only was I clumsy, but I had a severe speech problem too. I stuttered."

"Really?" Joe's mother said in surprise. "I never would have guessed."

"I don't talk much about it," Pastor Martin said. "It was an awful struggle for years. The Lord has really helped me. I don't have any problem with it now."

"So how did you become a preacher?" Joe asked, amazed. "Weren't you afraid people would laugh at you?"

[2]compounded—made worse

"I sure was," Pastor Martin said. "For a while I was more afraid of that than of anything else. I was sure the Lord could never use me to do anything for Him. I decided not to go to college and study the Bible. Instead, I planned to just stay home and work for my dad in his welding shop."

Pastor Martin paused to take another piece of fried chicken.

"But you didn't," Joe said, "or you wouldn't be here."

"No," Pastor Martin said. "I didn't. I was unhappy at the shop. I had promised the Lord that I would serve Him wherever He needed me, and I knew I was breaking my promise. I guess I finally started car-ing more about what God thought of me than about what other people thought of me. I told the Lord that if He gave me an opportunity, I would serve Him, even if I couldn't do a very good job. Then I decided to work and study and do the very best job I could for Him."

Joe's dad said, "I never would have guessed any of that. You cer-tainly do a fine job now."

"Thank you," Pastor Martin said. "I've always believed that God em-powers the weak things. And I am certainly one of the weakest. The im-portant part for us is to be empty and willing. Then God is free to do His work, His way."

Joe didn't hear much of what the adults talked about during the rest of the dinner. He kept thinking about what the pastor had said. He watched Pastor Martin, trying to imagine what he must have been like when he was young and clumsy. After supper, his mother winked at him and told him he didn't need to help clear the table. She leaned close and whispered in his ear, "We'll get your eyes checked before you help in the kitchen again."

While Mrs. Martin helped clean up, the men went back into the living room and began talking about politics and the national debt.

Joe went back to his room and sat down on his bed. He thought about the prayer he had prayed that afternoon. God had answered it. He hadn't sent a voice or writing in the sky or an angel. But God had sent a messenger: Pastor Martin.

"Mrs. Taylor could have asked Glen or Rodney or another boy in the class to be in the play," Joe thought. "I'm still not sure why she didn't. But when she asked me to take the part, that must have been God's way of giving me an opportunity to serve."

Joe knew it wouldn't be easy. It would take work to memorize all the lines, but that wouldn't be the hardest part. He was sure he'd embarrass everyone if he tripped or bumped scenery on the stage. New glasses

might help, but he couldn't be sure of that. Joe took a deep breath. What was it Pastor Martin had said? Joe decided he would do the same thing—he'd work and study and do the very best job he could for God.

That cold, hard feeling Joe had had inside was gone. He felt as if he had started on an exciting journey that would take him to wonderful places.

"Joe," his dad called, "come here a minute."

Joe ran out into the living room. "Yes, Dad?"

"I was telling Pastor how hard you've been working on your basketball. I told him I'd never played much and couldn't help you. Pastor Martin says he used to play a lot."

"Come on outside with me," Pastor Martin said. "I'll give you a few pointers before it gets dark. Getting your eyes checked may help your basketball playing too."

Joe and the pastor walked out to the basketball goal in the back yard. Joe took a deep breath and looked up at Pastor Martin. "Did you know I'm going to be in the school play?" he asked. "Mrs. Taylor asked me today, and I'm going to tell her tomorrow that I'll do it."

Pastor Martin shook Joe's hand and looked him straight in the eye. "Congratulations," he said. "I know you'll do a great job."

"I'll do the best I can," Joe said, smiling. "Thank you."

Joe picked up the basketball and passed it to Pastor Martin. The pastor dribbled to the basket and shot a lay-up.

"How did you do that?" Joe asked.

"I'll show you the technique[3] my coach showed me," the pastor said. "I've practiced it a lot because I played forward under the basket. Lay-ups were vital shots for me. You'll learn, Joe. Everybody has an important part to play."

---

[3]technique—a method or way of doing something

516

The Redheaded LEAGUE

From The Adventures of Sherlock Holmes
by Sir Arthur Conan Doyle
illustrated by Timothy N. Davis

Sir Arthur Conan Doyle made the detective story a permanent part of fiction with his brilliant literary character, Sherlock Holmes. A master of the minute and very detailed, Sherlock Holmes solved many crimes from his armchair, simply by "deducing" logical conclusions from facts given. In this story, you will see how he made the mysterious seem simple and apparent. As usual, the story is narrated by Holmes's good friend and admirer, Dr. Watson.

Mysterious Employment

I had called upon my friend, Mr. Sherlock Holmes, one day in the autumn of last year, and found him in deep conversation with a very stout, florid[1]-faced, elderly gentleman with fiery red hair.

The gentleman half rose from his chair, and gave a bob of greeting, with a quick little questioning glance from his small, fat-encircled eyes.

"Try the settee,"[2] said Holmes, relapsing into his armchair, and putting his fingertips together, as was his custom when in judicial moods. "I know, my dear Watson, that you share my love of all that is bizarre and outside the conventions and humdrum routine of everyday life. Now, Mr. Jabez Wilson here has been good enough to call upon me this morning and to begin a narrative that promises to be one of the most singular which I have listened to for some time. Perhaps, Mr. Wilson, you would have the great kindness to recommence[3] your narrative. In the present instance I am forced to admit that the facts are, to the best of my belief, unique."

The portly client puffed out his chest with an appearance of some little pride and pulled a dirty and wrinkled newspaper from the inside

---

[1]florid—flushed; red in color
[2]settee—a type of sofa
[3]recommence—start again

pocket of his greatcoat. As he glanced down the advertisement column, with his head thrust forward, and the paper flattened out upon his knee, I took a good look at the man, and endeavoured[4] after the fashion of my companion to read the indications which might be presented by his dress or appearance.

I did not gain very much, however, by my inspection. Our visitor bore every mark of being an average commonplace British tradesman, obese, pompous, and slow. He wore rather baggy grey shepherds' check trousers, a not over-clean black frock-coat, unbuttoned in the front, and a drab waistcoat. A frayed top-hat, and a faded brown overcoat with a wrinkled velvet collar lay upon a chair beside him. Altogether, look as I would, there was nothing remarkable about the man save his blazing red head and the expression of extreme chagrin[5] and discontent upon his features.

Sherlock Holmes's quick eye took in my occupation, and he shook his head with a smile as he noticed my questioning glances. "Beyond the obvious facts that he has at some time done manual labour, and that he has done a considerable amount of writing lately, I can deduce[6] nothing else."

Mr. Jabez Wilson started up in his chair, with his forefinger upon the paper, but his eyes upon my companion.

"How in the name of good fortune did you know that, Mr. Holmes?" he asked. "How did you know, for example, that I did manual labor? It's true, I began as a ship's carpenter."

"Your hands, my dear sir. Your right hand is quite a size larger than your left. You have worked with it, and the muscles are more developed."

"Ah, of course, but the writing?"

"What else can be indicated by that right cuff so very shiny for five inches, and the left one with the smooth patch near the elbow where you rest it upon the desk?"

Mr. Jabez Wilson laughed heavily. "Well, I never!" said he. "I thought at first you had done something clever, but I see that there was nothing in it after all."

"I begin to think, Watson," said Holmes, "that I make a mistake in explaining. My poor little reputation, such as it is, will suffer shipwreck if I am so candid.[7] Can you not find the advertisement, Mr. Wilson?"

"Yes, I have got it now," he answered, with his thick, red finger planted halfway down the column. "Here it is. This is what began it all. You just read it for yourself, sir."

---

[4]endeavoured—made a major effort or attempt
[5]chagrin—embarrassment caused by failure or disappointment
[6]deduce—to conclude from known facts or circumstances
[7]candid—open and honest

I took the paper from him and read as follows:

To the Redheaded League—

On account of the bequest of the late Ezekiah Hopkins, of Lebanon, Penn., U.S.A., there is now another vacancy open which entitles a member of the League to a salary of four pounds a week for purely nominal[8] services. All redheaded men who are sound in body and mind, and above the age of twenty-one years, are eligible. Apply in person on Monday, at eleven o'clock, to Duncan Ross, at the offices of the League, 7 Pope's Court, Fleet Street.

"What on earth does this mean?" I exclaimed, after I had twice read over the extraordinary announcement.

---

[8]nominal—small; insignificant

Holmes chuckled, and wriggled in his chair, as was his habit when in high spirits. "It is a little off the beaten track, isn't it?" said he. "And now, Mr. Wilson, off you go at scratch, and tell us all about yourself, your household, and the effect which this advertisement had upon your fortunes. You will first make a note, Doctor, of the paper and the date."

"It is *The Morning Chronicle*, of April 27, 1890. Just two months ago."

"Very good. Now, Mr. Wilson?"

"Well, it is just as I have been telling you, Mr. Sherlock Holmes," said Jabez Wilson, mopping his forehead, "I have a small pawnbroker's business at Coburg Square, near the City. It's not a very large affair, and of late years it has not done more than just to give me a living. I used to be able to keep two assistants, but now I only keep one; and I would have a job to pay him, but that he is willing to come for half wages, so as to learn the business."

"What is the name of this obliging youth?" asked Sherlock Holmes.

"His name is Vincent Spaulding, and he's not such a youth either. It's hard to say his age. I should not wish a smarter assistant, Mr. Holmes; and I know very well that he could better himself, and earn twice what I am able to give him. But after all, if he is satisfied, why should I put ideas in his head?"

"Why, indeed? You seem most fortunate in having an employee who comes under the full market price. It is not a common experience among employers in this age. I don't know that your assistant is not as remarkable as your advertisement."

"Oh, he has his faults, too," said Mr. Wilson. "Never was such a fellow for photography. Snapping away with a camera when he ought to be improving his mind, and then diving down into the cellar like a rabbit into its hole to develop his pictures. That is his main fault; but on the whole, he's a good worker. There's no vice[9] in him."

"He is still with you, I presume?"

"Yes, sir. He and a girl of fourteen, who does a bit of simple cooking, and keeps the place clean—that's all I have in the house, for I am a widower, and never had any family.

"The first thing that put us out was that advertisement. Spaulding, he came down into the office just this day eight weeks with this very paper in his hand, and he says:

" 'I wish, Mr. Wilson, that I was a redheaded man.'

" 'Why that?' I asked.

" 'Why,' says he, 'here's another vacancy in the League of Redheaded Men. It's worth quite a little fortune to any man who gets it, and I understand that there are more vacancies

---

[9]vice—corruption; dishonesty

520

than there are men, so that the trustees are at their wits' end what to do about the money. If my hair would only change color, here's a nice little crib[10] all ready for me to step into.'

" 'Why, what is it, then?' I asked.

" 'Have you never heard of the League of the Redheaded Men?' he asked, with his eyes open wide.

" 'Never.'

" 'Why, I wonder at that, for you are eligible yourself for one of the vacancies.'

" 'And what are they worth?' I asked.

" 'Oh, merely a couple of hundred a year, but the work is slight, and it need not interfere much with one's other occupations.'

"Well, you can easily think that that made me prick up my ears, for the business has not been over good for some years, and an extra couple hundred would have been very handy.

" 'Tell me all about it,' said I.

" 'Well,' said he, showing me the advertisement, 'you can see for yourself that the League has a vacancy, and there is the address where you should apply for particulars. As far as I can make out, the League was founded by an American millionaire, Ezekiah Hopkins, who was very peculiar in his ways. He was himself redheaded, and he had a great sympathy for all redheaded men; so, when he died, it was found that he had left his enormous fortune

---

[10]crib—a comfortable situation, especially financially

in the hands of trustees, with instructions to apply the interest to the providing of easy berths[11] to men whose hair is of that color. From all I hear it is splendid pay, and very little to do.'

" 'But,' said I, 'there would be millions of redheaded men who would apply.'

" 'Not so many as you might think,' he answered. 'You see, it is really confined to Londoners, and to grown men. This American had started from London when he was young, and he wanted to do the old town a good turn. Then, again, I have heard it is no use applying if your hair is light red, or dark red, or anything but real, bright, blazing, fiery red. Now, if you cared to apply, Mr. Wilson, you would just walk in; but perhaps it would hardly be worth your while to put yourself out of the way for the sake of a few hundred pounds.'

"Now, it is a fact, gentlemen, as you may see for yourselves, that my hair is of a very full and rich tint, so that it seemed to me that, if there was to be any competition in the matter, I stood as good a chance as any man that I had ever met. Vincent Spaulding seemed to know so much about it that I thought he might prove useful, so I just ordered him to put up the shutters for the day, and to come right away with me. He was very willing to have a holiday, so we

shut the business up, and started off for the address that was given us in the advertisement.

"I never hope to see such a sight as that again, Mr. Holmes. From north, south, east, and west, every man who had a shade of red in his hair had tramped into the City to

[11]berths—jobs

answer the advertisement. I should not have thought there were so many in the whole country as were brought together by that single advertisement. When I saw how many were waiting, I would have given it up in despair; but Spaulding would not hear of it. How he did it I could not imagine, but he pushed and pulled and butted until he got me through the crowd, and right up to the steps, which led to the office. There was a double stream upon the stair, some going up in hope, and some coming back dejected; but we wedged in as well as we could, and soon found ourselves in the office."

"Your experience has been a most entertaining one," remarked Holmes. "Pray continue your very interesting statement."

"There was nothing in the office but a couple of wooden chairs and a deal table,[12] behind which sat a small man, with a head that was even redder than mine. He said a few words to each candidate as he came up, and then he would disqualify them. Getting a vacancy did not seem to be such a very easy matter after all. However, when our turn came, the little man was more favourable to me than to any of the others, and he closed the door as we entered, so that he might have a private word with us.

" 'This is Mr. Jabez Wilson,' said my assistant, 'and he is willing to fill a vacancy in the League.'

" 'And he is admirably suited for it,' the other answered. 'He has every requirement. I cannot recall when I have seen anything so fine.' He took a step backwards, cocked his head on one side, and gazed at my hair until I felt quite bashful. Then suddenly he plunged forward, wrung my hand, and congratulated me warmly on my success.

" 'My name,' said he, 'is Mr. Duncan Ross, and I am myself one of the pensioners[13] upon the fund left by our noble benefactor.[14] Are you a married man, Mr. Wilson? Have you a family?'

"I answered that I had not.

"His face fell immediately.

" 'Dear me!' he said gravely, 'that is very serious indeed! I am sorry to hear you say that. The fund was, of course, for the propagation[15] and spread of the redheads as well as for their maintenance. It is exceedingly unfortunate that you should be a bachelor.'[16]

"My face lengthened at this, Mr. Holmes, for I thought that I was not to have the vacancy after all; but

[12]deal table—one made from a specific type and size of wood
[13]pensioners—persons receiving a sum of money, usually after retirement
[14]benefactor—supporter
[15]propagation—multiplication in number
[16]bachelor—a man who is not married

after thinking it over for a few minutes, he said that it would be all right.

"'In the case of another,' said he, 'the objection might be fatal, but we must stretch a point in favor of a man with such a head of hair as yours. When shall you be able to enter upon your new duties?'

"'Well, it is a little awkward, for I have a business already,' said I.

"'Oh, never mind about that, Mr. Wilson!' said Vincent Spaulding. 'I shall be able to look after that for you.'

"'What would be the hours?' I asked.

"'Ten to two.'

"Now a pawnbroker's business is mostly done of an evening, Mr. Holmes, especially Thursday evening, which is just before payday; so it would suit me very well to earn a little in the mornings. Besides, I knew that my assistant was a good man, and that he would see to anything that turned up.

"'That would suit me very well,' said I. 'And the pay?'

"'Is four pounds a week.'

"'And the work?'

"'Is purely nominal.'

"'What do you call purely nominal?'

"'Well, you have to be in the office, or at least in the building, the whole time. If you leave, you forfeit your whole position forever. The will is very clear upon that point. You don't comply with the conditions if you budge from the office during that time.'

"'It's only four hours a day, and I should not think of leaving,' said I.

"'No excuse will avail,' said Mr. Duncan Ross, 'neither sickness, nor business, nor anything else. There you must stay, or you lose your billet.'[17]

"'And the work?'

"'Is to copy out the *Encyclopedia Britannica.* There is the first volume of it in that press. You must find your own ink, pens, and blotting-paper, but we provide this table and chair. Will you be ready tomorrow?'

"'Certainly,' I answered.

"'Then good-bye, Mr. Jabez Wilson, and let me congratulate you once more on the important position which you have been fortunate enough to gain.' He bowed me out of the room, and I went home with my assistant, hardly knowing what to say or do, I was so pleased at my own good fortune."

---

[17]billet—a job

524

Fraud or Fortune?

"Well, I thought over the matter all day, and by evening I was in low spirits again; for I had quite persuaded myself that the whole affair must be some great hoax[18] or fraud, though what its object might be I could not imagine. It seemed altogether past belief that anyone could make such a will, or that they would pay such a sum for doing anything so simple as copying out the *Encyclopedia Britannica*. Vincent Spaulding did what he could to cheer me up, but by bedtime I had reasoned myself out of the whole thing. However, in the morning I determined to have a look at it anyhow, so I bought a penny bottle of ink, and with a quill pen, and seven sheets of foolscap[19] paper, I started off for Pope's Court.

"Well, to my surprise and delight everything was as right as possible. The table was set out ready for me, and Mr. Duncan Ross was there to see that I got fairly to work. He started me off upon the letter A, and then he left me; but he would drop in from time to time to see that all was right with me. At two o'clock he bade me good day, complimented me upon the amount that I had written, and locked the door of the office after me.

"This went on day after day, Mr. Holmes, and on Saturday the manager came in and planked down four golden sovereigns for my week's work. It was the same next week, and the same the week after. Every morning I was there at ten, and every afternoon I left at two. By degrees Mr. Duncan Ross took to coming in only once of a morning, and then, after a time, he did not come in at all. Still, of course, I never dared to leave the room for an instant, for I was not sure when he might come, and the billet was such a good one, and suited me so well, that I would not risk the loss of it.

"Eight weeks passed away like this, and I had written about Abbots, and Archery, and Armour, and Architecture, and Attica, and hoped with diligence that I might get on to the B's before very long. It cost me something in foolscap, and I had pretty nearly filled a shelf with my writings. And then suddenly the whole business came to an end."

"To an end?"

"Yes, sir. And no later than this morning. I went to my work as usual at ten o'clock, but the door was shut and locked, with a little square of cardboard hammered on to the middle of the panel with a tack. Here it is, and you can read for yourself."

---

[18]hoax—false story
[19]foolscap—(British) type of paper approximately 13" × 16" in size

He held up a piece of white cardboard, about the size of a sheet of note-paper. It read in this fashion:

THE REDHEADED LEAGUE IS DISSOLVED
Oct. 9, 1890

Sherlock Holmes and I surveyed this curt announcement and the rueful face behind it, until the comical side of the affair so completely overtopped every other consideration that we both burst out into a roar of laughter.

"I cannot see that there is anything very funny," cried our client, flushing up to the roots of his flaming head. "If you can do nothing better than laugh at me, I can go elsewhere."

"No, no," cried Holmes, shoving him back into the chair from which he had half risen. "I really wouldn't miss your case for the world. It is most refreshingly unusual. But there is, if you will excuse me saying so, something just a little funny about it. Pray what steps did you take when you found the card upon the door?"

"I was staggered,[20] sir. I did not know what to do. Then I called at the offices round, but none of them seemed to know anything about it. Finally, I went to the landlord, who is an accountant living on the ground floor, and I asked him if he could tell me what had become of the Redheaded League. He said he had never heard of any such body. Then I asked him who Mr. Duncan Ross was. He answered that the name was new to him.

"'Well,' said I, 'the gentleman at No. 4.'

"'What, the redheaded man?'

"'Yes.'

"'Oh,' said he, 'his name was William Morris. He was a solicitor, and was using my room as a temporary convenience until his new premises[21] were ready. He moved out yesterday.'

"'Where could I find him?'

"'Oh, at his new offices. He did tell me the address. Yes, 17 King Edward Street, near St. Paul's.'

"I started off, Mr. Holmes, but when I got to that address it was a manufactory of artificial kneecaps, and no one in it had ever heard of either Mr. William Morris, or Mr. Duncan Ross."

"And what did you do then?" asked Holmes.

"I went home to Saxe-Coburg Square, and I took the advice of my assistant. But he could not help me in any way. He could only say that if I waited I should hear by post. But that was not quite good enough, Mr. Holmes. I did not wish to lose such a place without a struggle, so, as I had heard that you were good enough to give advice to poor folk who were in need of it, I came right away to you."

"And you did very wisely," said Holmes. "Your case is an exceedingly remarkable one, and I shall be happy to look into it. From what you have told me I think that it is possible that graver issues hang from it than might at first sight appear."

"Grave enough!" said Mr. Jabez Wilson. "Why, I have lost four pounds a week."

"As far as you are personally concerned," remarked Holmes, "I do not see that you have any grievance against this extraordinary league. On the contrary, you are, as I understand, richer by some thirty pounds, to say nothing of the minute[22] knowledge which you have gained on every subject which comes under the letter *A*. You have lost nothing by them."

"No, sir. But I want to find out about them, and who they are, and what their object was in playing this prank—if it was a prank—upon me. It was a pretty expensive joke for

---

[20]staggered—shocked; stunned
[21]premises—someone's land or building
[22]minute (mī nyoōt´ or mī nyoŏt´)—careful and detailed

them, for it cost them two-and-thirty pounds."

"We shall endeavor to clear up these points for you. And, first, one or two questions, Mr. Wilson. This assistant of yours who first called your attention to the advertisement—how long had he been with you?"

"About a month then."

"How did he come?"

"In answer to an advertisement."

"Was he the only applicant?"

"No, I had a dozen."

"Why did you pick him?"

"Because he was handy, and would come cheap."

"At half wages, in fact."

"Yes."

"What is he like, this Vincent Spaulding?"

"Small, stout-built, very quick in his ways, no hair on his face, though he's not short of thirty. Has a white splash of acid upon his forehead."

Holmes sat up in his chair in considerable excitement.

"I thought as much," said he. "Have you ever observed that his ears are pierced for earrings?"

"Yes, sir. He told me that a gipsy had done it for him when he was a lad."

"Hum!" said Holmes, sinking back in deep thought. "He is still with you?"

"Oh, yes, sir; I have only just left him."

"And has your business been attended to in your absence?"

"Nothing to complain of sir. There's never much to do of a morning."

"That will do, Mr. Wilson. I shall be happy to give you an opinion upon the subject in the course of a day or two. Today is Saturday, and I hope that by Monday we may come to a conclusion."

"Well, Watson," said Holmes, when our visitor had left us, "what do you make of it all?"

"I make nothing of it," I answered, frankly. "It is a most mysterious business."

"Sarasate[23] plays at the St. James's Hall this afternoon," he remarked. "What do you think, Watson? Could your patients spare you for a few hours?"

"I have nothing to do today. My practice[24] is never very absorbing."

"Then put on your hat, and come. I am going through the City first, and we can have some lunch on the way. I observe that there is a good deal of German music on the programme, which is rather more to my taste than Italian or French. It is introspective,[25] and I want to introspect. Come along!"

---

[23]Sarasate (sä′ dä sä′ tä)—famous Spanish violinist
[24]practice—the group of people who use the services of a doctor; a professional business
[25]introspective—thoughtful; meditative

We travelled by the Underground as far as Aldersgate; and a short walk took us to Saxe-Coburg Square, the scene of the singular story that we had listened to in the morning. It was a pokey, little, shabby-genteel place, where four lines of dingy two-storied brick houses looked out into a small railed-in enclosure, where a lawn of weedy grass and a few clumps of faded laurel bushes made a hard fight against the smoke-laden and uncongenial[26] atmosphere. Three gilt balls and a brown board with JABEZ WILSON in white letters, upon a corner house, announced the place where our redheaded client carried on his business. Sherlock Holmes stopped in front of it with his head on one side and looked it all over, with his eyes shining brightly between puckered lids. Then he walked slowly up the street and then down again to the corner, still looking keenly at the houses. Finally he returned to the pawnbroker's, and, having thumped vigorously upon the pavement with his stick two or three times, he went up to the door and knocked. It was instantly opened by a bright-looking, clean-shaven young fellow, who asked him to step in.

"Thank you," said Holmes, "I only wished to ask you how you would go from here to the Strand."

"Third right, fourth left," answered the assistant promptly, closing the door.

"Smart fellow, that," observed Holmes as we walked away. "He is, in my judgment, the fourth smartest man in London and for daring I am not sure that he has not a claim to be third. I have known something of him before."

"Evidently," said I, "Mr. Wilson's assistant counts for a good deal in this mystery of the Redheaded League. I am sure that you inquired your way merely in order that you might see him."

"Not him."

"What then?"

"The knees of his trousers."

"And what did you see?"

"What I expected to see."

"Why did you beat the pavement?"

"My dear Doctor, this is a time for observation, not for talk. We are spies in an enemy's country. We know something of Saxe-Coburg Square. Let us now explore the paths which lie behind it."

The road in which we found ourselves as we turned round the corner from the retired Saxe-Coburg Square presented as great a contrast to it as the front of a picture does to the back. It was one of the main arteries that convey the traffic of the City to the north and west. The roadway was blocked with the immense stream of commerce[27] flowing in a double tide inwards and outwards, while the

---

[26]uncongenial—unfriendly
[27]commerce—trade; business

footpaths were black with the hurrying swarm of pedestrians. It was difficult to realize as we looked at the line of fine shops and stately business premises that they really abutted[28] on the other side upon the faded and stagnant[29] square which we had just quitted.

"Let me see," said Holmes, standing at the corner, and glancing along the line; "I should like just to remember the order of the houses here. It is a hobby of mine to have an exact knowledge of London. There is Mortimer's, the tobacconist, the Suburban Bank, the Vegetarian Restaurant, and McFarlane's carriage-building depot. That carries us right on to the other block. And now, Doctor, we've done our work, so it's time we had some play. A sandwich, and a cup of coffee, and then off to violin land, where all is sweetness, and delicacy, and harmony, and there are no redheaded clients to vex[30] us with their conundrums."[31]

• •

"You want to go home, no doubt, Doctor," he remarked, as we emerged.

"Yes, it would be as well."

"And I have some business to do which will take some hours. This business at Coburg Square is serious."

"Why serious?"

"A considerable crime is in contemplation. I have every reason to believe that we shall be in time to stop it. But today being Saturday rather complicates matters. I shall want your help tonight."

"At what time?"

"Ten will be early enough."

"I shall be at Baker Street at ten."

"Very well. And, I say, Doctor! There may be some little danger, so kindly put your army revolver in your pocket." He waved his hand, turned on his heel, and disappeared in an instant among the crowd.

---

[28]abutted—lay alongside; adjoined
[29]stagnant—inactive; lifeless
[30]vex—to annoy
[31]conundrums—puzzling problems

Considerable Crime

It was a quarter past nine when I started from home and made my way across the Park, and so through Oxford Street to Baker Street. Two hansoms[32] were standing at the door, and, as I entered the passage, I heard the sound of voices from above. On entering his room, I found Holmes in animated conversation with two men, one of whom I recognized as Peter Jones, the official police agent; while the other was a long, thin, sad-faced man with a very shiny hat and oppressively respectable frock-coat.

"Ha! Our party is complete," said Holmes, buttoning up his pea-jacket, and taking his heavy hunting-crop from the rack. "Watson, I think you know Mr. Jones of Scotland Yard? Let me introduce you to Mr. Merryweather, who is to be our companion in tonight's adventure."

"We're hunting in couples again, Doctor, you see," said Jones in his consequential[33] way. "Our friend here is a wonderful man for starting a chase. All he wants is an old dog to help him to do the running down."

"I hope a wild goose may not prove to be the end of our chase," observed Mr. Merryweather gloomily.

"You may place considerable confidence in Mr. Holmes, sir," said the police agent loftily. "He has his own little methods, which are, if he won't mind my saying so, just a little too theoretical[34] and fantastic, but he has the makings of a detective in him."

"Oh, if you say so, Mr. Jones, it is all right!" said the stranger with deference.

"I think you will find," said Sherlock Holmes, "that you will play for a higher stake tonight than you have ever done yet, and that the play will be more exciting. For you, Mr. Merryweather, the stake will be some thirty thousand pounds; and for you, Jones, it will be the man upon whom you wish to lay your hands."

"John Clay, the murderer, thief, smasher, and forger. He's a young man, Mr. Merryweather, but he is at the head of his profession, and I would rather have my bracelets[35] on him than on any criminal in London. He's a remarkable man, is young John Clay. His grandfather was a Royal Duke, and he himself has been to Eton and Oxford.[36] His brain is as cunning as his fingers, and though we meet signs of him at every turn,

[32]hansoms—horse-drawn carriages
[33]consequential—self-important; showy
[34]theoretical—based on theory; imaginative; exploratory
[35]bracelets—handcuffs
[36]Eton and Oxford—prestigious schools in England

we never know where to find the man himself. I've been on his track for years, and have never set eyes on him yet."

"I hope that I may have the pleasure of introducing you tonight. I've had one or two little turns also with Mr. John Clay, and I agree with you that he is at the head of his profession. It is past ten, however, and quite time that we started. If you two will take the first hansom, Watson and I will follow in the second."

Sherlock Holmes was not very communicative during the long drive, and lay back in the cab humming the tunes that he had heard in the afternoon. We rattled through an endless labyrinth[37] of gas-lit streets until we emerged into Farringdon Street.

"We are close there now," my friend remarked. "This fellow Merryweather is a bank director and personally interested in the matter. I thought it as well to have Jones with us also. He is as brave as a bulldog, and as tenacious as a lobster if he gets his claws upon anyone. Here we are, and they are waiting for us."

We had reached the same crowded thoroughfare in which we had found ourselves in the morning. Our cabs were dismissed, and, following the guidance of Mr. Merryweather, we passed down a narrow passage, and through a side door, which he opened for us. Within

there was a small corridor, which ended in a very massive iron gate. This also was opened and led down a flight of winding stone steps, which terminated at another formidable gate. Mr. Merryweather stopped to light a lantern, and then conducted us down a dark, earth-smelling passage, and so, after opening a third door, into a huge vault or cellar, which was piled all round with crates and massive boxes.

"You are not very vulnerable[38] from above," Holmes remarked, as he held up the lantern and gazed about him.

"Nor from below," said Mr. Merryweather, striking his stick upon the flags which lined the floor. "Why, dear me, it sounds quite hollow!" he remarked, looking up in surprise.

"I must really ask you to be a little more quiet," said Holmes severely. "You have already imperiled the whole success of our expedition. Might I beg that you would have the goodness to sit down upon one of those boxes, and not interfere?"

The solemn Mr. Merryweather perched himself upon a crate, with a very injured expression upon his face, while Holmes fell upon his knees upon the floor, and, with the lantern and a magnifying lens, began to examine minutely the cracks

---

[37]labyrinth—maze
[38]vulnerable—exposed to attack

premises, and felt that I had solved my problem. When you drove home after the concert I called upon Scotland Yard, and upon the chairman of the bank directors, with the result that you have seen."

"And how could you tell that they would make their attempt tonight?" I asked.

"Well, when they closed their League offices, that was a sign that they cared no longer about Mr. Jabez Wilson's presence; in other words, that they had completed their tunnel.

But it was essential that they should use it soon, as it might be discovered, or the bullion might be removed. Saturday would suit them better than any other day, as it would give them two days for their escape. For all these reasons I expected them to come tonight."

"You reasoned it out beautifully," I exclaimed in unfeigned[46] admiration. "It is so long a chain, and yet every link rings true."

---

[46]unfeigned—not false; not pretended

Olympian

Dawn L. Watkins
illustrated by Paula Cheadle

A barreling start and a jump
Over porch rail and peonies,
Five long strides before the stump
Slides beneath, gone, the long drive
Grinding under the striving heels,
Up the hill past the gate, the barn,
Pounding heart and pumping knees,
Over the creek fence posts flash—steel
For the last hurrah of the marathon,
Slapping past corn as crowds roar, "Boy,
Hold on, do it, for gold, the prize!"
Hear cheers, and collapse into joy.

Sing the song, stand on glory rare:
Take roses, take medals with a bow.
Walk back, now breathing real air,
Planning for someday, somehow.

A Visit with a POET: Dawn L. Watkins

Eileen M. Berry

Interviewer: With what does a poem usually begin for you—an idea, an image, an unusual or musical word or phrase?

Watkins: It can begin in any of those places. Something I read or see or hear stirs me to write it down as a poem. But most often I believe a poem begins in the emotion of any of the above causes.

Interviewer: Are some subjects more "poetic" than others, or can anything be a good subject for a poem?

Watkins: There are, to be sure, some topics that are not worthy of a Christian writer's time. And of course every writer has topics that he finds inspiring that may not inspire others. I was born in Cogan House, Pennsylvania, and I tend to like the things I knew growing up— stars and mountains and snow. But overall, a good writer can find

beauty enough to inspire him nearly anywhere.

Interviewer: What is your favorite place to be when writing a poem? What surroundings do you find most inspiring?

Watkins: I don't have a favorite place. What I need is an idea. If I have an idea I really want to write a poem about, I think I could write it in the middle of a highway. I will say this, though: thinking about places where I grew up can put me in a good frame of mind for writing. But actually being in those places does not necessarily do the same thing.

Interviewer: Do your poems usually contain rhyme?

Watkins: Yes, most of my poems rhyme. But not in a formal pattern usually. I like every line to have a "partner" somewhere in the poem— it's like a game to find the best places for the rhymes to occur in the poem. I do use quite a bit of slant rhyme.[1]

Interviewer: In what other ways do you give your poems a musical quality?

Watkins: I don't think of my poems as being musical. At least, not in the ways that one usually thinks of musical writing with lovely liquid lines. When I write a poem, I am out for meaning mostly. But I do pay attention to line lengths and rhythm. I like poems to have a spoken quality. That is, to sound as though a person might just be talking to you.

Interviewer: Do you usually write poetry or free verse?

Watkins: I guess you could call what I write mostly a form of free verse. Although it has rhyme usually, it is not a standard pattern. And the rhythms usually serve that particular piece. I did invent a form, though, for fun, based on how bell ringers play their bells.

Interviewer: How do you determine the type of form you will use?

Watkins: That's a huge question. If the topic is very important, I think it's best to use a formal form, like a sonnet. If the poem is not for a particular occasion, but just to capture an idea, then I guess I ask myself first: does this seem to need a big space or just a small space? After that, the question is what will the tone be: serious, silly, or what? And then the fun begins—just playing with sound and tinkering with lines and the looks of the poem. It's then that meaning and form help invent each other.

Interviewer: Do you prefer to write serious or humorous poetry—or both?

Watkins: Oh, serious. It hardly ever just occurs to me to write something funny, even though I know most readers under twenty years old really prefer that kind. Serious poems just present themselves. Funny ones I have to be asked to write or purposely set out to do.

Interviewer: What goals or objectives do you have in writing poetry?

Watkins: I want to get better in my craft.[2] I really should be reading more poetry and studying more. I want to be able to write as well as I can, by God's grace. I think that

---

[1]slant rhyme—partial or imperfect rhyme
[2]craft—skill or occupation requiring skill

when God gives you a desire to do something, and you do it for the right reasons, it's a joy to you. Writing poetry is also a service to other people because it seems to make people happy to read poems that express thoughts they've had themselves.

Interviewer: What poets have you learned from in your own reading and study?

Watkins: Robert Frost, Gerard Manley Hopkins, George Herbert, and Emily Dickinson are the big ones. Also T.S. Eliot, Ezra Pound, and William Butler Yeats. The list could go on and on. Imitating poets you admire is a good way for beginning poets to learn.

Interviewer: What other advice would you give to young poets?

Watkins: Read the dictionary! Read the definitions.

Read the derivations.[3] Words are everything to a writer. If he were a carpenter, words would be the tools as well as the wood. I don't think it's possible for a writer to know too many words. If you don't find joy in just looking at words as words, you probably will have a hard time writing poetry.

And the other thing is to write from the outside and *then* the inside. Always be more aware of what's around you than you are aware of yourself. When something strikes you as needing a poem written about it, *then* you can look into your own experience to write about that universal[4] idea from a personal angle. This makes you useful. To start with yourself makes you less useful and, in the end, boring.

---

[3]derivations—roots; origins
[4]universal—applying to all members of a group

illustrated by Preston Gravely

Medals at the Paris Olympics

Steffi C. Adams

The best sprinters from England, Scotland, and Ireland took their places on the track for the 440-yard race. When the starting pistol fired, each runner scrambled for the inside lane. During the mad dash a Scottish runner was knocked off the track.

The fallen runner waited for a signal that he was not disqualified before jumping up and chasing the other runners, who were now twenty yards ahead of him. Swinging his arms wildly, the runner passed his opponents one by one. Soon he was in third place but appeared ready to drop. Then, forty yards from the fin-ish line, he threw back his head, opened his mouth, and ran even harder. He collapsed at the tape, having won the race by two yards in 51.2 seconds. As he was carried from the track, the crowd cheered the runner's bullheaded determination.

The runner, 21-year-old Eric Liddell, was a science student at the University of Edinburgh in Scotland. Although Eric excelled in all sports and was a champion short-distance runner, he planned to follow in his parents' footsteps by becoming a missionary to China. Running on the racetrack was important to Eric, but "running the Christian race" was even more important. At one race Eric, who had drawn the inside lane, offered to change places with a less-experienced runner. Another time, he talked with a runner whom the other runners ignored. And at every race he shook hands with all his competitors while they waited for the gun.

A friend once asked Eric if he had prayed about winning. He replied, smiling, "No, I have never prayed that I would win a race. I have, of course, prayed about the athletic meetings, asking that in this, too, God might be glorified."

When the British athletes were chosen for the 1924 Olympics, Eric Liddell was included. He would run in the 100-meter sprint and 200-meter races as well as in two relays. The 100-meter sprint was one of the most outstanding races in the games, and Eric wanted to win it for the glory of God and his country.

Then, a few months before the games began, Eric received the timetables for the events. The heats for several races, including the 100 meters and the relays, had been scheduled for Sunday. Eric did not hesitate. He just said quietly but firmly, "I'm not running on a Sunday."

His statement shocked the British athletic officials. Eric Liddell was the British champion. He was their best hope to win the 100 meters for the first time since the Olympic games had been revived in 1896. "You're throwing away a gold medal for Scotland and Britain," they said to him.

Pressure from all sides was put on Eric to change his mind. The newspapers criticized him harshly. Some of the athletes wondered aloud why he could not glorify God by winning the race for Him. The rest of the public taunted[1] Eric about his national honor, and some even called him a traitor.[2]

Though deeply wounded by the criticism, Eric remained steadfast. "The Sabbath is God's day," he replied to his critics. "I will not run."

Finally the officials asked Eric to train for the 400 meters, although it was not his best race. Eric eagerly agreed and sandwiched training time between his studies and his preaching at student rallies. A few weeks before the Olympics, his time for the 400 was 49.6 seconds, still almost 2 seconds behind the champions from other nations.

The Paris Olympics opened on Saturday, July 5, 1924, in the middle of a scorching heat wave. More than three thousand athletes marched into Colombes Stadium during the open-

[1]taunted—ridiculed or made fun of; harassed
[2]traitor—a person who betrays his or her country, a cause, or an idea

ing ceremony. These men and women from forty-four nations were the best in their fields.

As the games began, Eric was still under pressure to run in the 100 meters. Though impressed by his firm stand on his principles, most of his teammates still wanted him to win the gold medal for Britain. One of the British nobles even said to the team, "To play the game is the only thing in life that matters."

On that Sunday, July 6, Eric preached at a Scots church in Paris while another British athlete ran in the 100-meter heats. Then on Monday, the day of the final race, he sat in the stands and cheered the teammate to victory. The athlete received the gold medal that Eric might have won, had he run.

By Friday morning, July 11, Eric had won his own medal for the 200 meters. He had also won the quarterfinal heat of the 400 meters in 49.0 seconds. His critics, however, pointed out that he had won only a bronze medal and that at least three other athletes had better times in the 400-meter heats.

"He's lost any chance for the gold," they said, shaking their heads.

That Friday morning, when Eric left his hotel, the masseur³ for the British team handed him a note.

"Read this when you get to the stadium," he said.

As Eric dressed for the semifinal heat of the 400 meters, he remembered the note. Opening it, he read, "In the old book it says, 'He that honours me I will honour.' Wishing you the best of success always." These words stayed with him as he won the morning heat, then prepared for the final race later that day.

The stadium was like a furnace when the six finalists walked onto the cinder track for the 400-meter final. While Eric shook hands with his opponents before the race, the

³masseur—a man who massages athletes to relax their muscles and improve the circulation of their blood

2nd Queen's Own Cameron Highlanders marched around the stadium playing "The Campbells Are Coming" just to lift Eric's spirits.

The sound of the bagpipes faded away in the still air, and the runners took their assigned places on the track. Muscles tensed, Eric strained to hear the signal from his position in the outside lane.

The pistol cracked, and the runners thrust off from their starting holes. For the first half of the race Eric ran with electrifying speed. At the 200-meter mark he was three meters ahead of his nearest competitor.

"He can't keep running all out," said one spectator. "He'll drop back soon."

"I don't understand how he runs at all," said another man. "Such a poor, ungainly[4] style—hands clawing the air, legs wobbling, and face toward the heavens."

While the crowd watched, the runners came out of the bend. The American champion made his move and was soon only two meters behind Eric. Eric just threw back his head, opened his mouth, and spurted forward. He broke the tape at 47.6 seconds, his best time ever.

The crowd cheered and waved small Union Jacks. The loudspeaker crackled as the announcer said, "Hello, hello. Winner of the 400 meters: Liddell of Great Britain. The time, 47.6, is a new world's record."

The British and American flags were raised. Bands played anthems of both nations. Then Eric walked across the grass and down the stairs to the dressing room while the spectators applauded.

The masseur was waiting for him. "Aren't you going to the victory party?" he asked as Eric lay on the treatment table.

Eric smiled. "On Sunday I must deliver an address to all the athletes at a special church service, and I must pray and study the Scriptures. I can do no less after reading your most encouraging note."

When Eric returned to Scotland for his graduation from the University of Edinburgh, crowds cheered him, newspapers praised him, and dinners were held in his honor.

"Can you tell us the secret of your running success?" they would ask.

"The first half I run as fast as I can," Eric usually replied, "and the second half I run faster with God's help.

"The great thing for me," he often added, "is that when I stood by my principles and refused to run in the 100 meters, I found that the 400 meters is really my race. I would never have known that otherwise."

---

[4]ungainly—awkward in movement

The Prize of the High Calling

Laurie McBride

Fan mail poured in from all over. Many people expressed congratulations and asked for Eric's picture or his autograph. Good-naturedly, he sent off photographs to all his enthusiastic fans. In his spare time Eric spoke at crowded evangelistic meetings. He kept running, too, and won several more races after the Olympics. But Eric's heart turned more and more toward China. For a long time he had wanted to be a missionary. Now, as soon as his schooling was finished, he could join his parents and his brother Rob in their work with the Chinese people.

One night, after another celebration dinner, Eric announced his plans to become a missionary. The results were what he had expected. He received encouragement from his family, but there were also those people who thought he was throwing away a promising athletic career.

"Throwing away." That expression reminded Eric of Christ's words in Matthew 10:39: *He that findeth his life shall lose it: and he that loseth his life for my sake shall find it.* In his heart he felt a quiet peace: he would find his life in China.

Eric spent a busy year attending classes, preaching at meetings, and preparing for the mission field. Then, early in the summer of 1925, after a noisy farewell party at the train station, he left for China.

His first missionary assignment was to teach science and English at a college known as the foremost British school in northern China. The Anglo[5]-Chinese College was located in Tientsin. This large city sprawled along both banks of the Haihe River. Eric found that the people of Tientsin—merchants, sailors, coolies,[6] university professors, shopkeepers, and beggars—merely tolerated[7] the foreigners who lived among them. As the young missionary settled into his work, he found that under the formal politeness of the Chinese lay a growing anger. Unable to forget how the Western nations had cheated them out of their land, they included the missionaries in their bitterness toward any representatives of the West.

Although he arrived in the midst of this uneasy political situation, Eric became a popular speaker with the Chinese boys at the college, for they were attracted by his straightforward talks. He organized the sports activities and soon had his runners winning races. At the same time he won several sprints himself,

---

[5]Anglo—English speaking or of England
[6]coolie—a Chinese laborer
[7]tolerated—put up with; endured

racing against the soldiers from other countries that guarded the Europeans' houses.

One day, after winning a 400-meter race at an international sports meeting in Japan, he had only twenty minutes left to catch his boat back to China. Although he rushed off in a taxi, it arrived just as the boat pulled away from the wharf. But Eric was never one to give up. He threw his bags on deck and jumped for the boat with a flying leap that covered almost fifteen feet of water. It is no wonder that he was nicknamed the "Flying Scotsman." When people asked why he won so many races, he smiled and replied that he didn't like to be

beaten. He showed the same tenacity[8] in the way he went about courting Florence McKenzie, the lively, dark-haired daughter of Canadian missionaries. Eric had known her family for several years, but dating her was a problem. The custom of the day frowned upon the idea of a seventeen-year-old girl going out alone with a man. He handled the situation by inviting a whole group of her classmates along wherever he wanted to take Florence. His friends began to wonder at his new enthusiasm for escorting[9] a crowd of young people to

---

[8]tenacity—persistence; determination
[9]escorting—going along with; accompanying

tennis parties or to picnics, or to drink tea at a certain Tientsin café.

Eric kept it up until he was sure that Florence was the girl for him. Then, on one of their long walks, he told her how he felt. Even Florence was surprised to find out that he wanted to marry her, but she had admired him for a long time and agreed immediately. Eric lost no time in sending to Edinburgh for an engagement ring. He wanted one just like his mother's, with five diamonds in a row.

The young couple had to wait four long years while Florence finished her nurses' training in Canada. Meanwhile, when Eric took a year's furlough[10] in Scotland, the people gave him a heartwarming welcome, although it had been seven years since he'd won his Olympic medals.

He returned to China and his ministry. Five weeks after Florence returned from Canada, Eric married her. They settled happily into his newly redecorated house in Tientsin.

Eric enjoyed family life and was as proud as any father when his daughters, Patricia and Heather, were born. He wrote detailed letters to Scotland about the little girls' accomplishments and described the bicycle trips that they all took together.

During this time he learned more about the hundreds of Chinese who lived in the villages outside of Tientsin. The country had been thrown into turmoil by civil war. The armies of both the Nationalists and the Communists fought back and forth across the land, destroying it as they went. The careless marching feet of soldiers flattened the wheat crop. Whatever escaped the soldiers withered in the drought that gripped all of northern China. Marauding[11] bandits took advantage of the general confusion and robbed travelers and farmers alike.

When Eric visited Siaochang, where his brother Rob and a handful of other missionaries worked, he found that the tiny village houses hid whole families of terrified peasants who were both sick and starving. He had to do something to help, even though it meant separation from Florence and the girls. At the very least he could ease the villagers' suffering; perhaps he could show them the way to the One who could give them peace. Once again he had to listen to arguments from those who thought he would be wasting his talents on the simple peasants. After praying about his decision, he left his young family in the comparative[12] safety of Tientsin

---

[10]furlough—time off from missionary or military work to return home

[11]marauding—going through a land and robbing its inhabitants

[12]comparative—measured in relation to something else

and joined the mission work at Siaochang.

By now the Japanese had invaded northern China. The countryside was caught in the middle of a conflict between the Japanese troops and Chinese guerrilla units[13] that were trying unsuccessfully to force them back. The Japanese controlled the railways and many of the villages. The Chinese still had not given up the land in between, so the fighting continued. The hospital in the mission compound was always crowded, and the small church often sheltered frightened peasants during an attack.

Eric did the work of a traveling evangelist, bicycling on long treks with his interpreter to visit the fledgling Chinese churches. Usually he preached outdoors. This meant standing under the burning sun in summer or the pouring rain in winter. At the same time he had to keep out of the way of the Chinese guerrillas, the Japanese soldiers, and the roving bandits.

The Chinese came to love this quiet man with the shining blue eyes. In one of the dimly lit village homes he would share a meal of *chiao-tzus,*[14] and then, as visitors gathered, he would teach them hymns and tell Bible stories. They called him Li Mu Shi and eagerly welcomed his visits.

One time Eric took a twenty-mile trip over rutted roads, dodging Japanese troops along the way, to bring a wounded man to the hospital at Siaochang. He had found the man lying on a thin mattress on the dusty floor of a temple where he had suffered five days. No one had dared to take him into their home for fear of being shot by the Japanese. On the way back to Siaochang, Eric received an urgent message about another wounded man. He decided to make a detour to pick him up as well.

Villagers led him to a small, dark hut where a middle-aged man lay with dirty bandages wrapped around his neck. Eric was amazed to learn that the man, an artist, was still alive after having his neck slashed by a Japanese executioner's[15] sword. The wounded artist survived the jolting trip to the hospital in Siaochang, and the doctors managed to save his life. He became a Christian and painted several beautiful pictures to thank the missionaries for what they had done.

---

[13]guerrilla units—groups of soldiers fighting to overthrow an established government
[14]chiao-tzus—Chinese dumplings stuffed with meat, vegetables, and spices
[15]executioner—someone who puts condemned prisoners to death

When the time came in 1939 for Eric's next furlough, he took Florence and the two little girls to visit their families in Canada and Scotland. They returned to China and found that conditions had grown worse in Siaochang. The Nationalists and the Communists were still battling each other and trying to slow down the Japanese invasion at the same time. The Japanese were fighting both Chinese armies and getting closer and closer to Tientsin.

It soon became clear to Eric that his young family would not be safe in Tientsin, so he sent them home to Canada. But he stayed on in China, along with several other missionaries.

After the Japanese bombing of Pearl Harbor in December of 1941, the missionaries were taken to another part of the city. A little more than a year later—March 30, 1943—they marched the missionaries down to the railroad station and sent them to the Weihsien internment camp.[16] Held as prisoners, they would remain at the camp until the end of the war. It was a discouraging moment for the missionaries when they entered the camp. It was located in the gray buildings of an old, deserted mission. The furnishings and the plumbing had been destroyed, and someone had tossed broken desks, pipes, and beds into the streets. The compound itself was far too small for the hundreds of foreigners and their children who crowded into it.

That first night their meal consisted of bread and thin soup. After waiting in line for forty-five minutes, Eric ate it thankfully. He soon found that all the cleaning, cooking, and repairs in the camp had to be done by the prisoners themselves. Besides his chores, Eric taught classes in math and science and developed a camp sports program. Many people watched him with wide-eyed respect after hearing the whispered comment, "He's an Olympic champion—won a gold medal." He was shy about his accomplishments, however, and did not often talk about them.

Eric saw that the hundreds of children in the camp, especially the restless teenagers, needed a challenge to keep their minds off the boring routine of prison life. He organized a program of activities that ranged from chess tournaments to puppet shows. He sewed up their baseballs and tore his sheets into strips to mend their broken hockey sticks. At one time he almost sold his prized gold watch in order to buy softball equipment for the camp. The youngsters in the camp soon learned that they could count on Eric to join in a game or to arrange a round of baseball, even though he looked more tired every day.

[16]internment camp—prisoner of war camp

Those who wondered how he could do it all with such good spirits might have watched him early in the morning and found an answer. Eric had a lifelong habit of getting up at 6:00 A.M. for a quiet time with God. He would climb down from his top bunk and sit at a small Chinese table to pray and read his Bible by the light of a peanut-oil lamp. Only then would he face the demands of the busy day that lay ahead.

Eric Liddell did not live to see the end of the war. In January of 1945, he began to have headaches that grew worse and worse. Finally he had to lie in the camp hospital with his eyes bandaged to keep out the light. The stream of children and teenagers that came to cheer him found that he wasn't feeling the least bit sorry for himself. Instead, he wanted to talk about their problems, not his.

In February, a few short weeks later, he died of a brain tumor. Unable to believe that such a thing had happened, the whole camp reeled[17] with shock and grief. When the rest of the world heard of his death, countless admirers and friends mourned him deeply. Many of them sent his family messages that told how their lives had been touched by his powerful example.

As he lay dying, Eric whispered, "It's complete surrender." His words reveal the secret of a man who met every challenge by putting God first. He pressed toward the mark for the prize of the high calling in Christ Jesus. It was in surrender that Eric Liddell truly was a winner.

---

[17]reeled—staggered

552

Periodical Literature

Suppose you want to find out more about sports records or about mile running events. Your use of the card catalog or of the electronic database by computer would provide a list of many helpful books. But have you considered researching magazines or newspapers? They also publish a mass of information and photographs.

Periodicals for research

The publishing industry distributes magazines or newsletters that appeal to almost every hobby, profession, or special-interest group. There are magazines for doctors, fishermen, teachers, stockbrokers, architects, pilots, and so on.

The reading range is almost as broad as the subject matter. Some magazines are designed just for children. Others are designed for the interest and education of adults. There are also magazines for highly specialized professional or technical groups.

One specific advantage of using magazines is that they offer an emphasis on the present. This focus is helpful for ever-changing subjects such as medicine and technology.

Many times information on current events can be found only in magazines or electronic media. Books may not have been written yet on the subject you are researching. Other times it is interesting to read old magazines to find out what people thought about events and ideas at the time they were *news*.

We call magazines and newspapers *periodicals* because they come out at regular times, or periodically. As you visit the periodical room of the library, you will soon find those magazines that have special interest to you. Often the title of the magazine can be a good clue to the level of reading and technicality. For example, the word *digest* in the title indicates that the content is less technical, but the word *journal* indicates a higher reading level.

If the magazine is a recent issue, you will be able to get the individual magazine from the library. However, the issues for the previous years will be bound together by year in a hard cover like a book. You may even find older magazines and newspapers on microfiche or on microfilm.

The *Readers' Guide to Periodical Literature*

How do you find the precise information you need in stacks and stacks of magazines? Look for the *Readers' Guide to Periodical Literature.* Since 1898, editors at the H. W. Wilson Company have kept a record of articles published in many periodicals. Today this company continues to list currently released articles in the monthly paperback volumes of the *Readers' Guide.* At the end of each year, these volumes are combined and reissued as a single large hardbound volume.

The book *Readers' Guide to Periodical Literature* has one main section in which entries are recorded alphabetically by subject and by author. Look for the first word of the title, disregarding initial articles such as *a, an,* or *the.*

A smaller section in the back of the book lists book reviews.

In order to keep the book small enough to be usable, the authors of the guide use abbreviations. To assist the novice researcher, these authors provide a list of abbreviations that are used in the guide. Some of the common abbreviations are listed below.

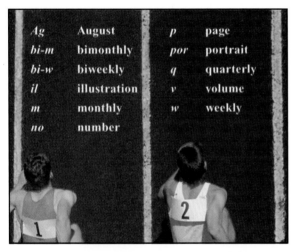

Ag	August	p	page
bi-m	bimonthly	por	portrait
bi-w	biweekly	q	quarterly
il	illustration	v	volume
m	monthly	w	weekly
no	number		

To find an article about a particular subject, first determine a time frame and keyword for your search. Remember that online services offer a wider range of dates in your search. For example, the paperback volume contains only the current month, and the bound volume for the particular year gives the records for only that year; but the online services can access records for several years.

A keyword may only be the beginning of your search. The term *See also* followed by another reference indicates related subject headings. When you look at the entry in *ATHLETICS,* you might find something like the following:

> ATHLETICS   *See also*
>   Athletes
>   Coaches
>   Track and field athletics

To learn about running events you would try the new entry word *Track and field athletics.*

When you do locate the entry that lists the articles you need, you will find each entry organized consistently. For instance, if an author has both *written* articles and had articles *written about him,* the titles of articles that the author wrote will come before the titles of those written about him.

Example:

> THURSTON, Paul, 1961-
>   Life of a Runner. il *Daily Life Digest* v51 no9 p110-13 S 21 2001
>
>   *about*
>
> Running for Gold [prospective medalist] T. Armstrong. por *Marathon Monthly* v93 no2 p25-6 F 2000

Subdivisions of a subject will be recorded alphabetically under the subject.

Examine the sample entry listings below.

TRACK & FIELD ATHLETICS
    See also
      Decathlon
      Javelin throwing
      Mile running

Accidents & injuries

Lighting the way [emphasis on safety when running] H. Carver. il *Marathon Monthly* v93 no6 p44-51 Je 2000

Competitions

Run for glory [Paralympic Games] D. Brown. il *Daily Life Digest* v35 no6 p90-5 Ag 24 2000

To the finish [preview to Olympic hopefuls] D. Sunderman. por *Marathon Monthly* v93 no7 Jl 2000
    See also
      Olympic Games

Equipment

If the shoe fits [guide for purchasing footwear] L. Haney. il *Fitness Weekly* v212 no10 p32-5 Mr 16 2001

In the above example, the subject—track and field athletics—is followed by several subdivisions, which are alphabetized. After you find the heading *Track and field athletics*, you can select from the subheadings: *Accidents and injuries, Competitions,* and *Equipment.* To find special information about Olympic runners, you could look at the articles listed under *Competitions.*

You may want to investigate further the topics of mile running and Olympic games. Look again at the example above. *See also* indicates other article titles or subjects that relate to the heading subject. In the entries shown, "*See also* mile running" and "*See also* Olympic games" give other subjects that might be of additional interest to those researching articles about track and field athletes.

You will also notice that information in the entries is always recorded in a certain order. The title will always come first, and it is sometimes followed by brackets that enclose an explanation of the title. Notice that the author's name is next and is punctuated by a period. If the article has illustrations or portraits, the abbreviation *il* or *por* will then be given. Then the name of the magazine is listed, which may or may not be abbreviated. The entry ends with numbers to show the volume number or date of the magazine, along with the page numbers of the article. The date may be given as the month and year or the month, day, and year.

article title—*Do sports activities build character?*

Do sports activities build character?
[evaluating the purpose of recreational sports]
S. O'Niel. il por *Fitness Weekly* v53 no7 p8-11+ S 14 2001

author—*S. O'Niel*

includes illustrations—*il*

includes portraits—*por*

magazine title—*Fitness Weekly*

date—*S 14 2001*

article continues on other pages—*+*

beginning page number—*8*

number—*7*

volume—*53*

Now you need to know whether or not the library you are using subscribes to the particular periodical you need. The librarian will have a list of the periodicals available.

Try choosing a subject that has been in the news within the past few years. Then research the subject using the *Readers' Guide*. Though your research will be directed by the subject matter, you may find yourself led down some interesting paths.

Laura Bridgman

John A. Matzko

Laura Bridgman (1829-1889)

The scarlet fever epidemic[1] of 1832 killed her brother. It killed two of her sisters. It nearly killed her. But two-year-old Laura Bridgman survived—just barely. The scarlet fever left her bedridden for five months—and totally deaf and blind forever.

Little Laura never again saw her mother's smile or heard her father's voice. She lived in a world as dark and silent as a cave. Her only communication was through simple touches. If someone pulled on her, she knew that someone wanted her to move. If she felt a pat on the head, she knew she had done something someone approved of. She could tell her mother by her smell and her father by the feel of his face. But most of the time, she was left alone in her silent black world.

Not knowing how to discipline a child with such special needs, Laura's parents soon found a strong-willed and hot-tempered seven-year-old in their house. She defied[2] everyone except her powerful New Hampshire farmer father. He held her tight when she flew into rages. Sometimes he stamped the floor himself, hard enough for her to feel the vibrations and realize he demanded obedience.

In the 1830s, few people tried to communicate with anyone deaf and blind. Most thought such a thing was impossible. Many people with disabilities were locked away with the insane, in places rarely cleaned and often not heated in the winter. But Samuel Gridley Howe of Boston thought differently. The same winter that Laura had been fighting scarlet fever, he had been opening the Perkins Institution, the first American school for the blind. It

---

[1]epidemic—a disease that spreads rapidly and widely
[2]defied—went against openly; challenged boldly

was an immediate success. And Dr. Howe was now, as always, looking for a new challenge.

When Dr. Howe heard about Laura in 1837, he drove his carriage to Hanover, New Hampshire, determined to bring her back to Perkins and to teach her to use language. He told her parents that not only would he be helping their daughter but he would also be proving to the world that people with special needs like Laura could learn to read and communicate with others. Although Laura's parents loved her dearly, they saw that they would not be able to help her as Dr. Howe could. They agreed that she should go to Perkins. But Laura, able to understand only that a stranger was taking her from her home, had to be almost dragged away.

Laura soon adjusted to her new surroundings at Perkins. Dr. Howe decided not to teach her any more signs like being patted on the head. Rather he set out to teach her the alphabet. He invented a system of raised type to represent letters and made labels for common objects. (The system originated by Louis Braille was not commonly used until later in the 1800s.) Then he brought the objects to Laura—a knife, a spoon, a key. Laura felt the items and their labels. Then Dr. Howe gave her a set of labels with the same words on them, but no objects.

Almost immediately, Laura realized that the word *key* on the separate label was the same as the word on the label attached to the key. She put the label on the already labeled key.

Laura quickly learned many words by this method of matching. Then one day, almost in a moment, she understood the combinations of raised type stood for *words,* not just objects, that she could use them to communicate her thoughts to others.

Laura Bridgman was extremely intelligent and proved to be an excellent student. Dr. Howe could not have hoped for a better proof for his theory that the physically disabled could learn to use language. Laura learned so fast that even he was surprised. She learned to use the manual alphabet (the method of forming letters by moving fingers against another person's hand). Within a year, only experts could follow the swift succession[3] of letters she pressed into their hands. She exhausted her teachers on walks—not because of the pace but because of the torrent[4] of questions Laura asked all five miles out and five miles back.

Like other students at Perkins, Laura learned to write on grooved paper. She wrote letters and kept records of her studies in literature, arithmetic, and geography. She also became skilled in needlework—so

[3]succession—series
[4]torrent—any rapid or rushing flow

skilled that her work sold well and made her money to live on.

Although Laura was quick in her studies and communicative, she still had trouble with quirks of language that sighted and hearing people take for granted. She asked how a river could run when it had no feet. She became indignant when someone told her that a preacher had gone to "marry a couple." She thought he had left to marry two wives. After learning the word *alone,* she described being with another person as *al-two*.

Dr. Samuel G. Howe (1801–1876)

Laura became famous, although she probably never realized how famous because Dr. Howe and his assistants tried to keep her from knowing how much attention her progress was attracting. They thought it would make her vain. News spread from the United States to Europe. The British writer Charles Dickens came to visit her. The King of Prussia awarded Dr. Howe a medal for his work. So many Americans came to see her on exhibition[5] days at Perkins that Dr. Howe had a barrier built to protect her from the crowds.

Dr. Howe was pleased with his success. He believed that man was naturally good. He saw his work with Laura as proof that given the right circumstances, human beings could better themselves no matter what obstacles[6] they faced. He was an upright person, even religious, but he was not a Christian. He dismissed the Devil and hell as superstitions and the Bible as interesting but full of errors. When Laura began to ask questions about religion and God, he ordered his assistants not to talk to her, but to tell her to ask him. He insisted that Laura could find a true knowledge of God by herself.

Laura knew she was a sinner. Her temper was still with her. Occasionally she struck another blind student

[5]exhibition—a public display
[6]obstacle—anything that blocks the way

or even a teacher. Once she broke a glass and lied about it. When confronted, she felt guilty. "Why do I have two thoughts?" she asked. "Why do I not do what my conscience tells me is right?"

Just as Laura had wanted to learn about the world around, she now wanted to learn about the world beyond her. She badgered[7] her teachers for answers. When one of the other students died, she asked Dr. Howe point blank: "Why does not God take us? Does He not want you and me? Why did God kill Orrin?" Dr. Howe could no longer avoid her questions, but his answers did not satisfy her.

Dr. Howe married Julia Ward (who later became famous herself as the author of "The Battle Hymn of the Republic"), and they went to Europe on a honeymoon. While they were away, Laura read a Bible that the American Bible Society had printed in Dr. Howe's raised letters. Another student in Perkins, a blind girl, may have told Laura the gospel for the first time as well during this time.

Later, when the Civil War began, Dr. Howe left Perkins to take on duties in the war. About the same time, Laura's sister Mary died. Laura was grief-stricken. A distant relative who was a Christian came to console her. She told Laura more about Jesus Christ who had died for all that they might accept Him as Savior. Laura listened raptly.[8] Later she wrote a letter to the pastor of the Baptist church in her hometown about her conversation that day with her relative: "Jesus spoke down from his throne into my heart . . .[and] I felt my soul fall into his hands."

Laura had never seen a baptism. When her pastor told her about it and asked her if she wanted to be baptized, she was afraid she would drown. But her mother and the pastor's wife reassured her. So Laura was baptized in a stream in Hanover on July 6, 1862. Dr. Howe was displeased with her decisions, but there is no evidence that he tried to change her mind or destroy her faith.

Laura's conversion was no mere intellectual experience. Her teachers saw a great change in her afterward. One wrote, "She never manifests anger now and is always kind and gentle. In speaking with me lately of her former experience and of the frequency with which she gave way to passion, she said, 'Sometimes I feel tempted to anger, but I can resist it now. God gives me strength.'"

Laura Bridgman wrote in other ways about her faith. She composed poems in praise of her Lord and out of joy for her new hope. Because of her handicaps, her poems have no regular rhythm or rhyme schemes. But they express her great faith and

---

[7]badgered—annoyed by asking many questions
[8]raptly—delightedly

her changed desires. Perhaps her most famous poem is "Holy Home."

Laura Bridgman went to her holy home on May 24, 1889. At her funeral at Perkins Institution, a bust[9] of Dr. Howe stood at the head of her coffin. He was the only man of his generation who could have reached her mind and taught her a way to communicate with the world. And despite his efforts to keep her from the gospel, his teaching her to communicate had helped her to find God.

[9]bust—sculpture of a person's head, shoulders, and the upper part of the chest

Holy Home

Heaven is holy home.
Holy home is everlasting to
   everlasting.
Holy home is summery.
I pass this dark home toward a light
   home.
Earthly home shall perish,
But holy home shall endure forever.
. . . .

By the finger of God my eyes and
   my ears shall be loosed.
With sweeter joys in heaven I shall
   hear and speak and see.
. . . .

Jesus Christ has gone to prepare a
   place for those who love and
   believe Him.
My zealous hope is that sinners might
   turn themselves from the power
   of darkness unto light divine.
When I die, God will make me
   happy.
In Heaven music is sweeter than honey,
   and finer than a diamond.

Moral Tone

Morgan Reed Persun
illustrated by Paula Cheadle

Did you recognize that the story of Laura Bridgman was a *biography?* Several people have written book-length biographies about this remarkable woman. But some people who have written biographies of her omitted everything about Laura's conversion to Christ.

Why is that? How could a biographer not mention Laura Bridgman's faith when it was central to her life? One answer is that authors write with certain ideas in mind. For instance, if an author wanted to write a book to show that deaf and blind people have achieved great things, he might focus his whole book on Laura Bridgman's accomplishments and never once mention her faith. Or an author who doesn't believe in God might leave out anything about Laura's faith because he thinks it unimportant.

The way an author handles a story will affect his reader. He can write stories that give people hope, or he can, if he chooses, write stories to make people despair. An author's work reflects his attitude. An author's attitude about what he writes creates the work's *moral tone.*

The Author's Attitudes

An author's moral tone usually will be affected by his beliefs. If he does not believe in God, he may look at life—at his experiences as well as the condition of the world—and perhaps he will think that life has no purpose. Perhaps he will think that man can never have peace or hope.

If he is a skilled writer, he can then write a story that says the same thing. He may write a book in which all the characters—even the hero—spend the rest of their lives in misery. However, the same characters in the hands of a writer who believes in God would be a very different story.

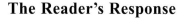

Authors write stories with specific purposes in mind. They want their stories to convince the reader of certain things. Christian writers want to convince their readers of the goodness, holiness, and mercy of God. They sometimes want to convince readers that all men need to be saved by faith in the blood of Christ. Just as Christian authors want to convince the reader of God's love, so some godless authors may want to convince their readers that life is hard and ultimately empty.

If you read something that goes against what you believe or think is right, you need to stop and consider the author's purpose. He may have engineered a whole story to convince you of something you disagree with.

The Reader's Response

Remember that all authors try to represent their own view of reality in their writing. Even if the setting of a story is something unreal like a fictional planet, an author still uses believable characters and causes us to care about them in order to make some point about real life. The reader's job is to judge the value of that point for himself.

Everything you read should be evaluated against some trusted standards. It is not wise to refuse to read anything that has a reference to something sinful in it. Where would that policy leave God's Word, with its many examples of sin, its results, and forgiveness for wrongdoing? It is better to ask "How does what I am reading compare to the way God's Word handles such things?"

One question to ask yourself is "Why is this here?" The Book of Esther, for example, says that Haman was "full of wrath" and plotted to "lay hands on Mordecai." Do you stop reading because plotting murder is evil? No, because since you are reading the Bible, you know that you will learn what happens to evil in the end. For other books and stories to measure up to the Bible's standards, they too should mention wrong in order to show it for what it is. So—should you read on to see what happens in some other book?

To help decide, ask yourself another question: "Is this bad thing mentioned just enough to let me know what's happening?" The Book of Esther does not spend a long time describing Haman's evil thoughts. To do so would be to give too much attention to the sin. Some books may make sin look bad in the end, but they give too much detail about the sin first, and so cannot measure up to God's way of thinking. Talk about the story to parents or your teachers and see what they think.

If you decide to finish the piece, at last ask, "How does the whole story make this bad thing look? Does it make sin look bad and show its terrible results? Does it make righteousness look appealing and show the pleasant end of right action?" When Haman plots against Esther, his evil repulses us and he is punished in the end. If such revenge had succeeded, the story would have a bad moral tone, rather than the perfect tone it does have. Do you not end the Book of Esther wanting to be like Esther rather than Haman?

Should a Christian read anything he wants then? Consider Philippians 4:8. "Of good report" means "having recognized value." There are books and magazines that you know immediately are not worthy of a Christian's mind. Those should be dismissed without question. Others, whether written by Christians or non-Christians, must be judged one by one against biblical standards. Every Christian must study and set such standards for himself before God. Always be asking yourself as you read, "Is this lesson, presented this way, something I would want to be reading if Christ walked in?"

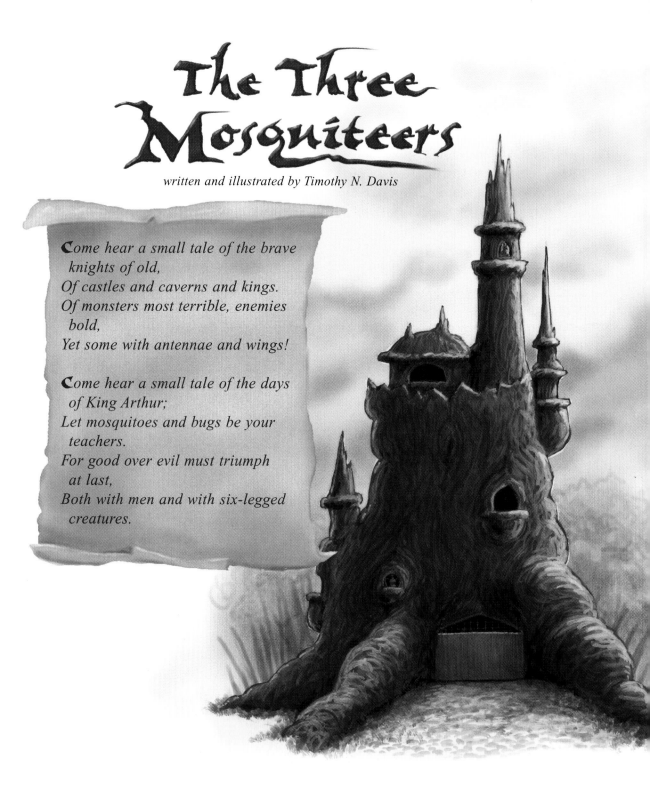

The Three Mosquiteers

written and illustrated by Timothy N. Davis

Come hear a small tale of the brave
   knights of old,
Of castles and caverns and kings.
Of monsters most terrible, enemies
   bold,
Yet some with antennae and wings!

Come hear a small tale of the days
   of King Arthur;
Let mosquitoes and bugs be your
   teachers.
For good over evil must triumph
   at last,
Both with men and with six-legged
   creatures.

Traitor in Towerwood

It seemed as if the clouds were lifting over Towerwood. The victorious mosquiteers[1] were returning home with yet another slain dragonfly to present to their gracious Queen Ladybug. As they approached the tree-stump castle, many insects rushed out to greet their heroes. Young aphids danced gleefully around the mosquitoes' feet while lady butterflies blushed at their courage and charm. The old walking stick struck up a joyous chorus, and everyone joined in. Before long, the happy commotion wafted up to the topmost tower of Towerwood, where Queen Ladybug waited, along with her stepdaughter, Princess Swallowtail, and the Queen's most trusted adviser, Sir Lucius Stinkbug.

Princess Swallowtail fluttered over to the window. "Mother, Mother! They're back! And they've killed another dragonfly!"

"That's wonderful, dear!" The Queen sighed. "Perhaps my husband's dream of a safe, peaceful kingdom in Towerwood may someday come to be." Then she closed her eyes, as if even those few words had been an effort.

"Ah, Milady," breathed Lucius, bending over the sickly Queen, "never was there a more noble king

than your husband—may he rest in peace."

Princess Swallowtail spoke again before Sir Lucius could say more. "Mother, they're just wonderful! So handsome and dashing!"

"Especially Marcelle," continued Queen Ladybug. "Am I right, dear?"

Princess Swallowtail blushed as only a royal butterfly could.

Just then the drawbridge was opened. Ant-knights riding fine white horseflies escorted the three heroes into Towerwood. Trumpets sounded and banners waved. Leaning on Princess Swallowtail's arm, the Queen entered the throne room, where everyone waited in respectful silence. Then the heroes, Marcelle, Jacques, and Pierre, entered the throne room with much pomp and circumstance.[2]

Marcelle, the eldest, spoke first. "Your royal Highness, in your service we have slain a dragonfly and thus hope your kingdom is the safer for it."

"I thank you most sincerely," said the Queen. "And my kingdom thanks you!" At that she stood, leaning on Sir Lucius's arm, and clapped, creating an eruption of

---

[1]mosquiteer (mŏs´ kē tēr´)
[2]pomp and circumstance—a show of splendor or formality

enthusiastic applause from all. Except for Sir Lucius. But then, of course, he was helping his Queen.

Suddenly a stern ant-knight entered. "Your Highness." His serious manner brought a sudden halt to the celebration.

"What is it, Captain?" asked the Queen.

"Your Highness," began the ant, "we have just captured a termite spy outside the gatehouse. A document was found hidden in his armor that we thought deserved your immediate attention. It mentions something of a traitor in Towerwood."

Traitor? The word raised many antennae in the room. Soon a loud whisper seemed to fill the chamber.

The Queen's eyes grew wide. "Quite right, Captain. Take the spy to the dungeon and bring me the document at once."

Whispers flew like the wind through the royal chamber. You see, many had suspected the possibility of a traitor for a long time. During the past several years, the termites' domain had been inching ever closer to Towerwood. Their advances at times had been surprisingly rapid, as if they had known just where and when to attack. And their wicked advances had culminated[3] in the capture—and most assured assassination,[4] for the termites never kept prisoners—of Towerwood's noble king. Yes, per-haps there really *was* a traitor in Towerwood.

The ant-knight returned before long, carrying the document with him. The Queen took it from him. As she read, her already pale face turned paler still, almost gray. "I—I hesitate to reveal what it says," she faltered.

"Perhaps you had best reveal it to me alone, your Ladyship." Sir Lucius sidled up to the Queen's side. She whispered in his ear, but Sir Lucius repeated the words aloud, as if over-come by amazement and horror. "The three mosquiteers? In the ser-vice of the terrible Queen Alexis?"

Uncertain mutters filled the chamber in the confusion that ensued.[5] "Our heroes? Employed by Alexis?"

"Can it be?"

Queen Ladybug was distraught. Carefully she scrutinized the three mosquito brothers before her. "And what have you to say to the charge of this incriminating[6] document?"

Marcelle responded solemnly. "Your royal Highness, your three humble servants are not traitors. We have never been in the employ of the wicked Queen Alexis."

"Very well," said the Queen, though her voice sounded uncertain.

---

[3]culminated—came to a climax
[4]assassination—the murder of a high official
[5]ensued—followed; resulted
[6]incriminating—accusing, causing to look guilty

She dismissed all the assembly except the Princess and the stinkbug. Then she leaned back heavily on her throne, as if the recent news had been too much for her.

As soon as the great hall was vacated, Princess Swallowtail cried out, "Certainly you cannot believe a word of any document that that grotesque[7] creature would be carrying, Mother!"

Sir Lucius moved in to calm the frustrated young butterfly. "Your gracious mother is most wise to be suspicious of any potential threat to her kingdom, my dear Princess. You must go rest and calm yourself, child. Perhaps then you can be more objective[8] concerning this matter."

"More objective? Mother, that's ridiculous!"

"Now, Swallowtail, Sir Lucius is right—you go calm yourself, dear." And the Princess left the room in a flutter, as only a royal butterfly could.

"These mosquiteers," Sir Lucius began. "They seem to be so loyal . . . and yet . . ." He paused and shook his head. "Forgive me my speculation, Milady, but doesn't it seem as if the mosquiteers have been more zealous of late against dragonflies than against our most threatening enemies, the termites . . . Ah, perhaps I speculate too much, your Highness."

"Perhaps," replied the Queen, almost in a trance.

"But maybe," continued Lucius, "it would be *easier* for the termites

themselves to attack Towerwood if they didn't have to concern themselves about dragonflies." The stinkbug crept over to the window. Yet still he watched the Queen from the corner of his eye.

Suddenly the Queen spoke. "I must know if Marcelle and his brothers are indeed loyal to me. But how can I ascertain[9] it?" She rubbed her furrowed brow.

"Perhaps a test," ventured Lucius. "A difficult test of their loyalty—maybe a quest of sorts."

"A quest. Yes," said the Queen. "Perhaps an attack on the termites themselves."

"Most royal Highness, forgive me, but if indeed they *are* employed by the termites, the termites could cooperate with them to bring about their success, and thus falsely restore your trust."

"Yes, you're right." The Queen paused, bewildered. "Lucius, could you develop an adequate quest? Then I shall present it to them on the morrow."

"Milady, I'd be most honored to serve you so," replied the stinkbug. Then silently he slipped out of the room.

---

[7]grotesque—very ugly or strange
[8]objective—impartial; open-minded
[9]ascertain—to find out

fore the furious survivor could figure out what had happened.

The mosquiteer had evened the odds. But now an enraged mantis hunted him, consumed not only with hunger but also with the desire for revenge.

Meanwhile, deep in the dark well of Nocturna Cave, Jacques prepared himself for a dramatic exit. Perhaps the bats were sound sleepers, but their large ears seemed to indicate otherwise.

Wings humming, Jacques flew up and out of the well, into the cavern

chamber. One look at the ceiling spelled trouble. One after another, the bats dropped into flight. Their high-pitched radar chirps honed in on the intruding mosquito. Jacques flew loops, zigzags, and swirls, avoiding a dozen bats or more, but scores more followed behind! He knew he would never make it out that way. Quickly he dove for a wall and found safety in a narrow crack.

The mosquiteer pressed against the cold rock wall. Several clawed wings scraped inside the crack in search of the tasty morsel. But in here their radar couldn't help them. All the same, this was no comfortable haven[22]—he had to get out! Jacques thought for a moment. Maybe he could hitch a ride.

He was glad that the cave was so utterly black. The darkness made the bats almost blind—they would have to rely on their radar to find such a tiny invader as he was.

Jacques tore a strip off his cloak and tied it to his sword. Then he wadded up another torn strip and threw it out of the crack. The bats dove after it. The brave mosquiteer then leapt onto one of the searching wings just as it was retreating from the crack. He was on board—and hanging on for all he was worth! Gradually he inched his way onto the bat's neck. Then he reached his sword out in front of the bat's mouth

and fluttered the cloth tied to the blade's tip.

The bat perceived the cloth as an insect flying just out of reach, and so it flew furiously to apprehend[23] the morsel. Jacques flicked the cloth back and forth—the bat darted right and left after it. "Hi, ho, Nellie! Let's get out of here!" cried the mosquiteer, and he steered the bat right out of the cave. So fast did the bat fly after the elusive[24] cloth that his comrades were left far behind him.

Once out of the cave and in the dazzling glare of the late afternoon sun, Jacques stuffed first one of the blinded bat's ears and then the other with remaining bits of his cape. "Don't want you following me that hard, now do I," he said, hopping off the confused creature's back and leaving the radarless bat to bump and bounce its way back home.

While Jacques was completing his quest, Pierre remained in a rather tight spot, held captive in a woodsman's beard by a crow's unresting eye. When the woodsman's snores stopped, Pierre didn't want to still be in that beard. But neither did he want to be in the stomach of a certain crow.

---

[22]haven—place of safety and rest
[23]apprehend—catch
[24]elusive—difficult to catch

Suddenly an idea struck the mosquiteer. He tied a loop in one strand of the woodsman's long beard. Grasping it, he flew up in full view of the crow. When the bird swooped in for attack, Pierre flipped the looped hair around its beak and hung on tight. When the bird jerked, the hair came loose. Pierre slipped the hair free from the crow's beak and flew upward with it in hand. The confused crow looked around for its prey.

The bleary-eyed woodsman sprang up from his nap and gave the crow a clout with his knobby hand. Pierre darted toward the window, hair in hand. "What's this?" the angry man bellowed when he saw his precious hair floating away. The woodsman scrambled to the window and lunged after the mosquiteer and his prize. "Come back with that hair! Crow, after him!" But the crow had awkwardly landed on the hearth, its head still ringing.

Pierre fled from Starkwood speedily. The last thing he heard was the heavy footsteps of the woodsman in clumsy pursuit.

Back in Deadfern Forest, Marcelle took to the air. The mantis unfolded her wings and leapt up to follow, chasing him relentlessly. But Marcelle's constant dodging and weaving through the junglelike undergrowth kept her back. Her wings were too long for many nooks and crannies that Marcelle squeezed through.

But no matter how strong and quick he was, Marcelle couldn't keep up the chase forever. Apparently the furious mantis could.

Temporarily losing his beastly pursuer in a patch of briars, Marcelle dove into some tall grass to rest. He had scarcely caught his breath when he heard a rustle behind him. An insect sprang from the grass toward Marcelle. It was Jacques!

"My dear Marcelle, that's a mighty mean mantis up there." Jacques laughed and brushed off his cloak. "Took after me with a vengeance."[25]

"Jacques! I'm thankful you've come! You've completed your quest?"

"Yes. It nearly drove me batty, though. Can I help you out here?"

"Most assuredly, good fellow. By myself I'd have been completely worn out before long. But together perhaps we can turn the tables on her. Especially if she thinks there's only *one* mosquito out here."

"Ah, yes. Sounds good. One of us can turn her in circles up there, while the other meanders peacefully

[25]vengeance—viciousness; violence

through the underbrush. But how can we *rid* ourselves of this nasty wench?"[26]

Marcelle looked thoughtful. "Perhaps we can put her wrath to some good purpose before we get to that. Let's lead her toward Mortazylum."

Jacques responded with a smile. "A stroke of genius, my brother. Here, you take it easy. I'll tend to sister mantis for a while." And with that, Jacques shot up into the air. Soon the irate[27] mantis was tailing him tirelessly. The mosquiteer dodged and looped through a host of aerial maneuvers. Briars and sticks clipped the larger winged mantis in her attempt to follow. Jacques kept up his furious pace until his wings ached; then he dove for the underbrush. After a moment, Marcelle emerged, and the chase was on again. Thus, gradually, they worked their way toward the termites' domain.

At the edge of Deadfern Forest, Pierre joined them. The third mosquiteer was glad to take his turn as acrobatic bait, luring the angry mantis onward. Marcelle and Jacques buzzed along slowly together.

"How glad I am that Pierre showed up," sighed Jacques. "It seems that mantis is as strong as a yoke[28] of oxen. She nearly caught me my last turn at it."

"I only hope she still has something left for the termites," responded Marcelle with a weary smile as he took his turn at the mantis relay flight.

"Hope *she* has something left? What about us? I feel as if my wing sockets are out of joint!" Pierre was rubbing his sore shoulders.

As the last bit of sunlight hovered on the horizon, the mosquiteers (with their angry traveling companion) arrived at Mortazylum. Its craggy towers loomed black against the darkening sky.

Without a moment's delay, the three mosquiteers enacted their plan of attack. All three joined together in flight, mocking the mantis. As they expected, she was even more enraged by the trickery that now unfolded before her. Straight toward the castle wall they flew, the mantis's hot breath on their backs. At the last moment, they split apart, Marcelle left, Pierre right, and Jacques straight up. Sudden confusion overtook the mantis. Her wings twisted and she made an awkward landing on the wall— THUD!

Immediately a termite guard below signaled the alarm—mantis

---

[26]wench—a cruel and malicious woman
[27]irate—furious
[28]yoke—a pair of animals joined by a crossbar on a harness and working together

582

attack! Every weapon in the termites' mighty arsenal was directed against the crazed predator.[29] The mosquitoes now forgotten, the terrible mantis turned her wrath against her new tormentors. It was instant bedlam![30]

"I say, she'll give them a good fight," said Jacques.

"I hope she takes a good many of those assassins down with her," panted Pierre.

"We must leave them to themselves, good fellows," Marcelle said. "For if ever we're to find the evidence to clear our name before the Queen—"

"And Sir Lucius," sneered Jacques.

"Yes, the 'noble' stinkbug—the time and place is here and now!"

Into an open portal crept the three mosquiteers. Mortazylum, the very domain of Alexis and her murderous band of termites, seemed to hold the only hope for proof of their innocence. This dark castle could turn a key to their success, if it did not become instead a doorway to their doom.

---

[29]predator—an animal that lives by catching and eating other animals
[30]bedlam—chaos; noisy uproar

Hearts Great and Bold

The hours passed. After a long, restless night, the hopeful Princess Swallowtail gazed anxiously out her window into the misty early-morning dawn. Just after sunrise, she observed two silhouettes gliding through the morning mist.

"It must be they," the Princess breathed. She ran for her mother's room. "Mother, they're returning! I'm nearly sure I saw them coming! There were only two of them, but the appointed hour has not yet arrived. I'm sure all will return by then."

A great reception[31] was quickly prepared. As the members of the court gathered in the throne room, two mosquiteers, Jacques and Pierre, appeared before them. The heroes looked weary and worn. Silently they bowed to the Queen.

"Gracious Queen," began Pierre, "though a strand from the woodsman's beard was plucked and your servant carried it away in safety, I now return without it, having had great need to use it along the way."

Sir Lucius Stinkbug stepped forward and declared, scoffing, "You carried it away in safety, did you? You could have rested in a swamp and come back with nothing but words! Besides, even if you did have it, only traitorous thought could have convinced you of a greater need than

presenting the woodsman's hair for a harp to quicken the spirits of your Queen. You have returned a failure at your given quest!" And he stepped back in triumph.

The Queen bowed her head. In a broken voice she asked, "And you, Jacques?"

"Gracious Queen, I fear that I have fared no better than my brother. For I escaped Nocturna, my bag filled with the water from the well. And yet I had need to give it away."

"What!" shouted Lucius. "Give away a gift intended for the Queen? You are indeed no better than your brother!" Sir Lucius then turned to the Queen. "Most gracious Highness, these mosquiteers have proven themselves disloyal. Not only by action but also by the very words of their mouths they are condemned. The darkest dungeon would be a merciful sentence."

"No!" shouted the Princess. "There is still time before the appointed hour. And Marcelle has not yet returned." The butterfly pleaded with Queen Ladybug. "Surely, Mother, you can wait just that much longer before passing sentence."

The Queen covered her face in a tear-stained handkerchief. Sir Lucius slid to her side. "Milady, Marcelle

---

[31]reception—a social gathering in honor of someone

has without doubt fled, a traitor as the rest." The stinkbug narrowed his eyes and sneered at Princess Swallowtail's devotion.

Just then there was a great commotion by the gate of Towerwood. The noise of it sounded even in the throne room.

"What's that?" Antennae lifted in anticipation all around the room.

"Marcelle!" cried the Princess. "It's got to be Marcelle!" Princess Swallowtail rushed to the window and strained to see through the still-shrouding mist. There was a great crowd of insects bustling about and cheering.

The expectant throne room buzzed with speculation—until with the blast of a trumpet the doors opened wide.

Triumphantly, the herald[32] announced the arrival. "HIS MOST ROYAL MAJESTY, *THE KING!*"

Indeed it was the noble King of Towerwood, Queen Ladybug's long-lost husband. He was followed by none other than Marcelle, the mosquiteer.

The whole room stood speechless, wide-eyed, and open-mouthed. The Queen looked as if she were about to faint as the King stepped up beside her. Then he spoke with a deep, clear voice. "Only one need fear my return. Rejoice with me, loyal subjects, for I am no ghostly apparition,[33] but your true King, es-

caped from the dark dungeon of Mortazylum, sole prisoner of the evil Alexis. I escaped with the help of these three brave mosquiteers here before you.

"Last night, Mortazylum was attacked by a dying mantis, led to the place by my rescuers. Entering discreetly[34] in the midst of the turmoil, they happened upon my dark prison within. They bound my guards with a cord so strong, methought it must be a strand of the mighty old woodsman's beard. Then they gave me refreshing drink, so clear I took it to be from deep Nocturna's well. With stealth we all escaped to stand before you now."

"Then 'tis true," sighed Queen Ladybug as she stood to embrace her beloved husband, and her spirits revived within her. And the hall was suddenly filled with shouts of joy and "Long live the King!"

Then the King held up his arms. The room quieted. He spoke again. "I mentioned that *one* need fear my return." The King suddenly pointed toward the back wall. "That one now creeps toward yonder door. Guards! Apprehend him!"

Immediately Sir Lucius Stinkbug was shackled and bound in chains by four palace guards.

"Tomorrow," continued the King, "you, Sir Lucius, shall be released—

---

[32]herald—a person who proclaims important news
[33]apparition—a haunting or disturbing image
[34]discreetly—secretly; quietly

released to your beloved termite queen, Alexis! We shall see how *she* deals with your failures."

As guards escorted the white-faced stinkbug to prison, the celebration was rekindled.

"Long live the King!"

The crowd honored their brave heroes. "Three cheers for three brave mosquiteers!" they shouted.

"All for one and one for all!" came from the three triumphant brothers.

All day long and on into the night, the castle Towerwood rejoiced in its wonderful turn of events. There were feasts and music, singing and laughing such as hadn't been heard in years.

Even today you might hear some minstrel singing of that happy time, the beginning of Towerwood's great kingdom.

Here ends a small tale of three
    brave knights of old,
Mosquiteers Jacques, Marcelle,
    and Pierre.
With minds that were keen and
    with hearts great and bold
They won fame and renown
    everywhere.

Here ends a small tale of a
    kingdom returned,
Restored to a true, noble king.
The good were rewarded; the
    lessons were learned.
Thus endeth the song that I sing.

IT MUST NOT FAIL!

Gloria Repp

illustrated by Chris Koelle

Abbie Burgess stood on tiptoe, high up on the balcony of the lighthouse at Matinicus Rock, and strained her eyes to watch the glinting speck that was her father's sail. As it disappeared into the endless ocean blue, she sighed and turned to leave. It must be time for Mother's medicine. Suddenly she felt the cold fingers of a freshening breeze against her face. She studied the gulls soaring high overhead into scudding[1] gray clouds, and she frowned. A storm was coming.

Before Father had set sail today, he had talked to her very seriously. Mother was too sick to be told how low they were on supplies—dangerously low—with the long winter still ahead. Father knew Abbie could tend the lighthouse for the few days it would take him to sail twenty-five miles to the mainland for food, oil,

and chicken feed. She'd never forget his quiet words: "I can depend on you, Abbie."

She glanced at the gleaming light beside her, at the sturdy home below that housed her invalid[2] mother and three little sisters, and at the other lighthouse, built into the far end of their house. "It's a good thing Father taught me to take care of the lights while he was away on lobstering trips," Abbie thought. "I can do it. I'll keep the lights burning until he comes back."

That stormy January of 1856, Abbie Burgess was only seventeen years old.

She hurried down the steeply curving steps of the lighthouse to fix supper and prepare for the coming storm. After supper, she took a few handfuls of chicken feed out to the

[1]scudding—moving quickly
[2]invalid—sick, weak, or disabled

old wooden building that sheltered her pet chickens.

"Come, Anna, Emma, Martha; come, Jane and Priscilla," she called. "Oh, Priscilla, when will you learn to obey?" she scolded the old hen sulking in the corner. A blast of icy wind shook the coop, reminding Abbie of the rising storm. "Good night, girls," she called hastily over her shoulder.

The next day the storm grew more violent, the sound of its roaring filling the house. Abbie hurried through her housework; then she polished and filled the twenty-eight lamps in the twin lighthouses so that they would shine brightly that night.

As the tide came in, great breakers surged wildly around the rocky ledge that was Matinicus Rock Station, and Abbie began to worry about her chickens. They were such precious pets in this lonely place; and besides, the family needed their eggs. She looked out of the window at the towering waves pounding the rocks, the waters driven higher and higher by the howling wind.

Suddenly she couldn't bear the thought of losing them. Snatching up a basket, she splashed her way to the chicken coop. Anxiously she called them as she always did, "Anna, Emma . . ." But where was Priscilla? No time to hunt for her now. Abbie quickly stuffed the four squawking hens into her basket and struggled

back to the house through knee-deep water. Just as she burst through the door, her sister cried, "Abbie, look!" A great wave had crashed against the chicken house, shattering it. Thankfully, Abbie hugged the bedraggled hens to her. At least she had saved these four.

That night, after tucking her younger sisters into bed, Abbie wearily climbed the tower stairs to check on the light. "Stay awake," she commanded herself. "Remember the light. It must not fail." Carefully, she refilled the lamps with oil and trimmed their wicks. Then, through the long, icy hours of darkness, her only company the thundering waves, Abbie watched over the light—her light now.

It guarded the entrance to Penobscot Bay and beamed a warning to all the ships sailing up and down the Maine coast. She thought of the graceful clipper ships she had seen skimming the waves on their way to China, and the sturdy schooners, busily carrying people and cargo to Boston and New York, or even Europe. All these depended on her light to warn them of the dangerous reefs[3] near the rock. If the light should fail . . . Abbie shuddered as she remembered the tales she had heard of mighty ships that

---

[3]reefs—strips or ridges of rock, sand, or coral at or near the surface of a body of water

588

had been smashed against rocks just like these.

On the fourth morning at dawn, as Abbie stumbled sleepily down the lighthouse stairs, she discovered that the sea had swept completely over her rocky island. To her dismay, not a stick was left of the old wooden house or the chicken coop. And her own house was flooded with water. Swiftly she moved her small family into one of the stone lighthouse towers, hoping that it could withstand the battering of the sea that swirled around its base.

And then the weary days and nights dragged into a week of exhausting work. Still the storm raged. She knew her father was desperately trying to get back to them, and proudly, doggedly,[4] she tended the lights. That week became two, three, then four weeks; not once did the light fail. At last the sea calmed down enough for Captain Burgess to land his little dory on the slippery rocks below the lighthouse. How proud he was of his daughter's bravery during that terrible storm.

Only a year later, Abbie was stranded by another storm and again was responsible for keeping the light. For twenty-one dismal[5] days, Abbie stayed at her post while caring for her mother and sisters, hoping her father hadn't drowned on his trip for supplies. As their small supply of food dwindled,[6] she rationed[7] the family to one cup of cornmeal and one egg each day, so they managed to stay alive until her father returned.

By 1861, when Captain Burgess resigned his post as keeper of Matinicus Rock Light, Abbie was twenty-two and had come to love her barren little island, inhabited only by gulls and strutting puffins. So when the new lightkeepers, the Grants, moved in, she was happy to stay and help them get used to the twin lights. A year later she married their son, Isaac. Soon she was officially appointed Assistant Keeper to the light and was rearing her four children while performing her duties.

For more than thirty-five years Abbie tended the lights, at Matinicus Rock and later at White Head Light. She died in 1892 at the age of fifty-three, after spending all her life as a lighthouse keeper. A miniature lighthouse marks her grave in Spruce Head Cemetery, not far from the lights she loved so well.

Today, Abbie Burgess Grant is remembered as the youngest heroine of the U.S. Light Service, and we honor her for her courage and her faithfulness in serving those who depended on her for their very lives.

---

[4]doggedly—not giving up; persistently
[5]dismal—showing or causing gloom or depression; dreary
[6]dwindled—grew less; became smaller
[7]rationed—limited the amount of something each person could use or have

SONS OF A MIGHTY FATHER

Jeri Massi   *illustrated by Preston Gravely*

Trial of the Faith

Aesculapius Gaius looked over the gardens and hedges of the plain. Shadows had fallen; the trees looked like spires. The first stars were still pale. The boy drew fresh spring air into his lungs as a thirsty man drinks water, for it was all he would get until the next day.

He slung the leather bag over his shoulder and groped through the tangled undergrowth of the deserted field. At last he touched cool, rough mortar.[1]

Careful not to stub his sandaled toes, he climbed around the broken and moldering rim of the entrance.

---

[1]mortar—a building material made of sand, water, lime, and sometimes cement

He felt his way along a steeply slanting passageway. Almost instantly the tunnel became dark, and the hot, dry air from below came up against him like a wall.

The city's own guard, encountering the darkness that weighed down on a man's shoulders like bags of sand, usually turned back after only a few paces. Almost stifled in the hot underworld, they would retreat, clawing for light and fresh air. Aesculapius had also feared the catacombs,[2] but "The people that do know their God shall be strong, and do exploits," he told himself. He raced through the now narrow tunnels as though he were back in his father's villa by the Via Appia. He almost smiled at the thought of the stories his brother Barnabas had told him—stories of this group of soldiers and that group of soldiers stumbling around in the entranceways, scarcely two arms' lengths from the very men they were hunting, making excuses as to why their prey had surely escaped beyond hope of capture.

But then he remembered his own plight. One might laugh at the soldiers who trembled in the catacombs, but above the ground, the soldiers were swift, efficient, and often merciless. And they had arrested his sister.

At last the wall led the boy around a corner to a sputtering torch. It illuminated very little—its light throwing round splotches on the wall where it hung and on the wall opposite.

He took the torch in hand and followed the tunnel, which became narrower, the roof sloping downward. Most of the men had to stoop quite a bit at this point, but not he. On either side were long, narrow indentations like slots: the tombs, built like bunks in the walls and sealed over with terra cotta or marble.

Aesculapius knew little of the history of the catacombs except that they represented the truth that Rome had not always been there; nor would she always be. Someday, perhaps, men and women and their children could return to their villas, their gardens, their markets, and studies, and resume life.

But the boy would gladly have given up the villa, his schoolwork, his days of sports and play, if only— if only that one thing on earth most precious to him had not been taken away. That one life he had promised to protect.

He had passed several entrances to other tunnels on either side— some of them beginning with stairways going lower, and some going higher. The catacombs had three levels in most places. His own tunnel now widened again, and he descended a flight of seven steps and

[2]catacombs—in ancient Rome, underground tunnels in which graves were dug

then took the first right. For a moment he stopped to rest and set the leather bag on the floor. He lifted the torch higher, inspecting a slab of terra cotta that had been mortared over one of the tombs. There was an inscription on it. Of all the many inscriptions to be found down there, it was the one he always stopped to read:

> Timothy, beloved son in the faith,
> His the cross, the grave, the skies,
> Lord, we follow to Paradise!

Timothy was unknown to the younger Christians living in the catacombs—an early quarrier,[3] probably, entombed before persecution had spread to include the rich as well as the humble, the famous as well as the anonymous.

After a moment the Roman boy moved on. Most of the other inscriptions were brief—"Flavia, in peace" came right after Timothy's tomb, then "Justinius, alive two days, at rest in God"; "Marcus, laid here by his wife, in peace"; and then an inscription for a martyr,[4] "Timeritus, meek on earth, frail in flesh, a lion of the faith. In peace despite torments, he departed."

---

[3]quarrier—one who cuts stone from an open place called a quarry

[4]martyr—a person who chooses to die rather than give up a religion or belief

"A lion of the faith," the boy repeated to himself. He himself was not a lion of the faith.

Up ahead, footsteps echoed in the dry tunnel.

"Young Peter?"

"*Ave!*[5] the boy called. "I am here, Barnabas!"

His older brother appeared after a moment, also carrying a torch. His real name was Fortunatis, but he was more commonly called Barnabas after the Apostle Paul's companion. Roman Christians, whose old names of the gods or the fates no longer fit them, adopted the names of apostles or patriarchs.[6] Aesculapius took the name of Peter for himself. His sister Claudia became Deborah.

Barnabas, six years older than his younger brother, was not tall, but he was broad and muscular. He looked as ready and fit as any pugilist[7] or gladiator[8] trained for the arena. Indeed, his training had early been in the arts of war, for their father, Marcus Gaius, was a centurion.

"You are spent, little brother. Shall I carry you on my back?"

"No, only take the bag if you will, Barnabas." Peter handed over the heavy bag.

"Come along then." Barnabas shouldered the bag with no effort and put his other hand on Peter's shoulder.

They were silent as they walked. Barnabas and Peter rarely needed to speak to feel the warm friendship that they shared. Without thinking, Peter sighed and heaved his shoulders up and then down.

"I know your thoughts," Barnabas said. "It is a heavy weight to bear, Peter."

"Perhaps today they have passed judgment on our sister, Barnabas," Peter said faintly. He couldn't speak outright about her, for the thought of losing her brought tears to his eyes. And then he would cry.

From the first, Barnabas had decided that they must leave their sister to God's care and not try anything foolish like a rescue or a bribe to free her. But sometimes Peter broke down and cried for her. Barnabas tried to reason with Peter from Scripture and pray with him.

Peter was ashamed of himself. He *did* worry and fret and beg God to spare her. And when he persisted in worrying and fretting, Barnabas seemed to doubt his own decision not to do anything foolish.

Young Peter had braved everything that God had allowed to befall him. There had been arguments with his father to dissuade[9] him from his new faith. Ultimately, Marcus Gaius had disowned his Christian children.

---

[5]Ave (ā´ vā)—greeting
[6]patriarchs—ancestors of the Israelites
[7]pugilist—a boxer
[8]gladiator—one who fought to the death for entertainment of Roman audiences
[9]dissuade—discourage; persuade against

There had been long, exhausting conversations with uncles who had tried even more intense methods of winning Peter back. And, hardest of all, their mother had died in the catacombs.

Yet how joyful those days had been too—in spite of the pain—just knowing that the grace of God would bring him through trouble to heaven. Why, Peter asked himself, did he not have that faith now?

For a long time Barnabas was silent, and Peter wondered if the older boy would speak. At last, Barnabas gave a sigh and said, "Aye, little brother, they have passed judgment on our sister."

"Oh! What have they said—you know—"

Barnabas raised his hand. "Peace! For now, peace. Judgment is passed, Peter, and we have before us several choices to make. I bid you now, before the brethren, to be silent about this, for our sister's own sake. Trust in God to keep her safe in hand until we can talk."

Peter's chest was heaving. Surely she was condemned to death! It was in Barnabas's eyes—the judgment was terrible. But Peter caught himself. "Aye. I will wait until we can talk. Only hurry, Barnabas, please."

Then they stepped from the passage into one of the larger rooms of the catacombs. About twenty people were gathered there, most of them on their knees, the older ones sitting or standing. Over all hung a gloomy torchlight. Peter and Barnabas waited on the edge of the prayer meeting.

Their friends stood up and sang a hymn, which the boys joined. Barnabas set the bag on the floor and opened it up.

There was no severe lack of food in the tombs. Few believers stayed down in the tunnels for more than a few weeks at a time. Many people received food from Christians living in the city or from relatives and friends who were not converted but had sympathy. The elderly came forward first, followed by women with babes and then whoever else needed food. There was no shoving or ill will. Most of these people had been rough and poor all their lives; yet the Spirit of Christ had given them a gentleness and a goodwill better than any noble manners.

Barnabas turned the remainder over to the deacon for storing. Then he and Peter quickly excused themselves and hurried through the black passageways to the small chapel. Barnabas held a torch aloft to guide them, though they had traveled this part of the catacombs so often that they could have found their way in total dark.

Up narrow stairways, through winding turnoffs, past row after row of tombs they went in silence. At last they came to an alcove where the tunnel widened. They turned aside, and Barnabas hung the torch in a bracket. Young Peter sat down on a bench hewn out of the rock. Barnabas stayed standing. He dropped a hand on Peter's shoulder.

"Dear Aesculapius, how well you know the faint hope of a Christian who has been found guilty of treason."[10]

"Aye. I know."

"Rightly, then, you must have guessed what the judge's sentence for our sister would be. You know that, don't you, little brother?"

Young Peter's lips trembled, and his sight blurred. He wanted to plead with Barnabas about an appeal or

---

[10]treason—the betraying of a person's country by helping an enemy

perhaps even a bribe to free her, but his throat worked against him, wanting him to cry instead. Then he heard himself blurt out, "Only tell me not the circus! Not the circus, Barnabas?"

"Nay, not that, and I thank God she has been spared that. I couldn't have borne it, either—" And then Barnabas started to cry, too, shocking Peter into calmness. Through everything—their sister's arrest on one of her trips to the city, her cruel interrogation,[11] and her long imprisonment—Barnabas had been strong and confident that God knew best. And now he was crying too. But he quickly regained control of himself.

"Pardon me, little brother. Don't fear because I cry. I had prayed in my own great weakness that God would spare her from being thrown to the animals in the circus. I weep because in mercy He answers the prayer of a coward."

"Why do you call yourself that?" Peter demanded.

"Because I saw Deborah today in the jail. She's not afraid of the beasts—why should I have been? She's willing to pass through any affliction to give the great glory to Christ. And aye, I tell you this, Peter, her testimony is sweeter than the song of angels. Her own jailer, and those cutthroats and thieves bound with her, are greatly gentled and humbled by her. For before she came

in there in bonds, you had never seen such an unruly pack, including the guards and jailer. Yet now order rules, and they are much subdued."

Peter felt a moment's envy that Barnabas had seen her. It was possible, though risky, for the Christians to visit in the prisons. The truth was that many Christians in Rome were not persecuted at all. A Christian had to be accused by a private citizen of disloyalty to the gods, and most people preferred to mind their own business rather than bother with the long process of the law.

"Oh, that He would hear my prayer!" Peter exclaimed. "And free her! I would gladly go in her place!"

"Peter!" Barnabas said. "Even she herself doesn't ask to be freed. She is content to pass on to heaven through whatever fires God allows here on earth."

"I ask because she is my sister— for the same reason that you prayed for her not to be sent to the circus!" Peter cried. He leaped to his feet. "Aye, it's cowardly! Aye, it shows no faith! But I still can't bear it, and I can't change! I don't want her to die! If you're ashamed, then leave me here! But I can't lie, for God knows my heart!"

Barnabas stepped back, and his face was grave. At last he said, "I cannot bear to see you suffer so,

[11]interrogation—questioning

596

Peter. Sit down." And Peter sat, trembling from his outburst. Barnabas went on, "May God forgive me if I have prayed amiss; yet doesn't He command that we pour ourselves out before Him and lay bare every fear and every torment?" These words Barnabas said to himself, but then he spoke gently to his brother. "Stop crying, Peter. For your sake I asked God to show us a way to save her. Mayhap it will not work, but in that case we shall all pass on to glory together. Death doesn't frighten you, does it?"

"Not my own!" Peter said earnestly. "Barnabas! Have you thought of a way to rescue her? To bring her out of jail?"

"There may be a way. Vincens is also overwrought[12] at the thought of her death. This very day he contacted me through Artoris, the deacon's son."

Peter stood up again. Vincens was their oldest brother, the only one left in their father's good graces, one who followed the gods with all the carelessness and tongue-in-cheek reverence of a true soldier. He had rejected his mother and agreed with disinheriting Barnabas, Peter, and Deborah.

"What could Vincens want? He would betray us!"

"Nay," Barnabas said. "You were too young to understand, little brother. Vincens was so loud in denouncing[13] us only because he was so hurt and so frightened, especially at the thought of losing Mother. And then she died in the catacombs. Vincens could not bear the separation. And he was outraged that we would let Christianity become our rule—he who has never been religious in any belief. He did all that he did to hide his pain and make himself believe he hated us. You must forgive him. He sent me word today—he wants our help. Forgive Vincens and work with him now, when our sister's life is in the balance."

Peter raised his eyes to Barnabas. The older boy smiled, encouraging him. "We forgive because we are forgiven. Isn't that right?"

"How can you, after what he did?" Peter asked.

"Peter, for shame," Barnabas said. "You ask, and I tell you—I forgive Vincens because in his wrong I see my wrong. In his sin I see my sin, and God in His mercy forgave me. Therefore, I forgive my older brother. And you should do the same."

"I cannot lie and say that I do."

"Don't you see that God in His mercy could very well be answering your prayer? Vincens can help us. He *wants* to help us. Do you reject God's way even now?"

---

[12]overwrought—very worried
[13]denouncing—accusing in public

"I will go with Vincens—I will do what he asks me to in order to free our sister, Barnabas," Peter said. "But I cannot lie and tell you I forgive him. If he were ever to strike me again—now that I be thirteen and sturdy, I would strike him down!"

For a long moment the silence in the great catacombs weighed down on them while the darkness pressed in. "Truly you are just a boy," Barnabas said at last. "Sometimes I forget your youth when you carry yourself so long with so much manliness." He reached up to the torch and took it from the bracket. "Now I believe that God will answer your prayer because He knew—before I knew—that you are but a boy. He will give you your sister back and will keep Vincens from hurting you again. If you fear Vincens, then I can go up alone and meet him."

"Nay, Barnabas, I will go," Peter said. He was glad that Barnabas couldn't see him blushing with shame.

"Come then," Barnabas said. "Artoris, the deacon's son, has agreed to run messages between me and Vincens. I will tell him to give Vincens word that we will meet him. We must travel all the way up to the entrance by the Via Salaria. It will take a long time. Let us get some food and torches, and we will camp near the entrance and wait until tomorrow evening for our brother."

"Aye." Peter fell into step beside Barnabas. "I am a soldier who fights well," Peter told himself bitterly, "but Barnabas is the champion. I have run the marathon,[14] too, but he is the winner of the race. Why can I not be a Christian as strong as Barnabas?"

Barnabas seemed to know his little brother's thoughts.

"You are overwrought now. Spare yourself a little, and when the time is ready, pray for God's guidance, Peter," Barnabas said kindly.

They collected a bag of food for themselves, and while Peter found some torches, Barnabas made arrangements with his friend Artoris.

---

[14]marathon—a long race

598

Lion of the Faith

Travel through the heart of one of the catacombs was dangerous. But Barnabas knew most of the network. They traveled throughout the rest of that long night, walking first underground, then above ground, and later below again. Above the ground the moon set, the stars paled, and the sky again turned purple and red on the edges as morning came.

Rarely did light pierce the tunnels where they walked. Every now and then they ascended to one of the higher levels where people had cut out airshafts—*luminaria cryptae,* as they were called. These welcome places provided a little bit of fresh air.

At last Barnabas called them both to a halt. "The entrance is only a little farther. Let us stop and rest. Have a little food."

They gave their morning thanks and ate hungrily on dried figs, hard cheese, and old bread. Not far away, a natural spring in the rock provided a small pool of water for drinking.

"I have something to say to you," Barnabas said when they had finished eating. "I think your thoughts go very hard with you."

Peter nodded and bowed his head.

"Little brother, I'm going to tell you something about our heavenly Father."

"What is it?"

"He often lets us be pressed sore—as a wrestler is pressed by one stronger. And this is not to break us, nor even to let us lose the match, but to show us where we are weak."

"I'm weak all over," Peter confessed.

"Nay. You have weathered many a storm, and God has kept you through them all. But now you have come to those things you hold most dear: your love for your sister and your fear of Vincens. God knows that we are dust, and He forbears[15] with our weaknesses. You must believe that God will give you grace to endure whatever trials He sends you. He will not give you what you cannot bear, though He may stretch you to the very end of yourself."

"I thought I was at the end of myself," Peter said. "Why does He stretch us so?"

"I don't always know the answer to that," Barnabas said, leaning his curly head back against the tunnel wall. "But in some ways, God is rather like Mother was when we were young. When I was a boy, in tears from a fall or after losing a game or wrestling match, I always ran to Mother to be comforted. And now when I suffer falls and losses, I

---

[15]forbears—is patient with

run to God for the same reasons. He stretches us to turn us to Himself."

Peter pushed the food bag over. "Do you always run to God? Don't you ever think He might be displeased or disgusted with us, Barnabas, and these are the sign of His displeasure?"

"No, Peter, never," Barnabas said. "I used to, until I understood that God is my Father. Does that make sense?"

"I think so," Peter said.

"God is not an earthly father like Marcus Gaius. Even when we are weak and afraid, Peter, we are His." Barnabas looked at him for a moment, then patted the floor. "Well, lie down and rest for now. I'll keep watch."

Peter woke up much later. Their second-to-last torch was guttering in a wall bracket. Barnabas was washing up in the tiny spring.

"Soon Vincens will be coming. Hurry," Barnabas said.

Peter quickly made himself as presentable as his ragged tunic would allow. They picked up the food bag, cramming bread into their mouths as they hurried up the tunnel. Soon a cool evening breeze wafted past, and in another instant Barnabas was pushing aside some heavy foliage,[16] making a way out for Peter. They emerged into the underbrush and looked around, their eyes slowly adjusting to the upper world.

"*Ave!*" A hearty voice called. The voice made them jump.

It was Vincens, standing on a narrow strip that bordered two overgrown vineyards. The setting sun gleamed dully on his armor.

"*Ave!*" Barnabas called. "Are you alone, brother?"

"Call me anything but that," Vincens commanded. "Yes, I come alone, Fortunatis."

"As you wish, Vincens. Come, Aesculapius." Aesculapius and Fortunatis stepped through the leafy foliage and joined him on the path.

"You have been promoted!" Barnabas said. "You are now a centurion!"

---

[16]foliage—the leaves of plants or trees

"Nay, Fortunatis. I have borrowed father's armor."

Barnabas blurted, "Father knows? Did he say—"

Vincens said, "Be silent. Now listen. As to Claudia, I know the soldier guarding her. He's a blond-haired pup from overseas, who speaks bad Latin, and she's got him half-listening to all her Christian ways. Tonight he will desert the Roman army, with a little present from me to speed him on his way home. He has promised to escort her away with him as though he were moving her to a different cell. He will pass her into my custody,[17] and I in turn will pass her into yours. And then the lot of you can be off and done as far as I'm concerned."

Barnabas nodded. Peter noticed that Vincens had long knives thrust through his belt. Vincens pulled these knives out and held them hilt first toward his brothers. "Here—in case we have trouble."

"Nay," Barnabas said quickly. "We will not kill—"

"Take these weapons as men called back into service. For once in your lives, do your duty!"

"Killing other soldiers who are obeying orders, even to rescue our sister, is impossible for us!"

"You had best consider some of the parts of the city we must pass through before we reach the prison by the prefecture.[18] Take them, I say!"

Reluctantly, Barnabas took one and thrust it into his belt. Peter did likewise.

"Well," said Vincens as though noticing Peter for the first time. "Living in a cave has not stopped Aesculapius from growing up, eh?"

Peter answered nothing.

"Are *you* ready to strike a blow for your sister?" Vincens asked.

"If you have not planned any treachery,[19] yes," Peter answered.

Vincens's smile faded.

"Nay, there shall be no treachery," was all he said. "Come then."

They set off across the vineyard to the road. There were horses waiting—three of them.

"Does the boy remember how to ride?" Vincens asked Barnabas.

"I believe so," Barnabas said.

Vincens steadied the smallest horse for Peter to mount. Barnabas exclaimed in pleasure, recognizing his old mount from his father's stables. Peter hurriedly mounted. Last of all, Vincens swung up into his own saddle.

"You still are the fairest rider," Barnabas said to the oldest brother.

"A man feels free on a horse, eh?" Vincens asked. Peter was surprised at the pang in his own heart, at the flood of memories of riding

---

[17]custody—protection; guardianship
[18]prefecture—place where the prefect, a high military official, lives
[19]treachery—deceit; betrayal

with Vincens, at how Vincens had taught him to mount up right away after he'd been thrown.

"O Lord, please convert my brother," Peter prayed silently as they started off. Barnabas had been right. God was working out His answer to their prayers. With the realization, Peter felt a small thrill of genuine gratitude, and in sudden remorse he added to his first prayer, "If only I could trust You more!"

They rode south down the Via Salaria, toward the prefecture and prison on the edge of the capitol. The moon had come out and cast a silvery sheen over the fields and vineyards. At last the villas came more closely together. The three brothers passed large houses, then smaller houses, until they were at last passing tenements.[20]

Two sturdy men such as Vincens and Barnabas were unlikely to be disturbed, even in that rough quarter. Peter rode between them. Every now and then came a drunken halloo from a doorway, but otherwise the ride was uneventful. At last, when Peter could see the arches of the capitol building silhouetted against the sky and catch a little of the faint gleam of torchlight on marble, Vincens reined them in.

"Wait here," he said. He dismounted and entered an alley. In a few moments he came hurrying back, supporting a cowled[21] figure on his arm.

"Deborah!" Peter whispered, ready to dismount.

"Stay there!" Vincens whispered hoarsely. "The soldier tells me he was observed; he thinks he may have been followed by others who would capture her back for a reward. Lady, I ask you, can you ride before me on the saddle?"

"Yes, Vincens. I can," she said, and the hood fell away from her face. It was Deborah all right, but weak from her months in the prison.

"Come then." He swung up into the saddle and lifted her onto it in front of him. "Fortunatis, we cannot go back the way we came. Word may be spreading, and we must go faster than the spoken word. Where shall we go?"

"East," Barnabas said. "The Via Tiburtina. There is an entrance less than a mile beyond the city gate. Can you get us through?"

"I'll bribe the soldiers if I have to." The Via Tiburtina gate was guarded by men who would wonder at a centurion leaving the city with strangers. But there was nothing else to do. They spun the horses and rode swiftly away, as men with deadly important business.

---

[20]tenements—cheap apartments in a poor part of a city
[21]cowled—hooded

They quickly passed through the Subura, another rough quarter of the city, and rode onto the Esquilinus, dangerously close to the military district, where Vincens might be recognized by any soldiers on patrol or officers returning from a late night in the city.

They were passing a small clearing on their right. This was the clearing near the Porta Esquilinus set aside for executing criminals. Many of the Christians had been put to the sword there.

Just past the Esquilinus, Barnabas turned to look back. "We are not alone, Vincens," he said.

Vincens turned. "Run for it to the gate, and beyond that to the catacombs! These be the best horses in all Rome!"

They urged their horses on. Peter glanced back once. The riders behind them had increased to a gallop too!

It turned into an all-out race for the wall and the Campagna beyond. Vincens had spoken truthfully about the horses. They kept their lead to the gate, but Peter worried. Surely the gate would be closed.

Ahead of them, the Servian Wall, a dark bulwark[22] in the moonlight, loomed up. As they came nearer, Vincens boldly bawled out, "Open the gates! Open the gates in the name of Rome!"

Seeing the armor of the centurion, the guards hastened to obey, lifting aside the bar and opening one of the huge doors. Barnabas and Peter galloped through. Vincens slowed down, pushing his imaginary authority to the limit.

"Stop that pursuit! Swords out, in the name of Mars![23] Or this noble lady's blood shall be on your heads!"

Then he thundered by, too, right behind his brothers, and the gates closed behind them.

"Hurry!" he cried. "It won't take long for them to realize we fooled them."

Deborah said something, but Peter couldn't hear what she said over the beating hooves and Vincens's rattling armor. Vincens gave her a gruff reply. "Think nothing of that. Marcus Gaius will protect his only son."

"They come!" Barnabas exclaimed, looking back.

"They'll follow us to the secret entrance!" Peter called.

But Barnabas shook his head. "We will not fear!"

Already, Vincens's horse was falling behind, wearied from carrying an armored soldier and an extra person.

"Fortunatis!" Vincens called to his brother. "Take her! Take her! They may push a fight."

With pursuit barely a bend in the road behind them, Barnabas quickly slowed his horse, stopped, and took their sister on the front of his own saddle.

"Go! By the feet of Mercury,[24] you should still make good speed! I will bring up the rear!"

Vincens loosened the sword in its sheath, and they started off again. But Vincens stayed a few lengths behind, watchful of the pursuit.

Peter's heart felt another stab. Vincens meant to fight them alone. He would be killed if he fought.

---

[22]bulwark—a wall built for protection
[23]Mars—mythical Roman god of war
[24]Mercury—mythical Roman messenger of the gods

They galloped on, and the men behind them gained no more ground.

"Up there!" Peter called back to him, pointing to the white mile marker where they would turn off the road.

Barnabas slowed his horse a little and turned off the Via Tiburtina. Peter glanced back beyond Vincens. At last the pursuit was gaining, joined now by at least one man whose armor gleamed under the moonlight.

Quickly Peter followed Barnabas down through leafy foliage, through a sandy patch, and down a steep dip that twisted around a stand of poplar trees. The poplars were up on a rise of the ground. A cave entrance opened up at their roots, hidden from the road. Barnabas swung off and lifted their sister down. Peter slid off so unexpectedly that Vincens nearly trampled him. Vincens turned his mount around, ready to make a stand at the entrance.

"Go!" he shouted, pulling out his heavy sword.

"Come, both of you!" Barnabas called to Vincens and Peter. He helped Deborah inside.

Already came the pounding of hooves through the leaves on the other side of the poplar stand above them. In seconds Vincens would be discovered, an impostor[25] dressed as a centurion, one who had aided an escape from the prison.

"Vincens!" Peter called. "Come with us!"

"Go in!" Vincens called from his horse. "They'll chase you unless you get a head start!"

He didn't understand that nobody could be chased in the catacombs, not for very long. "Come with us!" Peter cried.

There were shouts from above the dip. Two horsemen appeared and roared in delight at seeing Vincens make a stand.

"Come on then!" Vincens shouted at them. "By the spear of Mars, you'll rue[26] this night!"

Peter prayed silently, "Oh Lord, he's my brother! Have mercy on us! I cannot fight, but I cannot leave him, either!"

Then he knew that Vincens was just as much a part of everything they were. He was in danger; he needed help.

"Vincens!" Peter shouted. He drew his knife and ran at Vincens's horse. One quick swipe of steel against leather, and the girth[27] was cut. Vincens and the saddle toppled over. The war horse, too well trained to trample his rider, reared up at the men above, who hesitated before tackling a horse in those close quarters.

---

[25]impostor—one who pretends to be something he is not
[26]rue—to regret
[27]girth—the strap that holds a saddle on a horse

Peter nimbly slipped in between Vincens and the rearing horse.

"Up, brother, up! It's your only chance! Come with me, and I will lead you out another exit!" he cried, pulling on Vincens's shoulder.

Vincens stumbled to his feet, picked up his sword, and gave his horse a swat with the flat of it. The horse reared again, and the two brothers slipped into the cave.

"Silently now!" Peter said, guiding him along by the hand.

"Claudia and Fortunatis are in here?" Vincens asked.

"Aye," Peter whispered. "He got her in safely. This way."

There was already a sound of men invading the entrance, calling to them to give up and come out. The invaders might hear Vincens's armor rattling faintly and follow the sound. In the darkness, Peter quickly pulled him in one turnoff and down another, stopping in an alcove in the complete darkness. For several seconds they stood in silence as their enemies poked a little bit farther into the tunnel, muttering. It was amazing how quickly even the most hot-blooded soldiers were subdued in the dry and terrifying stillness of the catacombs. After several seconds the muttering turned to questions as the men looking for them wondered how to go on without lights. Then at last they gave up and turned to go back to the night outside. Peter stayed absolutely still while the men and the soldier clanked out.

"Sorry I spilled you and lost your horse, Vincens," Peter whispered. "But I couldn't bear the thought of the numbers against you."

"The horses will return home without me. You saved my life, little brother. It is enough. Where has Fortunatis gone?"

"Come, we will check the main passage." Still gripping Vincens's hand, Peter groped along in the blackness and led him to the main passage. They walked on until they had rounded a few turns, and then they saw the gleam of a torch.

"*Ave!*" Peter called. Vincens hesitated.

Yet he let Peter lead him to where their sister sat with Barnabas stooping over her. She was weak, her face white, but she was alive. Peter dropped by his sister's side and embraced her. Behind him, Vincens slipped his sword back into its sheath.

"God was merciful and didn't take you away," Peter said.

"Aye, and He brought me my brother back," she added, and she looked up over Peter's head at Vincens.

"For tonight, anyway," Vincens said. "It was not for the magistrate to condemn you. And now I must go back to my duty."

"Will you stoop for a kiss? Will you allow that?" she asked him.

"Aye." He hurriedly bent down and let her kiss his cheek. "Come, Aesculapius. Lead me out some other way."

"Aye." Peter stood up. Barnabas gave him the torch.

"There is another one at the next turnoff for Deborah and me," Barnabas said. "You take this."

Barnabas and Vincens looked at each other for a moment.

At last Vincens said, "Come along, Aesculapius."

Peter led Vincens deeper into the maze of tunnels. "The nearest entrance is at the Via Nomentana," he said. "Just outside the city."

In the low, narrow tunnel, Vincens removed the high-crested helmet. "Dawn is not far off. I will enter the gates with the rabble."[28]

They wound through the darkness. Peter wondered at himself. Funny how he had hated Vincens earlier—or thought he had hated him. Yet God had heard his prayer to spare Vincens, too, and had given Peter the courage and wit to cut the horse's girth.

"Aesculapius," Vincens said at last, and his voice was not gruff.

"Aye?"

"Do you hate me, little brother, for the meanness that I showed toward you once?"

So Vincens had been thinking of it too.

"I thought I hated you, Vincens. But God has changed my heart—"

He stopped, lifted the torch a little to see Vincens's face, and said, "I could not bear to see you slain or punished. God heard my prayer for you."

"He seems to hear your prayers." And this time Vincens wasn't mocking.

"I am His son. If nothing else this night, God has taught me that I am His son, and He bears with me as a father would."

They came to the entrance. The sky was paling outside.

"Farewell," Vincens said. "You are a worthy brother for courage."

"Thank you." He looked up at Vincens. "If you came to this very entrance by night, Vincens, I would be here to meet you," Peter said.

"Perhaps, I will find the time and come," Vincens told him. Then he added, "I could bring you food."

"Thank you," Peter told him. Then Vincens was gone.

In the musty interior Peter paused.

"Lord, it's been worth everything to be Your son," he whispered. Perhaps he and Barnabas had suffered much in the last few years, but Christ had been near through every loss—and all on their account.

"Thank you," he whispered again before he hurried on. "Thank you, for now surely I know you are my Father." And as he hurried back to Deborah and Barnabas, he was already praying that Vincens and their father would come to know that too.

---

[28]rabble—lower-class people

Glossary

This glossary has information about selected words found in this reader. You can find meanings of words as they are used in the stories. Certain unusual words such as foreign names are included so that you can pronounce them correctly when you read.

The pronunciation symbols below show how to pronounce each vowel and several of the less familiar consonants.

ă	pat	ĕ	pet	îr	fierce		
ā	pay	ē	be	ŏ	pot		
âr	care	ĭ	pit	ō	go		
ä	father	ī	pie	ô	paw, for, ball		

oi	oil	ŭ	cut	zh	vision
o͝o	book	ûr	fur	ə	ago, item,
o͞o	boot	*th*	the		pencil, atom,
yo͞o	abuse	th	thin		circus
ou	out	hw	which	ər	butter

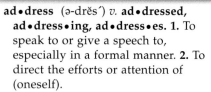

a•ban•don (ə-băn´dən) *v.* **1.** To withdraw help or assistance in spite of duty. **2.** To give way completely to emotion. —**a•ban´don•ment** *n.*

a•brupt (ə-brŭpt´) *adj.* **1.** Unexpected; sudden. **2.** Moving from one subject to another with no transition. —**a•brupt´ly** *adv.*

ab•sorb (əb-sôrb´, əb-zôrb´) *v.* **ab•sorbed, ab•sorb•ing. 1.** To take in or soak up. **2.** To take the full attention of.

ab•surd (əb-zŭrd´, əb-zûrd´) *adj.* Ridiculously inappropriate or unreasonable; foolish.

a•bun•dance (ə-bŭn´dəns) *n.* A supply that is more than enough; a great amount.

a•bun•dant (ə-bŭn´dənt) *adj.* In great amounts; plentiful.

a•but (ə-bŭt´) *v.* **a•but•ted.** Lie alongside; adjoin.

a•byss (ə-bĭs´) *n.* A very deep and large hole; an immeasurable chasm.

a•ca•cia (ə-kā´shə) *n.* A tree with flowering branches.

ac•cess (ăk´sĕs) *n.* A means of reaching; a passage.

ac•ces•si•ble (ăk-sĕs´ə-bəl) *adj.* Easily reached or entered.

ac•com•plice (ə-kŏm´plĭs) *n.* A person who helps someone else in a crime.

ac•cord•ing•ly (ə-kôr´dĭng-lē) *adv.* Because of that; therefore.

ac•count•ant (ə-koun´tənt) *n.* A person who keeps or inspects the money records of a business or person.

a•chieve (ə-chēv´) *v.* **a•chieved.** To accomplish something desired or attempted.

ac•knowl•edge (ăk-nŏl´ĭj) *v.* **ac•knowl•edged.** To recognize as being valid or having force or power.

ad•dress (ə-drĕs´) *v.* **ad•dressed, ad•dress•ing, ad•dress•es. 1.** To speak to or give a speech to, especially in a formal manner. **2.** To direct the efforts or attention of (oneself).
—*n.* **1.** (*also* ăd´rĕs´) The house number, street name, city, state, and zip code where a person lives, works, or receives mail. **2.** A formal speech.

a•dept (ăd´ĕpt) *n.* An expert; professional.
—*adj.* (ə-dĕpt´) Very good at something; skillful.

ad•e•quate (ăd´ĭ-kwĭt) *adj.* Enough to meet needs; sufficient.

a•dieu (ə-dyōō´) *interj.* French for "farewell."

ad•join (ə-join´) *v.* **ad•join•ing.** To be next to; be side by side.

ad•min•is•ter (ăd-mĭn´ĭ-stər) *v.* **ad•min•is•tered. 1.** To be in charge of; direct; manage. **2.** To give as a remedy or treatment.

a•do•be (ə-dō´bē) *n.* **1.** Brick or bricks made of clay and straw that dry and harden in the sun. **2.** A building made of these bricks.

ad•vance (ăd-văns´) *v.* **ad•vanced, ad•vanc•es.** To move forward, onward, or upward.

ad•verse (ăd-vûrs´, ăd´vûrs´) *adj.* Harmful or unfavorable.

aer•i•al (âr´ē-əl, ā-îr´ē-əl) *adj.* High in the air.

af•firm (ə-fûrm´) *v.* To insist; maintain to be true.

af•fir•ma•tion (ăf´ər-mā´shən) *n.* The act of affirming.

ag•gra•vate (ăg´rə-vāt´) *v.* **ag•gra•vat•ing.** To make angry or exasperated; provoke.

a•ghast (ə-găst´) *adj.* Horrified or amazed.

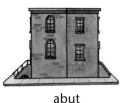

abut

adobe

610

ag•ile (ăj´əl, ăj´īl´) *adj.* Capable of moving quickly and easily; nimble.

a•gil•i•ty (ə-jĭl´ĭ-tē) *n.* The ability to move quickly and easily.

ag•o•nize (ăg´ə-nīz´) *v.* **ag•o•niz•ing.** **1.** To experience great pain or anguish. **2.** To struggle.

ag•o•ny (ăg´ə-nē) *n.* **1.** Great pain of body or mind. **2.** Intense emotion.

ag•ri•cul•ture (ăg´rĭ-kŭl´chər) *n.* Having to do with farms or farming. —**ag•ri•cul´tur•al** *adj.*

ail (āl) *v.* **ail•ing.** To be ill; feel sick.

a•jar (ə-jär´) *adj.* Not closed all the way; partly open.

a•lac•ri•ty (ə-lăk´rĭ-tē) *n.* Enthusiasm; cheerful readiness.

al•cove (ăl´kōv´) *n.* An inset or recessed part of a room.

a•li•en (ā´lē-ən, āl´yən) *n.* An outsider; someone from a very different place and culture.

a•loft (ə-lôft´, ə-lŏft´) *adv.* In or into a high place; up in or into the air.

am•ble (ăm´bəl) *v.* **am•bled.** To walk unhurriedly, as an animal using both legs on one side alternately with both on the other; to stroll.

am•bush (ăm´boosh) *v.* **am•bushed.** To attack from a hidden position.

a•mend•ment (ə-mĕnd´mĕnt) *n.* A change in a law.

a•men•i•ty (ə-mĕn´ĭ-tē, ə-mē´nĭ-tē) *n., pl.* **a•men•i•ties.** Pleasant or polite conversation; "small talk."

am•e•thyst (ăm´ə-thĭst) *n.* The shade of a purple or violet form of quartz used as a gemstone.

am•i•a•ble (ā´-mē-ə-bəl) *v.* Friendly and good-natured.

a•miss (ə-mĭs´) *adj.* Improper; faulty. —*adv.* Improperly; in a faulty or mistaken way.

am•ple (ăm´pəl) *adj.* **1.** Large in size. **2.** Large in quantity; more than enough.

an•a•lyze (ăn´ə-līz´) *v.* To separate something into its basic parts in order to examine it very carefully.

an•ces•tor (ăn´sĕs´tər) *n.* Any person from whom one is descended, especially one who is further removed than a grandparent.

an•es•thet•ic also **an•aes•thet•ic** (ăn´ ĭs-thĕt´ĭk) *n.* a drug or other substance that makes the body unable to feel pain, heat, cold, or other sensations.

An•glo (ăng´glō) *n.* English speaking or of England.

an•guish (ăng´gwĭsh) *n.* **an•guished.** Very great pain or suffering of body or mind.

an•i•mat•ed (ăn´ə-mā´tĭd) *adj.* Full of spirit; lively.

a•non•y•mous (ə-nŏn´ə-məs) *adj.* A person whose identity is not known or does not stand out in any way.

an•ten•na (ăn-tĕn´ə) *n., pl.* **an•ten•nae** (ăn-tĕn´ē) One of a pair of long, thin feelers on the head of insects and some animals.

an•tic (ăn´tĭk) *n.* A funny act or action intended to draw attention.

an•tic•i•pa•tion (ăn-tĭs´ə-pā´shən) *n.* The act of looking forward to in expectation.

an•tique (ăn-tēk´) *n.* Something made a long time ago.

an•vil (ăn´vĭl) *n.* A heavy block of iron or steel with a smooth, flat top where metal articles are hammered into shape.

anx•i•e•ty (ăng-zī´ĭ-tē) *n.* **1.** An uneasy feeling about what will happen; worry. **2.** An eager feeling mixed with worry.

ap•er•ture (ăp´ər-chər) *n.* An opening such as a crack or slit.

ă	pat	ĕ	pet
ā	pay	ē	be
âr	care	ĭ	pit
ä	father	ī	pie
îr	fierce	oi	oil
ŏ	pot	oͦo	book
ō	go	oͦo	boot
ô	paw,	yoͦo	abuse
	for	ou	out
ŭ	cut	ə	ago,
ûr	fur		item,
th	the		pencil,
th	thin		atom,
hw	which		circus
zh	vision	ər	butter

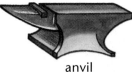

anvil

ă pat	ě pet
ā pay	ē be
âr care	ĭ pit
ä father	ī pie
îr fierce	oi oil
ŏ pot	ŏŏ book
ō go	ŏŏ boot
ô paw,	yŏŏ abuse
for	ou out
ŭ cut	ə ago,
ûr fur	item,
th the	pencil,
th thin	atom,
hw which	circus
zh vision	ər butter

ap•o•plex•y (ăp′ə-plĕk′sē) *n.* A stroke or sudden attack on the brain.

ap•pall (ə-pôl′) *v.* **ap•palled.** To fill with surprise and dismay.

ap•pa•ri•tion (ăp′ə-rĭsh′ən) *n.* **1.** A haunting or disturbing image. **2.** A sudden, surprising appearance.

ap•peal (ə-pēl′) *n.* A request to have a law case tried again by a higher court.
—*v.* To attract; interest.
—*adj.* **ap•peal•ing.** Attractive or interesting.

ap•pease (ə-pēz′) *v.* **1.** To make calm or quiet, especially by giving what is demanded. **2.** To satisfy or relieve.

ap•praise (ə-prāz′) *v.* **ap•prais•ing.** To estimate or judge the value of.

ap•pre•hend (ăp′rĭ-hĕnd′) *v.* To arrest or capture; seize.

ap•pre•hen•sion (ăp′rĭ-hĕn′shən) *n.* Fear of what may happen.

ap•pren•tice (ə-prĕn′tĭs) *n.* A person who learns a skill or trade by working for a skilled craftsman.
—**ap•pren′tice•ship′** *n.*
—*v.* **ap•pren•ticed.** To place or hire as an apprentice.

aq•ui•fer (ăk′wə-fər, ä′kwə-fər) *n.* An underground water-holding rock formation.

ar•bor (är′bər) *n.* A shaded place or garden area closed in by trees, bushes, or vines growing on lattices.

ar•chae•ol•o•gy or **ar•che•ol•o•gy** (är′kē-ŏl′ə-jē) *n.* The science of studying the remains of past civilizations. —**ar′chae•o•log′i•cal** (är′kē-ə-lŏj′ĭ-kəl) *adj.*

a•re•na (ə-rē′nə) *n.* In ancient Rome, an enclosed area or stadium where gladiators fought and other sporting events were held.

ar•mor•y (är′mə-rē) *n.* A storehouse where weapons are kept.

a•rouse (ə-rouz′) *v.* To awaken.

arbor

ar•rest (ə-rĕst′) *v.* **ar•rest•ed. 1.** To seize and hold under the law. **2.** To stop the movement or development of; hold back; check.
—*n.* The act of arresting.

ar•ro•gant (ăr′ə-gənt) *adj.* Feeling that one is much better or more important than everyone else; having too much pride.

ar•sen•al (är′sə-nəl) *n.* Stock of weapons.

ar•ter•y (är′tə-rē) *n.* A main road or way.

ar•ti•fact (är′tə-făkt) *n.* An ancient manmade object.

as•cent (ə-sĕnt′) *n.* **1.** The act of climbing or rising upward. **2.** An upward slope.

as•cer•tain (ăs′ər-tān′) *v.* To find out; make certain.

a•scribe (ə-skrīb′) *v.* **as•cribed.** To give credit to a specific cause.

a•skew (ə-skyŏŏ′) *adv. & adj.* Not lined up or straight; awry.

as•pire (ə-spīr′) *v.* To have a great ambition; strive toward.

as•sas•sin (ə-săs′ĭn) *n.* One who murders a public official.

as•sas•si•na•tion (ə-săs′ə-nā′shən) *n.* The murder of a public official.

as•sem•ble (ə-sĕm′bəl) *v.* **as•sem•bled.** To gather together.

as•sem•bly (ə-sĕm′blē) *n.* A group gathered together for a special purpose.

as•sent (ə-sĕnt′) *n.* Consent; agreement.

as•sess•ment (ə-sĕs′mənt) *n.* Judgment; opinion.

at•tire (ə-tīr′) *n.* Clothing or costume.

at•tune (ə-tŏŏn′, ə-tyŏŏn′) *v.* **at•tuned.** In agreement; understanding.

au•di•ble (ô′də-bəl) *adj.* Loud enough to be heard.

au•ger (ô′gər) *n.* Tool for boring holes.

aught (ôt) *pron.* Anything.

a•vail (ə-vāl´) *v.* **a•vailed.** To be of use, help, or advantage. —*idiom* **avail oneself of.** To make use of.

av•a•lanche (ăv´ə-lănch´) *n.* A large mass of rocks sliding down a hill.

a•ve (ä´vā) *n.* A Latin greeting.

a•vert (ə-vûrt´) *v.* To keep from happening; prevent.

awe (ô) *v.* Emotion of wonder or fear about something that is mighty or majestic.

awe•some (ô´səm) *adj.* Remarkable; inspiring awe.

awe•struck (ô´strŭk´) *adj.* Filled with wonder or awe; amazed.

awn•ing (ô´nĭng) *n.* A canvas screen that looks like a roof.

ax•i•om (ăk´sē-əm) *n.* An accepted universal truth or saying.

az•ure (ăzh´ər) *adj.* Light to medium blue.

bach•e•lor (băch´ə-lər, băch´lər) *n.* A man who is not married.

bac•te•ri•a (băk-tîr´ē-ə) *n.* Tiny plants that can be seen only with a microscope. Some bacteria cause diseases.

bac•te•ri•ol•o•gist (băk-tîr´ē-ŏl´ə-jĭst) *n.* One who studies bacteria, especially in relation to medicine and agriculture.

bade (băd, bād) *v.* A past tense of the verb **bid.**

badg•er (băj´ər) *n.* A digging member of the weasel family, often gray in color. —*v.* **badg•ered.** To annoy by asking many questions.

bail•iff (bā´lĭf) *n.* One who keeps order in a courtroom.

bale (bāl) *n.* A large, tightly wrapped bundle of raw or unfinished material.

bal•last (băl´əst) *n.* Any heavy material carried in a vehicle to give it weight to control balance.

ban (băn) *v.* **banned.** To forbid by law or decree; prohibit.

ban•is•ter also **ban•nis•ter** (băn´ĭ-stər) *n.* The railing supported by posts along a staircase.

bank•rupt (băngk´rŭpt´, băngk´rəpt) *v.* **bank•rupt•ed.** To cause to become financially ruined; penniless.

ban•ner•et (băn´ər-ĭt, băn´ə-rĕt´) *n.* A knight who led others under his own banner.

bare (bâr) *adj.* **bar•est. 1.** Without covering. **2.** Revealed to view; undisguised. **3.** Without the usual supplies or furnishings. —*v.* To open up to view; uncover. —*adj.* **bared.** Opened up to view; uncovered.

bar•ren (bâr´ən) *adj.* **1.** Not able to bear children. **2.** Having no vegetation.

ba•salt (bə-sôlt´, bā´sôlt´) *n.* A hard volcanic rock, often having a glassy appearance.

bate (bāt) *v.* To take away; subtract.

bat•ter (băt´ər) *v.* **bat•tered. 1.** To strike or pound again and again with heavy blows. **2.** To hurt or damage by rough treatment or hard wear. —*n.* In baseball, a player who is or will be batting.

bat•tle•dore (băt´l-dôr´) *n.* A flat wooden paddle used in an early form of badminton.

bawl (bôl) *v.* **bawled, bawl•ing.** To cry out or call in a loud, strong voice; bellow.

bed•lam (bĕd´ləm) *n.* Chaos; noisy uproar.

be•drag•gled (bĭ-drăg´əld) *adj.* **1.** Wet; drooping. **2.** Shabby and deteriorating.

badger

be•guile (bē-gīl´) *v.* To distract or amuse.

be•half (bĭ-hăf´, bĭ-häf´) *n.* Interest, support, or benefit.

belch (bĕlch) *v.* **belch•ing.** To erupt violently.

bel•low (bĕl´ō) *v.* **bel•lowed, bel•low•ing.** To yell or make a loud roaring noise.
—*n.* A loud roar.

bench (bĕnch) *n.* **1.** A long seat for two or more people. **2.** A judge or position of a judge.

ben•e•fact•or (bĕn´ə-făk´tər) *n.* One who gives support, especially financially.

be•quest (bĭ-kwĕst´) *n.* The act of passing something on to another.

berth (bûrth) *n.* A job.

be•seech (bĭ-sēch´) *v.* To beg or plead earnestly.

be•stow (bĭ-stō´) *v.* **be•stowed, be•stow•ing.** To give as a gift or an honor. —**be•stow´al** *n.*

be•wil•der (bĭ-wĭl´dər) *v.* **be•wil•dered.** To confuse.

be•wil•der•ment (bĭ-wĭl´dər-mənt) *n.* The condition of being confused.

bi•ased (bī´əst) *adj.* Preferring one opinion over another; prejudiced.

bid (bĭd) *v.* **bade** (băd, bād) or **bid, bidding. 1.** To tell someone to do something; command. **2.** To say as a greeting or farewell.

bil•let (bĭl´ĭt) *n.* A well-paid position; a job.

bi•zarre (bĭ-zär´) *adj.* Strange; out of the ordinary.

blear•y (blîr´ē) *adj.* Blurry.

boar (bôr, bōr) *n.* A wild pig with a thick coat of dark bristles.

board (bôrd) *n.* The side of a ship.
—*v.* **board•ed. 1.** To give shelter or food, usually for pay. **2.** To enter a vehicle.

board•ing school (bôr´dĭng skool, bōr´dĭng skool) *n.* A school at which students live and take their meals as well as attend classes.

bob•by (bŏb´ē) *n.* British nickname for a policeman.

bob•o•link (bŏb´ə-lĭngk´) *n.* An American songbird with black, white, and tan feathers.

bod•ice (bŏd´ĭs) *n.* A woman's vest worn over a blouse.

bog (bôg, bŏg) *n.* A soft, wet area of land; marsh; swamp.

bois•ter•ous (boi´stər-əs, boi´strəs) *adj.* Loud; noisy. —**bois´ter•ous•ly** *adv.*

bol•ster (bōl´stər) *n.* A long, narrow pillow or cushion.
—*v.* To support or buoy up.

boon (boon) *n.* Benefit; blessing.

boo•ty (boo´tē) *n.* Stolen possessions, usually taken by force in time of war.

bore (bôr, bōr) *v.* **bor•ing. 1.** To make a hole in. **2.** To make weary by being uninteresting or dull.

bos•om (booz´əm, boo´zəm) *n.* The chest.

bot•a•nist (bŏt´n-ĭst) *n.* One who specializes in the study of plants.

bough (bou) *n.* A large branch of a tree.

bout (bout) *n.* A contest between two opponents; attack; session.

bow•er (bou´ər) *n.* An arbor.

brace•lets (brās´lĭts) *n.* Handcuffs.

bran•dish (brăn´dĭsh) *v.* **bran•dished, bran•dish•ing.** To wave about as a weapon.

brawl (brôl) *v.* **brawl•ing.** To fight loudly.

bra•zen (brā´zən) *adj.* Bold; unashamed.

breach (brēch) *n.* The breaking of a rule or contract.

ă	pat	ĕ	pet
ā	pay	ē	be
âr	care	ĭ	pit
ä	father	ī	pie
îr	fierce	oi	oil
ŏ	pot	oo	book
ō	go	oo	boot
ô	paw,	yoo	abuse
	for	ou	out
ŭ	cut	ə	ago,
ûr	fur		item,
th	the		pencil,
th	thin		atom,
hw	which		circus
zh	vision	ər	butter

breast•plate (brĕst′plāt′) *n.* A piece of armor that covers the chest.

breech•es (brĭch′ĭz, brē′chĭz) *n.* Short trousers that are fastened at or just below the knees.

bribe (brīb) *n.* Money or another valuable that is offered or given to make a person do something dishonest or illegal.

bri•dle (brīd′l) *n.* The straps, bit, and reins that fit over a horse's head and are used to control the animal. —*v.* To express resentment by holding the head high.

brim•stone (brĭm′stōn′) *n.* Sulfur.

bris•tle (brĭs′əl) *n.* A short, coarse, stiff hair. —*v.* **1.** To raise the bristles stiffly. **2.** To show anger or irritation.

brooch (brōch, brooch) *n.* A large pin worn as an ornament.

brook (brook) *v.* To put up with; bear; tolerate. —*n.* A small stream or creek.

buff (bŭf) *v.* **buffed.** To polish or shine with a hard piece of wood covered with leather or with any strong, soft material.

buff•er (bŭf′ər) *n.* Something that separates and protects.

bulk•head (bŭlk′hĕd′) *n.* A wall that divides a ship into several compartments.

bul•lion (bool′yən) *n.* Gold or silver in bar form.

bul•wark (bool′wərk, bool′wôrk′, bŭl′wərk) *n.* A wall built for protection.

bung (bŭng) *v. Chiefly British.* **bung•ing** To fling or toss unceremoniously.

Bun•sen burn•er (bŭn′sən bûr′nər) *n.* A kind of small gas burner usually used in laboratories, consisting of a vertical metal pipe on a base attached to a gas source.

bunt (bŭnt) *v.* To bat a baseball lightly so that it rolls slowly and does not go very far. —*n.* The act of bunting.

buoy (boo′ē, boi) *v.* **buoyed.** To raise or keep up one's spirits.

burgh•er (bûr′gər) *n.* A citizen of a small village.

burgh•er's pate (bûr′gərz pāt) *n.* A villager's mind.

bur•nish (bûr′nĭsh) *v.* To polish.

bust (bŭst) *n.* Sculpture of a person's head, shoulders, and the upper part of the chest.

bus•tle (bŭs′əl) *n.* **bus•tled.** Busy, excited activity.

butt (bŭt) *v.* **butt•ed.** To hit or push as with the head or horns. —*n.* The thicker end of a tool, weapon, or piece of meat.

byre (bīr) *n.* A barn.

ca•dence (kād′ns) *n.* A steady, rhythmic flow.

cal•lous (kăl′əs) *adj.* **cal•loused.** Having calluses or toughened skin.

cam•paign med•al (kăm-pān′ mĕd′l) *n.* An award given for military accomplishment.

can•did (kăn′dĭd) *adj.* Open and honest; sincere.

can•o•py (kăn′ə-pē) *n.* A covering like a tent.

cap•i•tal (kăp′ĭ-tl) *n.* **1.** A city where the government of a state or country is located. **2.** Money or property that is invested to produce more money. —*adj.* Calling for a penalty of death: *capital punishment.*

cap•size (kăp′sīz′, kăp-sīz′) *v.* **cap•siz•ing.** To turn bottom side up; overturn.

breeches

bust

Bunsen burner

cap•sul•ize (kăp´sə-līz´, kăp´syoo-līz´) *v.* **cap•sul•ized, cap•sul•iz•ing.** To put into capsule form; encase.

car•a•van (kăr´ə-văn) *n.* A large covered vehicle.

car•go (kär´gō) *n.* The goods carried by a ship, airplane, or other vehicle.

cask (kăsk) *n.* A barrel of any size for holding liquids.

cast (kăst) *v.* **1.** To throw; hurl. **2.** To search or look for. **3.** To contrive; devise. —*n.* The actors in a play.

cat•a•comb (kăt´ə-kōm´) *n.* In ancient Rome, an underground tunnel in which graves were dug.

cat•a•pult (kăt´ə-pŭlt´, kăt´ə-poolt´) *n.* An ancient military machine for hurling boulders at an enemy.

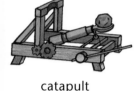

catapult

cen•tu•ri•on (sĕn-toor´ē-ən, sĕn-tyoor´ē-ən) *n.* A commander of 100 soldiers.

cha•grin (shə-grĭn´) *n.* Embarrassment caused by failure or disappointment.

cham•ber (chām´bər) *n.* A room.

cha•os (kā´ŏs´) *n.* Great confusion; disorder.

char•ac•ter•i•za•tion (kăr´ək-tər-ĭ-zā´shən) *n.* The way an author represents a character in writing.

charg•er (chär´jər) *n.* A horse trained specifically for battle.

chas•tise (chăs-tīz´, chăs´tīz´) *v.* To admonish severely; rebuke.

chiao•tzus (jyou´dzu´) *n.* Chinese dumplings stuffed with meat, vegetables, and spices.

chis•eled (chĭz´əld) *adj.* Shaped as if from stone.

chor•tle (chôr´tl) *v.* **chor•tled.** To chuckle in a snorting way.

chron•o•log•i•cal (krŏn´ə-lŏj´ĭ-kəl, krō´nə-lŏj´ĭ-kəl) *adj.* In order of time.

cin•der (sĭn´dər) *n.* A piece of partly burned coal or wood that cannot be burned further.

cir•cus (sûr´kəs) *n.* In ancient Rome, a large, enclosed arena where gladiators fought to the death, Christians were thrown to the lions, and other wicked events were displayed to entertain the Romans.

civ•il (sĭv´əl) *adj.* **1.** Of a citizen or people within a community. **2.** Polite.

civ•il ac•tion (sĭv´əl ăk´shən) *n.* People within a community acting without authority of the law.

clam•ber (klăm´bər) *v.* To climb clumsily, especially on all fours.

clam•or (klăm´ər) *n.* A loud noise. —*v.* To complain or insist.

clan (klăn) *n.* A group of families tracing descent from a common ancestor.

cli•ent (klī´ənt) *n.* A person who uses the services of a professional person.

clout (klout) *n.* **1.** A blow, as with the fist. **2.** A powerful hit in baseball.

coax (kōks) *v.* **coax•ing.** To get something by being nice or gentle. —**coax´ing•ly** *adv.*

cob•ble (kŏb´əl) *n.* **cob•bled.** A round stone once used to pave streets; a cobblestone.

cock (kŏk) *n.* The adult male of chickens and other fowl; a rooster. —*v.* **1.** To tilt or turn up to one side. **2.** To raise the hammer of a firearm in preparation to fire.

cock•pit (kŏk´pĭt´) *n.* The part of an airplane where the pilot and copilot sit.

co•her•ent (kō-hîr´ənt, kō-hĕr´ənt) *adj.* Understandable.

com•mence (kə-mĕns´) *v.* To begin; to start.

grudge (grŭj) **grudg•ing•ly** *adv.* To be unwilling or hesitant to give or acknowledge.

guard•i•an (gär´dē-ən) *n.* A person who is given the responsibility of looking after someone who cannot take care of himself.
—**guard´i•an•ship´** *n.*

guer•ril•la or **gue•ril•la** (gə-rĭl´ə) *n.* Member of a small, loosely organized group of soldiers fighting to overthrow an established government.

guil•der (gĭl´dər) *n.* A unit of currency; money.

gules (gyōolz) *n.* Vertical lines that indicate the color red on a coat of arms.

gul•let (gŭl´ĭt) *n.* The throat.

gut•ter (gŭt´ər) *n.* A ditch along the side of a street for carrying off water.
—*v.* **gut´tered, gut´ter•ing.** To burn low; flicker.

hab•i•ta•tion (hăb´ĭ-tā´shən) *n.* A dwelling place; a place to live.

haft (hăft) *n.* Handle.

han•som (hăn-səm) *n.* A horse-drawn carriage.

har•bor (här´bər) *n.* A sheltered place along a coast serving as a port for ships.
—*adj.* **har´bor•ing.** Giving shelter to; taking in.

har•dy (här´dē) *adj.* Strong and healthy; robust.

har•ry (hăr´ē) *v.* **har•ried.** To worry or harass.

has•ten (hā´sən) *v.* **has•tened, has•ten•ing.** To hurry.

haugh•ty (hô´tē) *v.* Too proud of oneself; superior in one's own mind; arrogant.

haul (hôl) *v.* To pull or drag with force.

haunch (hônch, hŏnch) *n., pl.* **haunch•es.** The hindquarter of an animal.

ha•ven (hā´vən) *n.* Place of safety and rest.

hav•oc (hăv´ək) *n.* Disorder.

haz•ard (hăz´ərd) *v.* **haz•ard•ed.** To attempt.

head (hĕd) *n.* Critical point or crisis.

hear•ing (hîr´ĭng) *n.* Official meeting to listen to arguments.

hearse (hûrs) *n.* A car or wagon for carrying a dead person to a church or cemetery.

hearth (härth) *n.* The floor of a fireplace and the area around it.

heart•y (här´tē) *adj.* **1.** Showing warm, friendly feeling; strong and cheerful. **2.** Vigorous; energetic.
—**heart´i•ness** *n.*

heath (hēth) *n.* A grassy, open field.

heave (hēv) *v.* **heaved. 1.** To raise, lift, or throw with effort or force; hoist. **2.** To utter with a long, deep breath.

hedge (hĕj) *n.* A row of closely planted shrubs or small trees.

her•ald (hĕr´əld) *n.* A person who proclaims important news.

hewn (hyōon) *adj.* Carved or cut.

hilt (hĭlt) *n.* The handle of a sword or dagger.

Hin•du•sta•ni (hĭn´dōo-stä´nē) *n.* A group of Indian dialects.

hitch•hike (hĭch´hīk´) *v.* **hitch•hi•king.** To travel by standing by the sides of roads and getting free rides from passing cars.

hoarse (hôrs, hōrs) *adj.* Low and rough in sound or voice.

hoax (hōks) *n.* False story or report made up to deceive people.

gules

hansom

hilt

hob (hŏb) *n.* A shelf inside a fireplace.

hoist (hoist) *v.* **hoist•ed.** To raise up or lift.

ho•ly (hō′lē) *adj.* **1.** Set apart for God; godly. **2.** Of or having to do with God; sacred.

hon•or•ar•y (ŏn′ə-rĕr′ē) *adj.* Title or position given as an honor.

hos•tile (hŏs′təl, hŏs′tīl) *adj.* Unfriendly or unfavorable to health or well-being.

hov•er (hŭv′ər, hŏv′ər) *v.* **hov•ered, hov•er•ing. 1.** To stay in one place in the air; float or fly without moving much. **2.** To stay or wait nearby; linger.

hue (hyōō) *n.* A color; shade.

hue-and-cry (hyōō ən krī) *n.* An exclamation intended to excite people to chase after someone believed to have stolen something or committed some other crime.

hu•mane (hyōō-mān′) *adj.* Not cruel; kind.

hu•mor•ist (hyōō′mər-ĭst) *n.* Writer of humorous, or funny, material.

hus•band•man (hŭz′bənd-mən) *n.* A farmer.

hy•dro•pho•bi•a (hī′drə-fō′bē-ə) *n.* Rabies.

hy•per•bo•le (hī-pûr′bə-lē) *n.* A figure of speech using exaggeration.

hy•po•der•mic (hī′pə-dûr′mĭk) *adj.* Injected beneath the skin.

hys•ter•i•cal (hĭ-stĕr′ĭ-kəl) *adj.* Excited beyond control.

i•dol (īd′l) *n.* **1.** A statue, picture, or other object that is worshiped as a god. **2.** A person who is admired and loved very much.

il•lu•mi•nate (ĭ-lōō′mə-nāt′) *v.* **1.** To shine light on. **2.** To make understandable.

im•mense (ĭ-mĕns′) *adj.* Of great size, extent, or degree.

im•mi•grant (ĭm′ĭ-grənt) *n.* A person who comes to a country in order to live there permanently.

im•pact (ĭm′păkt′) *n.* **1.** An important effect or impression. **2.** The action of one object striking against another; collision.

im•pass•a•ble (ĭm-păs′ə-bəl) *adj.* Impossible to cross.

im•pas•sive (ĭm-păs′ĭv) *adj.* Expressing no emotion.

im•per•a•tive (ĭm-pĕr′ə-tĭv) *adj.* Necessary.

im•per•il (ĭm-pĕr′əl) *v.* **im•per•iled** or **im•per•illed.** To put in peril; endanger.

im•per•son•ate (ĭm-pûr′sə-nāt′) *v.* **im•per•son•at•ing.** To pretend to be something or someone else.

im•per•ti•nent (ĭm-pûr′tn-ənt) *adj.* Rude; disrespectful; insulting; impolite.

im•plant (ĭm-plănt′) *v.* **im•plant•ed.** To establish firmly in the mind; instill; embed.

im•ple•ment (ĭm′plə-mənt) *n.* A tool or piece of equipment.

im•plore (ĭm-plôr′, ĭm-plōr′) *v.* **im•plored.** To beg; plead with.

im•ply (ĭm-plī′) *v.* **im•plies.** To suggest without stating.

im•port (ĭm-pôrt′) *v.* **im•port•ed.** To bring in goods or products from a foreign country for sale or use.

im•pose (ĭm-pōz′) *v.* **im•posed.** To put on or assign to a person something that is a burden.

im•pos•ing (ĭm-pō′zĭng) *adj.* Awe-inspiring.

im•pos•tor (ĭm-pŏs′tər) *n.* One who pretends to be something he is not.

im•po•tent (ĭm′pə-tənt) *adj.* Powerless.

im•preg•na•ble (ĭm-prĕg´nə-bəl) *adj.* Unable to be broken into.

im•prob•a•bil•i•ty (ĭm-prŏb´ə-bĭl´ĭ-tē) *n., pl.* **im•prob•a•bil•i•ties.** Something that is not likely to happen.

im•pro•vise (ĭm´prə-vīz´) *v.* **im•pro•vised.** To build or make from whatever things or materials are available.

in•ac•ces•si•ble (ĭn´ăk-sĕs´ə-bəl) *adj.* Difficult or impossible to reach.

in•ca•pa•ble (ĭn-kā´pə-bəl) *adj.* Not having a certain ability; not capable.

in•cense (ĭn´sĕns´) *n.* A substance that gives off a sweet smell when burned.

in•cite (ĭn-sīt´) *v.* **in•cit•ing.** **1.** Provoke; push. **2.** To put in motion; provoke.

in•cli•na•tion (ĭn´klə-nā´shən) *n.* The act of lowering the head or nodding.

in•cline (ĭn-klīn´) *adj.* **in•clined.** Having a preference or tendency.

in•cred•u•lous (ĭn-krĕj´ə-ləs) *adj.* Shocked and unbelieving. **—in•cred´u•lous•ly** *adv.*

in•crim•i•nate (ĭn-krĭm´ə-nāt) *v.* **in•crim•i•nat•ing.** To accuse; cause to look guilty.

in•del•i•ble (ĭn-dĕl´ə-bəl) *adj.* Permanent.

in•di•ca•tion (ĭn´dĭ-kā´shən) *n.* Something that indicates; a sign or symptom.

in•dif•fer•ent (ĭn-dĭf´ər-ənt, ĭn-dĭf´rənt) *adj.* Having or showing no interest; not caring one way or the other.

in•dig•nant (ĭn-dĭg´nənt) *adj.* Angry about something that is unfair, mean, or bad. **—in•dig´nant•ly** *adv.*

in•dis•tinct (ĭn´dĭ-stĭngkt´) *adj.* Not clearly understood.

in•dulge (ĭn-dŭlj´) *v.* **in•dulged.** To allow oneself or someone else to have something that is desired but not needed.

in•dul•gence (ĭn-dŭl´jəns) *n.* **1.** The act of indulging. **2.** Tolerance; generosity.

in•dus•tri•ous (ĭn-dŭs´trē-əs) *adj.* Hard working; diligent.

in•fect (ĭn-fĕkt´) *v.* **in•fect•ed.** To give or transfer a disease to.

in•fec•tion (ĭn-fĕk´shən) *n.* A disease in the body or part of the body.

in•fec•tious (ĭn-fĕk´shəs) *adj.* Able to cause infection.

in•fu•ri•ate (ĭn-fyʊr´ē-āt´) *v.* To make very angry; enrage.

in•gen•ious (ĭn-jēn´yəs) *adj.* Clever; skillful in inventing things.

in•glo•ri•ous (ĭn-glôr´ē-əs, ĭn-glōr´ē-əs) *adj.* Without dignity or honor; disgraceful. **—in•glo´ri•ous•ly** *adv.*

in•i•ti•ate (ĭ-nĭsh´ē-āt´) *v.* **in•i•ti•at•ed.** To begin; start.

in of•fice (ĭn ô´fĭs, ĭn ŏf´ĭs) *n.* Referring to those in governmental positions.

in•quire (ĭn-kwīr´) *v.* **in•quir•ing, in•quired.** To ask.

in•scrip•tion (ĭn-skrĭp´shən) *n.* Words or letters engraved or written on something.

in•sen•si•ble (ĭn-sĕn´sə-bəl) *adj.* Unconcious.

in•sig•nif•i•cant (ĭn´sĭg-nĭf´ĭ-kənt) *adj.* Not important; small.

in•sin•u•a•tion (ĭn-sĭn´yʊ-ā´shən) *n.* Something that is implied.

in•so•lent (ĭn´sə-lənt) *adj.* Rude and disrespectful.

in•stinc•tive (ĭn-stĭngk´tĭv) *adj.* Automatic; without thinking. **—in•stinc´tive•ly** *adv.*

in•sti•tute (ĭn´stĭ-tōōt´, ĭn´stĭ-tyōōt´) *v.* **in•sti•tut•ing.** To begin.

in•sti•tu•tion (ĭn´stĭ-tōō´shən, ĭn´stĭ-tyōō´shən) *n.* An organization, especially one that has been set up for public service.

inscription

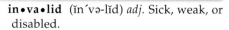

ă	pat	ě	pet
ā	pay	ē	be
âr	care	ĭ	pit
ä	father	ī	pie
îr	fierce	oi	oil
ŏ	pot	o͞o	book
ō	go	o͞o	boot
ô	paw,	yo͞o	abuse
	for	ou	out
ŭ	cut	ə	ago,
ûr	fur		item,
th	the		pencil,
th	thin		atom,
hw	which		circus
zh	vision	ər	butter

in•suf•fer•a•ble (ĭn-sŭf´ər-ə-bəl, ĭn-sŭf´rə-bəl) *adj.* Difficult to endure; unbearable.

in•te•gral (ĭn´tĭ-grəl, ĭn-tĕg´rəl) *adj.* Essential.

in•te•gra•tion (ĭn´tĭ-grā´shən) *n.* The act or process of making something open to all groups.

in•ter•est (ĭn´trĭst, ĭn´tər-ĭst, ĭn´trĕst) *n.* Money paid or charged for the use of someone else's money. Banks pay interest on money that is put into them for saving. Banks charge interest for money that is borrowed from them.

in•ter•fere (ĭn´tər-fîr´) *v.* To meddle in the business of others.

in•ter•ject (ĭn´tər-jĕkt´) *v.* To put in, as a remark.

in•ter•nal (ĭn-tûr´nəl) *adj.* Coming from the inside; inner.

in•tern•ment camp (ĭn-tûrn´mənt kămp) *n.* Prisoner of war camp.

in•ter•ro•gate (ĭn-tĕr´ə-gāt´) *v.* To question. —**in•ter´ro•ga´tion** *n.*

in•ter•sect (ĭn´tər-sĕkt´) *v.* To come together or cross.

in•ter•vene (ĭn´tər-vēn´) *v.* To come between groups in order to change a situation.

in•tol•er•a•ble (ĭn-tŏl´ər-ə-bəl) *adj.* Impossible to bear or submit to. —**in•tol´er•a•bly** *adv.*

in•tri•cate (ĭn´trĭ-kĭt) *adj.* Complicated; complex.

jews'-harp

in•trigue (ĭn´trēg´, ĭn-trēg´) *v.* **in•trigued.** To catch the interest or increase the curiosity of; fascinate.

in•tro•spect (ĭn´trə-spĕkt´, ĭn´trə-spĕkt´) *v.* To look inward and examine one's thoughts.

in•tro•spec•tive (ĭn´trə-spĕk´tĭv, ĭn´trə-spĕk´tĭv) *adj.* Thoughtful; meditative.

in•tu•i•tive•ly (ĭn-to͞o´ĭ-tĭv-lē, ĭn-tyo͞o´ĭ-tĭv-lē) *adv.* Knowing or sensing something without needing to ask.

in•va•lid (ĭn´və-lĭd) *adj.* Sick, weak, or disabled.

in•ven•tive (ĭn-vĕn´tĭv) *adj.* Clever; ingenious.

i•rate (ī-rāt´, ī´rāt´) *adj.* Furious.

irk•some (ûrk´səm) *adj.* Annoying.

i•ron•ic also **i•ron•ic•al** (ī-rŏn´ĭk) *adj.* Opposite the literal meaning; sarcastic.

i•so•la•tion (ī-sə-lā´shən) *n.* The condition of being separated from others.

jaun•ty (jôn´tē, jän´tē) *adj.* Perky; cheerful; energetic.

jeer (jîr) *v.* To mock or taunt loudly.

jes•ter (jĕs´tər) *n.* In the Middle Ages, a person kept by kings, queens, and other nobles to entertain or amuse them.

jews'-harp also **jew's-harp** (jo͞oz´härp´) *n.* A small, metal instrument held between the teeth that makes a soft twanging sound.

jock•ey (jŏk´ē) *v.* **jock•ey•ing.** To maneuver.

jo•cose (jō-kōs´) *adj.* Jolly; humorous. —**jo•cose´ly** *adv.*

jos•tle (jŏs´əl) *v.* To push or bump.

junc•ture (jŭngk´chər) *n.* Point in time.

jus•tice (jŭs´tĭs) *n.* Fair treatment according to law or honor.

ka•chi•na (kə-chē´nə) *n.* **1.** Hopi term for an imaginary spirit, believed to bring rain. **2.** A masked dancer in costume representing an imaginary spirit.

keel (kēl) *n.* A strong piece or beam of wood or metal that runs down the center of the bottom of a ship or boat. —*v.* To fall down.

keen (kēn) *adj.* Piercing; sharp. —**keen´ly** *adv.*

kins•man (kĭnz´mən) *n.* Relative.

kirk (kûrk) *n.* Church.

kith and kin (kĭth´ ən kĭn´) *n.* Friends and family.

kiva (kē´və) *n.* Hopi term for an underground room where men of the tribe hold meetings and ceremonies.

la•bo•ri•ous (lə-bôr´ē-əs, lə-bōr´ē-əs) *adj.* Involving hard work. —**la•bo´ri•ous•ly** *adv.*

lab•y•rinth (lăb´ə-rĭnth´) *n.* Maze.

lad•en (lād´n) *adj.* Loaded or filled with something.

la•goon (lə-gōōn´) *n.* A shallow body of water connected to the ocean.

lair (lâr) *n.* The den or home of a wild animal.

la•ment (lə-mĕnt´) *v.* **la•ment•ed.** To mourn.

lance (lăns) *n.* A weapon made of a long spear with a sharp metal head.

land•scape (lănd´skāp´) *n.* A piece of land or countryside that has its own special appearance.

la•pel (lə-pĕl´) *n.* Either of the two flaps that go down from the collar of a coat or jacket and fold back against the chest.

lapse (lăps) *v.* **lapsed.** To pass by.

lar•der (lär´dər) *n.* A place to store food.

lat•i•tude (lăt´ĭ-tōōd´, lăt´ĭ-tyōōd´) *n.* Distance north or south of the equator, expressed in degrees. On a map or globe, latitude lines are drawn running east and west.

lat•tice (lăt´ĭs) *n.* **lat•ticed.** Framework of strips of wood or metal woven with spaces between.

laur•el (lôr´əl, lŏr´əl) *n.* An evergreen tree.

la•va (lä´və, lăv´ə) *n.* Hot melted rock that flows from a volcano.

lav•ish (lăv´ĭsh) *adj.* Extravagant; abundantly furnished. —**lav´ish•ly** *adv.*

lay-up (lā´ŭp´) *n.* A shot made with one hand from near the basket in basketball.

league (lēg) *n.* **1.** A group of people working together for a common purpose. **2.** An association of sports teams that compete mainly among themselves. **3.** Unit of distance equal to three miles.

lei•sure•ly (lē´zhər-lē, lĕzh´ər-lē) *adj.* Without haste; not hurried. —*adv.* At a slow or moderate rate of speed.

le•ni•ent (lē´nē-ənt, lēn´yənt) *adj.* Not strict or severe. —**le´ni•ent•ly** *adv.*

lilt•ing (lĭlt´ĭng) *adj.* Lively; rhythmic.

li•no•le•um (lĭ-nō´lē-əm) *n.* A durable, smooth flooring material.

lisp (lĭsp) *v.* **lisp•ing.** To speak with difficulty in pronouncing words.

list (lĭst) *n.* Stadium for jousting.

lit•er•a•cy (lĭt´ər-ə-sē) *n.* The ability to read and write.

lit•er•ar•y (lĭt´ə-rĕr´ē) *adj.* Having to do with writing or literature.

lithe (līth) *adj.* Easily bent; flexible.

liv•er•y (lĭv´ə-rē, lĭv´rē) *n.* Uniform worn by male servants of a household.

loath (lōth, lōth) *adj.* Unwilling.

loathe (lōth) *v.* **loathed.** To despise; hate.

lattice

lodge (lŏj) *v.* **lodged. 1.** To live in a place. **2.** To present or submit a complaint to the proper official.

log•ic (lŏj´ĭk) *n.* A way of thinking or reasoning.

log•i•cal (lŏj´ĭ-kəl) *adj.* Able to think clearly and sensibly; reasonable.

loi•ter (loi´tər) *v.* **loi•ter•ing.** Standing about in an idle manner.

loom (lo͞om) *n.* Machine for weaving threads to make a cloth.
—*v.* **loomed, loom•ing.** To come into view as large and dangerous.

loot (lo͞ot) *v.* **loot•ing.** To steal valuable things, especially in a time of war or chaos.

lot (lŏt) *n.* **1.** A large amount or number. **2.** A kind, type, or sort. **3.** A piece of land. **4.** One's fortune in life; fate.

Lou•vre (lo͞o´vrə) *n.* One of the largest art museums in the world, located in Paris, France.

lub•ber•ly (lŭb´ər-lē) *adj. & adv.* Clumsy.

lu•di•crous (lo͞o´dĭ-krəs) *adj.* Absurd or ridiculous.

lull (lŭl) *n.* Brief period of quiet or calm.
—*v.* **lulled.** To make or become quiet; calm.

lunge (lŭnj) *v.* **lunged.** To move forward suddenly.

lurch (lûrch) *v.* **lurched.** To move suddenly and violently.

lure (lo͝or) *v.* To attract; tempt.

lu•rid (lo͝or´ĭd) *adj.* Bright; vivid.

lurk (lûrk) *v.* **lurk•ing.** To sneak around waiting for something.

lux•u•ri•ant (lŭg-zho͝or´ē-ənt, lŭk-sho͝or´ē-ənt) *adj.* Abundant or rich.

lux•u•ri•ous (lŭg-zho͝or´ē-əs, lŭk-sho͝or´ē-əs) *adj.* Very rich, comfortable, splendid, or costly.

loom

manor

mack•in•tosh (măk´ĭn-tŏsh´) *n.* Raincoat.

mag•is•trate (măj´ĭ-strāt´, măj´ĭ-strĭt) *n.* A judge with limited authority.

mail (māl) *n.* **1.** Letters, packages, and other items sent and received through a postal system. **2.** Armor made of connected metal rings, chain loops, or scales.

main•te•nance (mān´tə-nəns) *n.* The act of maintaining or taking care of.

make•shift (māk´shĭft´) *adj.* Put together quickly from materials at hand.

mal•ice (măl´ĭs) *n.* Ill will; spite.

ma•lign (mə-līn´) *adj.* Evil.

man•date (măn´dāt) *n.* An order.

ma•neu•ver (mə-no͞o´vər, mə-nyo͞o´vər) *n.* A clever movement; skillful trick.

mang•y (mān´jē) *adj.* Having bare or dirty spots; shabby.

man•or (măn´ər) *n.* The large main house of an estate.

man•u•fac•ture (măn´yə-făk´chər) *v.* **man•u•fac•tured.** To make a product in large quantities, usually by using machinery.
—*n.* The making of goods in large quantities.

mar (mär) *v.* **marred.** To damage, especially the looks of.

mar•a•thon (măr´ə-thŏn´) *n.* A long race.

ma•raud (mə-rôd´) *v.* **ma•raud•ing.** To go through a land and rob its inhabitants.

ma•roon (mə-ro͞on´) *v.* To leave a person helpless and alone on a deserted shore or island.

mar•row (măr´ō) *n.* The soft material inside bones.

Mars[1] (märz) *n.* The mythical Roman god of war.

Mars[2] (märz) *n. colloquial* Abbreviation of "Master" used in the southern U.S.: *"Mars Tom."*

marsh (märsh) *n., pl.* **marsh•es.** An area of low, wet land; swamp.

mar•tin•gale (mär´tn-gāl´) *n.* A strap between a horse's girth and nosepiece used to steady the head.

mar•tyr (mär´tər) *n.* A person who chooses to die rather than give up a religion or belief.

mas•seur (mă-sûr´, mə-sûr´) *n.* A man who massages athletes to relax their muscles and improve their blood circulation.

may•hap (mā´hăp´, mā-hăp´) *adv.* Maybe.

mea•gre or **mea•ger** (mē´gər) *adj.* Lacking in quantity; poor.

mean (mēn) *adj.* **1.** Common; low in status. **2.** Hard to handle; troublesome.

me•di•e•val (mē´dē-ē´vəl, mĕd´ē-ē´vəl) *adj.* Applying to anything in the Middle Ages (A.D. 500-1500).

mel•an•chol•y (mĕl´ən-kŏl´ē) *n.* Sadness; gloominess.

mel•low (mĕl´ō) **mel•lowed.** *adj.* Seasoned with age.

mem•o•ra•ble (mĕm´ər-ə-bəl) *adj.* Unforgettable.

men•ace (mĕn´ĭs) *adj.* To threaten with harm; endanger. **—men´ac•ing•ly** *adv.*

me•nag•er•ie (mə-năj´ə-rē, mə-năzh´ə-rē) *n.* A collection of strange animals; a zoo.

Mer•cu•ry (mûr´kyə-rē) *n.* The mythical Roman messenger of the gods.

merge (mûrj) *v.* **merg•ing.** To blend together gradually.

me•ri•no (mə-rē´nō) *n.* A fine wool used to make certain articles of clothing.

mer•it (mĕr´ĭt) *n.* Value; worth.

met•ro (mĕt´rō) *n.* Subway system.

min•strel (mĭn´strəl) *n.* A court musician.

mi•nute (mī-nyo͞ot´ or mĭ-nyo͞ot´) *adj.* Careful and detailed.

mi•ser (mī´zər) *n.* A stingy person who lives like a poor person to save money.

mis•for•tune (mĭs-fôr´chən) *n.* **1.** Bad luck. **2.** An unlucky event.

mod•er•ate (mŏd´ər-ĭt) *adj.* Not too much or too little; not extreme or excessive.

mon•o•logue (mŏn´ə-lôg´, mŏn´ə-lŏg´) *n.* A long speech by one person.

mon•o•tone (mŏn´ə-tōn´) *n.* Unchanging tone of voice.

mo•not•o•nous (mə-nŏt´n-əs) *adj.* Never changing; dull.

moon (mo͞on) *n.* A month.

moor (mo͞or) *v.* **moored.** To tie down or make secure with ropes.

mo•roc•co (mə-rŏk´ō) *n.* Type of leather.

mor•row (môr´ō, mŏr´ō) *n.* Tomorrow; the next day.

mor•tal (môr´tl) *adj.* Having to do with death.

mor•tar (môr´tər) *n.* A building material made of sand, water, lime, and sometimes cement. **—v. mor•tared.** To build with mortar.

mor•ti•fi•ca•tion (môr´tə-fĭ-kā´shən) *n.* Extreme embarrassment; shame.

Mos•lem (mŏz´ləm, mŏs´ləm) *n.* A person who believes in the religion of Islam.

mot•to (mŏt´ō) *n.* A saying that expresses what is important to a state, nation, family, group, person, or organization.

muck (mŭk) *v.* To clean the dirt or manure from.

metro

ă	pat	ĕ	pet
ā	pay	ē	be
âr	care	ĭ	pit
ä	father	ī	pie
îr	fierce	oi	oil
ŏ	pot	o͝o	book
ō	go	o͞o	boot
ô	paw,	yo͞o	abuse
	for	ou	out
ŭ	cut	ə	ago,
ûr	fur		item,
th	the		pencil,
th	thin		atom,
hw	which		circus
zh	vision	ər	butter

ă pat	ĕ pet
ā pay	ē be
âr care	ĭ pit
ä father	ī pie
îr fierce	oi oil
ŏ pot	o͝o book
ō go	o͞o boot
ô paw,	yo͞o abuse
for	ou out
ŭ cut	ə ago,
ûr fur	item,
th the	pencil,
th thin	atom,
hw which	circus
zh vision	ər butter

mus•ket (mŭs´kĭt) *n.* An old gun with a long barrel, used before the invention of the rifle.

mute (myo͞ot) *adj.* Choosing not to speak. —**mute´ly** *adv.*

mu•ti•nous (myo͞ot´n-əs) *adj.* Rebellious.

mut•ton (mŭt´n) *n.* The meat of a fully grown sheep.

muz•zle (mŭz´əl) *n.* The projecting part of an animal's face that includes the nose and mouth; snout.

myr•i•ad (mĭr´ē-əd) *n.* An extremely large number.

myr•tle (mûr´tl) *n.* A shrub with evergreen leaves, white or pinkish flowers, and blackish berries.

nan•ny (năn´ē) *n.* A person who cares for the children of one family in exchange for pay.

nar•ra•tive (năr´ə-tĭv) *n.* A story.

na•sal (nā´zəl) *adj.* Produced through the nose.

nau•ti•cal (nô´tĭ-kəl) *adj.* Of ships, sailors, or navigation.

nav•i•gate (năv´ĭ-gāt´) *v.* To plan and/or control the course of a ship or aircraft.

nav•i•ga•tion (năv´ĭ-gā´shən) *n.* The act or practice of navigating.

neg•lect (nĭ-glĕkt´) *v.* **1.** To fail to care for or give proper attention to. **2.** To fail to do.

nes•tle (nĕs´əl) *v.* **nes•tled.** To situate oneself comfortably.

net•work (nĕt´wûrk´) *n.* A system or pattern.

new•fan•gled (no͞o´făng´gəld, nyo͞o´făng´gəld) *adj.* Something original and novel.

newt (no͞ot, nyo͞ot) *n.* A type of salamander.

newt

nig•gling (nĭg´lĭng) *adj.* Troublesome.

nim•ble (nĭm´bəl) *adj.* Moving or able to move quickly, lightly, and easily. —**nim´bly** *adv.*

Ni•zam (nĭ-zäm´, nĭ-zäm´, nī-zäm´) *n.* Former title of a ruler in India.

no•bil•i•ty (nō-bĭl´ĭ-tē) *n.* **1.** A social class having titles of rank and often wealth and power. Queens, kings, princes, and princesses are all part of the nobility. **2.** Fine character.

nod•dy (nŏd´ē) *n.* A fool.

nom•i•nal (nŏm´ə-nəl) *adj.* Small; insignificant.

not•with•stand•ing (nŏt´wĭth-stăn´dĭng) *adv.* Even so; in spite of.

nov•ice (nŏv´ĭs) *n.* A person who is new to a field or activity; a beginner.

nui•sance (no͞o´səns, nyo͞o´səns) *n.* Someone or something that annoys or is not convenient; a bother.

nunch•eon (nŭn´chən) *n.* A snack.

nu•tri•tive (no͞o´trĭ-tĭv, nyo͞o´trĭ-tĭv) *adj.* Nutritious; nourishing.

o•bese (ō-bēs´) *adj.* Very fat.

ob•jec•tive (əb-jĕk´tĭv) *adj.* Impartial; open-minded. —*n.* Goal; purpose.

o•blige (ə-blīj´) *v.* **o•bliged, o•blig•ing. 1.** To force to act in a certain way. **2.** To make grateful or thankful. **3.** To satisfy the wishes of; do a favor for.

o•bliv•i•on (ə-blĭv´ē-ən) *n.* Nothingness.

o•bliv•i•ous (ə-blĭv´ē-əs) *adj.* Inattentive; unaware.

ob•nox•ious (ŏb-nŏk´shəs, əb-nŏk´shəs) *adj.* Very disagreeable.

ob•scure (ŏb-skyo͝or´, əb-skyo͝or´) *v.* **ob•scured.** To hide from view.

ob•sta•cle (ŏb´stə-kəl) *n.* Anything that blocks the way.

ob•sti•nate (ŏb´stə-nĭt) *adj.* Stubborn; unwilling to give up.
—**ob´sti•nate•ly** *adv.*

ob•tain (əb-tān´, ŏb-tān´) *v.* **ob•tained.** To get by means of planning or effort; acquire; gain.

oc•cu•pant (ŏk´yə-pənt) *n.* A person who is living in or holding a place or position.

of•fi•cious (ə-fĭsh´əs) *adj.* Overly eager to perform one's duties.
—**of•fi´cious•ly** *adv.*

off•spring (ôf´sprĭng´, ŏf´sprĭng´) *n.* A descendant.

o•mit (ō-mĭt´) *v.* To leave out; not include.

on my ac•count (ŏn mī ə-kount´) *prep. phrase.* For me; because of me.

on•set (ŏn´sĕt´, ôn´sĕt´) *n.* Assault; attack.

ope (ōp) *v.* To open.

op•por•tune (ŏp´ər-tōōn´, ŏp´ər-tyōōn´) *adj.* Taking place at a good time.

op•pose (ə-pōz´) *v.* **op•posed.** To be against.

op•po•si•tion (ŏp´ə-zĭsh´ən) *n.* **1.** The act or condition of opposing or being against; resistance. **2.** Something that is an opposing obstacle.

or•deal (ôr-dēl´) *n.* A very difficult or painful experience or test.

out•house (out´hous´) *n.* A small building that houses a toilet, for use when there is no indoor plumbing.

out•land•ish (out-lăn´dĭsh) *adj.* Foreign or strange.

out•rid•er (out´rī´dər) *n.* A rider who goes before; escort.

o•ver•girth (ō´ver-gûrth´) *n.* Strap that holds a saddle on a horse.

o•ver•rule (ō´ver-rōōl´) *v.* To disallow actions or arguments.

o•ver•whelm (ō´ver-hwĕlm´, ō´ver-wĕlm´) *v.* **o•ver•whelmed, o•ver•whelm•ing.** To overcome completely; overpower.

o•ver•wrought (ō´ver-rôt´) *adj.* Very worried.

pad (păd) *n.* Small cushion-like parts on the bottoms of the feet of certain animals.
—*v.* **pad•ded.** To line, stuff, or cover with soft, firmly packed material.

pad•dock (păd´ək) *n.* A fenced field.

pains•tak•ing (pānz´tā´kĭng) *adj.* Needing or showing great care; careful.

pal•a•din (păl´ə-dĭn) *n.* A knightly hero; renowned champion.

pale horse (pāl hôrs) *n.* Symbol of death from Revelation chapter six.

pall (pôl) *n.* A covering.

par•a•pet (păr´ə-pĭt, păr´ə-pĕt´) *n.* Low wall built to protect soldiers.

par•cel (pär´səl) *n.* A package.

parch•ment (pärch´mənt) *n.* Writing material of sheepskin or goatskin.

par•ing (pâr´ĭng) *n.* The outer portion that is removed from fruit, vegetables, or cheese.

pa•rish (păr´ĭsh) *n.* A church district in the Anglican, Roman Catholic, and some other churches.

pa•rish•ion•er (pə-rĭsh´ə-nər) *n.* Member of a parish.

par•lor also **par•lour** (pär´lər) *n.* A room for entertaining visitors.

par•son (pär´sən) *n.* A clergyman or minister.

par•son•age (pär´sə-nĭj) *n.* House provided for the pastor of a church.

pate (pāt) *n.* Head or mind.

parapet

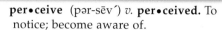

pa•thet•ic (pə-thĕt´ĭk) *adj.* Causing or making one feel pity or sorrow; pitiful. —**pa•thet´i•cal•ly** *adv.*

pa•tri•arch (pā´trē-ärk´) *n.* An ancestor of the Israelites.

pa•tron (pā´trən) *n.* A person who helps or supports another by giving him money or things.

pat•sy (păt´sē) *n.* Something or someone easily taken advantage of.

paul•dron (pôl´drən) *n.* Armor that covers the shoulder.

paunch (pônch, pänch) *n.* Stomach.

pau•per (pô´pər) *n.* One who is very poor.

pa•vil•ion (pə-vĭl´yən) *n.* A fancy or elaborate tent.

pa•viour (pāv´yər) *n.* A man who paves streets.

pawn•bro•ker (pôn´brō´kər) *n.* One who lends money, exchanging it for personal items to hold until the money is paid back.

peach (pēch) *v.* **peached.** To tattle.

pe•cu•liar (pĭ-kyōōl´yər) *adj.* **1.** Unusual or odd; not normal; strange. **2.** Belonging to a special or particular person, group, place, or thing.

pe•des•tri•an (pə-dĕs´trē-ən) *n.* Person who travels on foot.

pel•let (pĕl´ĭt) *n.* A kind of bullet for certain kinds of guns.

pelt (pĕlt) *n.* An animal skin with the hair or fur still on it.

pen•e•trate (pĕn´ĭ-trāt´) *v.* To go into or through.

pen•i•cil•li•um (pĕn´ĭ-sĭl´ē-əm) *n.* Fungus from which the medicine, penicillin, is made.

pen•sion•er (pĕn´shə-nər) *n.* Person receiving a sum of money, usually after retirement.

per•am•bu•la•tor (pə-răm´byə-lā´tər) *n.* A baby carriage.

perambulator

per•ceive (pər-sēv´) *v.* **per•ceived.** To notice; become aware of.

per•cep•tive (pər-sĕp´tĭv) *adj.* Having keen discernment and understanding.

per•il (pĕr´əl) *n.* Danger

per•il•ous (pĕr´ə-ləs) *adj.* Full of peril; dangerous.

per•pet•u•al (pər-pĕch´ōō-əl) *adj.* Going on without stopping.

per•se•vere (pûr´sə-vîr´) *v.* **per•se•vered.** To keep on; persist.

pes•ti•lence (pĕs´tə-ləns) *n.* A plague.

pe•ti•tion (pə-tĭsh´ən) *v.* **pe•ti•tion•ing.** To make a formal request to.

pe•tri dish (pē´trē dĭsh) *n.* A small, flat, covered dish used to grow microorganisms.

pet•ri•fy (pĕt´rə-fī´) *v.* **pet•ri•fied.** To daze with fear or surprise; paralyze.

pet•ty (pĕt´ē) *adj.* Of low rank.

pew•ter (pyōō´tər) *n.* A kind of metal made from tin, copper, and lead.

phil•o•soph•i•cal (fĭl´ə-sŏf´ĭ-kəl) *adj.* Of philosophy.

phi•los•o•phy (fĭ-lŏs´ə-fē) *n.* A person's beliefs about life and the world.

phys•i•cal ther•a•py (fĭz´ĭ-kəl thĕr´ə-pē) *n.* Treatment consisting of special exercises and massaging the body to restore proper movement of muscles and limbs.

pic•tur•esque (pĭk´chə-rĕsk´) *adj.* Interesting or very attractive.

pie•bald (pī´bôld´) *adj.* Spotted or patched in color.

pied (pīd) *adj.* Having splotches of color.

pig•my (pĭg´mē) *adj.* Unusually small.

pi•ki (pē´kē) *n.* Thin bread made from corn.

pil•fer (pĭl´fər) *v.* **pil•fered.** To steal, usually small things.

pil•lar (pĭl´ər) *n.* A column that is used to hold up a building. —*fig.* Used figuratively to describe one who has an important position.

pin•nace (pĭn´ĭs) *n.* A small sailing boat.

plac•id (plăs´ĭd) *adj.* Calm or peaceful. —**plac´id•ly** *adv.*

plague (plāg) *n.* A very serious disease that spreads rapidly from person to person.

plat•i•num (plăt´n-əm) *n.* A silver-white metallic element.

plight (plīt) *n.* A difficult situation.

plume (plo͞om) *n.* A large or showy feather, often used for decoration. —*v.* To pride oneself.

plunge (plŭnj) *v.* **plunged, plung•ing. 1.** To throw suddenly into something. **2.** To thrust. —*n., pl.* **plung•es.**

poach (pōch) *v.* **poach•ing.** To hunt illegally.

poach•er (pō´chər) *n.* One who hunts illegally.

point (point) *n.* **points.** Movable part of a railroad switch.

poise (poiz) *v.* **poised.** To balance or be balanced.

poke (pōk) *n.* A sack.

pom•mel (pŭm´əl, pŏm´əl) *n.* The raised front of a saddle.

pomp and cir•cum•stance (pŏmp ən sûr´kəm-stăns´) *n.* A show of splendor or formality.

pom•pous (pŏm´pəs) *adj.* Overly conscious of one's importance.

pop•u•lace (pŏp´yə-lĭs) *n.* The common people.

pop•u•late (pŏp´yə-lāt´) *v.* **pop•u•lat•ed.** To supply or be supplied with inhabitants.

pop•u•la•tion (pŏp´yə-lā´shən) *n.* The number of people or animals that live in a certain place.

po•rous (pôr´əs, pōr´əs) *adj.* Allowing liquid or air to pass through.

port (pôrt, pōrt) *n.* **1.** A place along a river, lake, ocean, or other body of water where ships may dock or anchor; harbor. **2.** A city or town with a harbor. **3.** The left side of a ship.

por•tal (pôr´tl, pōr´tl) *n.* Doorway or entrance.

por•ter (pôr´tər, pōr´tər) *n.* A person hired to carry or move luggage at a station, airport, or hotel.

port•ly (pôrt´lē, pōrt´lē) *adj.* Fat or stout in a dignified way.

po•ten•tial (pə-tĕn´shəl) *adj.* Not yet real or definite, but possible in the future.

prac•tice (prăk´tĭs) *n.* The group of people who use the services of a doctor; a professional business.

prag•mat•ic (prăg-măt´ĭk) *adj.* Interested only in the desired result of an action rather than in the correctness of the action.

pre•cede (prĭ-sēd´) *v.* **pre•ced•ed, pre•ced•ing.** To come or go before.

prec•i•pice (prĕs´ə-pĭs) *n.* A steep cliff.

pre•cip•i•tate (prĭ-sĭp´ĭ-tāt´) *v.* To throw down from a high place.

pre•cip•i•ta•tion (prĭ-sĭp´ĭ-tā´shən) *n.* The amount of rain, snow, sleet, or hail that falls from the sky to the earth's surface.

pre•cise•ly (prĭ-sīs´lē) *adv.* Exactly.

pre•ci•sion (prĭ-sĭzh´ən) *adj.* The condition of being precise or exact; accuracy.

pred•a•tor (prĕd´ə-tər, prĕd´ə-tôr) *n.* An animal that lives by catching and eating other animals.

pred•e•ces•sor (prĕd´ĭ-sĕs´ər, prē´dĭ-sĕs´ər) *n.* Someone or something that came before or had a function before another.

ă	pat	ĕ	pet
ā	pay	ē	be
âr	care	ĭ	pit
ä	father	ī	pie
îr	fierce	oi	oil
ŏ	pot	o͝o	book
ō	go	o͞o	boot
ô	paw,	yo͞o	abuse
	for	ou	out
ŭ	cut	ə	ago,
ûr	fur		item,
th	the		pencil,
th	thin		atom,
hw	which		circus
zh	vision	ər	butter

ă pat	ĕ pet
ā pay	ē be
âr care	ĭ pit
ä father	ī pie
îr fierce	oi oil
ŏ pot	o͝o book
ō go	o͞o boot
ô paw,	yo͞o abuse
for	ou out
ŭ cut	ə ago,
ûr fur	item,
th the	pencil,
th thin	atom,
hw which	circus
zh vision	ər butter

pre•face (prĕ´fĭs) *n.* An introduction to a book.

pre•fec•ture (prē´fĕk´chər) *n.* The place where the prefect, a high military official, lives.

pre•ma•ture (prē´mə-tyo͝or´, prē´mə-to͝or´) *adj.* Occuring too early. —**pre•ma•ture´ly** *adv.*

prem•is•es (prĕm´ĭs-ĕz) *n.* Someone's land or building.

pre•oc•cu•pied (prē-ŏk´yə-pīd´) *adj.* Distracted; lost in thought.

pre•scribe (prĭ-skrīb´) *v.* **pre•scribed.** To set; prearrange.

pres•ti•gious (prĕ-stē´jəs, prĕ-stĭj´əs) *adj.* Respected; valued as important.

pre•sume (prĭ-zo͞om´) *v.* **1.** To act without permission or authority. **2.** To suppose to be true.

prey (prā) *n.* Someone or something that is hunted.

prim (prĭm) *adj.* Showing proper manners. —**prim´ly** *adv.*

prime (prīm) *adj.* The best or highest stage or condition.

prim•i•tive (prĭm´ĭ-tĭv) *adj.* Of an early stage of history; simple; crude.

pri•or•i•ty (prī-ôr´ĭ-tē, prī-ŏr´ĭ-tē) *n.* Importance.

priv•i•ly (prĭv´ə-lē) *adv.* Privately.

priv•y to (prĭv´ē to͞o) *adj.* Aware of.

pro•cure (prō-kyo͝or´, prə-kyo͝or´) *v.* To obtain; acquire; get. —**pro•cur´a•ble** *adj.*

pro•fess (prə-fĕs´, prō-fəs´) *v.* **pro•fessed.** To declare to others; to claim.

pro•found (prə-found´, prō-found´) *adj.* **1.** Having or showing great knowledge and understanding of something; wise. **2.** Felt very deeply. —**pro•found´ly** *adv.*

pro•fuse (prə-fyo͞os´, prō-fyo͞os´) *adj.* More than is normal; excessive. —**pro•fuse´ly** *adv.*

psaltery

pro•fu•sion (prə-fyo͞o´zhən, prō-fyo͞o´zhən) *n.* Abundance; surplus.

prom•i•nence (prŏm´ə-nəns) *n.* Importance; distinction.

prom•i•nent (prŏm´ə-nənt) *adj.* Important.

prompt (prŏmpt) *adj.* Done at once, or without delay; quick. —**prompt´ly** *adv.* —*v.* To cause someone to act.

prop•a•ga•tion (prŏp´ə-gā´shən) *n.* Multiplication in number.

pro•pose (prə-pōz´) *v.* **pro•posed.** **1.** To bring up something or someone for consideration; suggest. **2.** To intend to do something.

pros•e•cu•tor (prŏs´ĭ-kyo͞o´tər) *n.* One who formally accuses another of a crime in court.

pros•per•i•ty (prŏ-spĕr´ĭ-tē) *n.* Success, especially in money matters.

pro•voke (prə-vōk´) *v.* **pro•vok•ing.** To make angry; annoy.

prowl (proul) *v.* **prowled, prowl•ing.** To move about quietly, as if in search of prey.

psal•ter•y (sôl´tə-rē) *n.* Ancient stringed musical instrument.

pub•lish (pŭb´lĭsh) *v.* **pub•lished.** To print material to be sold to the public.

pu•gi•list (pyo͞o´jə-lĭst) *n.* A boxer.

punch•eon (pŭn´chən) *n.* A cask or container.

pun•gent (pŭn´jənt) *adj.* Having a sharp, biting taste or smell.

pur•i•fy (pyo͝or´ə-fī´) *v.* **pur•i•fied.** To make clean and pure.

quack (kwăk) *adj.* Characteristic of a person or thing that lacks qualified medical information.

quaint (kwānt) *adj.* Strange; old-fashioned.

quan•da•ry (kwŏn´də-rē, kwŏn´drē) *n.* A perplexing situation.

quar•rel (kwôr´əl, kwŏr´əl) *n.* An angry argument.
—*v.* To have a quarrel; argue angrily.

quar•rier (kwôr´ē-ər, kwŏr´ē-ər) *n.* One who cuts stone from an open place called a quarry.

quar•ry (kwôr´ē, kwŏr´ē) *n.* A person or animal that is hunted; prey.

quest (kwĕst) *n.* Mission; search for something of value.

rab•ble (răb´əl) *n.* Lower-class people.

ra•jah (rä´jə) *n.* A ruler of India.

ram•ble (răm´bəl) *n.* A stroll.

rank (răngk) *n.* A high or important position in a group.
—*adj.* Abundant.

rap•pel (ră-pĕl´) *v.* **rap•pelled, rap•pel•ling.** To climb down the side of a high, steep place by using a rope.

rapt (răpt) *adj.* Absorbed attention; delight. —**rapt´ly** *adv.*

rap•tur•ous (răp´chər-əs) *adj.* Delighted; overjoyed.

ra•tion (răsh´ən, rā´shən) *v.* **ra•tioned.** To limit the amount of something each person can use or have.

rav•en•ous (răv´ə-nəs) *adj.* Very hungry.

ra•vine (rə-vēn´) *n.* A deep, narrow opening in the ground.

re•cede (rĭ-sēd´) *v.* To move farther and farther away.

re•cep•tion (rĭ-sĕp´shən) *n.* A social gathering in honor of someone.

re•cess (rē´sĕs´, rĭ-sĕs´) *n.* A small hollow place or indentation.

rec•i•ta•tion (rĕs´ĭ-tā´shən) *n.* The act of reciting.

re•cite (rĭ-sīt´) *v.* **re•ci•ted.** To repeat something memorized in front of an audience.

re•coil (rĭ-koil´) *v.* **re•coiled.** To kick back, as a fired gun.
—*n.* The act of kicking back.

re•com•mence (rē´kə-mĕns´, rĕk-ə-mĕns´) *v.* To start again. **See commence.**

rec•on•cile (rĕk´ən-sīl´) *v.* **rec•on•ciled.** To come to accept.

re•con•noi•ter (rē´kə-noi´tər, rĕk´ə-noi´tər) *v.* To inspect an unknown area.

re•con•sti•tu•ted (rē-kŏn´stĭ-tōōt´ĭd, rē-kŏn´stĭ-tyōōt´ĭd) *adj.* Put back in its original form by adding water.

re•count (rē-kount´) *v.* **re•count•ed.** To describe; tell what happened.

re•deem (rĭ-dēm´) *v.* **re•deemed, re•deem•ing.** To rescue or pay for.

re•demp•tion (rĭ-dĕmp´shən) *n.* Man's salvation.

reef (rēf) *n.* A strip or ridge of rock, sand, or coral at or near the surface of a body of water.

reek (rēk) *v.* **reeked.** To smell strongly.

reel (rēl) *v.* **reeled.** To walk unsteadily; stagger.

re•frain (rĭ-frān´) *n.* A phrase repeated several times in a poem or song; chorus.

ref•uge (rĕf´yōōj) *n.* A place where one can go for protection.

ref•u•gee (rĕf´yōō-jē´) *n.* A person who flees from his own country to find protection or safety.

re•gain (rē-gān´) *v.* **re•gained, re•gain•ing.** To get back; recover.

re•ga•lia (rĭ-gāl´yə, rĭ-gā´lē-ə) *n.* The emblems and symbols of royalty; fancy clothing.

reg•is•ter (rĕj´ĭ-stər) *n.* An official written list or record.
—*v.* **reg•is•tered. 1.** To record in the mind. **2.** To officially write on a list or record.

regalia

ă	pat	ĕ	pet
ā	pay	ē	be
âr	care	ĭ	pit
ä	father	ī	pie
îr	fierce	oi	oil
ŏ	pot	o͝o	book
ō	go	o͞o	boot
ô	paw,	yo͞o	abuse
	for	ou	out
ŭ	cut	ə	ago,
ûr	fur		item,
th	the		pencil,
th	thin		atom,
hw	which		circus
zh	vision	ər	butter

relic

reservoir

640

reg•u•late (rĕg´yə-lāt´) *v.*
reg•u•la•ted. 1. To control or direct according to certain rules. **2.** To adjust a machine or device so that it works properly.

reg•u•la•tion (rĕg´yə-lā´shən) *n.* A law or set of rules by which something is regulated.

reign (rān) *n.* The period of time that a monarch rules.
—*v.* To have or hold the power of a monarch; rule.
—*adj.* **reign•ing.** Holding the power of a monarch; ruling.

re•kin•dle (rē-kĭn´dl) *v.* **re•kin•dled.** To restart.

re•lapse (rĭ-lăps´) *v.* **re•lapsed, re•laps•ing.** To fall back into a previous condition.

re•lay (rē´lā) *v.* **re•lay•ing.** To pass or send along.
—*n.* A race between groups of runners or swimmers in which each member goes only part of the total distance.

re•lent (rĭ-lĕnt´) *v.* **re•lent•ed.** To give in.

re•lent•less (rĭ-lĕnt´lĭs) *adj.* Persistent; not giving up.
—**re•lent´less•ly** *adv.*

rel•ic (rĕl´ĭk) *n.* Something that survives from the distant past.

re•lieve (rĭ-lēv´) *v.* **re•lieved.** To lessen or reduce pain or anxiety; ease.

rel•ish (rĕl´ĭsh) *v.* **rel•ished, rel•ish•ing.** To enjoy.

re•lo•cate (rē-lō´kāt) *v.* The act of moving from one place to another.
—**re´lo•ca´tion** *n.*

re•luc•tance (rĭ-lŭk´təns) *n.* Unwillingness; lack of enthusiasm.

rem•e•dy (rĕm´ĭ-dē) *n., pl.* **rem•e•dies.** Something that cures a disease or relieves pain.

re•mon•strate (rĭ-mŏn´strāt) *v.* **re•mon•stra•ted.** To object; protest.

re•morse (rĭ-môrs´) *n.* Regret; repentance.

re•morse•ful (rĭ-môrs´fəl) *adj.* Characterized by remorse.
—**re•morse´ful•ly** *adv.*

re•mote (rĭ-mōt´) *adj.* Far away.

ren•der (rĕn´dər) *v.* **ren•dered.** To cause to become; make.

re•nown (rĭ-noun´) *n.* Honor; fame.
—*adj.* **re•nowned.** Having honor and fame.

re•pose•ful (rĭ-pōz´fəl) *adj.* Restful.

re•pug•nant (rĭ-pŭg´nənt) *adj.* Repulsive; disgusting.

re•sent (rĭ-zĕnt´) *v.* To feel angry or bitter about.

re•sent•ment (rĭ-zĕnt´mənt) *n.* A bitter or angry feeling.

re•serve (rĭ-zûrv´) *n.* A supply of something for later use.
—*adj.* **re•served.** Quiet; not eager to talk.

res•er•voir (rĕz´ər-vwär´, rĕz´ər-vwôr´, rĕz´ər-vôr´) *n.* A body of water that has been collected and stored for use.

re•sign (rĭ-zīn´) *v.* **re•signed.** To give up.

res•in (rĕz´ĭn) *n.* A thick, clear liquid that some plants produce.

res•o•lute (rĕz´ə-lo͞ot´) *adj.* Firm; determined. —**res´o•lute´ly** *adv.*

res•o•lu•tion (rĕz´ə-lo͞o´shən) *n.* **1.** The ending of a story where the plot comes together. **2.** A formal statement put before an assembly for a decision.

re•solve (rĭ-zŏlv´) *v.* **re•solved. 1.** To make a firm decision. **2.** To bring to a conclusion.
—*n.* Determination.

re•sort (rĭ-zôrt´) *n.* Means of achieving something.

re•splen•dent (rĭ-splĕn´dənt) *adj.* Splendid; brilliant.

re•strain (rĭ-strān´) *v.* **re•strained.** To hold back by physical force.

re•straint (rĭ-strānt´) *n.* Something used to hold back or restrain.

re•strict (rĭ-strĭkt´) *v.* **re•strict•ed.** To keep within limits; confine.

re•sume (rĭ-zōōm´) *v.* **re•sumed.** To begin again; continue.

ret•i•nue (rĕt´n-ōō, rĕt´n-yōō´) *n.* Group of servants.

re•treat (rĭ-trēt´) *v.* **re•treat•ed, re•treat•ing.** To withdraw. —*n.* **1.** The act of withdrawing under enemy attack. **2.** A quiet and private place.

re•trieve (rĭ-trēv´) *v.* To get back; recover.

re•veal (rĭ-vēl´) *v.* **re•vealed, re•veal•ing.** To make known.

rev•el (rĕv´əl) *v.* **re•vel•ing.** To delight.

rev•e•la•tion (rĕv´ə-lā´shən) *n.* The act of making known.

re•ver•ber•ate (rĭ-vûr´bə-rāt) *v.* **re•ver•ber•a•ting.** To echo.

rev•er•ence (rĕv´ər-əns) *n.* A feeling of deep respect.

rev•er•ent (rĕv´ər-ənt) *adj.* Feeling or showing reverence. —**rev´er•ent•ly** *adv.*

rev•er•ie (rĕv´ə-rē) *n.* Daydream.

re•vive (rĭ-vīv´) *v.* **re•vived.** To bring back.

re•voke (rĭ-vōk´) *v.* **re•voked.** To take back or take away.

re•volt (rĭ-vōlt´) *v.* **re•volt•ed.** To be filled with disgust; be repulsed by.

re•vul•sion (rĭ-vŭl´shən) *n.* A strong change in feeling; disgust.

rib•ald (rĭb´əld, rī´bôld´) *n.* An offensive person.

ric•o•chet (rĭk´ə-shā´, rĭk´ə-shā´) *v.* To rebound from a surface.

rid•i•cule (rĭd´ĭ-kyōol´) *n.* Words or actions that make fun of something or someone.

rit•u•al (rĭch´ōō-əl) *n.* A regularly observed way of doing things.

rogue (rōg) *n.* A dishonest person; a cheat.

rouse (rouz) *v.* **roused, rous•ing.** To cause to become active or alert.

roust (roust) *v.* To wake; stir up.

rove (rōv) *v.* **roved, rov•ing.** To wander.

roy•al•ty (roi´əl-tē) *n.* Kings, queens, and other members of a royal family.

rue (rōō) *v.* To regret.

rue•ful (rōō´fəl) *adj.* Causing one to feel pity or sorrow; regret. —**rue´ful•ly** *adv.*

rum•mage (rŭm´ĭj) *v.* **rum•maged.** To search thoroughly by moving things around or turning them over.

run•way (rŭn´wā´) *n.* A strip of pavement along which an airplane runs in preparation for takeoff.

rut•ted (rŭt´ĭd) *adj.* Filled with tracks or grooves made by the passage of a wheel or foot.

sack•cloth (săk´klôth´, săk´klŏth´) *n.* A rough cloth worn as a symbol of mourning.

Sa•hib (sä´ĭb, sä´ēb, sä´hĭb) *n.* Term used in India to address a European man.

sa•laam (sə-läm´) *n.* A respectful greeting; a low bow.

sal•ly (săl´ē) *v.* **sal•lied.** To set out.

sanc•tu•ar•y (săngk´chōō-ĕr´ē) *n.* An area where wild animals and birds are protected; place of protection and safety.

sackcloth

saun•ter (sôn´tər) *v.* **saun•ter•ing.** To walk casually.

sav•age (săv´ĭj) *adj.* **1.** Not tamed; wild. **2.** Cruel and fierce; ferocious; frightening. —**sav´age•ly** *adv.* —*n.* One who is wild or uncivilized.

sa•vor•y (sā´və-rē) *adj.* Appetizing to the taste or smell.

scab•bard (skăb´ərd) *n.* A sheath for a sword.

schol•ar (skŏl´ər) *n.* **1.** A person who has a great deal of knowledge. **2.** A pupil or student.

scoff (skŏf, skôf) *v.* **scoffed, scoff•ing.** To scorn; make fun of.

score (skôr, skōr) *n.* **1.** Debt; amount owed. **2.** A set or group of twenty items.

scorn (skôrn) *v.* **scorned, scorn•ing.** To treat someone or something as worthless or bad; look down on. —**scorn´ful** *adj.*

scour (skour) *v.* **1.** To scrub. **2.** To search thoroughly.

scrap•per (skrăp´ər) *n.* A person who gets into fights easily.

scru•ti•nize (skrōōt´n-īz´) *v.* **scru•ti•nized, scru•ti•niz•ing.** To examine closely.

scru•ti•ny (skrōōt´n-ē) *n.* Close inspection.

scud (skŭd) *v.* **scud•ding.** To move quickly and smoothly; run.

scull (skŭl) *n.* An oar. —*v.* **sculled.** To row.

scul•ler•y (skŭl´ə-rē) *n.* A room for cleaning kitchen dishes and utensils.

scut•tle (skŭt´l) *n.* A container for carrying coal. —*v.* **scut•tled.** To scurry.

se•clude (sĭ-klōōd´) *v.* **se•clud•ed.** To keep apart from everything else.

seed•y (sē´dē) *adj.* Shabby; inferior.

seize (sēz) *v.* **seized.** To take hold of suddenly and quickly; grab.

sem•i•nar•y (sĕm´ə-nĕr´ē) *n.* **1.** A private school for girls. **2.** A school that trains people to become ministers, priests, or rabbis.

sen•ior (sēn´yər) *n.* One who is older or has a higher rank than another.

sen•nit (sĕn´ĭt) *n.* A cord formed by braiding plant fibers.

sen•tence (sĕn´təns) *n.* The punishment given to a person who has been found guilty.

sen•ti•men•tal (sĕn´tə-mĕn´tl) *adj.* The quality of being easily moved by emotions.

sen•ti•men•tal•i•ty (sĕn´tə-mĕn-tăl´ĭ-tē) *n.* Condition of being overly sentimental.

sep•ti•ce•mi•a (sĕp´tĭ-sē´mē-ə) *n.* A disease of the blood that affects the whole body.

se•quence (sē´kwəns, sē´kwĕns´) *n.* Order; arrangement.

se•rene (sə-rēn´) *adj.* Peaceful and calm; without trouble, noise, clouds, or other disturbances. —**se•rene´ly** *adv.*

set•tee (sĕ-tē´) *n.* A type of sofa.

sev•er•al•ly (sĕv´ər-əl-ē, sĕv´rəl-ē) *adv.* One at a time.

se•ver•i•ty (sə-vĕr´ĭ-tē) *n.* Strictness and harshness.

shaft (shăft) *n.* **1.** A long, narrow passage that goes up and down, not sideways. **2.** The long, narrow rod of a spear or arrow. **3.** A long bar that is part of a machine.

sham (shăm) *n.* Something that is not real; a fake. —*v.* **sham•ming.** To fake something; pretend.

sheath (shēth) *n.* A case that fits tightly over the blade of a knife, sword, or other sharp object.

sheen (shēn) *n.* Shiny appearance.

sheer (shîr) *adj.* Pure; complete.

settee

shin•ny (shĭn´ē) *v.* **shin•nied.** To climb.
—*n.* An informal game of field hockey.

shoal (shōl) *n.* A shallow area in a body of water.

shod (shŏd) *adj.* Equipped with shoes.

shrew (shro͞o) *n.* An ill-tempered woman.

shrine (shrīn) *n.* A temple; place of worship.

shroud (shroud) *v.* **shroud•ing.** To enfold, as in a burial cloth.

shunt (shŭnt) *v.* To change the course.
—*n.* The directional track used for changing course.

sid•ing (sī´dĭng) *n.* A short length of railroad track that goes off the main track.

si•dle (sīd´l) *v.* **si•dled.** To move in a way that will not attract attention.

sil•hou•ette (sĭl´o͞o-ĕt´) *n.* A dark outline of something against a light background.
—*adj.* **sil•hou•et•ted.** Shown as a dark outline.

sim•ple•ton (sĭm´pəl-tən) *n.* A person without good sense; a fool.

sin•cere (sĭn-sîr´) *adj.* **sin•cer•est.** Without lies; real; honest.

singed (sĭnjd) *adj.* Lightly burned.

sin•gle (sĭng´gəl) *adj.* Not with another or others; only one.
—*n.* In baseball, a hit that allows the batter to reach first base.

sink•hole (sĭngk´hōl´) *n.* A depression in the ground connected with an underground passageway.

sir•rah (sĭr´ə) *n.* Term used to address a person of lower status. (This term is no longer in use.)

skir•mish (skûr´mĭsh) *n.* A small fight.

slant rhyme (slănt rīm) *n.* Partial or imperfect rhyme.

slip (slĭp) *n.* A place to park a ship or boat.

smelt[1] (smĕlt) *v.* **smelt•ing.** To melt and blend.

smelt[2] (smĕlt) *v.* A past tense and past participle of the verb **smell.**

smith•y (smĭth´ē, smĭ*th*´ē) *n.* A blacksmith's shop.

smock (smŏk) *n.* A garment that is made like a long, loose shirt.

smoul•der (smōl´dər) *v.* **smoul•der•ing.** To burn very low.

sneer (snîr) *n.* A look or statement of contempt or scorn.
—*v.* **sneered.** To show contempt or say with a sneer.

snig•ger (snĭg´ər) *n.* Combination of a giggle and a snort.

so•ber (sō´bər) *adj.* Serious; solemn.
—**so´ber•ly** *adv.*

so•lic•i•tor (sə-lĭs´ĭ-tər) *n.* One who seeks donations.

sol•i•tar•y (sŏl´ĭ-tĕr´ē) *adj.* Existing or living alone.

sol•i•tude (sŏl´ĭ-to͞od´, sŏl´ĭ-tyo͞od) *n.* Loneliness; isolation.

sought (sôt) *v.* Past tense of **seek.** Looked for.

sow (sou) *n.* A female pig that is fully grown.

span (spăn) *v.* **spanned.** To stretch across.

span•ner (spăn´ər) *n.* A wrench.

spare (spâr) *v.* **spared, spar•ing. 1.** To deal gently with. **2.** To avoid or keep from destroying or harming. **3.** To save or free someone. **4.** To do without.
—*adj.* Free for other use.

spec•ta•tor (spĕk´tā´tər) *n.* Someone who watches an event but does not take part in it.

spec•u•late (spĕk´yə-lāt´) *v.* **spec•u•lat•ed, spec•u•lat•ing.** To guess without having complete knowledge.

shinny

silhouette

ă	pat	ĕ	pet
ā	pay	ē	be
âr	care	ĭ	pit
ä	father	ī	pie
îr	fierce	oi	oil
ŏ	pot	o͝o	book
ō	go	o͞o	boot
ô	paw,	yo͞o	abuse
	for	ou	out
ŭ	cut	ə	ago,
ûr	fur		item,
th	the		pencil,
th	thin		atom,
hw	which		´circus
zh	vision	ər	butter

spec•u•la•tion (spĕk´yə-lā´shən) *n.* Theory; supposing.

spe•lunk•ing (spĭ-lŭng´kĭng, spē´lŭng´kĭng) *n.* Exploring caves.

spe•lunk•er (spĭ-lŭng´kər, spē´lŭng´kər) *n.* One who explores caves.

spig•ot (spĭg´ət) *n.* Faucet.

spire (spīr) *n.* The top part of a steeple or other structure that tapers upward.

spir•it•ed (spĭr´ĭ-tĭd) *adj.* Lively.

spite (spīt) *n.* Anger or ill will that causes a person to want to hurt or embarrass another person. —*idiom* **in spite of.** Even though; regardless.

spite•ful (spīt´fəl) *adj.* Vicious; mean. —**spite´ful•ly** *adv.*

spor•tive (spôr´tĭv, spōr´tĭv) *adj.* Playful; teasing.

sprat (sprăt) *n.* A small fish.

spright•ly (sprīt´lē) *adj.* Lively.

spur (spûr) *n.* A sharp metal piece in the shape of a small wheel with spikes that is worn on the heel of a person's boot. It is used to make a horse go faster. —*adj.* **spurred.** Moved to action; urged on.

squan•der (skwŏn´dər) *v.* **squan•dered.** To waste.

stag•ger (stăg´ər) *v.* **stag•gered. 1.** To move or stand in an unsteady way. **2.** To overwhelm with a severe shock, defeat, or misfortune.

stag•nant (stăg´nənt) *adj.* Inactive; lifeless.

stake (stāk) *n.* **1.** A stick or post with a sharp end for driving into the gound as a marker, support, or part of a fence. **2.** A share or interest in a business or enterprise. **3.** A gamble or risk.

stal•wart (stôl´wərt) *adj.* Strong of body and character.

staph•y•lo•coc•cus (stăf´ə-lō-kŏk´əs) *n., pl.* **staph•y•lo•coc•ci** (stăf´ə-lō-kŏk´sī). A bacteria that causes boils or other severe infections.

star•board (stär´bərd) *n.* The right side of a ship facing forward.

state•ly (stāt´lē) *adj.* Elegant, dignified, or grand in manner or appearance; majestic.

sta•tion (stā´shən) *n.* **1.** A place or location where a person or thing stands. **2.** A place or special building where certain services or activities are provided or carried on. **3.** A stopping place along a route for taking on or letting off passengers. **4.** Social position; rank.

stat•ure (stăch´ər) *n.* Height; build.

sta•tus (stā´təs, stăt´əs) *n.* Position or rank.

staunch (stônch, stänch) *adj.* Firm and strong; loyal.

stave (stāv) *v.* **staved.** To break.

stead•fast (stĕd´făst´, stĕd´fəst) *adj.* Unfaltering; persistent. —**stead´fast´ly** *adv.*

stealth (stĕlth) *n.* The act of behaving or maneuvering in a secretive manner.

stealth•y (stĕl´thē) *adj.* Cautious or sneaky. —**stealth´i•ly** *adv.*

steed (stēd) *n.* Horse.

ster•e•o•type (stĕr´ē-ə-tīp´, stîr´ē-ə-tīp´) *n.* A fixed view of something which does not allow for individuality. —**ster´e•o•typ´i•cal** *adj.*

ster•il•ize (stĕr´ə-līz´) *v.* **ster•il•ized, ster•il•iz•ing.** To make free from germs or dirt.

stern (stûrn) *adj.* Grave; severe. —*n.* The rear part of a ship or boat.

stew•ard (stoo´ərd, styoo´ərd) *n.* **1.** A person who manages another's household. **2.** A male attendant on a ship or airplane who waits on passengers.

spires

ă	pat	ĕ	pet
ā	pay	ē	be
âr	care	ĭ	pit
ä	father	ī	pie
îr	fierce	oi	oil
ŏ	pot	oo	book
ō	go	oo	boot
ô	paw,	yoo	abuse
	for	ou	out
ŭ	cut	ə	ago,
ûr	fur		item,
th	the		pencil,
th	thin		atom,
hw	which		circus
zh	vision	ər	butter

sti•fle (stī´fəl) *v.* **sti•fled. 1.** To cause to feel uncomfortable because of a lack of air. **2.** To hold back.

stim•u•late (stĭm´yə-lāt´) *v.* **stim•u•lat•ed.** To temporarily make more active.

stint (stĭnt) *n.* A certain period of work.

stir (stûr) *v.* **stir•ring. 1.** To mix something by moving it around in a circular motion with a spoon or other similar object. **2.** To change or cause to change position slightly. **3.** To excite the emotions of.

stir•rup (stûr´əp, stĭr´əp) *n.* A loop hung from either side of a horse's saddle to hold the rider's foot.

sti•ver (stī´vər) *n.* Something of little value.

stol•id (stŏl´ĭd) *adj.* Showing no emotion. —**stol´id•ly** *adv.*

stow (stō) *v.* To put or place; store.

strafe (strāf) *v.* **strafed.** To fire at with machine guns from airplanes flying close to the ground.

straight•a•way (strāt´ə-wā´) *n.* The straight part of a road or track.

strait•ened (strāt´nd) *adj.* Limited.

strife (strīf) *n.* Conflict; fighting.

striped (strīpt) *v.* Marked with a stripe; streaked.

stu•por (stoo´pər, styoo´pər) *n.* Daze.

sub•due (səb-doo´, səb-dyoo´) *v.* **sub•dued. 1.** To bring under control. **2.** To lessen the intensity of.

sub•side (səb-sīd´) *v.* To sink to a lower or more normal level.

sub•ter•ra•ne•an (sŭb´tə-rā´nē-ən) *adj.* **sub•ter•ra•ne•ous.** Underground.

suc•ces•sion (sək-sĕsh´ən) *n.* Series.

suf•fice (sə-fīs´) *v.* To be what is needed; enough.

suit•or (soo´tər) *n.* A man who seeks the affection of a woman.

sulk (sŭlk) *v.* **sulk•ing.** To pout; act quiet and sullen out of displeasure. —*adj.* **sulk•y.** Cross; grouchy. —**sulk´i•ly** *adv.*

sul•len (sŭl´ən) *adj.* Silent and angry; glum. —**sul´len•ly** *adv.*

sum•mar•i•ly (sə-mĕr´ə-lē) *adv.* Quickly and without care for detail.

sum•mon (sŭm´ən) *v.* **sum•moned.** To call up; stir up.

sum•mons (sŭm´ənz) *n.* A call or order to appear or do something.

sump•tu•ous (sŭmp´choo-əs) *adj.* Suggesting great expense; lavish.

sun•dry (sŭn´drē) *adj.* Various.

su•per•fi•cial (soo´pər-fĭsh´əl) *adj.* Only presenting the obvious; on the surface; artificial.

sup•press (sə-prĕs´) *v.* **sup•pressed.** To hold back from expressing.

sur•face (sûr´fəs) *n.* The outermost or top layer of an object. —*v.* **sur•faced. 1.** To rise or come to the surface. **2.** To appear after being hidden.

surge (sûrj) *v.* **surged.** To rise and move forward with force, as rolling waves do.

sur•ly (sûr´lē) *adj.* Rude; short-tempered.

sur•vey (sər-vā´, sûr´vā´) *v.* **sur•veyed, sur•vey•ing.** To look over and examine; investigate in detail.

sus•pend (sə-spĕnd´) *v.* **sus•pend•ed. 1.** To attach something so that it hangs down. **2.** To temporarily take away a person's position or privileges.

sus•tain (sə-stān´) *v.* To keep alive.

sus•te•nance (sŭs´tə-nəns) *n.* Nourishment; food that supports life or health.

swarth•y (swôr´thē) *adj.* Dark-colored.

swath (swŏth, swôth) *n.* A strip cut through grass or trees, as if by a mower.

stirrup

talon

tapestry

thatch

swear (swâr) *v.* **1.** To make a solemn statement or promise while calling on God or some sacred object or person to show or prove the honesty or truth of what is said. **2.** To issue an oath as in a courtroom.

swell (swĕl) *v.* **1.** To increase in size or volume; expand. **2.** To cause to increase in size or volume.
—*n.* A long wave or series of waves that move without breaking or rising to a crest.
—*adj.* Excellent.

tack rail (tăk rāl) *n.* A place to hang bridles and harnesses and other gear for horses.

taint (tānt) *v.* **taint•ed.** To pollute.

tal•on (tăl´ən) *n.* A claw.

tam•a•rind (tăm´ə-rĭnd) *n.* The fruit of a tropical tree.

tan (tăn) *v.* **tanned. 1.** To make animal hides into leather by soaking them in certain chemicals or mixtures. **2.** *figurative* To spank or beat up.
—*n.* A light yellowish-brown color.
—*adj.* **tanned.** Of the color tan.

tan•ner (tăn´ər) *n.* One who tans animal skins.

ta•per (tā´pər) *v.* **ta•pered.** To make or become gradually thinner.

tap•es•try (tăp´ĭ-strē) *n.* A heavy cloth with designs or pictures woven in it.

tar•nish (tär´nĭsh) *v.* **tar•nished.** To become dull; lose color or luster.

tar•pau•lin (tär-pô´lĭn, tär´pə-lĭn) *n.* A waterproof canvas cover.

Tar•ta•ry (tär´tə-rē) *n.* Area of Europe and West Asia.

taunt (tônt) *v.* **taunt•ed, taunt•ing.** To ridicule or make fun of; harass.

taw•ny (tô´nē) *adj.* Light orange-brown.

tax•i (tăk´sē) *v.* **tax•i•ing.** To move slowly over the surface of the ground or water before taking off or landing.

tech•nique (tĕk-nēk´) *n.* A method or way of doing something.

te•di•ous (tē´dē-əs) *adj.* Long and tiring.

tel•e•graph (tĕl´ĭ-grăf´) *n.* A system of sending messages over wires or radio to a special receiving station.

tem•per•a•men•tal (tĕm´prə-mĕn´tl, tĕm´pər-ə-mĕn´tl) *adj.* Unpredictable; moody.

tem•per•ate (tĕm´pər-ĭt, tĕm´prĭt) *adj.* **1.** Moderate weather, neither too hot nor too cold. **2.** Restrained; sensible.

tem•pest (tĕm´pĭst) *n.* **1.** Storm. **2.** Uproar.

tem•pes•tu•ous (tĕm-pĕs´chōō-əs) *adj.* Stormy.

tem•po•rar•y (tĕm´pə-rĕr´ē) *adj.* Lasting or used for a short time only; not permanent.

te•na•cious (tə-nā´shəs) *adj.* Persistent; determined.

te•nac•i•ty (tə-năs´ĭ-tē) *n.* Persistence; determination.

ten•der•foot (tĕn´dər-fōōt´) *n.* A beginner; inexperienced person.

ten•e•ment (tĕn´ə-mənt) *n.* A cheap apartment in the poor part of a city.

ter•mi•nate (tûr´mə-nāt´) *v.* **ter•mi•nat•ed.** To come to an end.

ter•ra cot•ta (tĕr´ə kŏt´ə) *n.* A type of clay.

ter•rain (tə-rān´) *n.* The nature of the countryside.

teth•er (tĕth´ər) *v.* **teth•ered.** To tie up.

thatch (thăch) *n.* Straw, reeds, or palm fronds, used to cover a roof.
—*v.* **thatched.** To cover with thatch.

wretch•ed (rĕch´ĭd) *adj.* **1.** Very unhappy or unfortunate. **2.** Evil or wicked; despicable.

yawl (yôl) *n.* A small boat launched from a ship.

yeo•man (yō´mən) *n.* A commoner who works the land.

yield (yēld) *v.* **yield•ed. 1.** To give forth; produce; provide. **2.** To give way to pressure or force.

yoke (yōk) *n.* **1.** A pair of animals joined by a crossbar and harness and working together. **2.** Part of a piece of clothing that fits closely around the neck and shoulders or over the hips.

yon•der (yŏn´dər) *adv.* Over there.

zeal•ous (zĕl´əs) *adj.* Filled with dedication and enthusiasm.

yoke

ă	pat	ě	pet
ā	pay	ē	be
âr	care	ĭ	pit
ä	father	ī	pie
îr	fierce	oi	oil
ŏ	pot	o͝o	book
ō	go	o͞o	boot
ô	paw,	yo͞o	abuse
	for	ou	out
ŭ	cut	ə	ago,
ûr	fur		item,
th	the		pencil,
th	thin		atom,
hw	which		circus
zh	vision	ər	butter

Index

the End